# Resonances

# Resonances: Noise and Contemporary Music

EDITED BY

MICHAEL GODDARD,

BENJAMIN HALLIGAN AND

NICOLA SPELMAN

BLOOMSBURY
NEW YORK · LONDON · NEW DELHI · SYDNEY

**Bloomsbury Academic**
An imprint of Bloomsbury Publishing Plc

| 1385 Broadway | 50 Bedford Square |
| New York | London |
| NY 10018 | WC1B 3DP |
| USA | UK |

www.bloomsbury.com

First published 2013

© Michael Goddard, Benjamin Halligan, and Nicola Spelman, 2013

All rights reserved. No part of this publication may be reproduced or transmitted in any form or by any means, electronic or mechanical, including photocopying, recording, or any information storage or retrieval system, without prior permission in writing from the publishers.

No responsibility for loss caused to any individual or organization acting on or refraining from action as a result of the material in this publication can be accepted by Bloomsbury Academic or the authors.

**Library of Congress Cataloging-in-Publication Data**
Resonances : noise and contemporary music/edited by Michael Goddard, Benjamin Halligan and Nicola Spelman.
    pages ; cm
Includes bibliographical references and index.
ISBN 978-1-4411-5937-3 (pbk. : alk. paper)– ISBN 978-1-4411-1054-1 (hardcover : alk. paper) 1. Noise music–History and criticism. 2. Avant-garde (Music)–History–20th century. 3. Music–20th century–Philosophy and aesthetics. 4. Music–Social aspects. I. Goddard, Michael, 1965- II. Halligan, Benjamin. III. Spelman, Nicola.
    ML3534.R387 2013
    780.9'04–dc23
    2013005989

ISBN: HB: 978-1-4411-1054-1
    PB: 978-1-4411-5937-3

Typeset by Fakenham Prepress Solutions, Fakenham, Norfolk NR21 8NN
Printed and bound in the United States of America

# CONTENTS

*Acknowledgements* viii
*Contributors* ix

Introduction 1
Michael Goddard, Benjamin Halligan and Nicola Spelman

**PART ONE** Noise, Rock and Psychedelia 11

1  'Kick Out the Jams': Creative Anarchy and Noise in 1960s Rock 13
   Sheila Whiteley

2  Recasting Noise: The Lives and Times of *Metal Machine Music* 24
   Nicola Spelman

3  Shoegaze as the Third Wave: Affective Psychedelic Noise, 1965–91 37
   Benjamin Halligan

4  To Be Played at Maximum Volume: Rock Music as a Disabling (Deafening) Culture 64
   George McKay

## PART TWO  Punk Noise: Prehistories and Continuums  79

5   Sounds Incorporated: Dissonant Sorties into Popular Culture  81
    Stephen Mallinder

6   Stairwells of Abjection and Screaming Bodies: Einstürzende Neubauten's Artaudian Noise Music  95
    Jennifer Shryane

7   Make a Joyous Noise: The Pentecostal Nature of American Noise Music  107
    Seb Roberts

8   Roars of Discontent: Noise and Disaffection in Two Cases of Russian Punk  121
    Yngvar B. Steinholt

9   Noise from Nowhere: Exploring 'Noisyland's' Dark, Noisy and Experimental Music  134
    Michael Goddard

    Archive: Indestructible Energy: Seeing Noise  153
    Julie R. Kane

## PART THREE  Noise, Composition and Improvisation  181

10  Xenakian Sound Synthesis: Its Aesthetics and Influence on 'Extreme' Computer Music  183
    Christopher Haworth

11  Sound Barriers: The Framing Functions of Noise and Silence  198
    Alexis Paterson

12  Listening Aside: An Aesthetics of Distraction in
    Contemporary Music  209
    David Cecchetto and eldritch Priest

13  Using Noise Techniques to Destabilize Composition and
    Improvisation  222
    Eric Lyon

14  Noise as Mediation: Adorno and the Turntablism of Philip
    Jeck  242
    Erich Hertz

## PART FOUR  Approaching Noise Musics  255

15  Noise as Music: Is There a Historical Continuum? From
    Historical Roots to Industrial Music  257
    Joseph Tham

16  Noise as Material Impact: New Uses of Sound in Noise-
    related Movements  273
    Rafael Sarpa

17  Into the Full: Strawson, Wyschnegradsky and Acoustic
    Space in Noise Musics  286
    J.-P. Caron

18  Gossips, Sirens, Hi-Fi Wives: Feminizing the Threat of
    Noise  297
    Marie Thompson

19  Beyond Auditive Unpleasantness: An Exploration of Noise
    in the Work of Filthy Turd  312
    James Mooney and Daniel Wilson

*Notes*  326
*Bibliography*  347
*Index*  366

# ACKNOWLEDGEMENTS

The Editors thank: David Barker and his team; the Communication, Cultural and Media Studies Research Centre of the School of Arts and Media at the University of Salford; Professors George McKay, David Sanjek and Ben Light, and Dr Deborah Woodman; Stephen Lawrie, Stuart Braithwaite and Paul Hegarty; the staff and habitués of the Salford King's Arms, and especially Livy and Ken for their assistance with facilitating the noise gig associated with University of Salford conference 'Bigger than Words, Wider than Pictures: Noise, Affect, Politics', from which this collection, along with *Reverberations: The Philosophy, Aesthetics and Politics of Noise*, emerged.

Work on the conference and this book was partly supported by a Research and Innovation Strategic Fund grant from the Faculty of Arts and Social Sciences at the University of Salford.

Images/diagram credits: of Metal Machine Trio, in Chapter 2 (Daniel Boud); of back cover detail, in Chapter 5 (Stephen Mallinder); of Einstürzende Neubauten, in Chapter 6 (Kieran Shryane and Jennifer Shryane); of Japanese street noise, in Chapter 7 (Seb Roberts); of distressed vinyl, in Chapter 19 (Benjamin Halligan). All diagrams are the authors' own unless otherwise stated. All images in the Archive section: Julie R. Kane. Cover image: *The Burning World* (July 2011), Julie R. Kane (fstopqueen.blogspot.com).

# CONTRIBUTORS

**J.-P. Caron** (aka Jean-Pierre Caron) is active on both the contemporary classical and the noise scenes. His musical output is divided between indeterminate music, fully notated works and noise groups such as -notyesus> (with Rafael Sarpa) and Epilepsia (with Henrique Iwao). Studies of composition were made at the Universidade Federal do Estado do Rio de Janeiro (UNIRIO). He also took a Master's degree in music at the same university with a thesis about time and space in the music of Giacinto Scelsi and La Monte Young. His (second) master's dissertation in philosophy, pursued at Universidade Federal do Rio de Janeiro (UFRJ) deals with different approaches to problems of musical ontology/morphology. His current doctorate, being pursued at the University of Paris 8 in collaboration with the University of São Paulo, under supervision of philosophers Antonia Soulez and Vladimir Safatle, deals once again with the morphology of the musical work from a Wittgensteinian perspective.

**David Cecchetto** is Assistant Professor of Critical Digital Theory at York University (Canada). He has published a number of chapters and articles, co-edited a collection, and his monograph *Humanesis: Sound and Posthumanism* is published by the University of Minnesota Press. As an artist working with sound, David has presented work internationally. www.davidcecchetto.net

**Michael Goddard** is Senior Lecturer in Media and PGR Coordinator in the School of Arts and Media at the University of Salford. He has published research in media and aesthetic theory, Eastern European film and visual culture and anomalous forms of popular music. His book *Impossible Cartographies: The Cinema of Raúl Ruiz* is currently at press and he is co-editor, with Jussi Parikka, of the recently published special issue of *Fibre Culture* journal, *Unnatural Ecologies*. Michael has also published articles on Throbbing Gristle and Laibach as well as co-editing, with Benjamin Halligan, *Mark E. Smith and The Fall: Art, Music and Politics* (Ashgate, 2010). Currently Michael is working on a research project on radical media ecologies in radio, music and radical politics in the 1970s. Michael co-convened the international conference 'Bigger than Words, Wider than

Pictures: Noise, Affect, Politics' with Benjamin Halligan at the University of Salford in Summer 2010.

**Benjamin Halligan** is the Director of Postgraduate Research Studies for the College of Arts and Social Sciences, University of Salford. His publications include *Michael Reeves* (Manchester University Press, 2003), *Mark E. Smith and The Fall: Art, Music and Politics* (Ashgate, 2010; co-edited with Michael Goddard), *Reverberations: The Philosophy, Aesthetics and Politics of Noise* (Continuum, 2012; co-edited with Michael Goddard and Paul Hegarty) and *The Music Documentary: Acid Rock to Electropop* (Routledge, 2013; co-edited with Robert Edgar and Kirsty Fairclough-Isaacs). Ben has published chapters and articles on the Sarajevo Documentary School, Frank Zappa, 1970s television science fiction, and film aesthetics and ideology. Ben co-convened the international conference 'Bigger than Words, Wider than Pictures: Noise, Affect, Politics' with Michael Goddard at the University of Salford in Summer 2010.

**Christopher Haworth** is a postdoctoral researcher on the ICASP project at McGill University, Montréal. He writes about emotion, subjectivity, and the mediumship of the listener in music and sound art, 'presentness' and the aesthetics of immediacy, and the social and technological aesthetics of technologically mediated improvisation practices. This is informed by Christopher's work as a sound artist, which recently has focused on the use of psychoacoustic phenomena as a compositional material in computer music. His publications include 'Ear as Instrument: Sound at the Limits of Audition' and 'Composing with Absent Sound'. Outside of his academic work Christopher makes electronic music under the moniker Littl Shyning Man, and has released three records on London-based electronica label Head+Arm (Sonic 360).

**Erich Hertz** is an Associate Professor of English at Siena College in New York where he teaches courses in contemporary culture, film and literature. Erich has published on Adorno, Benjamin, Surrealism, and the aesthetics of music documentaries. He is currently co-editing a volume entitled *Write in Tune: Contemporary Music and Fiction*.

**Julie R. Kane** is a Delaware-born photographer/publisher who moved to London in 2003, seizing the opportunity to photograph various sounds. She is currently inspired by developments in the London underground scene embodied by This is DIY, a collective of like-minded promoters, musicians, record labels and artists. Julie's work includes: *Colorless Green Ideas* (2009–12), limited edition prints and sleeve art for One Unique Signal (*Villains To A Man*, 2009), The Telescopes (*Live. Aftertaste*, 2010) and Cherry But No Cake (*Unveiling*, 2011).

**Eric Lyon** is a composer and computer music researcher. Major areas of focus include computer chamber music, spatial orchestration, and articulated noise composition. Recent compositions include 'Spirits', a 43-channel electroacoustic piano composition for the ZKM Kubus (supported by the Giga-Hertz Preis 2011), 'Variations on Psycho-Killer' for violinist Pauline Kim-Harris, and 'Noise Variations' for ensemble mise-en. Eric plays piano with the Noise Quartet, and computer with the Biomuse Trio. His music is commercially available on Everglade Records, Capstone Records, EMF, Isospin Labs Records, Sound's Bounty, Centaur Records, Smart Noise Records, Ash International and Bohn Media. Lyon has taught computer music at Keio University SFC, the International Academy of Media Arts and Sciences, Dartmouth College, Manchester University, and currently teaches in the School of Creative Arts at Queen's University Belfast.

**George McKay** is Professor of Cultural Studies at the University of Salford. He is author or editor of over ten volumes, mostly around popular music, social movements or cultural politics, including *Senseless Acts of Beauty: Cultures of Resistance since the Sixties* (Verso, 1996), *Circular Breathing: The Cultural Politics of Jazz in Britain* (Duke University Press, 2005), *Radical Gardening: Politics, Idealism & Rebellion in the Garden* (Frances Lincoln, 2011), and *Shakin' All Over: Popular Music and Disability* (Michigan University Press, 2013). He was founding co-editor in 2002 of *Social Movement Studies: Journal of Social, Cultural and Political Protest* (Routledge). In 2012 George was appointed to an Arts and Humanities Research Council Leadership Fellowship, for the Connected Communities Programme. His website is georgemckay.org

**Stephen Mallinder** is a founder member of pioneering electronic act Cabaret Voltaire, who are regarded as one of the key influences on contemporary electronic and popular music culture. The group's first release, *Extended Play* in 1979, represented the first domestic release for Rough Trade Records, the UK's foremost independent label. This was followed by *A Factory Sampler*, the debut release for the seminal British record label, Factory Records. Cabaret Voltaire went on to produce more than 30 albums for these and other groundbreaking independent labels, with chart and club successes around the world. Stephen has worked with numerous artists, film and record producers including Afrika Bambaataa and early electro producer John Robie. He has recorded albums with legendary dub producer Adrian Sherwood and became the first UK act to record an album in Chicago in the late 1980s with the 'originator of house', Marshall Jefferson. Stephen continues to record, perform and DJ, collaborating under the Wrangler and Hey, Rube! names. Stephen completed his PhD in popular music culture, *Movement: Journey of the Beat* and has written numerous journal articles. He currently works at the International College of Art and Design at the University of Brighton.

**James Mooney** is a researcher, writer and musician based at the School of Music, University of Leeds. His research addresses historical, critical and interdisciplinary approaches to music technology and electronic music. He has published texts on musical tools and affordance theory, and developed and written about multi-loudspeaker systems for electroacoustic music sound diffusion. His current project explores the work of Hugh Davies (1943–2005), his influence upon electronic music culture from the 1960s onwards, and his association with composers including Stockhausen, Cage, Oram, and others. www.james-mooney.co.uk

**Alexis Paterson** studied at Exeter University before completing her PhD, 'The Minimal Kaleidoscope: Exploring Minimal Music through the Lens of Postmodernity', at Cardiff University in 2010. As well as teaching at Cardiff University and the University of Salford, Alexis has worked in arts administration with the Bournemouth Symphony Orchestra (and its new music ensemble Kokoro), as a freelance arranger and copyist, and at Presteigne Festival of Music and the Arts. She is currently manager of the Cheltenham Music Festival.

**eldritch Priest**'s writing on aesthetics and experimental music has appeared in various journals and collected volumes. He is also the author of *Boring Formless Nonsense: Experimental Music and the Aesthetics of Failure* (Bloomsbury, 2013). In addition to his academic work, eldritch is active as a composer. He lives in Toronto, where he is co-artistic director of the experimental music collective Neither/Nor, and is currently a visiting scholar at York University's Faculty of Fine Arts. www.strangemonk.com

**Seb Roberts** is a Canadian composer, performer and audio engineer living in Tokyo, Japan.

**Rafael Sarpa** holds a Master in Media Studies from Rio de Janeiro State University. His thesis explored the connections between sound and body materiality focusing on Japanoise and Power Electronics singularities. Rafael is also a composer and performer, both solo and with the duo -notyesus> and the trio nulltraces. His interests range across contemporary music aesthetics and politics, the Brazilian school of psychoanalysis, materiality studies, performance art, and old and new forms of musicology.

**Jennifer Shryane** completed her first degree in English and History at the University of Cardiff in 1968. She went on to gain a postgraduate teaching qualification at King's College, University of London, focusing on drama and theatre, and taught until 2005. Jennifer gained her MA in Performing Arts from Liverpool University and completed her PhD in 2009. She has written several articles on Einstürzende Neubauten and her book on the group, *Blixa Bargeld and Einstürzende Neubauten: German Experimental Music* was published in 2011 by Ashgate.

**Nicola Spelman** is Senior Lecturer in Music at the University of Salford where she teaches popular musicology and composition. She has contributed to the development of popular music education at Salford for many years, designing and developing modules in a range of subject areas. Her research interests surround issues of representation within popular music, and she specializes in the field of anti-psychiatry and music. Nicola's *Popular Music & the Myths of Madness* was published by Ashgate in 2012.

**Yngvar B. Steinholt** is Associate Professor in Russian at the Institute of Culture and Literature, University of Tromsø, Norway. He has published a book and several articles on popular music in the Soviet Union and Post-Soviet Russia. Currently Yngvar is contributing to the research project Post-Socialist Punk, financed by the Arts and Humanities Research Council.

**Joseph Tham** is an educator based in Singapore. He graduated from the National University of Singapore in the Republic of Singapore, in History, in 1998 and is currently completing an MA in Asian Art Histories with LaSalle College of the Arts/Goldsmiths at the University of London. Joseph used to run a local record shop (Flux Us) selling and promoting experimental and avant-garde musics. Joseph was a member of Singaporean improvisation-based rock group, I.D., and now contributes regularly to www.s-pores.com and blogs at www.psychmetalfreak.blogspot.com.

**Marie Thompson** is a PhD candidate based at the University of Newcastle upon Tyne. Her research uses the Spinozist notion of affect to critically reconsider the correlation between noise, 'unwantedness' and 'badness'. She is the co-editor of *Sound, Music, Affect: Theorizing Sonic Experience* (2013, Bloomsbury). Marie is also regularly audible as a improviser and noisemaker. She plays solo as Tragic Cabaret and in the band Tragic Cabaret.

**Sheila Whiteley** is Professor Emeritus at the University of Salford, Visiting Professor at Southampton Solent University, and Research Fellow at the Bader International Study Centre, Queen's University (Canada), Herstmonceux. As a feminist musicologist with strong research interests in issues of identity and subjectivity, she is known for her work on gender and sexuality as well as for long-standing interests in popular culture and ideology. Sheila is author of *The Space Between the Notes: Rock and the*

*Counter Culture* (Routledge, 1992), *Women and Popular Music: Popular Music and Gender* (Routledge, 2000) and *Too Much Too Young: Popular Music, Age and Identity* (Routledge, 2005), and editor of *Sexing the Groove: Popular Music and Gender* (Routledge, 1996) and *Christmas, Ideology and Popular Culture* (Edinburgh University Press, 2008). She co-edited (with Andy Bennett and Stan Hawkins) *Music Space and Place: Popular Music and Cultural Identity* (Ashgate, 2002) and (with Jennifer Rycenga) *Queering the Popular Pitch* (Routledge, 2006). She is currently editing *Countercultures and Popular Music* with Jedediah Sklower (Ashgate, and Éditions Mélanie Séteun, Bordeaux) and, with Shara Rambarran, *Virtuality and Music*.

**Daniel Wilson** is a composer and musicologist based in Leeds. His doctoral research in composition deals with the concept of noise as Ontology, specifically looking at work of Alain Badiou and Michel Serres. His music has been performed in the UK and USA and his writing has been published in the UK and Australia.

# Introduction

*Michael Goddard, Benjamin Halligan and Nicola Spelman*

Contemporary histories of popular Western musics may be more usefully read as a series of debates concerning what, sonically and experientially, actually constitutes music in the commonly understood way, and what then constitutes, or can be termed as, and typically dismissed as, non-music. Such debates are class-ridden, evidence racial prejudices and profiling, continually undermine traditional musicological assumptions, radically problematize the commercial framings of music, mark all pivotal shifts in music across at least one hundred years, relentlessly advance the 'death of the author', are called upon to define time, place and national identity, and outmanoeuvre demarcations of high art and low culture. Answers provided have formed the methodological foundations of the conservatoire as well as journalistic and academic approaches to music, and now pull in their wake a judicial apparatus of ownership, censorship and reparations.

Technologies have been calibrated to answers provided too: reproductions of sound that invariably brag about 'noise reduction'. Noise, to music, is typically byproduct, accident, the unwanted, the unpleasant. And yet noise is inevitable and imminent to music: that inexorable presence that mixers and sound engineers do their best to exorcize, that gig-goers reflexively block out, plugging fingers in ears, when it takes the form of feedback. The exception that proves the rule in terms of contemporary music is folk: 'natural' sounds and pre-modern instruments (and, often, affectations) as a respite from the noise of the real or urban world and the noise of the musics that the real or urban world taints – a kind of bucolic, aristocratic asceticism, and one that implicitly casts noise as detrimental to musical, and human, interactions.

Noise, however, cannot just be confined to the idea of music performed or reproduced. In recent times, the watershed moment in the above process could be said to be a case of noise meeting noise: Beatlemania as both the

2  RESONANCES

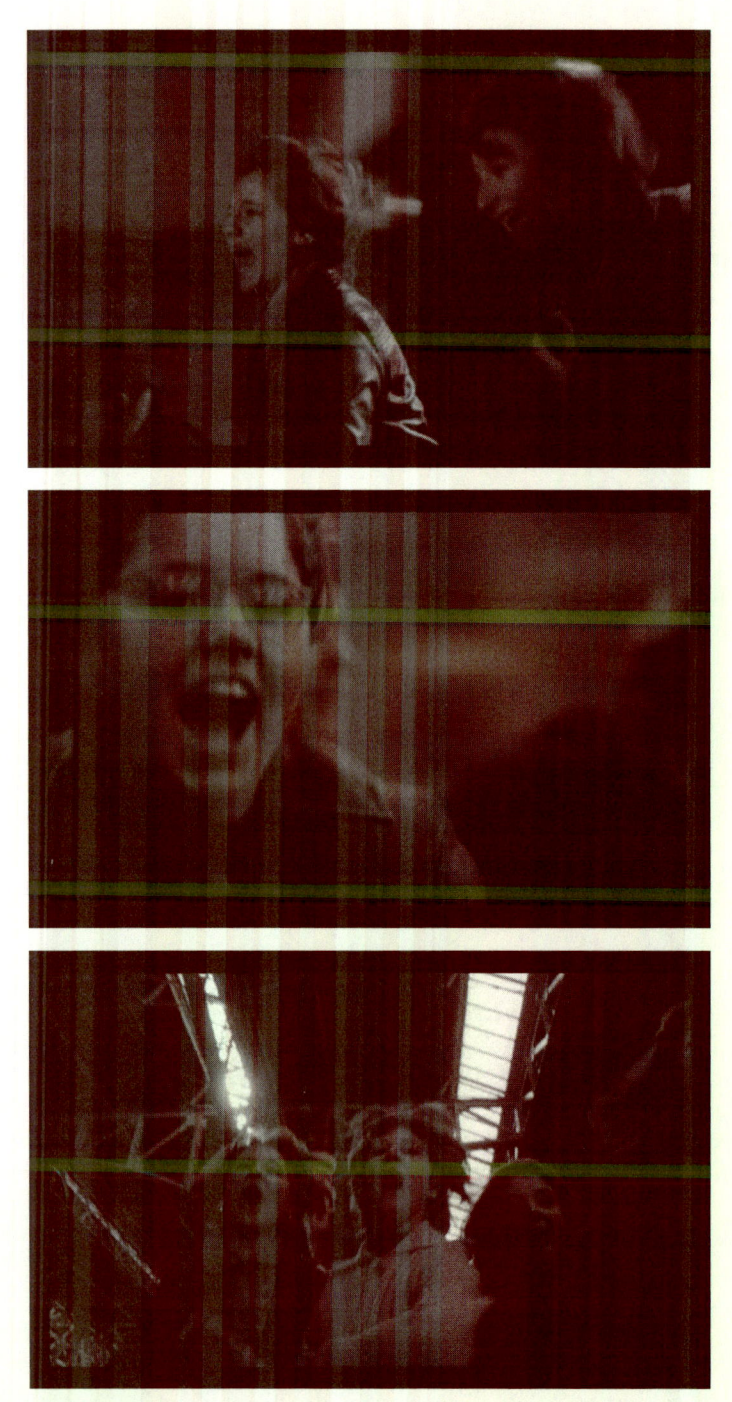

*Exit, pursued by fans; stills from* A Hard Day's Night *(Richard Lester, 1964)*.

sounds of the Fab Four in the mid-1960s (complete with crescendos of yelling-singing, 'naïve' drumming, the hardness of the sound of the guitar) and the sounds of their screaming audiences.

The cacophony that resulted baffled cultural commentators and alarmed moral guardians: respectively – where was the experience of the music that spoke to so many, when it was drowned out by the sounds of hysteria? and where were the old proprieties of the calm or passive enjoyment of popular culture? The questions raised here are directly articulated by noise theorist-activist Mattin, writing in 2009 in respect to the power relations that are established and nurtured by live music, this 'prime site of the spectacle'

> [...] where production and consumption are enacted at the level of experience. What is passivity? What is activity? Is the distinction that clear? What would it require to emancipate oneself from the situation and the roles that we accept when we enter such a space? How are social spaces produced in a given situation? What are the accepted conventions? Can we challenge them? Can we change them? Can we dare together by abandoning old conventions? (Mattin, 2011, n.p. ['Prologue to Unconstituted Praxis'])

The progressive cultural nature of the phenomenon of Beatlemania is still in advance of current thinking, and still represents a sonic-aesthetic assault on conceptions of art. To whisper or cough or sneeze in a classical concert or during a performance of a play, or have your mobile phone inopportunely ring or buzz or bleep, is taken as a form of disrespect to a collective established on – to employ Gerard Manley Hopkins's description – 'elected silence'. As Halligan has argued elsewhere (2009), the 'elected' is merely imposed, prompted by faltering notions of worthy art forms for institutions that have been, *pace* neoliberal business practices, 'hollowed out'. When the art movements of the twentieth century have attempted to break with the meek compliance of establishment art, and the institutions that form parasitical relationships to the practices and production of art, they have almost always initially sought to do away with the very rigidity of modes of acceptance or experience of that art. Such modes exist in dress and behavioural codes and, more insidiously, in a respect to be evidenced in apparent concentration and silence. The bodily paralysis that is required – not to cough or sneeze, to decline from talk, indeed not to slouch or sleep – is akin to Wilhelm Reich's notion of 'body armour': an unnatural, self-imposed immobilization of muscles, resulting in a repression of emotions and of thought. To 'twist and shout', in this context, represents a breaking of the armour, and a freeing of emotions, and allowing for communication between the music and the self. The enemy of music of progressive worth, then, is not a measure of noise, but of the acceptance of silence.

From these perspectives, it is clear why noise remains a pejorative term in two chief senses. First, noise as a negative aesthetic judgement, centred on that thing which is other than the authentic, organic creation of music. And, secondly, noise as the unwanted element for studio technicians, the evidence of the failings of technology, of dust on the tapehead, of the deterioration of reproductions, as denoting the technological limitations of yesteryear (and so in need of 'cleaning' for remastered reissues of albums). One could go further: noise is what generates complaints, and has become the basis for legislation (noise abatement, noise pollution); it has been claimed as one of the ills of contemporary urban existence, blamed for a variety of physical and mental disorders, and even applied for the purposes of torture. Philosophically, noise seems to stand for a lack of aesthetic grace, to be against enjoyment or pleasure, to alienate or distract rather than enrapture; it penetrates the body rather than transports the listener 'out of the body'. Enthusiasts of noise (particularly of the Second Summer of Love of 1989) tend to be termed 'survivors' now rather than seasoned connoisseurs. And yet the drones of psychedelia, the racket of garage rock and punk, the thudding of rave, the feedback of shoegaze and post-rock, the bombast of thrash and metal, the clatter of jungle and the stuttering of electronica, together with notable examples of avant-garde noise art, have all been inducted into the history of music, and recognized as key moments in its evolution. Postmodern theorizing about music lauds the DJ, the mixer or remixer, the very inauthenticity of sampling: the art 'after' the artist has vacated the artefact.

It is no exaggeration to say that it is the very opposite of melody and harmony – noise (dissonance, feedback, atmospherics and ambience, hiss and distortion), and the application and exploration of noise in and through music – that has overwhelmingly determined popular musics since at least the late 1960s. Indeed, as musicianship, musical virtuosity and prowess have faded from view, the sense of the indivisible totality of the noise of certain styles (most notably punk and post-punk, techno and rave) has become the primary point of reference. We tend to ask what it sounds like as much as, or rather than, who plays what, and when, and how. The enveloping experience of music determines popular music cultures, particularly those given over to gatherings, and to dance (or movement in general), rather than an appreciation of the sound of the bow, or plectrum, on the string. Sound is mixed for such environments, graded to fill and meet space and the potential for echo, to mingle with rather than exclude the sound of the masses rather than, or as much as to, showcase musicianship.

Noise, as the 'other' of music, has always been a concern of avant-garde artists and those who seek to operate on the margins of music, or outside its boundaries. A number of case studies can be found in this volume, from *Metal Machine Music* to 'noise rock', from turntablism to noise protest, that detail such experiments and interventions. In privileging noise in this manner – and inviting our contributors to consider music via noise – we hope, in the first instance, to assemble an overview of the noise foundations of contemporary popular music. We look to Mattin's foundational question: 'Can we use Noise as a form of praxis going beyond established audience/performer relationships?' (Mattin, 2011, n.p. ['Noise & Capitalism: Exhibition as Concert']).[1] In the second instance, we seek to establish an expanded sense of sonic aesthetics, conducting close analyses of noise music texts to enable a more developed understanding of their technological, compositional and performance practices. Specifically, this involves an investigation of experimental and alternative modes of sonic composition: purposeful disorganization/indeterminacy, spontaneous noise, improvised noise, the roles of space and silence, of durational extremes, and the ways in which particular sound synthesis and signal processing techniques are appropriated and employed by noise artists in novel and unforeseen ways. Thirdly, we are able to encounter and, we hope, to an extent 'recover' those still déclassé forms of contemporary music which renounce artistic-subjective expression and the elevation of the individual – typically by replacing the human with the computer. In this regard, we look to instances where indeterminacy and improvisation are determined and motivated by noise. We examine how noise elements may be installed to purposefully subvert conventional composer-directed modes of composition and performance, and how noise scores raise pertinent questions in relation to issues of musical notation and interpretation.

But our shared remit is not ultimately a matter of formulating new meanings, coining new terms, or expanding the lexicon of critical writing. It became apparent, in editing these chapters, that noise *per se* refuses fixed identities – an ontological equivocation often couched in semiotic terms. The debate is then forced open, and becomes radically ambiguous – not in the sense of a mystification, or the failing to provide an answer, but in the sense of indeterminateness. Pier Paolo Pasolini's film *Teorema*, which sought to address the revolutionary events of 1968 at the time of 1968 through the dramatization of the implosion of a bourgeois family, terminates at such a moment: the narrative is obscure, its stories unresolved, and the protagonist, in uncertain, volcanic surroundings, screams. Pasolini commented:

> So there are new problems, and these will have to be solved by the members of the bourgeoisie themselves, not the workers or the opposition. We dissident bourgeois cannot solve these problems, and neither can the 'natural' bourgeois. That is why [*Teorema*] remains 'suspended'; it ends up with a cry, and the very irrationality of this cry conveys the absence of an answer.
>
> (quoted in Stack, 1969, 157–8)

> *Teorema*... and *Porcile* [1969] are free, experimental films. They propose no outcome nor solutions. They are 'poems in the form of a desperate cry'. (quoted in Moravia, Betti, Thovazzi *et al.*, 1989, 129)

The presence of noise seems to offer the potential to radically problematize or suspend the traditional machinations of finding meaning, or making meaning, in popular music, and in the social sphere. In convening an international conference to probe this idea further, we adopted as a name a fragment of speech found in an early track from the post-rock group Mogwai.[2] 'Yes! I Am a Long Way from Home' (from 1997's *Young Team*) opens with a spoken description of the experience of the band live, delivered haltingly, and with some confusion. The music is described, counter-intuitively or as seemingly arising from non-native English, as 'bigger than words and wider than pictures'. Noise, we maintained, offered the potential to transcend correct adjectives too, so as to feel a way towards an expanded understanding of the sonic: to be louder than song, quicker than harmony, nearer than mixing, harder than sound.

Such an expanded understanding has remained difficult to locate in academic disciplines related to music. Traditional musicology, as applied to much classical music, has historically tended toward a near-exclusive consideration of melody and harmony. At the same time, popular music studies, especially as practised in academe, has been overly reliant upon its given foundation of lyrical poetry, allied with 'Eng Lit', as the artistic-subjective expression of the singer-songwriter, and the concomitant glorification of the individual (failings which are especially apparent in 'Dylanology'). And, while research emanating from the fields of popular and critical musicology has gone some way to redressing the balance, there still remains a general disparity with respect to the degree of detailed analysis ascribed to each musical parameter, as investigations of harmonic, melodic and rhythmic aspects still typically feature above more cursory explorations of sonic elements. So forms of music which privilege noise and rely upon high levels of sound manipulation continue to remain, to a significant extent, an unmapped territory in terms of contemporary musics.

By 2010, at the time of this conference, noise appeared to be a declining paradigm. Certainly there had been some key and relatively recent publications such as Douglas Kahn's *Noise, Water, Meat: A History of Sound in the Arts* (2001), or Paul Hegarty's *Noise/Music: A History* (2007), both following in the wake of Jacques Attali's seminal *Noise: The Political Economy of Music* (1985). And, at this point, many of the pioneering groups associated with noise-based popular musics discussed in this volume had met with wider acceptance and belated acclaim (the experience of seeing the reformed My Bloody Valentine had also prompted the convening of the conference), or stubbornly persisted, as with The Telescopes, in their sonic experimentation. And yet in other respects noise seemed to be increasingly

*Final moments of* Teorema (Theorem, *Pier Paolo Pasolini, 1968).*

disavowed in the smooth era of virtual communications and digital media. Typically noise was treated as if it were a strictly analogue phenomenon, to be consigned to the trash heap of history along with discarded vinyl records and phonographs, cassette tapes, video cassettes and floppy discs. Part of this rejection of noise was not just a passive abandonment but an active rejection of its transgressive assumptions and claims. So, although Simon Reynolds entitled a retrospective collection of his journalism *Bring the Noise* (2007; the title was also a nod to Public Enemy), the volume constituted a spirited attack on noise, both as a paradigm and in the practice of noise music as a pseudo-transgression that no longer offends anyone. Such sentiments were echoed in Steven Goodman's *Sonic Warfare: Sound, Affect, and the Ecology of Fear* (2010), which argues against the radicality of 'white noise' musics in favour of the bass-heavy dread of dub and dubstep, as well as in Ray Brassier's article 'Genre is Obsolete' (2009), that may as well have been entitled noise (music) is obsolete, were it not for a few exceptions made to the generic conformity of noise musics, and indeed Brassier's own collaboration with Mattin. A more promising sign was the then recently published *Noise and Capitalism* collection (Mattin and Iles, 2009), which situated noise practices politically beyond both the clichéd gestures of transgression and their equally clichéd critique, and in a profound relation with capitalism as both its co-opted product and immanent critique.

Since that time there has been a veritable flood of noise-related publications, falling into several distinct categories. One of these areas of research has been in relation to digital culture, and more specifically the phenomena of 'glitch' and the methodology of media archaeology. In terms of the former, the work of Rosa Menkman as glitch artist, curator and writer is a case in point, and one that has been taken up in a number of contexts.[3] Several recent books such as *Noise Channels: Glitch and Error in Digital Cultures* (Krapp, 2011) and *Error: Glitch, Noise and Jam in New Media Cultures* (Nunes, 2012) pursue these connections between noise and the digital via the concepts of glitch and error, showing that noise is hardly only an artefact of earlier, less perfect technologies and modes of communication. Indeed noise can be seen, in general, as a key concept of media archaeology, facilitating its non-linear histories of media, technologies and inventive practices. Other work on noise such as our own sister volume to *Resonances*, *Reverberations: The Philosophy, Aesthetics and Politics of Noise* (2012), along with Hillel Schwartz's mammoth opus *Making Noise – From Babel to the Big Band and Beyond* (2011) and Greg Hainge's *Noise Matters: Towards an Ontology of Noise* (2013) situate noise in cultural and philosophical contexts, showing how questions of noise go well beyond sonic phenomena to enter such fields as information theory, urban space, audiovisual practices and literature, to name but a few.

This expansion of noise 'studies' into multiple fields, while a timely riposte to its delimitation as a purely sonic and/or analogue phenomenon, does risk, however, a loss of focus on, or dispersal of the relation between, noise and music. The current volume aims to address this in the context of this expanded field of noise research, zeroing in on the specific relationships between a range of contemporary musics (post-classical, improvisatory, psychedelic, [post-]punk, industrial and noise music proper) and their respective deployments of noise, in order to extend some of the earlier work on noise and musics as well as to answer some of the critics who would seem to be arguing for the abandonment of noise as a useful paradigm for engaging with these musics.

Noise remains a lacuna in the vast majority of accounts of contemporary popular music, and in a critical exploration of noise lies the possibility of a new narrative – one that is wide-ranging (a continuum across numerous genres of music), connects the popular to the underground and avant-garde, posits the studio as a musical instrument, problematizes standards and assumptions about music and consumption/spectatorship, and prompts new critical and theoretical paradigms and approaches from those seeking to write about music. This edited collection addresses and traverses this untold story. It seeks to identify and analyse types of noise and noise-music, to understand noise as both applied and designed, and accidental and courted, to propose and test new theoretical frameworks for the discussion of noise, to highlight the way in which noise redefines and reshapes the relationship between the performer and audience, or artefact and appreciator, and to posit noise as an essential category in and for the writing about music.

# PART ONE
# Noise, Rock and Psychedelia

# CHAPTER ONE

# 'Kick Out the Jams': Creative Anarchy and Noise in 1960s Rock

## Sheila Whiteley

Unity is princely violence, is tyrannical rule. Discord is popular violence, is freedom.[1] (Panizza, quoted in Jelavich, 1985, 62)

It is not insignificant that Panizza's play 'The Council of Love' (1893) was revived in 1969 when a stage adaptation by Jean Bréjous was produced at the Théâtre de Paris. His challenge to the taboos surrounding religion and sex and his theory that genuine freedom is possible only at times of chaos and upheaval would appear apposite not only to the student revolution in Paris (May 1968)[2] but also to the extremes of noise that characterized certain genres of popular music associated with the 1960s counterculture. As I wrote in *The Space Between the Notes*:

> Initially there appears to be an underlying tension between the political activism of the student New Left and the 'Fuck the System' bohemianism of the hippies and the yippies. At a deeper level, however, both extremes were united in their attack on the traditional institutions that reproduce dominant cultural-ideological relations – the family, education, media, marriage and the sexual division of labour. There was a shared emphasis on the freedom to question and experiment, a commitment to personal action, and an intensive examination of the self. (Whiteley, 1992, 82)

As Roszak wrote at the time, 'Beat-hip bohemianism may be too withdrawn from social action to suit New Left Radicalism; but the withdrawal is a direction the activist can readily understand' (Roszak, 1970, 66). It would seem, then, that an acceptance of chaos and uncertainty can be interpreted as a prelude to rebirth, the ego temporarily destroyed before moving on to a changed form of consciousness. As Attali tellingly observed, noise contains prophetic powers. 'It makes audible the new world that will gradually become visible' (Attali, 1985, 11).

It is also relevant that the distinction between music for living by and music for leisure was of fundamental importance to the counterculture, highlighting the ways in which music and socio-cultural politics could fuse into a collective experience. As such, the impact of noise (inharmonious sound, distortion, dissonance, and the connotations surrounding discord itself) can be interpreted as underpinning a revolutionary agenda suggestive of a state of creative anarchy,[3] which is arguably distinct from the more soft-focus connotations of 'All You Need is Love' and the pacifist agenda implicit in such slogans as 'Make Love Not War'.[4] If, however, Roszak is correct in identifying 'beat-hip bohemianism as an effort to work out the personality and total life style that follow from New Left social criticism' (Roszak, 1970, 66), then a movement towards a communality based on love could appear a logical development. Discord and the darker extremes of 'noise' associated with performers such as Jimi Hendrix and the MC5 would thus come into focus as the first stage in the counter-cultural agenda of establishing a relevant and alternative lifestyle. As Jeff Nuttall observed, two of the aims of the Underground were to 'release forces into the prevailing culture that would dislocate society, untie its stabilizing knots of morality, punctuality, servility and property; and [to] expand the range of human consciousness outside the continuing and ultimately soul-destroying boundaries of the political utilitarian frame of reference' (Nuttall, 1970, 249). As the cartoon, Gandalf's Garden explained, 'Your minds are occupied territory! Take Over! Mind revolution is all happening!' (*International Times*, 1969, 24). With these thoughts in mind, my investigation explores three examples of the way in which noise was harnessed as a metaphor for musical resistance and disruption which challenged the politics of war, social and racial inequality and a culture in crisis.

## The politics of noise

As the saying goes, 'whenever a man's work is plugged into his times, it cannot help being political' (Hicks, 2000, 209) and Hendrix's performance of 'The Star Spangled Banner' at the 1969 Woodstock Festival provides a specific insight into the way in which his music became 'a symbol of solidarity and an inspiration for action' (Frith, 2000, 103) for those 'seeking to transform our deepest sense of the self, the environment' (Roszak, 1970, 156). As Bob Hicks wrote in his 1970 memorial dedication, 'at the time, his most obvious merit was strength, an awesome primeval power of the psyche more than capable of knowing, understanding, manipulating ... the torrent of infuriated fire careening through his equipment' (Hicks, 2000, 208). Charles Shaar Murray is in full agreement: 'When he used the onomatopoeic power of his guitar to evoke the sounds of urban riots and jungle fire fights as he did in 'Machine Gun' and 'The Star Spangled Banner' – he used every atom of that knowledge' (Shaar Murray, 1989, 23).

Hendrix was certainly aware of the problems confronting black servicemen in Vietnam: they represented 2 per cent of the officers and were assigned 28 per cent of the combat missions (Shaar Murray, 1989, 23). He was also aware of racial inequality on the home front and had dedicated 'Machine Gun' 'to all the soldiers that are fightin' in Chicago, Milwaukee and New York ... oh yes, and all the soldiers fightin' in Vietnam'[5] (Hendrix, quoted in Shaar Murray, 1989, 22). For example, 4 April 1968 had seen the death of civil rights activist Martin Luther King and there was a growing awareness that a political system that perpetuated inequality and racial injustice was untenable; that the war against Vietnam was itself symptomatic of wider social and moral issues. The timing of Hendrix's performance of 'The Star Spangled Banner' – considered by many to be the most complex and powerful work of American art to deal with the Vietnam War – at a festival dedicated to 'three days of peace with music' is thus significant. As Bob Hicks comments, 'It was a chillingly contemporary work, a vision of cultural crisis, of structural breakdown and chaos, screeching to an almost unbearable tension which must, somehow, burst' (Hicks, 1996, 209).

For Americans, 'The Star Spangled Banner' is the most familiar of all songs, one which speaks of 'the land of the free', 'the home of the brave' – sentiments that are intended to inspire a nation at war. By 1820 the melody had been used as a setting for about 50 American poems, almost all of a patriotic nature, including one by Francis Scott Key in which the phrase 'By the light of the star-spangled flag of our nation' appears. The melody thus brings with it strong associations with the patriotism associated with a nation at war,[6] and although those at Woodstock may have been unaware of its history, 'the ironies were murderous: a black man with a white guitar; a massive, almost white audience wallowing in a paddy field of its own making; the clear, pure, trumpet-like sounds of the familiar melody struggling to pierce through clouds of tear-gas, the explosions of cluster-bombs, the screams of the dying, the crackle of flames, the heavy palls of smoke stinking with human grease, the hovering chatter of helicopters ...' (Shaar Murray, 1989, 24)[7] evoked by Hendrix's performance. The straight melody finally comes through on 'gave proof through the night', and the anthem ends to the sounds of feedback and a final ear-shattering grind as the guitar strings are treated to a crude bottle-neck slide against the mike stand. As Shaar Murray writes:

There is no precedent in rock and roll, soul music or the blues for what Hendrix did to his national anthem that muddy Monday morning ... The sustain and feedback obtained by running his massive Marshall amplifiers at maximum volume to turn the bass growl of a 'dive-bomb' into higher and higher overtones gradually overwhelm[ing] the fundamental pitch of the original note ... (Shaar Murray, 1989, 194)

as the percussive distortion and crackling feedback aurally attack the original three-four meter of the neatly balanced phrases. 'Defiant and courageous in its ambition, deadly serious in its intent and passionately inspired in its execution ... it was a compelling musical allegory of a nation bloodily tearing itself apart' (Hicks, 1996, 195).

While there was, at the time, no comparable attack on the British National Anthem, it is nevertheless evident that the subversive use of noise as a political statement was recognized by the Beatles as evidenced in George Martin's musical arrangement of 'A Day in the Life', the final track on their 1967 album, *Sgt. Pepper's Lonely Hearts Club Band*. By 1967 their international status was unquestionable. The release of *Revolver* in August 1966 had, as Russell Reising writes, transformed rock and roll, inventing musical expressions, 'trends and motifs that would chart the path not only of the Beatles and a cultural epoch, but of the subsequent history of rock and roll as well' (Reising, 2002, 11). It included a string octet ('Eleanor Rigby'), the first Beatles' song adapted from a literary source ('Tomorrow Never Knows'/Timothy Leary's *Psychedelic Experience*), the first recorded use of reverse tape effects and ambient background sounds ('Tomorrow Never Knows', 'Yellow Submarine'). As such, it is no great surprise to note that the Beatles had been invited to perform at the June 1967 Monterey International Pop Festival, the first to headline rock and popular music. Having stopped touring, and currently working on the studio-based *Sgt. Pepper's* album, they had declined the invitation, but nevertheless contributed to the official festival programme by sending an original illustration in coloured pencil, felt marker and ink, with the header 'Peace to Monterey', signing it 'sincerely, John, Paul, George and Harold' – a possible reference to the current British Prime Minister, Harold Wilson.[8]

While there is little to suggest that the Beatles were directly involved in political protest, 1967 saw the release of two songs where the use of noise ('A Day in the Life'), and an extended bricolage of ambient background sounds and snippets of songs ('All You Need Is Love') challenged the complacency surrounding 'swinging London'. They also aligned them with the peace movement and the philosophy of love that characterized hippy philosophy, as suggested by Lennon's lyrics to 'Tomorrow Never Knows', the final track on the Beatles' 1966 album, *Revolver*: 'Love is all and love is everyone/it is knowing, it is knowing'. His vision of what might be – the importance of peace, love and understanding – also informed his thoughts about the power of music as a force for change as evidenced in 'All You Need is Love', which he composed as a 'singalong' for the international television programme, 'Our World', broadcast by satellite to 26 countries on 25 June 1967. The most distinctive feature of the song – apart from its simplistic repetition and frequent meter changes – comes in the extended coda, where such extramusical sounds as cowboy-style 'whoops', Baroque-style trumpet fragments, snatches of a big band version of 'In the Mood', 'Greensleeves' and a faint echo of the refrain of 'She Loves You' suggested to some that 'All You Need is Love' may itself be a parody of the so-called 'Love' generation (O'Grady, 1983, 142). Lennon, however, regarded it as a political song and, as such, the introduction, with its brass band version of the 'Marseillaise', provides a relevant context[9] in its associations with the French Revolution, the International Revolutionary Movement of the eighteenth and early nineteenth centuries, the Paris Commune, and anarchic leftist revolutionaries. Lennon's subsequent single, the blues-based 'Revolution' (B-side to 'Hey Jude') released in 1968, nevertheless makes what appears to be a more passive statement ('But when you talk about destruction,/Don't you know that you can count me out') and his much-publicized quest for peace in Vietnam continued with 'The Ballad of John and Yoko' and 'Give Peace A Chance', both released in 1969.

The musical distinction between contemplative, peaceful protest and the ear-shattering cacophony that accompanies apocalyptic chaos can be characterized by the polarization of consonance/dissonance. While the former provides a context for participation (in, for example, peace rally anthems), the latter overtly challenges and confronts. At its most extreme in the Coda to 'A Day In the Life', 'the spiralling ascent of sound' challenged 'the warm combination of acoustic guitar and piano' (Hannan, 2008, 60) that introduces the song, the complacency inherent in contemporary society ('A crowd of people stood and stared ...', 'A crowd of people turned away', Lennon's first and second verses) and the 'muzzy' effect on McCartney's vocal in the middle section of the song, which 'sounded as if he had just woken up from a deep sleep and hadn't yet got his bearings' (Hannan, 2008, 60). A climbing crescendo achieved by recording a small symphony orchestra four times on a separate four-track tape was used twice, following the line 'I'd love to turn you on' which ends both the first and final verses, while the final sustained piano chord (which involved two grand pianos, an upright piano, a Wurlitzer electric piano, a blond-wood spinet and a harmonium with a 43-second sustain) was created by a series of staggered overdubs of the chords, so allowing for cross-fading between them, while effecting an ever-changing timbre as the tonal emphasis seems to shift from the tonic to the third and then to the fifth and finally to the octave as the harmonics of the various overdubs interact and amplification is applied.[10]

The dramatic effect of the indeterminate textures of the ascending orchestral clusters is contextually anarchic in its intrusion into the passacaglia-like countermelody of the first two verses, albeit that Lennon's lyrical vocal 'features an unusually expressive use of non-harmonic tones, notably the leaps to dissonant notes in the latter part of the first and fourth bars ('I read the news to-day/oh- boy/a-bout a luck-y man who/ made the grade') (O'Grady, 1983, 138), so hinting at an underlying disillusionment. McCartney's second section is more frantic in its delivery, coming to an abrupt conclusion at the words 'Somebody spoke and I went into a dream', the vocal line becoming obscured by the progressively louder orchestral unisons on the root of each chord, before a two-bar unison brass motif plunges the key down a minor third for the return of the first section. This time, the bass leads to the intense orchestral build-up before the shifting timbres of the final sustained piano chord and its 30-second decay lead finally into 'a noisy 15kHz tone leading to a two second piece of gibberish which was cut into the run-out groove of the LP' (O'Grady, 1983, 61), so casting doubt as to whether the song's powerful imagery and disruptive musical aesthetics would inspire listeners to wake up and question (as suggested by the ringing alarm clock that heralds McCartney's middle section and the crowing cock in 'Good Morning, Good Morning')[11] or whether it would be interpreted as yet another example of the Beatles' love of the 'slicks and tricks of production' (Goldstein, 1967, 173).[12]

While the use of tone clusters suggests a certain comparison with Penderecki and his 'Threnody to the Victims of Hiroshima',[13] the Beatles' commercial obligations meant that they had to avoid overt political comments and, as such, what they did say about the UK's attitude towards the war in Vietnam was rather confusing and their lyrics move between the merits of political and personal change, without identifying any specific ideological solution. In contrast, Mick Jagger (Rolling Stones) was at the July 1968 Vietnam Solidarity Campaign demonstration at the American Embassy in Grosvenor Square, but his solution was to fall back on his rock credentials ('What can a poor boy do/'cept play for a rock 'n' roll band'; 'Street Fighting Man') and move towards a more Svengali-like image with 'Sympathy for the Devil', which related, to an extent, to the counterculture's stand against the established church and its support for what was seen as the West's exploitation of Third World countries and the USA's militant intervention in Vietnam. It is also evident from the introductory 'Please allow me to introduce myself' that the song also draws on Mikhail Bulgakov's *The Master and Margarita* (1967), a story about the devil's personal appearance in Moscow and his anarchic pranks, which was given to Jagger by Marianne Faithfull.

While all branches of the counterculture were united in their stand against the war in Vietnam, popular music played a largely symbolic role in challenging the political status quo. As Shaar Murray comments: 'The Beatles were lovably cheeky to authority'[14], albeit that 'the FBI considered

John Lennon and Yoko Ono a sufficient threat to US security to maintain surveillance on them ... The Rolling Stones slouched and sneered at [authority] ... Hendrix simply acted as if it wasn't there' (Shaar Murray, 1989, 18), and despite being courted by the Black Panther Party he consistently withheld any pubic endorsement of their activities. In contrast, the MC5's association with the White Panther Party and the often revolutionary rhetoric that accompanied the band throughout its career was sufficient for the Federal State Authorities to recognize them as a politically subversive threat. Yet, as Charles Shaar Murray asks, 'Were the MC5 a radical activist band or a band caught in a moment when their electric playing and act synergise with the time?' (Shaar Murray, 1972)

By 1968 the MC5 had become Detroit's leading underground band, performing at revolutionary rallies against a political backdrop of racial inequality and suppression, most notably the 1967 riots when confrontations with the US national guard and US army troops resulted in 43 deaths and over seven thousand arrests. The band's second single, 'Looking at You' was supposedly recorded in downtown Detroit 'sometime circa the 1967 riots', feeding the myth that 'the band were a group of "rock and roll guerrillas" who both fomented and embodied disorder with their rousing performances' (Waksman, 1998, 47) and feedback-laden sound. Further violence against protesters at the 1968 Democratic National Convention was highlighted by the MC5's revolutionary rallying cry, 'Kick Out the Jams, Motherfuckers', and a recording contract with the Elektra label.[15] Recorded live at Detroit's Grande Ballroom and released in 1969, *Kick Out the Jams* initially attracted an adverse review by Lester Bangs (*Rolling Stone*, 5 April 1969), which drew attention to its pretentiousness – the band's 'scrapyard vistas of clichés and ugly sounds' – and its Introduction by band manager John Sinclair, 'Minister of Information' for the White Panthers (Bangs, 1991, 226). While Bangs later withdrew his contempt for the album, claiming it to be one of his favourites, and the band itself a 'righteous minstrel ... rife with lamentations and criticisms of the existing order' (Bangs, 1991, 226), his identification of Sinclair is interesting. As a devotee of Beat culture and avant-garde jazz, and a founder of Trans-Love Energies, he recognized the potential of rock, and in particular the MC5, to influence social change and attract a growing youth counterculture to 'tune in, turn on, and drop out'. As Waksman observes, 'The stated goal was to turn the momentary synesthetic pleasure of musical experience into the basis for cultural revolution' (Waksman, 1998, 48).

Not least, the Trans-Love Collective delighted in taunting police and other symbols of authority with anti-establishment street theatre, often tongue-in-cheek writing in its underground press (*Creem*, for example, grew out of John Sinclair's White Panther Party and provided Lester Bangs with 'space for the farthest reaches of invective, scorn, fantasy, rage and glee' [Marcus, 1991, xii]), and inflammatory rhetoric at MC5 concerts.

With racial tensions high in Detroit, Sinclair's revolutionary invective and increasing focus on the high-profile potential inherent in the MC5's performances attracted increasing conflict with the authorities. Amplified music, for example, had been banned from city parks and Sinclair decided to hold an MC5 concert in defiance of the laws and was given permission to hold a series of concerts on the outskirts of the city, which were framed as multimedia events and punctuated by his radical speeches: 'Brothers and sisters, I want to see your hands up there! I want everybody to kick up some noise! I want to see some revolution out there!'[16] As rock journalist Dave Marsh wrote about his experiences with the band: '[S]o powerfully did the MC5's music unite its listeners leaving those 1968 and 1969 shows, one literally felt that anything, even that implausible set of White Panther slogans, could come to pass. In that sense, the MC5, with their bacchanalian orgy of high energy sound, was a truer reflection of the positive spirit of the counterculture than the laid-back Apollonians of Haight-Ashbury ever could have been' (Marsh, 1970).

The creation of the White Panther Party as the political wing of Trans-Love Energies on 1 November 1968 has been interpreted as a meeting of minds inside and outside the band in its call for total freedom. For Rob Tyner (vocals), the challenge was to safeguard the band's freedom of speech, and Wayne Kramer (guitarist) subsequently defended the band's revolutionary ideals: 'We not only talked about revolution, we believed it. The part about destroying the government and taking over and shooting it out with the pigs and all that – that didn't work. But the other part about the concept of possibilities, the revolution of ideas – that has changed the world' (quoted in DeRogatis, 2002). While the White Panther Party's call for a programme of 'rock and roll, dope and fucking in the streets' is reflected in the MC5's sexually explicit performances, its close identification with the Black Panther Party's armed self-defence strategy provided Sinclair with both radical credentials and credibility for the TLE as both a vanguard revolutionary organization and an arm of the Youth International Party. Its agenda for national visibility rested on the MC5, thus drawing attention to the significance of music in expressing a countercultural agenda of youth in revolt and hence, Sinclair's aim that the band should achieve national popular acceptance.[17] As Waksman writes, '[T]he energy that the Five generated was seemingly meant to break down the barriers between audience and performer and to radicalize the band's audience by awakening their deadened senses and compelling them to throw off the (mostly sexual) constraints imposed by the culture at large' (Waksman, 1998, 49).

The MC5's live album thus provides an insight into the construction of popular music as a force for political/cultural change while raising questions as to whether the band's revolutionary profile and militant posturing were distinct from Sinclair's inclusion of the White Panthers' core philosophies as liner notes on the album: 'The MC5 is the revolution ... the music will make you strong ... and there is no way it can be stopped now. Kick out the jams motherfuckers.' The title track, which opens with two power chords, segues into feedback over Dennis Thompson's pulsating drums. Its rousing hook and aggressive use of electric amplification is heightened by Kramer's guitar solo, where repetitive high-pitched sounds finally swerve into the final chorus 'Kickout the jaaaaams/I done kicked 'em out' against cries of 'MOTHERFUCKERS'. It is, however, 'Rocket Reducer No. 62 (Rama Lama Fa Fa Fa)', the closing song on side one of their album, that best conveys the live sound and inflated masculine dynamic of the MC5. 'I've gotta keep it up 'cause I'm a natural man' sets the tone and connotations of the song, which melds a one-chord blues vamp with maximum amplification, while Tyner's electric guitar hammers out 'the main musical figure over a wave of feedback generated by fellow guitarist Fred "Sonic" Smith'. In particular, the climactic finale to the song embodies cock-rock's[18] potency as 'the two guitarists take off on an orgasmic solo flight, pursuing each other on their respective fretboards while the rest of the band lays silent. A full minute of rapid distorted runs is capped by a final bluesy bend, and when the rest of the band rejoins for a final crash of the chords, the "rocket" is "reduced" to a state of detumescence, signified by the ensuing silence as both the song and the album's side come to an end' (Waksman, 1998, 63). The heat of the musical moment is summed up in Pam Brent's account of one of the MC5's shows for the first issue of *Creem*:

> The roaring vibrations and now-language combine to put the audience in an indescribable and frenzied mood. The voice of the Five resounds all that is the youth of today. An aura of all our sought-after goals: love, peace, freedom, and f-king in the streets – they are echos [*sic*], an incarnation of our will. We receive them with appropriate joy and rapture. (Brent, 1969)

While the anti-authoritarian title of the album and the title track hint at revolution – 'Let me be who I am and let me kick out the jams' – Kramer subsequently explained that the band's catchphrase was initially directed at bands (most specifically British bands) who the MC5 thought were not putting sufficient energy into their performances ... Kick out the jams meant 'get off the stage. Stop jamming'. He also commented that the band's commitment to 'revolutionary' politics was concerned with 'loving awareness' as opposed to the 'defensive awareness' implicit in manager Sinclair's politics. 'We knew it wasn't right, we knew it wasn't gonna change things ... In our stage show, in the things we say on stage, we wish to project this openness, this loving awareness, this sensitivity towards a higher level of communication' (Shaar Murray, 1972), so raising the question as to whether the ideological differences between Sinclair's machine-gun rhetoric and the band's 'armed love' stance was a matter of sonic anarchy rather than revolutionary zeal. Not least songs such as 'Come Together' suggests more a musical enactment of orgasm and a celebration of noise rather than radical activism, albeit that sexual freedom was high on the counterculture's agenda. Characterized by excess volume and an unchanging harmonic structure (a repetitive single note followed by two power chords, which repeat through the song), the line 'together in the darkness' and Tyner's muttered 'it's getting closer ... God it's so close now' create a palpable sexual undertow. Reinforced by the orgasmic connotations of the rising crescendo of the power chords and Tyner's concluding 'togetherness', the track 'ends with a progression of chords that ascends and then lunges back downward while becoming increasingly out of tune, the blur of the drums and the whirr of the feedback further contributing to the heightened disorder that immediately precedes the song's finish' (Waksman, 1998, 65–6). Little doubt, then, that the song is about physical pleasure, so fulfilling Sinclair's conceptualization of the politics of affect and its relationship to rock'n'roll's significance in achieving the White Panthers' goal of sexual freedom – 'fucking in the streets'.

As Shaar Murray comments, 'The band had that indefinable magic and music was the weapon for change not allied to guns ... They are the masters of kinetic excitement, they know how to open a song at maximum power and then build from there and that is what makes them a better show than many a band whose technical ability may be infinitely higher' (Shaar Murray, 1972). His identification of 'show' and its relation to 'showmanship' is interesting. The MC5 were famous for the shock effect of their high-decibel performances and their provocative stage image where they would often appear with unloaded rifles, with 'Motor City is Burning' suggesting a supportive reference to the 1967 Detroit riots and the role of the Black Panther snipers. Yet, as Kramer subsequently observed, 'The image of the gun was a mistake. The idea that we would use armed resistance was archaic' (Shaar Murray, 1972), and in retrospect it would seem that the MC5 were, as Matt Bartkowiak suggests, a band whose aggressive stance was largely created by an interweaving of self-generated propaganda, dominant media frames, and an unapologetic desire to become a popular rock band. The exploitation of noise as an anarchic and revolutionary tool can then be interpreted as a means of 'packaging subversion into usable forms for audiences who seek escape and social location in the subversion and criticism of dominant forces through the language of revolution' (Bartkowiak, 2009, 96). Above all, the MC5 celebrate subversion through their manipulation of electronic noise, and as Jacques Attali writes in his musicological tract *Noise: The Political Economy of Music* (1985), sound, noise and music are all fundamental to the concept of social order.

> With noise is born disorder and its opposite: the world. With music is born power and its opposite: subversion. In noise can be read the

codes of life, the relations among men. Clamour, Melody, Dissonance, Harmony [...] noise is the source of purpose and power, of the dream – Music. [...] [i]t is a means of power and a form of entertainment. (Attali, 1985, 6)

## Contextualizing noise

Although the deployment of noise had been a feature of popular music since the advent of rock'n'roll, the extremes of sound generated by Marshall amps, feedback, distortion and overload allied to an often aggressive performance style provided a new and subversive interplay between sound as physical force and sound as a symbolic medium. While it is recognized that such associations quickly become conventionalized – the connotations of noise, for example, set certain limits or defining parameters to meaning while, at the same time, being open to a performative exhibitionism which defuses its more radical implications – more precise social meanings are oriented both through context and historical location. As Simon Frith observes, 'rock can't just be consumed, but must be responded to like any other form of art – its tensions and contradiction engaged and reinterpreted into the listeners' experience' (Frith, 2000, 103).

The association of noise as both a cultural referent and a musical expression of chaos and uncertainty can thus be understood as a framework which both disrupts and destroys the internal consistency of established codes of music (the formalistic structure of 'The Star Spangled Banner', the radical disjunction of sound in the coda to 'A Day in the Life', the MC5's high-decibel impact on John Lee Hooker's urban blues 'Motor City is Burning') through an imposition of sound combinations, mental associations and imagery which conjure up moods and images of cultural, social and political crisis, so making 'music into a symbol of solidarity and an inspiration for action' (Frith, 2000, 103) while explaining how its radical connotations could be co-opted for their revolutionary potential.[19]

## CHAPTER TWO

# Recasting Noise: The Lives and Times of *Metal Machine Music*

## *Nicola Spelman*

Since its 1975 release, Lou Reed's double album *Metal Machine Music: The Amine ß Ring* has undergone a number of transformations and re-communications that negate its identity as a single cultural object, while allowing its constituent materials new contexts from which to function as tangible sources of intertextual meaning. The rearrangement of popular music texts often involves changing the channel through which such works are mediated: original recordings are frequently recast as performances which are subsequently refashioned as DVD 'live' recordings, and the process stands as a testament to the fluidity of popular music texts in general. Often such acts are theorized and illustrated as a part of debates concerning the advent of digital technologies and their various concomitant effects. However, *Metal Machine Music* constitutes a less typical case in point in that, following its twenty-fifth anniversary reissue, the work underwent a regression of sorts: moving from recorded composition to score/arrangement (by Ulrich Krieger and Luca Venitucci in 2002) to performance (at the Berlin Opera House, Haus der Berliner Festspiele, in 2002) and finally to an improvised performance exploring the compositional techniques utilized in the construction of the original work (by the Metal Machine Trio in 2008). A CD/DVD release of the 2002 live performance (Zeitkratzer featuring Lou Reed, 2007) contributed a further element to this spate of refashioning, and contains a pre-concert interview in which Reed outlines aspects of compositional intent and the circumstances surrounding its recent modification. Suffice it to say, each of the aforementioned acts elicits a new response from listeners; a further opportunity to ponder the work's transgressive nature with reference to issues of intertextuality and perceived genre distinctions. Through close examination of the original and its subsequent transformations, my chapter explores such issues in an attempt to pinpoint potential shifts in perception resulting from this successive recasting of noise.

The original *MMM* contravenes what Simon Reynolds later referred to as a bankruptcy of 'noise-as-threat' (Reynolds, 2004, 57), since many of Reed's fans purchased it assuming its content to be of a similar ilk to his previous albums. With limited pre-listening opportunities, they were effectively lured into an auditory experience few were prepared for. Thus followed an unprecedented number of album returns and the record's withdrawal just three weeks later. That its contents had disturbed was without doubt. A plethora of adjectives – mostly negative (unsettling, shapeless, antagonistic, relentless, unlistenable, confounding) – surrounded album and artist, prompting one reviewer to surmise the possibility of Reed orchestrating a form of career suicide.[1]

Although many accounts of the album's unpalatable nature rest on attempts to describe its arresting sonic properties, the discrete sounds and techniques of timbral manipulation explored within *MMM* (heavy distortion, feedback, amplifier hum, use of tremolo units, varied tape speed, EQ, reverb and tone controls) were already standard fare by the time of its conception and release. As such, the distinctly experimental aspects of Reed's noisescape are located not in the sounds themselves but rather in the way in which they are creatively and unconventionally employed: the extensive layering, unremitting duration, indeterminacy of structure and marked attentiveness to multiples of the same spewing sound source. As Marie Thompson articulates, such ventures 'push the question of what the guitar might be, what it can do, exploring its sonic potentialities beyond its conventional modes of existence' (Thompson, 2012, 216).

In terms of compositional design, *MMM* might best be described as an amorphous mass that Reed simply 'rides'; his eventual dismount signalling a moment of stoppage but not necessarily an (or the) end. Over the years, he has made various pronouncements regarding the composer-defined parameters essential to the work's creation (guitar tunings, the positioning of guitars in relation to amplifiers, the reverb settings and use of tremolo units).[2] When sound is made to feedback on itself, an element of randomness is inevitable, but the aforementioned parameters corral the potential outcomes, ensuring a degree of composer intervention throughout. The fact that the various technologies were functional contributors to the compositional process held evident appeal for Lester Bangs, who wrote: 'I realize that any idiot with the equipment could have made this album, including me, you or Lou. That's one of the main reasons I like it so much' (Bangs, 1976). At the same time, this indeterminate approach generated structural and formal properties that continue to challenge and perplex listeners seeking to impose a mode of hearing reliant upon the identification of structural markers and a sense of dialectic. Such an approach is clearly fruitless, since *MMM* rebuffs logical, causal development; there are no identifiable, opposing musical powers and the music is not teleological.[3] Indeed it is precisely the lack of such properties that enable its potential identification as noise: 'Noise offers the hope of times improper, the prospect of unending, of non-linearity' (Hegarty, 2012, 15).

Of course randomness observed will typically possess a sense of connectedness, and despite its lack of conventional melodic phrasing and structured time in accordance with Reed's previous stylistic output, *MMM* has a number of recurring sonic gestures which perform a cohesive function and, at points, ground the work in various ways. The instances of prolonged pitched feedback have the potential to function as a central axis against which the ephemeral nature of other gestures (screeches and distorted pitched fragments) is enhanced. Similarly, the various beating/pulsating sounds occasionally hint at the possible establishment of rhythmic syntax, but their transient nature and inability to permeate other timbral strands limits our evaluative response to one concerning only relative duration (as opposed to the possible assessment of rhythmic congruence/dissimilarity), thereby accentuating the work's drone-like qualities. *MMM* is relentlessly unpredictable at a micro level, being arrhythmic and devoid of ordered riffs/melodies or harmonic progression, but remains reassuringly consistent in terms of its overall form. This encourages recognition of its vertical, sonic complexity and frees the listener from a 'concentrated, memory dominated approach to listening' (Mertens, 2004, 17); the need to follow an unfolding musical argument dictated by a dialectical subdivision of time. As Torben Sangild notes, 'In minimal noise, the complexity is not at the horizontal level of development, but rather on the vertical level of sound textures' (Sangild, 2004, 4.4.5).

As an alternative to musical argument and its associated perspectives of tension and release, *MMM*'s persistent nebulous quality, its intensive exploration of a single instrument and abiding concentration upon depth of textural and timbral effect are thus suggestive of stasis. Moreover, it is precisely this character that informs Dave Thompson's conceptualization of the album as a 'frozen moment' from one of Reed's earlier works 'plucked off the stereo and dangled in perpetuity' (Thompson, 2012). In an effort to elucidate the work's *raison d'être* in his 2007 pre-concert interview, Reed also recalls: 'it was what I like about rock, freed from a song' (Reed, 2007). While some writers have interpreted the work as a ravaging of time – see, for example, Paul Morley's reference to its 'furious bitterness tearing time apart' (Morley, 2010), the significance of *MMM*'s final statement potentially undermines such a reading. The use of a locked groove[4] immediately carries associations of 'unendingness' but, in contrast to its antecedent materials, the chosen segment for repetition has a clearly discernable inner structure – a recognizable beat pattern that facilitates an awareness of meter. Its continuation connotes eternity while its evident audible patterning simultaneously suggests a definitive statement of closure. It is as if Reed's amorphous creation has finally run aground, inviting comparison with the previous 62 minutes to suggest the unexpected surfacing of clarity and order, albeit unresolved.

Returning briefly to the notion of *MMM* as a captured, elongated moment from one of Reed's earlier songs, it is clear that some of its formal and timbral elements have roots in his earlier compositions. Various bootlegs alongside songs like 'Heroin' (1967) and 'Sister Ray' (1968) attest to the Velvet Underground's penchant for long-held pitches and/or repetition techniques, feedback, intense volume and distortion.[5] Influences brought about by Reed's exposure to the ideas of La Monte Young and Tony Conrad, via John Cale, are equally apparent; Conrad's description of the compositional work of the Theater of Eternal Music clearly resonates with the musical concepts explored within *MMM*: 'they went on for hours in overdrive […] The music was formless, expostulatory, meandering […] arrhythmic, and very unusual' (Conrad, 2004, 315). In essence, *MMM* works on the open-minded listener in much the same way as Young's drone pieces, encouraging a recognition that sound is capable of sustaining interest in its own right without necessarily being engaged in the axiomatic act of conveying rhythm and pitch. Cale's experimental composition 'Loop' (1966) – devoid of vocals, employing timbral exploration of feedback and concluding with a locked groove – is perhaps closest to the conceptual aspects of Reed's noisescape and further attests to Reed's propensity for the utilization of avant-garde ideas that result in a questioning of contextual assumptions and expectations.

Yet viewing *MMM* as the radical progeny of earlier songs which capitalized upon the exploration of drones, feedback and structural laxness does not sufficiently account for the album's acute denigration at the time of its release. To understand this, one must additionally acknowledge the changed function of its 'noise' elements in comparison with Reed's earlier music. Here, Sangild's classification of noise gestures is pertinent, for *MMM* – cited by Sangild as an example of 'minimal' noise (Sangild, 2004, 4.4.2) – marked a definite departure from the arguably more expressive use of noise witnessed in Reed's previous repertoire. The distorted semiquaver guitar response in the chorus of 'Vicious' (1972) with its contrasting timbral quality and abrupt semiquaver interjection suggestive of purposeful harshness/volatility, and the dissonance resulting from the lack of conventional melodic resolution at the ends of vocal phrases in 'Kill Your Sons' potentially perceived as a metaphor for the loss of mental functioning caused by clinical electric shock treatment (EST) are just two cases in point. Devoid of the type of stylistic and musical contexts in which such gestures are capable of signifying, *MMM* instead offers an acutely insular projection of noise where, according to Sangild, 'the gestural subject is detached and minimized' (Sangild, 2004, 4.5). Here, the remnants of 1970s rock convention (with reference to lyric, vocal, and articulation of form and structure) are purposefully discarded, resulting in a significant change in the listener's ability to decode its constituent materials. As Richard Middleton explains, 'Establishment of "audibility" is [...] a necessary precondition for the coming into operation of the signification process' (Middleton, 1990, 184) and, in this respect, it is likely most listeners would have failed to determine its 'audibility' on two counts: non-recognition of codes, and the rapid realization that, in relation to the album's assumed purposive function, the music was doing things that were both inapt and unfamiliar.[6] If there is truth to be found in Reynolds's assertion that noise 'occurs when language breaks down. Noise is a wordless state ... The pleasure of noise lies in the fact that the obliteration of meaning and identity is ecstasy' (Reynolds, 2004, 56), it seems the majority of Reed's former audience were not yet ready to enter the unintelligible void. Hardly surprising, then, that the reissue, scoring, and subsequent acoustic performance and live touring of *MMM* should prompt the question: Why? 'Why reissue *Metal Machine Music* Now?' (Krapp, 2011, 60); why invest in its dynamic (re)production?

Through an accumulation of reworkings, *MMM* is effectively transformed into a 'master project'; the unique qualities and emphases of each rearrangement ensuring it adds up to more than simply the sum of its separate parts. It is irrelevant that such an outcome was not envisaged at the time of *MMM*'s original conception, for the inner dependencies of *MMM* artefacts (each comprising more than a mere act of replication) provide a useful illustration of how all musical experience is inherently intertextual in terms of its creation and reception. Thus, as Stan Hawkins reminds us, 'processes of intertextuality circumvent the domination of one interpretation over another, or, to put it differently, the totalisation of any specific singularity [...] intertextuality, in musical terms, relates to the sounding of one text in and through the other' (Hawkins, 2002, 27–8). Each reworking, be it score, live performance or DVD, is dependant upon the original *and* all other 'versions', supporting Bolter and Grusin's observation that 'media are continually commenting on, reproducing and replacing each other' (Bolter and Grusin, 2000, 55). As such, it is useful to consider how the various recastings of *MMM* impact upon potential interpretations of this 'master project'.

The CD/DVD release of Zeitkratzer's[7] acoustic performance incorporates and re-fashions *MMM* in a new digital medium and at the very least offers a new means of access to Reed's work. There is no attempt to achieve transparency/immediacy, for much of the desired appreciation of Zeitkratzer's achievement comes from a necessary comparison with the original recording. The interplay between media is conscious as Zeitkratzer's acoustic rendition highlights various performative aspects not contained within the original composition, yet from an aural perspective it seeks positive recognition for its closeness to it (particularly structurally).

Before reaching this point, the original *MMM* had already re-emerged in the form of a remastered CD and had been meticulously transcribed by Ulrich Krieger and Luca Venitucci, the latter process provoking statements of incredulity from both Reed[8] and the music press: 'That Zeitkratzer could even conceive of transcribing Reed's original album in the first place almost defies belief', wrote critic Janni Cole (Cole, 2007).[9] While the first act of recasting may appear somewhat unremarkable, presenting the work on CD (as opposed to vinyl) converted the listening experience into a conceivably more passive and ordered affair. The duration of the four parts, previously dictated by the individual LP sides, became presented as separate tracks of 16'01" and the final locked groove was allowed to continue for the final 2'21" of track 4 before being abruptly cut off. Now anyone wanting to absorb the work in its entirety simply had to press 'play'; the requirement to flip each side of vinyl and actively decide its end point (lifting the stylus from the locked groove) became unnecessary. Yet, at the same time, the digital reissue allows detailed consumption of the work in the sense of repeating, rewinding, forwarding, and sampling. Isolating moments of the digital reissue would also have assisted saxophonist, Ulrich Krieger, and accordion player, Luca Venitucci, in their previously inconceivable task of transcribing its contents.

In a 2010 interview, Krieger explained that his motivation for such a project stemmed from a perceived connection of *MMM*'s materials to the work of Xenakis, free jazz, and industrial music. And, that he had discovered an ensemble capable of realizing such a venture was equally significant: 'Not until I played with Zeitkratzer in Berlin and we did our first collaboration with noise artists (Merzbow, Karkowski) I realized this ensemble might be able to play *MMM*' (Eyles, 2010, 2). The instrumentation of Krieger and Venitucci's 2002 scored arrangement[10] consists of violin, viola, cello, contrabass, soprano and tenor saxophones, trumpet, tuba, piano, accordion, percussion, and for the Berlin performance a guest guitar appearance by Reed at the end of track three. Interviews given by Krieger have since provided details concerning the processes and challenges of such a task, the former consisting of two main stages: first, assigning compositional elements in the original work to those instruments best capable of mimicking them; second, notating perceived events within a score utilizing proportional time notation: 'Strings can play continuous yet varying sound, and have the closest overtones to the guitar. Wind instruments can create sounds with a feedback quality. Accordion, piano and percussion can have a noise-like quality and fill in with other instruments' explained Krieger (Inglis, 2007). The discernable intention was to enable Zeitkratzer's musicians to achieve a soundscape recognizable as an amplified acoustic version of Reed's original *MMM*, which involved formulating new ways of producing sounds from traditional instruments. Krieger directed the use of reverb and compression, and explained that the only compromise in terms of electrical processing was the use of guitar distortion on the four string parts to thicken the sound, claiming in hindsight, 'I wouldn't go below 8 to 10 string players these days' (Inglis, 2007). The scored arrangement of *MMM*'s first three parts for its Berlin premiere was eventually developed into four, with Krieger suggesting that, even at that point, the sheer density of the original work meant his own reworking was in constant flux as more and more particulars emerged from repeat listening: 'since then [2002] I have done three major revisions [...] adding more details, more precise timings, changing some of the arrangement around to make it even closer to the original' (Eyles, 2010).

In some ways this mitigates the view that such a recasting constitutes a resolute harnessing of the original work; an attempt to hold fast its unwieldy affectations in the traditional form of written notation. Clearly the proportional time notation used by Krieger and Venitucci represents a deviation from, and extension of, traditional scoring methods. And yet the act of transcribing, of producing that which Chris Cutler terms a 'written memory' of sound (Cutler, 1991, 28), is nevertheless suggestive of a form of veiled containment. *MMM*'s recasting as a score effectively reverses the popular music aesthetic by replacing its sense of fluidity with something more rigid. Here Tim Wise's observation concerning the different ideologies informing the creation of classical and popular arrangements is illuminating:

> In classical music, the text – that is, the score – is conceived to be a permanent artistic statement. Repeat performances of the same piece of music by different ensembles [...] will almost invariably use essentially the same text [...] In popular music, the notion of the musical text is much more fluid, and a song will reappear in the repertoire of another performer in a different arrangement almost as a matter of course. (Wise, 2003, 631)

At the same time, transcribing allows and encourages closer analysis of its subject, highlighting features of the original that were previously, if unwittingly, obscured or overlooked: as Tony Whyton reminds us, 'the score provides western art music with something to be studied and revered' (Whyton, 2010, 39). Jon Pareles's review of Krieger's completed score for the Fireworks Ensemble 2010 performance hints at this very issue: 'The transcription changes everything. It corresponds to some of the more perceptible events of the original' (Pareles, 2010), and Krieger himself confirmed that the act of transcription was focused on grasping the 'essential elements'[11] (Eyles, 2010, 2). As for reverence, Reed has consistently praised the score, insisting it be appreciated as an independent artefact worthy of admiration: 'His [Krieger's] transcription I think is a work of art and should be released as such. I wanted to have it printed. It's just too good' (Doran, 2010).

A final, more obvious observation is that the score engages its receiver in a different manner to the recording, and here Timothy Warner's comparison of the two mediums is pertinent: 'by representing the fleeting flow of a particular set of sounds organized in time as fixed signs on pages of paper, standard notation not only preserves musical invention, but also transposes it from the auditory to the visual sphere' (Warner, 2009, 139). The score is something to be *looked* at and followed as a means of creating, in this case, a further re-working of the original composition. Stored through notation, the work now possesses what Simon Frith defines as 'a sort of ideal or imaginary existence (against which any individual performance can be measured – and found wanting)' with the result being that, 'as in the appreciation of classical music, the musical mind is thus elevated over the musical body' (Frith, 1996, 227). Perhaps this is why much of the publicity surrounding the implementation of the score referred to both the intellect and mental effort required to produce it: Asphodel – the label under which Zeitkratzer's recorded 2002 performance of *MMM* was released – published quotes in which Reinhold Friedl referred to the 34-page score as a 'real masterwork of instrumentation', while Dave Simpson described it as 'the original's perhaps slightly more complex sibling' (Simpson, 2007). Most evident of the temptation to draw comparisons between the assumed thoughtlessness of the original and the meticulous effort involved in its transcription and rearrangement is Pareles's review for the *New York Times*, in which he claimed the 'countless work-hours involved in transcribing and orchestrating [...] moves *Metal Machine Music* into a context where, perhaps, it always belonged: as an avant-garde piece of bristling minimalism rather than a rock musician's bizarre experiment' (Pareles, 2007). Here reference to the scored arrangement is engaged as a preparatory device for the predictable act of deriding the radical and imprecise approach employed in the creation of the original artefact.

A score demands mental concentration in terms of its construction and utilization, and imparts an inevitable sense of formality to each. From a performance perspective, Zeitkratzer's use of scored parts emphasizes that there is an order of events to be followed and thus constrains the sense of indeterminacy and immediacy evoked by the original work. While this imposition of decorum might appear to limit or at least divert much of *MMM*'s intrinsic vigour, Zeitkratzer's performance compensates for such by offering a changed perspective – a potential humanizing of Reed's work. Again this appears to have been one of Krieger's aims: 'I wanted to emphasize the orchestral side of it and the human touch and group experience by having it performed live' (Inglis, 2007). It is also a contrasting feature capitalized upon by Pareles, who describes the original as an 'inhumanly generated composition' and its recasting (as performance) as 'flesh rather than machine' (Pareles, 2010). But it is worth noting that some critics have conversely strived to highlight the human element within the original: 'no matter how many things you use to distort, modify, and change the sound, it all has to pass through human hands at some point and be shaped and modulated [...] there's no denying the thought and creativity behind the work' (Marcus, 2010). Bangs was particularly vehement in this respect, using it as a means to criticize formulaic radio-formatted and orientated ('MOR') music:

> I have heard this record characterized as 'anti-human' and 'anti-emotional'. That it is, in a sense, since it is music made more by tape recorders, amps, speakers, microphones and ring modulators than any set of human hands and emotions. But so what? Almost all music today is anti-emotional and made by machines too [...] At least Lou is upfront about it [...] any record that sends listeners fleeing the room screaming [...] can hardly be accused, at least in results if not original creative man-hours, of lacking emotional content. (Bangs, 1976)

In other words, statements concerning the human element of *MMM* are usually couched in arguments of compositional agency. They are also informed by long-standing debates concerning the impact of technological mediation, as Hegarty notes: 'Electricity threatened music as purity of human expression, and also of innate "talent" as it first distanced the musician from the sound, and second, masked inadequacies of technique' (Hegarty, 2007, 59).

While discussions surrounding 'humanness' appear somewhat futile, Zeitkratzer's performance clearly resonates with that which Hegarty observes concerning the perceived estrangement between musician and sound, since the performance offers to restore the bond between audience and *MMM*'s creative source. Although Gracyk observed that 'rock music is not essentially a performing art' (Gracyk, 1996, 75), there remains, however, a requirement for rock's primary text (the recording) to conjure up visual representations: 'when sound is divorced from sight by virtue of technological mediation' Auslander notes, 'the aural experience nevertheless evokes a visual one' (Auslander, 2012, 85). As such, many listeners' disaffected response to the original *MMM* may have been informed by a distinct inability to visualize Reed 'performing' it.[12]

By presenting *MMM* as a visual experience, Zeitkratzer focuses attention on the mechanics of its production. The audience are now privy to the various performance techniques engaged in the mimicry of the original recording[13], and arguably much of the appeal of the performance lies in the spectacle and novelty of extreme instrumental techniques (Friedl playing inside the piano, for example). Indeed, the audience are able to derive a certain pleasure from attempting to identify the various roles of discrete sound sources: cellos frantically bowing in imitation of Reed's tremolo units; close-miked brass instruments sustaining notes that mimic drones/feedback, and so on. In terms of its aural impact, however, the performance's largely acoustic properties result in a sound that is clearly distinguishable from the original. The intention to mimic is comparable to Steve Reich's treatment of strings in *Different Trains* (1988) wherein they provide a composite anaphone (sonic and kinetic)[14] for the train's sound and movement but are still recognizably strings. Although the original *MMM* cannot be regarded as non-musical sound in the sense of Reich's trains, Krieger is nevertheless attempting to emulate its sound in a similar manner.

Sangild describes the distorted guitar as a 'metonymy of "abrasiveness"' (2004, 4.2) and its replacement with amplified acoustic sounds is inevitably less edgy and dense; we don't hear the full array of distorted sounds that saturate the original work because Zeitkratzer are simply performing Krieger's interpretation of the pitches he hears therein. The music is almost pointillist in texture as discrete sounds emanate from instruments to build depth of texture and timbre without recourse to linear progression or instrumental interplay. Some critics suggested Krieger's work had resulted in a smoother, more refined product ('the rough edges of the original – such as the sounds of tape recorders being switched on and off, and abrupt changes in dynamic – have been smoothed over' [Licht, 2007]; 'their [Fireworks Ensemble] combined efforts brought about something richer and more meditative than the album' [Pareles, 2010]), but it is equally the case that some of the original gestures become more conspicuous: certain textural shifts, swells in particular registers and melodic fragments achieving greater emphasis as a result of being detected and identified as significant elements during the transcription process. When asked how Krieger's arrangement had altered his own comprehension of the work, Reed highlighted this very issue: 'It was amazing to hear the pieces that he latched onto, as pit stops, or [as places] to take off from. There are a lot of things he could be listening to, and he picked this one or that one, and I found it fascinating – what he was doing, his way of listening' (Petrusich, 2007). The stopping and starting of parts also takes on a different quality, perhaps because of the visual evidence thereof but also because of inevitable changes in dynamic and attack, both of which impact upon possible interpretations of formal progression.

Krieger has described *MMM* as 'no-ego music' because of the novel role each musician is required to perform: 'if you don't play, it will be heard. If you play, the audience might not recognise you playing' (Inglis, 2007). Certainly there is no apparent hierarchy in terms of the conventional methods of foregrounding particular instruments, and the fact that there is an ensemble committed to *MMM*'s active production imbues the work with a unitary identity that functions as an active endorsement of the original. Philip Auslander's observation concerning the authenticating role of live performance is also relevant here, in that 'it has become the means by which mediatized representations are naturalized [...] if the mediatized image can be recreated in a live setting, it must have been "real" to begin with' (Auslander, 2008, 43). In this sense, the Metal Machine Trio (MM3)[15] reworking 'completes' *MMM* by providing its final ingredient for the attainment of rock authenticity – a live, electric performance. 'In rock culture,' Auslander argues, 'live performance is a secondary experience of the music but is nevertheless indispensable, since the primary experience cannot be validated without it' (Auslander, 2008, 185). It should be noted that neither Zeitkratzer nor MM3 can independently fulfil this function, since Zeitkratzer's performance works within an experimental chamber music aesthetic, while MM3 offer pieces that are simply inspired by the compositional approach of the original.[16] However, collectively Zeitkratzer and MM3 possess the potential to corroborate their creative source – the band name of the latter further endorsing the notion of *MMM* as the 'master project'.

While each instance of rejuvenation has offered a fresh musical perspective from which to re-evaluate the original *MMM*, together they have also provided ample opportunity for Reed to re-engage with his past: to perpetuate and embellish those aspects which best cast him in the role of creative visionary. Up until its reissue, Reed's pronouncements on the

The Metal Machine Trio rework Metal Machine Music. *Used by kind permission of Daniel Boud.*

album typically admonished those who failed to comprehend its contents, revealing his desire for a cerebral response; an awareness that *MMM*'s art music influences demand a certain effort and advanced theoretical understanding on the part of the listener: 'I don't expect anybody with no musical background to get it [...] But like I told some of the ad people at RCA, they said it's freaky. I said right, and Stravinsky's *Firebird* is freaky,' he told Bangs (quoted in Johnstone, 2005, 58). Stories about the album being both a calculated bid to terminate his recording contract with RCA and an affront to those fans who had avidly consumed *Sally Can't Dance* – and demanded endless live reiterations of his classic songs – have since been discredited. Indeed, his musings on such myths now seem keener to dismiss the notion of such puerile intentions in a bid to maintain a more apparent musical/creative focus:

> The myth is that I made it to get out of a recording contract. OK, but the truth is that I wouldn't do that, because I wouldn't want you to buy a record that I didn't really like … The truth is that I really, really, really loved it [...] I honestly thought 'Boy, people who like guitar feedback are gonna go crazy for this.' Count me among them. If you like loud guitars, here we are. (Reed quoted in Petrusich, 2007)

Unsurprisingly, Reed delights in *MMM*'s change of fate, for it provides undeniable sustenance to a star-identity which has long drawn upon, and in turn reinforced, the archetype of misunderstood artist (rejected, then vindicated). In essence, *MMM* now serves as the ultimate statement attesting to his versatility, daring and forward-thinking as a popular music composer.

With respect to Zeitkratzer, and Krieger in particular, the benefits of working on such a project are clear: *MMM* forms a crucial part of their own narrative of noise exploration, a testament to their commitment to initiating novel stylistic fusions within Europe's New Music scene. Their reworkings (score/arrangement and performance) constitute further examples of experimental music artists seeking new ways to challenge themselves, as with Joanna MacGregor's performance of Conlon Nancarrow's piano roll compositions, Bang on a Can All-Stars' rendition of Brian Eno's *Music for Airports* (1978) and the Balanescu Quartet's rearrangement of songs by Kraftwerk. Indeed, my opening reference to *MMM* undergoing a veritable regression is informed by the reverse chronology induced by Krieger's act of scoring (scores typically preceding acts of performance and recording), where what was deemed irreproducible is meticulously transcribed as a homage to the original text. It may be suggested that *MMM*'s distinctive blending of popular and art music elements is perpetuated and enhanced as a result of its various recastings – the latter elements arguably overtaking the former in Zeitkratzer's case, only to be reversed within Reed and

Krieger's subsequent manifestation of Metal Machine Trio. According to Ray Brassier, this type of genre meddling is typical of noise works in general:

> Noise not only designates the no-man's-land between electro-acoustic investigation, free improvisation, avant-garde experiment and sound art; more interestingly it refers to anomalous zones of interference between genres. (Brassier, 2009, 62)

It is possible to argue that *MMM*'s various reincarnations have rendered its effective noise status invalid due to the greater level of public acceptance surrounding its reprise (see, for example, GegenSichkollektiv, 2012, 194). However, as Hegarty makes clear, '[n]oise is not an objective fact' (Hegarty, 2007, 3) and such determinations are dependant upon far more than mere public acceptance: for example, the relationship of the work to musical conventions, and to its historical, geographical and cultural context (see Hegarty, 2007, ix and 3). Perceptions of *MMM* have indeed changed since its original conception, but its ability to challenge traditional assumptions pertaining to many aspects of popular music style, composition and performance remains intact. Moreover, it would seem odd to exclude a work from a genre whose most visible proponents have oftentimes cited it as a source of creative influence.[17] Due to the increased profile of noise music in general, *MMM*'s relevance as a representative early work has perhaps never been more acute.

In conclusion, the rearrangement potential of *MMM* has proven to be eminent and substantial. The aforementioned 'versions' capitalize on the properties afforded by the channels through which they are mediated and offer a variety of opportunities to re-engage with Reed's original work. Each has its own distinct character and relationship to *MMM*, and their interdependencies in turn underline the need for analysts to address intertextual meanings. Reed's abiding confidence in his most provocative creation – 'in time, it will prove itself' (quoted in Bockris, 1994, 299) – has been verified, and rewarded, for the album has provided a fruitful means of sustaining his own artistic creativity, inspiring later works such as 'Firemusic' (2003) and his MM3 album *The Creation of the Universe* (2008). *MMM* stands as a significant example of music's transformative potential: the insights it offers in relation to the mediation and recasting of popular music are distinctly valuable and enlightening.

# CHAPTER THREE

# Shoegaze as the Third Wave: Affective Psychedelic Noise, 1965–91

*Benjamin Halligan*

## Theorizing psychedelia

The idea of noise as aberrant or 'incorrect', unwelcome or unpleasant sound, particularly in respect to intrusions into soundscapes typically understood as given over to harmony or melody, offers a way into theorizing psychedelia that breaks with the paradigms of previous critical engagements. These paradigms were too often hampered by musicology and associated critical methodologies, privileged analyses of lyrics, were distracted by anecdotal drugs lore, or nostalgically dallied with the gestural politics of the time. This chapter identifies the noise of psychedelia which, in its affective qualities, then allows for the possibility of charting its evolution across two subsequent scenes or 'waves': from the counter-culture to that of rave and shoegaze. Charting this evolution allows for the possibility of both reconsidering what constituted psychedelic noise in the first place, and how it functioned, and extending this question of functioning, in terms of affect, ideology and even class, into these subsequent two waves.

## Wave one: psychedelia

In the mix, to increase the relative volume of one component of the music typically anticipates or, live, is prompted by, instrumental soloing: as the instrument takes the lead from the vocal, or takes over from another instrument. These are the variables comprehensively understood via Moore's notion of the 'sound-box', where the sound mix seeks to create a 'virtual textual space' of, for example, 'kit central, bass slightly to one side, guitars more extremely to either side' (Moore, 2001, 121, 124).[1] Studio and live mixing effectively work in the same 'virtual textual' way, and the mix reproduces the hierarchical positioning of instruments and presences associated with live music. And soloing, as such, in rock music, typically becomes the domain of musical prowess or virtuosity, or speed and dexterity, or (and as also applicable to jazz and classical music) a remaking or reimagining of the principal melodic elements, in addition to a notion of personal artistic expression at work in an allotted temporal space. Likewise, in the live circumstance, the musician steps forward, into the spotlight, and so presents him or herself as the centre of the music event, for that duration. Yet as rock lent increasingly towards the ragged and freeform, exhibiting both the influence of jazz improvisation, as Macan notes (1997, 17), and also the insouciant looseness of the Rolling Stones of the mid-1960s, these temporal limits began to change. Could it be said that the idea of popular music as artistic expression comes to the fore at this moment, privileging musical expression in the genre, so that musical expression became 'urgent' and in need of early beginnings and substantial temporal spaces, with the instrumental element increasingly then coming to sprawl across the better part of a rock track's duration?

Discernible trends that conform to this sensibility and tendency are particularly apparent by the late 1960s when the guitar seems to break from its confines. But with this break comes a series of additional changes, all of which can be read as alterations to popular music in terms of noise over melody or harmony. In this is a rebalancing of music in favour of the kind of guitar noise that only a few years previously would have been considered to have been inappropriate or unmusical, incorrectly mixed or evidencing the misuse of the instrument, rather than sonically innovative. It is this influx of noise that constitutes the foundation of psychedelic music, and these changes can be summarized and reviewed under five general headings.

### *In respect to increased volume*

The mixing of Eric Clapton's guitar for the opening track of the *Blues Breakers* LP, 'All Your Love', is jarringly loud – as particularly apparent in the main riff, which repeatedly announces itself as Clapton deliberately applies excessive pressure to the guitar strings as his fingers move towards their position on the fret board (the amusical squeak of 'string talk').[2] The guitar dominates the mix, enveloping the listener (especially so in the original mono release), and suggesting the sonic intimacy of being sat too close to the guitar amplifier in the studio.

## *In respect of positioning*

Clapton's first solo on 'All Your Love' begins before a minute and a half of the track have elapsed. Mick Taylor's guitar solo for 'Vacation', the opening track of John Mayall's *Blues from Laurel Canyon* (1968), begins in half that time, so that the album's first solo occurs after barely more than a dozen words have been sung. The thirteen-minute 'acid' guitar solos that close the Butterfield Blues Band's 1966 LP *East-West*, and that effectively run throughout the entirety of the 'Golgotha' movement of Kak's 'Trieulogy' (from the 1969 album *Kak*), can be taken as a logical extension of this tendency.

What is 'acid' about the playing can be taken to be the way in which there is little or no space between the notes or guitar sounds; as with the effect of an LSD-induced hallucination, solid surfaces melt and meld – a stream or flow of interconnections matched by the stream of guitar soloing. In this way, guitar noise tends to jostle with and usurp vocals as the principal element of the track (so that 'song', with its connotations of vocals, comes to seem to be an inadequate term). So, both in terms of temporal space and in terms of sonic density (the eradication of spaces 'between the notes'), the guitar elements of the tracks are radically and massively expanded.

## *In respect of playing*

Clapton's soloing on 'All Your Love' and the next album track, 'Hideaway', is defiantly expressionistic. For 'All Your Love' he lags behind the beat in order to tarry with the guitar sound as much as playing (an effect that is, again, overwhelming in the mono mix), speeds the track on in its middle section where he often begins some way ahead of the beat, and discreetly incorporates feedback between some of his lines. Such an ascendency of guitar sound can also be found in the way that Jimi Hendrix would break off from singing and allow the guitar to complete the vocal line, mimicking his voice, particularly live, as if the instrument was free to roam across and intervene in any aspect of a song and become interchangeable with his voice, despite its electrified and fabricated nature. In this way the guitar playing becomes an intrinsic part of Hendrix's presence but also his self. This dominance of guitar sound is further suggested by the way in which, as Auslander observes, singers during this psychedelic period were typically vocally weak – a weakness that denoted a naïve authenticity of expression (the untrained vocals of a *cri de coeur*, perhaps drawing inspiration from Bob Dylan) and a straight 'emphasis on instrumental rather than vocal virtuosity' (2009, 82). But Clapton, unlike Hendrix, seems to undo or undercut the sentiments of 'All Your Love' (a yearning for erotic intimacy; in Mayall's slurred, fragmented vocals: 'all the lovin' missed lovin'/all the kissin' missed kissin"). His solo does not seem to resonate so much with a sense of emotional need, as would be expected, but seems keener to become a space in which he can experiment with form and guitar noise: the way in which waves of sound are sustained or allowed to diminish, and the inclusion of feedback too – music that speaks to and of its noise rather than mimics and harmonizes emotional outpourings.

Whiteley, who gives Summer 1965 as the point of origin of acid rock,[3] discusses Clapton's playing in 'SWLABR' from the 1967 Cream album *Disraeli Gears* as fully psychedelic (Whiteley, 2004, 9, 13). But there is nothing in 'SWLABR' that is not already apparent in 'All Your Love' in terms of the playing. If anything, Clapton's playing for the Cream track – corralled bursts of blues licks between lyrics rich with ambiguous and psychedelic imagery and sentiment (the title is an anagram of 'she walks like a bearded rainbow') – is more conventional, albeit for a sound now filtered through effects pedals. Whiteley reads 'SWLABR' as a Hendrix-esque guitar/vocal dialogue, where the two elements, then, blend into a whole. In these terms, 'All Your Love' could be read as a guitar/vocal dialectic, where ambiguity exists in the form (the playing in relation to the lyrics: a negative correlation) rather than the content (the ambiguous lyrical imagery and sentiment: 'vocalized' too by the guitar).

## *In respect of repetition and drone*

This ascendency of guitar noise is also unapologetic in term of its positioning or imagining of the listener: what was once proffered as often just 'pleasant' (the pop song) now gives way to a challenging aural experience, effectively demanding a form of surrender on behalf of the listener, with a suspension of their preconceived aesthetic norms or standards. And to achieve surrender, often induced via a siege of repetition and drone, required a song duration longer that the three and a half minutes typical allotted by the industry and radio stations for the pop song.

Repetition and drone in psychedelic music are often credited to the Velvet Underground but can also be found on the Brian Jones recordings of the Master Musicians of Jajouka.[4] Here repetition and drone seem to function as mantra or incantation, lulling or even semi-hypnotizing the listener. The quasi-religious live performances of psychedelic drone music often emphasized this consciousness-enveloping aspect: the singer as shaman, the music as ceremony, the concert as collective happening. Liquid lightshows used to accompany the music have an affective aspect in this endeavour: inducing a seeming slowing down of cognitive functioning, and with this a lowering of defences in the face of the engulfing nature of the music – a process that can then take some time from which to recover. This was

*Syd Barrett and Pink Floyd, 'Astronomy Domine' live in 1967.*

true of Pink Floyd's live renditions of 'Astronomy Domine' but it is with 'Interstellar Overdrive' (both on *The Piper at the Gates of Dawn* of 1967) that the music fully gives way to soundscapes of drones and repetitions.

## *In respect of dissonance*

Quicksilver Messenger Service's *Happy Trails* (1969) culminates in the prolonged acid guitar playing of 'Calvary', which runs in excess of thirteen minutes. Such playing, while arguably not technically arresting, further extends those elements of Clapton's and Hendrix's playing that are given over to effect – the music that speaks to and of its noise rather than mimics and harmonizes emotional outpourings. This requires substantial space in the mix for echo and the diminution of sounds rather than the delivery of a musical line or theme. That is, the 'atmosphere' space of the mix, for these atmospherics, becomes foremost in the sonic make-up of the track. In terms of the sound-box model, it is akin to a more extreme use of the mixing variable in favour of the guitar while, at the same time, the size of the box is suddenly expanded in order to resonate not so much with the guitar playing but with the guitar's sound. And the point of audition is shifted to a position where such sounds become more audible.

In this, the ascendency of guitar sound is complete, and guitar noise comes to outflank previous conventions of playing. So the seemingly fumbled flurry of notes in Roger McGuinn's soloing on the Byrds' 'Eight Miles High' (a 1966 single from *Fifth Dimension*) suggests not so much an error of musical misjudgement but that some other guiding intelligence is at work, here cutting quite deliberately across the folksiness of the song with the attack and urgency of the playing.

These five tendencies evidence a moving beyond the ways in which pop or rock music was previously accepted and comprehended – that is, here, a movement beyond that former music's musicality. And these five tendencies fed into, or generated, psychedelic music, and came to represent an aspect of the unfettered, 'expanded' nature of psychedelic art forms. An example of the 'before' can now usefully be invoked: the mixing of Hank Marvin's guitar playing on 'Apache', a 1960 instrumental track by the Shadows, works to foreground the richness of the guitar sound, as sufficient 'voice' and drama in itself. And even in the few moments when Marvin embellishes his playing, he remains locked into the group's tempo, the guitar playing remains clear and 'clean' (even with his use of the tremolo arm), in terms of notes and spaces, and respects the shifts in rhythm across each section throughout.

## Psychedelic noise as affect

Psychedelic music was generally termed or identified as 'head music' (and its proponents 'heads'), and so taken as akin in some respects to Conceptual Art: the materiality of the artefact itself becomes irrelevant,

*Dr Hans Keller: 'Why has it got to be so terribly loud? For me I just can't bear it...'*

*Syd Barrett: 'I personally like quiet music just as much as loud music.'*

and any questions of 'correctness' or technique prompted by the artefact rendered irrelevant too, once it is understood that the artefact intends to speak directly to 'the head'. Indeed, those five tendencies listed above, all of which could be described as straight 'errors', inscribing noise into music, only work to further denote the invitation extended to bypass lucid cognition (as reasoning and aesthetic judgements) in favour of vague ideas of the self, or soul, or Id: the 'psyche'. Indeed, this dialogue occurred at the time, in the celebrated 1967 appearance by Pink Floyd on the BBC's *Look of the Week* (see previous page). This inscribed noise therefore seeks to affect the psyche. And, although the psyche is therefore the assumed goal of psychedelic music, this understanding has eluded academic writers, whose methodologies remain untroubled by this given.

Whiteley's approach is allied to that of poststructuralist analyses of cultural artefacts predominant in the early 1990s. Her *The Space Between the Notes* acknowledges 'the general trend towards a changed state of musical consciousness' (Whiteley, 2004, 2) in respect of psychedelic releases from the Beatles and the Rolling Stones at the end of the 1960s and assembles a textual reading (centred on the 'musical codes' involved and their interrelationships [Whiteley, 2004, 4]) while acknowledging methodological problems arising from the notion of a semiotics of sound. Decoding in this respect remains in constant flux at best and, at worse, still evidences a pitch queered by received interpretative frameworks that would seem to originate from the least disinterested of parties – the hippies themselves (Whiteley, 2004, 4–5). Hicks also touches on the problems of interpretive frameworks in this field, noting music from Frank Zappa and the Mothers of Invention, and the Yardbirds, that would seem to be deeply psychedelic but anecdotally originated from musicians not in the least inspired by LSD use (Hicks, 1999, 66). But a corrective isolation of the musical form and social or cultural context still proves unsatisfactory in terms of dealing with the question of what could be called a nominally psychedelic ambience and atmosphere, as with 'Coming Back to Me' by Jefferson Airplane. And the problem of the questionable grounds of imposed interpretative frameworks can be extended to texts that pre-date psychedelia and yet came to be perceived as psychedelic touchstones nonetheless: the writing of Tolkien, Lewis Carroll and Kenneth Grahame (whose 'Piper at the Gates of Dawn' chapter of *The Wind in the Willows* seems to very precisely narrate an LSD trip; the chapter lent the title to the first Pink Floyd album), *The Saragossa Manuscript* (Wojciech Has, 1965), or the 'straight' folk songs collected on the soundtrack of *Zabriskie Point* (Michelangelo Antonioni, 1969), for example. But for Cotner such a notion of a meta-definition of psychedelia, freely press-ganging artefacts into a subculture, is a defining characteristic, dividing the psychedelic from Prog Rock: psychedelia is *a priori* and 'directly mediated by the counter-culture' (Cotner, 2002, 86).

These musical codes are presented and read as a 'correlation' of 'drug experiences and stylistic characteristics' of the music, towards that which could be termed a literary conceit: the suggestion of '*alternative meanings*' (Whiteley, 2004, 8; Whiteley's italics). So the coding and music (that is, the music's subtext) 'suggests a state of "tripping"' (Whiteley, 2004, 8), or 'reflects the state of mind on an hallucinogenic trip' and creates 'feelings analogous' and 'a homology' to acid trips (Whiteley, 2004, 33). Terms employed to track this are typically therefore at one remove, and centre on how a listener or audience would read the music. Declensions of the verb 'to evoke' are repeatedly used in approaching the specifics of Pink Floyd's music at this time (Whiteley, 2004, 30, 34, 94), a music of 'connotations' (Whiteley, 2004, 31) and techniques designed to 'reflect' certain states (Whiteley, 2004, 33). And it is along just such metaphorical lines that Whiteley is able to deftly extract from the unexpected chord progression of the Beatles' 'Strawberry Fields Forever' not only a musical dramatization of an LSD trip (that is, a dramaturgy of musical form, rather than merely looking to the narrative information delivered in the lyrics) but also the implicit message that these seasoned LSD users, the Beatles, here offer themselves as guides for those now seeking to be newly initiated (see Whiteley, 2004, 65–7). But then Whiteley also notes, albeit in passing and without later development, that psychedelic music could operate in an affective manner in that 'the sheer volume of noise works towards the drowning of personal consciousness' (Whiteley, 2004, 20).

Likewise, Hicks's discussion of psychedelia is initially an outline of 'LSD-inspired music' (Hicks, 1999, 63), which is elaborated in terms of parallels between experimental music and recording techniques (i.e. the art and engineering of the creators of psychedelic music) and the nature of LSD trips. He delineates the resultant parallels under the headings of dechronicization, depersonalization and dynamization (Hicks, 1999, 63–4). The latter facet denotes the ways in which the tangible hardness of material objects is perceived to become unstable, which then finds its parallel with the liberties psychedelic music takes with previously rigid song forms: '[m]ore than anything else, psychedelic music dynamized musical parameters previously stable in rock' (Hicks, 1999, 66). Or, along the same lines, that the pitch-bending glissandi effect from the use of the guitar whammy bar can be read as equating string bending with 'mind bending' (Hicks, 1999, 67–8). A more clinically orientated but essentially similar methodological approach to the same subject matter – one of equivalences, evocations and parallels – is found in Baumeister (1984, 339–45).

In this way, Hicks's and Baumeister's pioneering readings, like Whiteley's, essentially concern psychedelia *qua* psychedelia: a semiotics of psychedelic noise, a vernacular of metaphors. And Hicks places his work in a line of development from Whiteley's in this respect (Hicks, 1999, 113). DeRogatis, however, merely unthinkingly reproduces and gilds the cliché, without ever attending to the question of hallucinogenics and musical form; his 2003 study begins in 'prehistoric times' with the use of plants to 'enlarge the scope of the mind' (DeRogatis, 2003, 1). And Bromell ([2000] 2002) is not much better: psychedelic music as springing from musicians under the influence, and first baffling and then enticing North American teens. Yet despite far-reaching historical and cultural contextualizations for the development of psychedelic music, all mostly unsourced, and autobiographical passages on LSD use, Bromell's study eschews questions of subjectivity in favour of vaguely phenomenological reminiscences. Hegarty and Halliwell's discussion of psychedelic music in 1966–7, however, offers more elaboration, with particularly attention to the increasing duration of performances, so that psychedelic music

> emerged as a response to the effects of LSD; it tried not simply to emulate drug-taking or provide a background to consumption but rather to replicate the sensory experience of a trip by creating a total environment. (Hegarty and Halliwell, 2011, 24)

What is not clear here is on whose part this replication is occurring (a shamanistic/didactic method whereby the seer articulates his personal vision, or a credo whereby the like-minded gather to collectively reactivate or relive a moment of altered consciousness), or the ontological nature of the replication itself. But a critical approach which considers psychedelic music in respect of the nervous system rather than questions of cognition suggests a way out of the textual/cultural/anecdotal *cul-de-sac*.

In this respect, volume and drone, which engender vibration, coupled with repetition, allow for the uncanny materialization of the unseen: pain in terms of hearing, but also the flapping of loose clothing and movement of hair, and the physical feeling of sound experienced on – and even in – the body. This, then, is not so much a matter of psychedelia *qua* psychedelia, but rather of psychedelics of affective noise.

Music and affect, which centres on ideas of the body as much as (or substantially more than) the mind – experience over interpretation – points directly to the dance floor. And this step, along the lines of music as a certain type of affective noise, producing new subjectivities, also questions a cultural history that positions Prog Rock as the natural successor to psychedelia.[5] But the question of affect then becomes radically problematic. On the one hand, to consider acid musics and affect is to raise questions of cultures of opposition that look to a fuller conception of the functioning of such music. In this instance, it is to wrench the question of 1968, psychedelic cultures and LSD use away from revisionist readings of the first Summer of Love (of 1967). Hardt and Negri note that

> 'Dropping out' was really a poor conception of what was going on in

Haight-Ashbury and across the United States in the 1960s. The two essential components were the refusal of the disciplinary regime and the experimentation with new forms of productivity. The refusal appeared in a wide variety of guises and proliferated in thousands of daily practices. (Hardt and Negri, 2001, 274)

The politics of rave could be understood from just such a post-autonomous perspective of a radical refusal of work: pushing the body's functioning to an extreme, across hours of activity, and so depleting abilities to engage (mentally or physically) with work subsequently. The spectrum runs from the adjusted opening hours of shops that catered to Acid House enthusiasts in the late 1980s (rarely on Mondays and Tuesdays), to the 'acid casualty', as found adrift in the weekday or, as Mark E. Smith observed, the subsequent decades: '[...] the living dead. Some essential trigger ceased functioning back when The Happy Mondays had another night out around 1992' (Smith, 2009, 6). And it is in this flight from working norms and social expectations, as the very basis of as a lifestyle, as MacKay (1996) argues with respect to New Age travellers and weekend ravers, that the politics then comes to cultures centred on music.

On the other hand, at the end of the second Summer of Love (of Acid House: the summer of 1988/89), the provocation that Jeremy Deller articulates in the installation *Open Bedroom, c.1988–c.1994* becomes difficult to settle.[6] Written beneath a fluorescent picture of the once-ubiquitous Acid House smiley face (found in a wardrobe and illuminated by a naked light bulb, and in the computer print typeface of those years) is the question: 'Did he change your life?' The inference is that Deller's own response is at best equivocal, and indeed Hardt and Negri do not read cultures of refusal as a radical break with capitalist norms (hence the 'new forms of productivity'). Rather, in such cultures, perversely, the beginnings of the remaking of the tertiary sector via immaterial labour can be seen in operation.

In both these questions, centred on the idea of subcultures engendering a radical refusal of work (1968) and a radical alteration of lifestyle (1988), affect represents the political functioning – for better or for worse – of acid musics.

## Wave one to wave two: the second Summer of Love

The very term 'electronic dance music' articulates the nature of the radical break between this genre (EDM) and former notions of musicality. EDM is music from the circuits, of electricity (rather than, as with electrification, electronics in service to amplification), so that the 'techno' subgenre can be taken quite literally: the sounds or noise of technology. Again, the head is now required to think or experience beyond lingering qualitative conceptions of musicality, but now – in contrast to the break represented by psychedelia – *also* beyond ideas of authenticity in performance, and beyond a still-popular sonic palette essentially founded on twelfth-century instruments of musical expression. Music is now to be found in the inorganic, placing machine over human. But, as with acid rock before it, the psyche is freed to explore, or aided in achieving this paradigm shift in acceptance, via artificial neurological stimulation. Both acid rock and Acid House had their own distinctive smorgasbords of hallucinogenics. And the uncertainties of the inclusion of Prog Rock in this psychedelic heritage, where Prog seems stripped of the countercultural and 'refusal' aspects of psychedelia (to apply Hardt and Negri's term), perhaps because of Prog's sobriety, becomes clearer in this light. So '[w]hereas Ecstasy was previously used to enhance the sounds and textures of dance music, the situation reversed, [so that] the continuous DJ set was used by Ecstasy consumers to heighten their weekend drug trip' (Metcalfe, 1997, 172). But both Metcalfe and acid exponent Nicholas Saunders (1997, 2), whose underground guide books covered and intervened in both Summers of Love, perceive Ecstasy as very different from LSD: essentially, Ecstasy does not provide a psychedelic experience. This understanding is apparent even in the earliest writing about the use of Ecstasy in clubbing; while Nasmyth is happy to discuss MDMA with reference to 1960s gurus Timothy Leary and R. D. Laing, he is at pains to note the distinctly non-1960s nature of the drug, drawing parallels with yuppie 'designer drugs' and New Age therapies (Nasmyth, [1985] 1997, 74–8). For all these authors, E is understood as a method of escapism that remains entirely materially grounded, and a decade later Metcalfe maintains the weekend use for those seeking relief from the 'stresses and strains of modern life' (Metcalfe, 1997, 176), and Saunders notes, jarringly, the successful business acumen he accrued through Ecstasy use (Saunders, 1997, 2). Thus when MacKay traces parallels between acid rock and Acid House cultures (and notes the defamatory use of the term 'rave' in relation to music events, from 1966), he continually questions the radical import of Acid House: too entrepreneurial (a critique also mounted by Redhead, 1990, 4–5, 27, and Clover, 2009), and with the political limitations of one-issueism (and where the issue was often merely the right to party) and which was, moreover, accidentally and unwittingly politicized by the external forces of the British state coming to it rather than as an expression flowing from the dissenting aspirations of ravers (MacKay, 1996, 103–26). Svenonius goes further: the DJ as 'designator-of-worth and handler-of-commodities', and so the music equivalent to monetarist policies in its fundamental disconnection from actual production (in addition to the DJ's 'display of contempt' – via scratching the product – 'for the labor of his subjects') (Svenonius, 2006, 218, 245).

Nevertheless, the framing of EDM in relation to psychedelia is founded on the way in which EDM and its variants remain psyche-centric. In this respect Acid House is understood to represent a second wave of psychedelia, but without the psychedelicism. And such a transition can be seen in the notion of 'state' over 'head': to find oneself in a certain or altered state of mind and body, or in an imagined, technology-enabled place that represents the melding of the mind and body, as with the ambient rave come-down of 'Pacific State' (1989) by 808 State. To be 'in a state', even with a derogatory vernacular use of the term, suggests a moment of being in a world that is materially grounded rather than spiritually calibrated: cold, wet, hung-over and penniless, say, rather than 'out there' and 'at one'.

Metcalfe, discussing and recalling the 'new Psychedelic warriors' (1997, 171) of the Ecstasy period, finds parallels (often via sampling) between the Summers of Love and proclaims: '[t]he comparisons were obvious, the second psychedelic wave was upon us' (Metcalfe, 1997, 170). Genesis P-Orridge dates his 'personal quest for a hyperdelic form of dance music' to 1987, and notes of his fledgling subgenre of 'techno acid beat' that it 'seemed inevitable that a form of dance music would occur that was contemporary but also psychedelic' (quoted in Reynolds, 1990, 181). Reynolds frames the KLF and the Orb in a sequence from Pink Floyd (Reynolds, 1997, 158, 161), and the work of Genesis P-Orridge as Jack The Tab, as illustrative of the wider ways in which '[…] acid house has revived the slang and cosmic imagery of psychedelia (if not the sound)', which he reports as occurring in Goa (Reynolds, [1987–89] 1990, 180, 186). Whiteley and DeRogatis also place P-Orridge at this juncture (Whitley, 1997, 130; DeRogatis, 2003, 447).

The Jack The Tab album *Acid Tablets Volume One*, although presented as an acid dance compilation, was in fact the sole work of P-Orridge and Richard Norris, as NON ('Noise or not'). Fictional band names were provided for each track, and the project can be read as an attempt to pseudo-curate and proactively anticipate this new wave before it had fully broken on UK shores.[7] Even tracks that are wide of the mark in respect of the coming sound (and song structure) evidence a psychedelic continuum across the periods under examination here: 'Rapid Bliss', in reproducing something akin to the improvisatory jazz-funk fusion workouts with which Miles Davis was engaging with his lead bass player, Foley, holds points of similarity with the shoegaze group A R Kane of this time, and their album *69* (1988). An earlier attempt to incubate a new wave of psychedelia by P-Orridge is found in his/her *Godstar* work[8] – the soundtrack to an anticipated (but unrealized) biopic of Brian Jones – which had anticipated elements of trance. But Jack The Tab is locked into more immediate, even if satirical, concerns: 'Meet Every Situation Head On', across the distinctive acid hi-hat beat, samples the intoned instruction 'take drugs: every drug' (followed by a chorus of 'hear, hear!' – the sampled sound of the House of Parliament in session), followed by the advice to 'make every situation head on' – both an exhortation and the suggestion of the heightening of perception to follow, one that allows for a greater engagement with (rather than flight from) the world. The alteration of the 'meet' of the track's title with the 'make' of the track as delivered is precise in this respect: not only to encounter, but to transform that encounter. It is a philosophical position later diagnosed by Diederichsen as a post-'68 allocation of controlled periods of 'intensity' (typically at weekends, and via clubbing) for the members of the bourgeoisie not content to dully organize their lives around the successful achievement of 'intentions' (Diederichsen, 2011, 9–29). The straighter fusions of dance and psychedelia that would follow shortly after, as with the Happy Mondays, World of Twist and Flowered Up's novella-like single 'Weekender' (1992), can also be appropriately positioned at this juncture.

EDM in some instances predates the first wave of psychedelia (in, for example, the pioneering experiments of Delia Derbyshire), but only came to the fore at the tail end of disco, and then in defiance of those who held that disco itself was an aberration – machine noise, lacking in human expression. Such sentiments could be said to be a re-run of criticisms made a decade earlier, centred on figures such as Bob Dylan and Miles Davis as they went 'electric' – understood as a perverse, counterproductive development: the sacrifice of distinctive and intimate timbres in favour of modish noise for reasons of commercial opportunism. Other electronic musics of the mid-1970s, notably Lou Reed's *Metal Machine Music* (1975) and David Bowie's collaborations with Brian Eno, could be said to have revisited experimental noise practices of the Modernist period: an avant-garde access to the idea of alienating (rather than danceable) noise. In the first instance Giorgio Moroder/Donna Summer collaborations provocatively combined the most biologically organic (the orgasmic groans of Summer, singing 'Love to Love You Baby' and 'I Feel Love', of 1975 and 1977 respectively) with the most electronically inorganic (synthetic sounds, drum machine beats). Synth pop and house, trance and techno musics logically spring from this synthesis. But the eradication of the human altogether, in the second instance, as with the 'mechanical' drumming of motorik, and then elements of Acid House and jungle, also occurs. And, in these musics, the trip is into the machine rather than into the head. Such a development can be seen as anticipated the final phases of psychedelia in the electronic remaking of the psychedelic journey for the Silver Apples album *Contact* (1969). For this the band members are pictured on the album sleeve in the cockpit of an aeroplane: this is a trip to be achieved with advanced technology rather than through a shunning of the technologies that the counterculture, in the bucolic manner of D. H. Lawrence, invariably held as dehumanizing and alienating. Elements of the soundtrack of *Performance* (Nic Roeg, Donald Cammell, [1968] 1970) reproduce psychedelic acid sounds electronically, as with the 'Harry Flowers' theme, as well as incorporating 'world music' elements denoting altered or non-Western consciousness, exhibiting the influence of Brian Jones, and Pink Floyd's 'Heart Beat, Pig Meat' (from *Zabriskie Point* soundtrack) curates a sequence of television-sourced found sounds (news broadcasts, advertisements, old films), as indexing the bad trip of contemporary North American media-saturated society.

Despite their sonic differences, EDM retained strong conceptual continuities with the first wave of psychedelia. Rave required duration: the beat uninterrupted for a dozen hours or more, courting the longueurs, lineaments and undulations of emotion in a way that necessitated a build-up over periods far longer than the length of an LP. The notion of the happening aspired to a similarly lengthy duration – all night long if need be, and even clocked for the 14-Hour Technicolor Dream event in Alexandra Palace in 1967. The DJ cultures of disco had already lengthened the song substantially (one mix of 'Love to Love You Baby' ran to seventeen minutes), and disco in general also aspired to a conception of the future that represented the full fruition and cultural entrenchment of the Summer of Love.[9] Repetition in EDM, from sampled hooks, or looped beats, offers a sonic compass for the raver as he or she travels ever further into altered states of waking consciousness. And rave promo videos, drawing on the aesthetics of projections at actual raves, often ignored the musicians in favour of computer-generated psychedelic visuals, now reworked as day-glo graphics (acid tabs, smiley faces, spiralling fractals, pulsing vortices of colour): here the technology visualizes the trip. As the Second Wave of Psychedelic, these musics could only occur after the realignment of the happening, away from the shamanistic band-leader figure and towards the DJ figure: selector rather than creator, and mixer rather than maker. In Bez's terms (where this was '[...] an era in which I was blissfully unaware of my [*sic*] catalystic qualities as a full-on hedonist' [Bez, 1998, ix]), to shift from the happening to the rave required the centrifugal force exerted from the presence of a catalyser rather than song-writer.

Psychedelic EDM noise, in this respect, wrests control of the body, destabilizing the mind. The mystical conjoining of gangster and hippie protagonists in *Performance* occurs with just such a sequence – a bank of electronic mixing gear, improvisatory layering of sounds, the exposed subject losing control at the behest of the burnt-out hippie rock star (played by Mick Jagger), mixing proto-EDM.

These connections, however, and the generation of a second wave of underground cultures that flow from them, are only noted here as a staging post between the first and third waves of psychedelia.

*Personality melding in* Performance.

## Wave three: shoegaze

### *Guitar-ism and revelry*

The reintroduction of the guitar to psychedelic music in the mid/late 1980s could only happen as finessed by aspects of EDM: with an anonymity and an amusicality, and as an agent of affectivity. Acid House is described, above, as psychedelia without psychedelicism. Shoegaze could be described as guitar-ism music rather than guitar music.

The origins of such a use of guitar can be found both in the tendencies apparent in Clapton's playing, as discussed above, and also in uses of the guitar by younger exponents of blues-based rock, including 'noise rock'. As King notes, North American groups such as Sonic Youth and Dinosaur Jr. can be said to have exerted musical (if not sartorial) influence on the British indie scene prior to shoegaze (that is, of C-86 and Twee Pop) in that such groups unapologetically heralded the return of the guitar (King, 2012, 298). This influence, in turn, can be traced back the rockier, garage elements of *Nuggets*, to the Velvet Underground, the MC5 and the Stooges (influences especially apparent on Loop) and, beyond this, Band of Susans and Galaxie 500. British influences are typically noted as the Cure, the Jesus and Mary Chain and the Cocteau Twins. And Azerrad notes that the 1987 Dinosaur Jr. tour of Europe, and the critical reception of the band of the UK, was formative to shoegaze bands (Azerrad, 2001, 365–6).

What exactly was influential in J Mascis's playing was the miasma of a sound where, in Azerrad's words, 'the volume and noise didn't symbolise power; it just created huge mountains of sound around the desolate emotions outlined in the lyrics' (Azerrad, 2001, 361). This sound was better described as coaxed guitar noise – Dinosaur Jr.'s 'Kracked', for example, features a guitar solo that seems to mimic the sounds of a tortured cat – or a quantitative layering of waves of guitar sound, so that the often non-specific guitar noise tends only to actually stop at the point of the end of the song, or even after. In this respect, the critical reception of Dinosaur Jr. and *You're Living All Over Me* (1987) could be said to work as a verification and emboldener of embryonic directions already apparent in My Bloody Valentine. Whereas this album is not, in itself, particularly shoegaze-like in terms of the construction of the songs or even in respect of much of its sound,[10] extant bootlegs of the 1987 shows capture a reticence on the part of Mascis to sing in favour of sculpting ever more uncompromising soundscapes. Mascis seems to vanish into them; an inlay photo that showed the band with a concert advert promising 'loud psychedelic rock' only really announced the point of departure.

The anonymity of shoegaze can be explained by the preference for sound over physical presence, or sound as allied to phenomenologies of feelings and moods rather than articulations understood to arise from the direct encounters of the seen individual with the world around (and where such encounters then represent a philosophical take on the world: the anger of punk, the diffidence of Goth, the loucheness of New Romanticism, the jitterings of jungle, and so forth). This lack of the personnel of the music, and of personalities in the wave – obscured at gigs, not pictured on releases or, in the case of Kevin Shields of My Bloody Valentine, discussed mostly in terms of his prolonged absences – freed the music to function in a non-individualized way. So the music is understood not to directly emanate from a particular person (sole singer, lead guitarist), or even the musical interactions of the group members (who often stood some way apart when performing live), but to speak more of a shared and collective state. This disarming approach was often and crucially achieved via mixing, where a multi-directional and total sound would be achieved: a sonic anarchy that sought to overwhelm the spatial organization of the sound-box model.[11] And, while the mixing emphasized the guitar sound, the guitar sound was often transmogrified into guitar noise; two rhythm guitars were often played without synchronicity, even when playing the same, so blurring the sequence of notes and de-emphasizing the musicality of the playing. Meanwhile the lyrics often adhered to a literal 'nothing to say' of vocal delivery: words as more interesting in terms of their sounds than carrying and communicating meanings (as Felder finds in the case of Slowdive [1993, 31]), or straight glossolalia (as with the opening of 69), or capitalizing disconcertingly on ambiguities of actual speech. 'Sueisfine' from My Bloody Valentine's *Isn't Anything* (1988) makes full use of its phonetic similarities to the word 'suicide'; the chorus is seemingly simultaneously sung as 'suicide' and 'sue is fine' (by Shields and Bilinda Butcher) but the vocal lines soon intertwine and confuse the syllables along the lines of '...fine/...cide/...sine'.

A side effect of these aesthetic strategies is noted by Wiseman-Trowse in respect to the influence exerted on shoegaze by the Cocteau Twins: the sense of an 'immersion' in the music (Wiseman-Trowse, 2008, 148–9). This would account for the term 'dream pop', also used at the time,[12] and which Wiseman-Trowse uses interchangeably with the term shoegaze. Dream pop is not a helpful term, although critics and journalists were clearly picking up on cues found in the music itself. The promo video for Curve's 'Clipped' (1991) explicitly suggests the events seen are a dream, as the singer's spirit is seen leaving her sleeping body to attend a party before returning to the sofa and rejoining the body – a literal version of My Bloody Valentine's '(When You Wake) You're Still in a Dream', and making good on the sensuality and surrealism of A R Kane's lyrics concerning 'here in my l s dream', and of 'l s dreamin' l s dream' (from 'spermwhale trip over' of 69). Since dreams, post-Freud, could be said to represent the 'active' part of sleeping (see Penzin, 2012, 8) and even, in the wake of new forms of cognitive work allied with virtual reality, the 'work' part of sleeping (see Lucas, 2010, 125–32), it is dreamless sleep that is more usefully placed as comparable: trance, oblivion, a state of losing awareness of the immediate surroundings, of no memory, a moment of the alteration of breathing and heart rate, and when time passing is no longer graspable. The latter, for Wiseman-Trowse, is also an element of the experience of shoegaze music (2008, 153) but more generally these aspects connect shoegaze to EDM, where memory loss is not atypical.[13] And if dreaming is also understood as a blissful surrender to the body – so that the music requires a comparably defenceless surrender to it – then the term still only tells half the story. Live, shoegazer groups, particularly My Bloody Valentine, the Telescopes and Swervedriver, were anything but somnolent. In this respect, the bipolarity of the music – either dreamy and ambient, or confrontational and extreme – points directly to the quiet/loud dichotomy of post-rock groups such as Earth, Hood and Mogwai.

Dreaming, here, suggests the vantage point of revelry, and there is in this, and in the therefore typical lyrical concerns of shoegaze music – where something past or not-present is recalled, and therefore becomes a matter of nostalgic meditation – a sense of critical reflection. Compared to the very presentness of rave – of a being in the moment, neurologically locked into the beats per minute as they occur – shoegaze would seem to exemplify an assumed middle-class trait: fond recollection, surveyed memories, revisiting the past to the ends of critical reflection. Revelry and daydreaming are a luxuriant access to 'contemplate grandeur', in Bachelard's phraseology of phenomenology, from which 'intimate immensity' could be aptly applied to the shoegaze sound (Bachelard, [1958] 1994, 183), as reflected in another journalistic description of the shoegaze sound: the 'sonic cathedral'.

Such processes are apparent, and in a linear, developmental fashion, in 'On Tooting Broadway Station' by Kitchens of Distinction (from 1992's *The Death of Cool*): the description of a breakdown in the dreary public location of the title, where the narrator tries to defy his feelings of loss in order to galvanize his lovelessness, so as to free himself of his lost lover ('I un-stitched the bindweed of love'). Instead, however, he finds himself holding dear the ashes of the bonfires he fancifully imagines, used to burn away his lover's belongings and his own feelings of loss. This fire is both a purging ('Benedictory fire') and a martyrdom ('my Joan of Arc' becomes the refrain, which here could refer to himself or the man he has lost). The final eighty seconds of the five minutes of the track, where the vocals fall silent (vocals that seem wilfully strained so as to avoid breaking) are given over to a reverb-bolstered guitarscape – suggesting the enormity of emotions as in need of (or, here, conjuring) what can be taken as a physically enormous sonic space. And while the echoing sound is enormous – and so seemingly not earthbound but universal, and cosmic – its point of origin, in lost love, is intimate and confessional. In this way, shoegaze noise comes to replace the faltering narrative or lyrical content as a directly phenomenological articulation, and in so doing renders the pastness of the subject (the matter of reflection) into the present. Such flows of feeling therefore oscillate across waking and dreaming states, the present and the past, are partly possible in terms of expression via lyrics and partly not, prompting noise to take over where lyrics fail. The only really materially certain element of the track becomes the location of its departure: Tooting Broadway Station. The lover may have gone, but in this noise these unresolved feelings live on, wresting control of the here and now.

## The problem of class in shoegaze aesthetics

Shoegazer music is more generously contextualized in direct relation to the five elements listed above as, after EDM, the third wave of psychedelia. The music itself conforms to these elements although rarely reproduces the sonic patina of late 1960s psychedelia.

Contextualization, and critical reactions at the time, seemed keener to make good on the disappointment in the countercultural figures of the late 1960s who, by the late 1980s, had long since made their peace with the establishment. Thus shoegaze groups were perceived as middle-class, originating from the relatively wealthy suburbs of the Thames Valley area, and Oxford and Reading among other southern cities,[14] and as providing a white music soundtrack for the lives of students of the late 1980s/early 1990s. As with their 1968 predecessors, there was a sense that, after an extended period of carefree diversions (study and/or chilling out; and extended in the sense of funded by the state), and with the entry into the world of work and professional responsibility, these students would willingly enter that establishment too. And so, as a musical culture of and for a privileged southern enclave, the shoegaze genre could be perceived as in direct opposition to the dangers inherent in the truly dissident lifestyles of 'northern' ravers. King writes that the 'licentious hedonism' of the Happy Mondays allowed their manager '[Tony] Wilson an opportunity to demonstrate the difference between Factory [Records] and the suburban, shoegazing, middle-class, indie-dancing south' (King, 2012, 358), while Wiseman-Trowse casts the two musical genres as the poles of his chapter 'Dream Pop and Madchester' (2008, 146). If the earliest phase of shoegaze music is placed in the mid-1980s, its avant-garde moment in the late 1980s, and its commercial success and elements of a pop phase in the first few years or so of the 1990s, then this divide seems somewhat arbitrary.[15] And Redhead, writing closer to the time, records the assumption that the raver demographic was (also) white and middle-class, and even rural (Redhead, 1990, 4), while Rapp's discussion of Berlin clubbers in recent years centres almost exclusively on professionals hopping from one European capital to another (Rapp, 2009).

The criticism was fair comment, however, in relation to the aesthetics – if not the sonics – of shoegaze, particularly as it entered its poppier phase in the early 1990s, and presumably sought to consolidate its fan base. The promo videos of various singles, dating from the moment that shoegaze

*From promo video for Ride's 'Like a Daydream'.*

began to chart commercially, exemplify both a middle-class milieu and unabashed romanticism.[16] Walks in autumnal woodlands, songs concerning vague yearnings for unusually named females, a failure on the part of bands to 'perform' as proletarian pop stars, and a calculated artiness all feature heavily. The House of Love's 'Christine' (1988) presents introspective band members, obscured by low lighting, video fuzz, and long fringes across bowed heads; all three sit near-motionless as they deliver the song. The promo for 'Destroy the Heart' (1988), borrowing the camera technique of Michael Snow's *La Région Centrale* of 1971 (a 360-degree pan, in this case around a recording studio) results in long stretches of blank screen with band members only sporadically, and briefly, veering into view. Ride's 'Like a Daydream' (from the 1990 *Play* EP) intercuts between a screaming woman (who would fit the description of their later single, 'Chelsea Girl', of 1990) with the band playing the song in a rapt and awkward fashion, as if unaware of the presence of a camera. They move and dress in a studiously uncool way (baggy tops, bed-hair), while Slowdive's 'Alison' (1993) seems to be have been shot at a student house party – a far cry from the 'temporary autonomous zones' needed for psychedelic happenings and raves. The *mise-en-scène* is entirely embryonic middle-class: over-large T-shirts and V-neck jumpers, unkempt fringes on the mildly inebriated and smiley guests, women 'natural' rather than made-up, a crush in the corridor, bottles of wine and cans of beer, candles and a chess board, and images from Jean-Luc Godard films on a wall. The band (with its male and female leads) are intercut and they, and the party-goers, are subject to aestheticization via superimposed, semi-psychedelic images.[17] As with the Boo Radleys's 'Finest Kiss' (1991), the female subject would seem to be absent (the chorus begins with 'have you seen her?'), but their return is anticipated. Loss is mitigated by security and certainty – also benefits of the middle classes.

Abstract, dreamscape-like imagery predominated on record and CD sleeves, underscoring the idea of close attention to minutiae (in the way that an LSD user might spend hours closely examining everyday objects), or day-dreamed fuzzes of colours and shapes, as if images from semi-consciousness states, or coloured by the play of light on half-opened eyelids. Early releases from Catherine Wheel and Swervedriver tended towards objects for contemplation: possibly an eye, possibly a circle of pineapple, for *Ferment* (1992), and light refracted across a lens and psychedelicized clouds for *Raise* (1991), respectively. For Ride, flowers for the *Ride* and *Play* EPs of 1990, and an ocean swell for *Nowhere* (1990) – but all three covers are essentially textured palettes and washes of single colours. This is also true of Curve's *Doppelgänger* of 1992 and *Cuckoo* of 1993 (severed parts of dolls rendered in burnt orange, and a murky purple for stones or eggs) and Slowdive's *Just for a Day* of 1991 (seemingly a blurred photo of a dancing woman, in bloodied orange). Flowers and oceans are also found on Kitchens of Distinction's *Strange Free World* (1991) and, as cupping a column of flame, Adorable's *Against Perfection* (1993) respectively. And nondescript psychedelic patterns are used for Lush's *Gala* (1990) and *Spooky* (1992) and, with a cat in the foreground, offsetting the psychedelic baroque, the Pale Saints' *The Comforts of Madness* (1990). Most of the releases from the Boo Radleys during their shoegaze phase feature just such a baroque, as do *Killing Time* by Bleach (1992; with a prawn) and ... *x, y and z* by Moose (1992; with a sunflower). Band members rarely figure or, where they do, are obscured, as looming figures with fluorescent-ized and bleached-out faces, as with My Bloody Valentine's *This Is Your Bloody Valentine* (1985) and *Isn't Anything* (1988) respectively. It is not entirely clear who the people on Lush EPs are, or the cartoon figures used for Blind Mr Jones's *Stereo Musicale* (1992) or the Drop Nineteen's *Delaware* (1992). Or blank-faced figures are lined up or bunched together artlessly, as if for a family photograph, for the Telescopes and proto-shoegaze group Loop.[18]

In addition to the *Comforts of Madness* cat, a curled, sleeping cat is found on the cover of Chapterhouse's *Whirlpool* (1990), and the recording of a cat's purring, and a discussion of that cat, ends *They Spent Their Wild Youthful Days in the Glittering World of The Salons* (1996) by the Swirlies.[19] In the same way that the image of the sheep is common for EDM releases at this time, the cat comes to typify shoegaze. The sheep, presumably exclusively living in the moment, and existing, as part of an undifferentiated mass, in a field, is an appropriate mascot for ravers in both these respects – and recalls William Holman Hunt's *The Scapegoat* (1854–6), which utilized a colourscheme that anticipated psychedelic art. And the cat – domesticated, spoilt, lethargic, keeping its own company, and prone to suddenly disappear – so embodies a shoegazer's qualities.

## The postmodernity of shoegaze sound

After a generation of British pop music that, often even at its most trifling, seemed naturally anti-Establishment, and running near-parallel to the concerted police and judicial actions against raves, shoegaze would have seemed to be entirely introspective, failing to engender any alternative thinking or critical distance, despite its 'indie' or alternative status. In its apoliticism, shoegazer music would then seem to be patterned after or represent a sonic equivalent to abstract expressionism,[20] and something of this sense of a complacent, bourgeois avant-gardism was communicated via the terms used to identify the genre. 'Shoegaze' itself was coined in respect to the tendency of shoegaze guitarists to stand immobile on the stage, looking down – as if at their shoes – so as to work the sizeable banks of pedals required to shape and temper guitar noise into shoegaze sound. Such a failure to project outwards, while looking back to the introspection of acid rock (so that, as Auslander notes, musicians, lost in their music, and whose movement often only amounted to swaying, behaved as if unaware of an audience, or even ungraciously turned their back to that audience [2009, 17]), was readily interpreted as passivity and surrender. Such surrender was clearly understood in the sense of 'giving in' to a sense of revelry, but also in the sense of abandoning potentials for political opposition, as well as in terms of failing to present an aggressively heterosexual or even discernible gender-specific vocal, or code music in terms of aggressive or impassioned expressions of sexual desire. So the gazing could also be said to be of the naval variety: musicians lost in their own particular revelry. Thus the genre ultimately became – in another journalistic slight – 'the scene that celebrates itself': self-contained and auto-referential (so that gigs reputedly drew an audience of other shoegazer group members, who also often shot promo videos for other groups). There was no class-based constituency of the disenfranchised, as with punk or, arguably, Acid House,[21] and shoegaze gig-goers seemed passive and spaced-out; singing along proved difficult and, for Felder, '[t]he way miasma fans dance – almost nondancing, nodding their heads, seemingly transported, druggily nodding-off – is an autonomic reaction' (Felder, 1993, 27). As with Acid House dancing, which Redhead contrasts starkly to the limber panache of disco dancing (a shift which is equally pronounced in the compendium of found dance footage of Mark Leckey's 1999 film *Fiorucci Made Me Hardcore*), shoegaze movement is a dance which requires 'no expertise whatsoever' (Redhead, 1990, 6).

Perhaps the short-lived nature of shoegaze can also be attributed to this contrarian nature, so that record labels and companies found themselves needing to sell a sound or vague attitude rather than a person or anthem, and then to individuals, for individual consumption, rather than to massed ravers. Shoegaze was also called 'the scene with no name' – also indicative of the lack of character and selling potential. And although politically progressive elements could be found, often unannounced, in the shoegazer scene (bands that were multi-ethnic, with openly gay members, and that fully incorporated female leads), the actual functioning of politics, as understood to occur in the majority of critically favoured popular music bands of that period and prior, was absent too: the bankable commodity of righteous and often personalized, even if non-specific or disorientated, anger. So shoegaze was understood not to have survived onslaughts from the self-proclaimed denizens of proletarian culture: firstly from grunge, followed by a counterpunch from Britpop. So complete was the routing that shoegaze has remained in danger of being written out of the histories of contemporary popular music altogether as little more than a brief interregnum.[22] Felder (1993) and Thompson (1998) overlap in the periods of their concern, in respect to the popular music scenes of 1991–1993, but assemble very different canons. For Felder (1993), the sounds of 'miasmic bands' is a defining characteristic, which she freely extends from shoegaze to grunge: the sonic template of the new decade is clear. Yet for Thompson, writing five years later, a 'year zero' effectively occurs in 1992, annexing and discarding all before: he initially refutes the idea that 'pop was dead' in 1992, but then notes the first tremors of Britpop as shaking the 'moribund domestic chart-scape' of the same year (Thompson, 1998, 20, 244).

And yet, even as a seemingly apolitical phenomenon, shoegaze failed to channel pop into postmodernity, and so eluded popular musicologists too. Postmodern pop with, as Auslander contends (2009), its 1970s glam rock roots, persisted in requiring a presence at the front of the stage, or in the foreground of group shots, in order for this person to engage in playfulness, be a subject to subvert the norms, or enact a knowing repackaging of the tropes of 'northern, working-class lads with vivid personalities' (Bracewell, 1997, 228). Such an inadequate utilization of postmodernism is the lacuna of Bracewell's survey, which explains why shoegaze is ignored altogether. The actual postmodernity of shoegaze music could be said to be less dogmatic. Firstly, a playing with the after-sound of music (the decay rather than the strum; the echo rather than the hit; the reverberation rather than the chord) – remaking, as it were, the detritus or cast-offs of the music-making process: the noise rather than the harmony. (For this reason, the blurry Fender Jazzmaster seen on the cover of My Bloody Valentine's *Loveless* of 1991 is an apt image: music that is losing its definition in terms of its point of origin.) Secondly, the lack of the artist or avant-garde creator of modernist art, or a general lack of a sense of one guiding or confessional intelligence behind the text, in favour of an *auteur*-less absence – albeit one which, unlike strains of machine-music (Krautrock, instrumental EDMs), nevertheless would seem to seek to express human emotion.

Felder (1993) and Shaviro (1997) both find a political critique in the confusions that arise from the scrambling or undermining of expectations in the music of My Bloody Valentine. For Felder, the challenges of dealing with the music resemble the confusions of a life elsewhere termed 'hyperreal', the '[...] miasma we all go through to make decisions or even just to survive' (Felder, 1993, 18), or the effects of drugs on the perception, and the tensions that arise from a sense of the murderous activities of the military-industrial complex abroad. This is a reading that Wiseman-Trowse finds to be true of swathes of popular music and not particularly specific to My Bloody Valentine or shoegaze (Wiseman-Trowse, 2008, 150). Shaviro finds the same, and finds a postmodern music in the uncertainties of the mix, but is more specific: this confusion as typifying the condition of modern life, where gender is blurred, and words begin to fail or become unnecessary or reductive, and so recalls experiences of chemically altered consciousness and anonymous homosexual encounters, or body modification (Shaviro, 1997, 30 and 31–2 respectively).

## *My Bloody Valentine, the Telescopes and third wave psychedelic affect*

The garage rock elements apparent in the debut LP from My Bloody Valentine, *This Is Your Bloody Valentine* (1985) give way to building guitar drones (at times augmented by organ) on 'Tiger in My Tank', 'The Love Gang' and 'Inferno': drones that, once they begin, remain constant throughout. What seems to be missing in this is the ability to stop or fade out elements of the sound: layers can only be added, not taken away. In this way the drumming, and to a lesser extent the vocals, become decorative to the overall sound, and the climax of each track is given over to instrumental rather than vocal passages: a wall of sound, with the guitar saturating the sonic spectrum (although it would take a few more years for production values to adequately meet and match this conception). Colm O'Coisig's drumming, which can seem eccentric, is better understood as counter-intuitive: expressionistic, and with a tendency to punctuate with a flurry rather than firm demarcation – akin, then, to Clapton's guitar in 'SWLABR'.

'Paint a Rainbow', the B-side to the 1987 single 'Sunny Sundae Smile', illustrates the transition from C-86 to this wall of sound: the jangle is distorted into, or collapses into, a constant, modulating guitar pitch of some aggression, counterpointing the feyness of the song. Although closer to the sound that would evolve and come to define the My Bloody Valentine of *Isn't Anything*, the EP compilation *Ecstasy and Wine* (1989) would attempt to marry the way in which the guitar is both constant and comes to dominate the audio spectrum of each song. In tracks such as 'Never Say Goodbye' (from the 1987 EP *Strawberry Wine*) and '(Please) Lose Yourself in Me' (from the 1987 EP *Ecstasy*) the sound of the guitar comes to structure each song, so that the sense is created that the shoegaze noise drives both vocals and the rhythm section. '(Please) Lose Yourself in Me' jarringly applies such noise to the intimacy of the confessional concerns of the song, so that any narrative, lyric-based sense must be extracted from vocals partially buried beneath the noise and, at any rate, sounding some distance away. In this way the song creates a form for its content: a siren song, of a promise and a threat (to lose oneself), and the 'me' could be the maelstrom of sound, and its disconcerting nature, as much as the suitor-singer. Such disorientation, and paradoxical combinations, would constitute the schizophrenic nature of the first album released by the Telescopes, *Taste* (1989), which repeatedly juxtaposed the lull with the frenetic.

In respect of this early and avant-garde phase of shoegaze, the next logical step would have been apparent: to begin to override vocals and rhythm section altogether with shoegaze noise – to further or fully extract that essence and allow the elements of the song to fall away, so shedding everything bar noise. This occurred in the 1988 track 'You Made Me Realise' (from the EP of the same name), in which a noise section lasts about 45 seconds of the three minutes and 44 seconds. But the noise was extended for live renditions at the time (albeit only to three minutes, as with the July 1990 gigs at the University of London), and for gigs in support of *Loveless*, and became the climax (or, for many in the audience, the final straw) of gigs in 2008 and 2009, where the noise typically occurred for between 20 and 30 minutes, and even longer for some European gigs, and at an unprecedented level of volume of around 130db.[23]

To experience 'You Made Me Realise' in this manner is to undergo an initial disorientation, and then reorientation, of the senses. The music is felt in and through the body – and in this sense 'becomes' flesh – as much as heard (many attendees augmented the earplugs given out by flattening their hands over their ears). And, as in situations of imminent physical danger, perceived reality alters. The sense of time slowing down, as in the feeling of slow motion, mid-car crash (which is understood to arise from the delay in cognitively processing an abundance of data, gathered as the body addresses the unfolding situation in as complete a manner of possible) occurs. In this instance too, a sharpening of sight and of smell occurs, further locking the experience of 'You Made Me Realise' into the very presentness of the situation – a presentness that seems existential rather than, as with rave, carefree.

In discussing the loudness of My Bloody Valentine, Shaviro turns to Deleuze and Guattari's concept of 'microperceptions', understood as coming into play at such moments, and which allow for a deeper reading of otherwise inaudible nuances and subtleties in the noise (Shaviro, 1997, 25). Wiseman-Trowse theorizes the noise of 'You Made Me Realise' in respect to semiotics and psychoanalysis, and provides other examples of as much (so that the 'breakdown' is a minor motif of shoegaze music): as a place 'beyond' signification – but in this respect, albeit perhaps in relation to the released rather than live version of the track, as 'sonic introspectiveness […] reaches a point of implosion' (Wiseman-Trowse, 2008, 152) For Felder, the effect of such volume is akin to the gig-goer feeling that they themselves are playing the instruments (Felder, 1993, 29). McGonigal begins his book on *Loveless* by recalling a 1992 rendition of the track and pushing 'through' the noise, as if to the 'other side', where he then experiences an '[…] array of overtones [which] can be heard bouncing about on top of the dirge. Everything goes into slow motion' (McGonigal, 2007, 7–8). McGonigal seems unable to shake the idea that this was a fanciful projection on his part, despite the evidence he assembles otherwise. Similarly, Shaviro outlines the journey through the volume: '[…] you can no longer make sense of such a gross opposition… You can't stand it, and you can't see beyond it; but for that very reason you get used to it after a while, and you never want it to end' (Shaviro, 1997, 24–5).

Such a courting of a counter-intuitive familiarity also occurs with the Telescopes, whose discography covers avant-garde, pop and contemporary phases of shoegaze. Variable members are often crouched on the floor, in the middle of a small room (unlike the sizeable venues occupied by their one-time Creation stablemates My Bloody Valentine upon their reform), and generate half-hour bursts of white noise through a variety of techniques (including drilling through the guitar). When reworking early 1990s hits, singer Stephen Lawrie is known to wander dazed through the audience, bumping into them, and adopting a foetal position on the floor, in their midst, while continuing to sing. It is a surrender of authority that recalls avant-garde theatre performance, and particularly those of the 1960s: inviting the audience in, refusing to occupy the ground allotted to the performer by the consumer, overturning the hierarchies of performance, as if acknowledging the democratic nature of the noise that engulfs all present equally.

As the noise of the third wave of psychedelia, shoegaze noise sought to materialize phenomenologies rather than create, nurture and sustain the subjectivities available 'on the other side' of 'dropping out' (of the first Summer of Love) or engender such subjectivities (as with the second Summer of Love). Noise, in this respect, operates affectively: assailing the body sonically, and returning it to states of emotional uncertainty. The charges historically levelled at shoegaze could be said have attached themselves to premature stopping-off points in this process: to return only to the state of dreams, or oblivion, or to that of bourgeois security and indifference, or infantile contentment. The destination state beyond these stages – and in this respect shoegaze represents a rupture with the counter-cultural if not EDM psychedelic music – is found in waking rather than hallucinated reality.

# CHAPTER FOUR

# To Be Played at Maximum Volume: Rock Music as a Disabling (Deafening) Culture

## *George McKay*

> [...] without your hearing, you have nothing.
>
> Ray Charles (n.d.)

This chapter looks at the terribly ironic *cripping* capacity of pop and rock as a deafening mode through music-induced hearing loss, the other symptom of which is mature regret. Here a number of rock artists are discussed, in particular from later life, when the occupational hazards of a career in the reckless and excessive industry of loud music are now presented as medical symptoms. Also the hearing loss of fans in relation to music technology (amplification, personal stereos) is discussed. For noise to achieve its dissonant, affective and troubling qualities, especially in the content of the otherwise pleasant or 'acceptable' sonic patina of popular music, volume is understood as necessary. The idea of playing at maximum volume could be said to be *the* way in which noise musics occur. Noise, in the ways discussed in this book, is therefore intimately connected to volume, and so this chapter seeks to examine volume as the essential vehicle of noise.

Music is first and foremost an aural cultural experience, and one which remains hugely popular with young people even in, and as part of, an interactive multimedia world. One recent survey of research into young people's exposure to loud music found that, '[o]n average, people in the group aged 14 to 20 years listen to over 3 hours of music per day'; further – in a key point to which we will return – 'the more they liked the music, the louder they preferred it' (Vogel et al., 2007, 124, 128). For the vast majority of people, central to the corporeal experience of music is the place of the ear – or rather, as Oliver Sacks corrects us in *Musicophilia*, 'the huge but often overlooked importance of having *two* ears' (2007, 146; emphasis added). Technological developments in recording and transmission (such as stereo or surround sound), or innovations in consumption such as the Walkman or iPod, infer a normative and fully functioning binaurality in a largely phonocentric globe. The shift from mono to stereo recording and records was popularized in the wake of rock and roll, one might argue effectively in parallel with the rise of popular music itself from the 1950s to the 1970s. Although stereo recordings were easier to transmit on tape, the first stereo records were produced for sale in America in 1957, and what 'started as a luxury good for the technically minded elite in the 1960s became a mass-produced consumer good in the 1970s' in the form of the home stereo system (Millard, 2005, 215, 222). Stereophonic sound, with its capacity for the listener to aurally discriminate between different instruments or sections in the recording by locating them in different soundspaces, has become such an industry standard and audience expectation that, during the digital era, vintage mono recordings are constantly being remastered for stereo consumption. This is not only a marketing innovation: such technological and industry developments dictate that it is not enough simply to hear popular music (which is often pretty loud anyway), one ought best be able to hear it stereophonically, via the two different ears and the two sets of sounds they simultaneously process.

According to Sacks, '[o]ur auditory systems, our nervous systems, are [...] exquisitely tuned for music' (Sacks, 2007, xi). Indeed, the very terms ear *drum* or *tympanic* membrane suggest a fundamental connection between physiology and musicality. For human beings, the 'functional utility' of the specialized organ of the ear is not so extraordinary as it is in, say, bats, with their sonar – indeed, humans may have 'the most limited range of all mammals' – but the utility does, according to A. J. Hood, 'find its highest expression in our ability to communicate by means of the spoken word *and in our appreciation of music*', not least because of 'the superlative pitch discrimination possessed by the ear' (Hood, 1977a, 32, emphasis added; 41). Although hearing is a neuro-physical operation of tremendous sensitivity, the hearing mechanism of the ear, the organ of Corti, is in fact rather 'well protected from accidental injury; it is lodged deep in the head, encased in the petrous bone, the densest in the body, and floats in fluid to absorb accidental vibrations' (Sacks, 2007, 132). But it remains the case that there are numerous ways in which our hearing can be affected by popular music: the use of very loud volume, the placing of the music source in or near the ear canal (as by using earphones or headphones), and the lengthy and regular duration of listening, for instance, all present potential hazards.

While deafness is often considered one of the invisible disabilities, this is not necessarily the case. It can combine with other associated symptoms to manifest in a physical manner; as Hood explains, because the ear is an organ of the sense of both hearing and balance, 'it is not unusual to find deafness accompanied by disorders of balance, the most classical example being Ménière's disease, in which fluctuating attacks of giddiness and deafness are the rule' (Hood, 1977a, 36). Also, as we will see, the technology of hearing aids was quite cumbersome in the early days of popular music – and remained so until the introduction of digital micro-technology in the field – and anyone who used one then would have been easily identifiable as hearing-impaired.

Yet, before going further, we do need to consider the extent to which, as my title suggests, *disabling* and *deafening* are related, or disconnected. Both the mobilizing history and the more recent impetus of identity politics have helped to produce a powerful community of people with hearing disorders, who in recent years have begun to self-identify as 'Deaf'. To be *Deaf rather than deaf* is to claim the identity of the Deaf as possessing and living a separate, distinctive and complete culture, with, vitally, its own (sign) language(s). As Lennard J. Davis puts it in *Enforcing Normalcy*, the Deaf 'feel that their culture, language and community constitute them as a totally adequate, self-enclosed, and self-defining subnationality within the larger structure of the audist state' (Davis, 1995, xiv). For American Sign Language speakers, the place signed and typographically represented as DEAF-WORLD is the nation they inhabit (Lane, 1995, 161–2). Further, many within the Deaf movement have not only questioned but rejected the inclusion of their own social and corporeal experience of hearing impairment within a discourse of disability (and even the term 'hearing *impairment*' as a part of that discourse). There is a 'political element' within Deaf identity groupings that, because of the self-identifying minority language status of Deaf culture, 'distances itself from both phonocentric society and from any suggestion that they are people with impairments or disabled people' (Scott-Hill, 2003, 89). Debates about the position of d/Deafness in relation to disability have become more compelling as the theoretical and social ideas of the two have become more sophisticated, and there is transatlantic consensus. One leading British Deaf activist, Paddy Ladd, has put the view from that community: 'We wish for the recognition of our right to exist as a linguistic minority group... [L]abelling us as disabled demonstrates a failure to recognise that we are not disabled in any way within our own community.' The American Deaf leader M. J. Bienvenu has asked: 'how can we fight for official recognition of A[merican] S[ign] L[anguage] and allow ourselves as "communication disordered" at the same time? [...] Disabled we are not!' (both quoted in Lane, 1997, 159). What Mairian Scott-Hill calls 'the tension-ridden relationships between Deaf and disabled people' is 'evidenced not only by the marginalisation of Deaf people from disability politics, and *vice versa*, but also by the separate evolution of Deaf studies and disability studies' (Scott-Hill, 2003, 88). In her view, Deaf people

> [...] perceive themselves to be excluded from the dominant areas of social and cultural production by the perpetuation of a phonocentric world-view. They may also feel excluded from the disability movement because the movement is seen to reflect this world-view in the way in which it is socially organised around phonocentric language 'norms'. (Scott-Hill, 2003, 89)

For Harlan Lane, the demands and expectations of each group, disabled and Deaf, are not only different but *mutually exclusive*: where disabled groups campaign for independence, the Deaf desire interdependence; rather than mainstreaming in education, the Deaf want dedicated institutions with their linguistic specialism; the Deaf reject medical intervention (for example, around cochlear implant surgery for Deaf children) and have little need of important areas for many disabled people such as personal assistance or rehabilitation (see Lane, 1997, 161–2).

Nonetheless, for a chapter such as this, concerned with a cultural form in which the activity of listening is an, if not *the*, essential corporeal behaviour, hearing impairment or absence can be – has been – understood as a reason to be fearful, to be denied admission to the party. For instance, the visually impaired singer Ray Charles has articulated starkly the common-sense view from within popular music about the centrality of hearing: 'I believe so strongly that without your hearing, you have nothing. Of course, that's especially true when it comes to music' (Charles, n.d.). This is perhaps the very kind of absolutist remark, *from the wider disabled community*, that betrays a lack of understanding and sensitivity about the experience of hearing impairment, and that would legitimate for the Deaf community its urge for separatism from the disability movement. But, in music, hearing helps – there is even a phrase for it: a gifted musician is said to have 'a good ear'. Practising a specific form of popular music – jazz – is predicated on the musicians' act of listening to each other as they improvise; the brilliant opening word and instructional sentence of trumpeter Miles Davis's autobiography is, after all, 'Listen' (1989, v). This is not to suggest, in disability studies, the return of the traditional deficit approach, but it is to acknowledge the legitimacy in Tom Shakespeare's observation that 'impairment is not neutral, because it involves intrinsic disadvantage [...] [P]eople with impairments will always be disadvantaged by their bodies' (Shakespeare, 2006, 43, 46). The extreme position of Ray Charles notwithstanding, we may assume a level of disadvantage in making music when one cannot hear it, accurately or without noise interference or indeed at all. That being so, the non-linguistic sonic order that is music does become the cultural limit case for the disability of hearing and deafness. Deafness has a special place within music, it being commonly understood by audiences since Beethoven as a symptom of a profound and pathetic lack – the never-ironic absolute limit case for the perception, let alone the pleasureful consumption, of music.[1]

## A *deafening mode* – music-induced hearing loss

> I have unwittingly helped to invent and refine a type of music that makes its principal proponents deaf.
> Pete Townshend of the Who (quoted in Anon, 2006)

Elsewhere I have explored ways in which the relation between popular music and disability is a positive, enhancing or empowering one, regardless of how complicated that might sometimes appear (McKay, 2009, 2013). So, for example, the repertoire of popular music lyrics includes the representation of the experiences of being disabled, its singing voices mark a connection with the extraordinary body, its bodies themselves find affirming space in the culture and performance of freakdom or deviance that some pops and subcultures have innovated, and sometimes its musical forms are capable of denoting a physical difference. In ways like these, even while we may be surprised by the generous fact, the culture can include the marginalized disabled. But we need also to consider situations in which popular music can function as a *disabling* culture. What should strike us is the extent to which some consumption and production practices in pop and rock have begun consistently to contribute to an experience of disability. Varieties and degrees of hearing impairment, tinnitus, difficulty with the auditory discrimination of simultaneous sounds, and deafness figure prominently here. Pop crips. It really can. While, '[t]ypically, people with NIHL [noise-induced hearing loss] complain of loss of perceived clarity of speech and greater difficulty than normal following speech in a background of noise' (SCENIHR, 2008, 34), musicians with music-induced hearing loss experience these and the anxiety of professional instability. This is confirmed in the plaintive tone adopted above by Pete Townshend, guitarist and songwriter for the Who, who in 1976 claimed the record as 'officially The Loudest Band in the World', playing live at levels consistently at 126 decibels (dB) (Barnes, 2009, 3). A seemingly perverse situation is an increasingly common one, due primarily to the popularity of extremely loud amplified music at live concerts and nightclubs on the one hand (an issue or danger for musicians and fans alike) and technological innovations in personal music consumption, from Walkman to iPod, on the other (an issue for fans). How unique or unusual is this situation? In the consumption of cultural forms, how many are potentially dangerously and irreversibly disabling? Watching a film, reading a novel, looking at a painting – none of these are usually strongly connected with visually impairing the spectator. By and large, more or less, generally speaking, most culture does not crip, its consumption or production is not disabling. But pop – and more specifically, rock – seems to have developed a self-negating potential. The irony is indeed profound; it's heavy. The very discriminating organs that make most possible profession and pleasure *in* popular music are those under threat of dysfunction *by* popular music. Lennard J. Davis has written of the way in which the activity and phenomenon of critical 'writing [is] a deafened mode' – dependent on silence and thought in both production (reading and writing) and consumption (reading, thinking) (Davis, 1995, 181, n. 64); my approach, in the critical context of popular music, is to explore the extent to which *music is a deafening mode* – with the echo (we need not hear it to understand it) of mode as a musical scale. The average loudness discomfort level, as otologists term it – the level of sound intensity which one would find unpleasantly (though not painfully) loud – is around 100 dB (Hood, 1977b, 329), though prolonged exposure to 80 or 90 dB and above is generally accepted as having the potential to cause hearing damage. Indeed,

> [I]ndustrial regulations require employers to take action whenever their workers are exposed to noise over 85 dB for 8 hours a day […] Listeners using portable music players can expose themselves to the same level of loudness in 15 minutes of music at 100 dB that an industrial worker gets in an 8-hour day at 85 dB […] A recent study found that, in a typical nightclub, the sound intensity ranged from 104 to 112 dB. (Daniel, 2007, 226–7)

It should be acknowledged that music, along with everyday sound and noise more generally, has become louder in recent decades: a Hear Education and Awareness for Rockers (HEAR) campaign organization leaflet from 2004 points out that 'Americans are increasingly exposed to noisier lifestyles'. So, while the pain threshold for hearing is at 125 dB, a rock concert nowadays, with improved amplification technologies, may be up to 130 dB – mundanely above the exceptional loudness of rock concerts such as the Who's record-breaking event of 1976 (HEAR, 2004, 7).[2]

As noted, the experience of music-induced hearing loss in the context of popular music belongs in the main to two groups: practitioners and enthusiasts of very loud popular music forms (typically, though as we will see not exclusively, hyper-amplified rock music and some experimental genres), and listeners to personal stereos. The cultural and technological innovations that have made these possible date from the 1960s and 1970s (the early popularity of rock and then heavy metal music), the 1980s (the popularization of the Sony Walkman personal stereo cassette and then CD player), the 1990s (introduction of MP3 personal stereos) and the 2000s (the introduction of the Apple iPod). We can postulate from this both that there are now generations of middle-aged and older people affected by music-induced hearing loss, and that there is a significant health concern for younger music fans about their levels of consumption and volume via iPods and other MP3 personal music devices. Surveys of recent studies have shown that, as Ineke Vogel et al. report, some 'musicians consider playing louder than any other group to be prestigious' (2007, 128). From a quick scan among my old albums and singles (actually it took me an entire morning, for I was diverted and ended up re-listening to my youth), I was reminded that the back cover of David Bowie's 1972 album *The Rise and Fall of Ziggy Stardust and the Spiders from Mars* contains the instruction TO BE PLAYED AT MAXIMUM VOLUME, for example. The more contemporary Anglo-Irish experimental rock band My Bloody Valentine were notorious for employing loud volumes in live performances; their reunion concerts in 2008 and 2009 were noteworthy for the controversy around the extreme loudness, with earplugs on offer at the doors and some audience members leaving because they felt 'physically distressed' by the noise (Barnes, 2009, 3). Bandleader Kevin Shields (who has tinnitus) has defended the band's sonic aesthetic – which includes trying to induce a state of physical unbalance or disorientation via the volume and frequency of the sounds produced – but also acknowledged the difficulty.

> We play with low frequencies that are nothing like anyone has ever heard before – it's a chaos that sets off a kind of inbuilt alarm system [...] We'd like to say that it is cool to wear earplugs; it's not cool to get your hearing damaged. And anyway, feeling the music is a great experience. (quoted in Barnes, 2009, 3)

Elsewhere I recently saw for sale some personal stereo earphones called Monster Jamz; the associated advertising copy tempts buyers with the promise of 'eardrum beating bass punch [...] You'll be shocked how big your music can sound'. (Elsewhere on the company's website are the 'safety tips', which include 'Avoid listening at high volume levels for prolonged periods. This may cause permanent hearing damage or loss'. You may one day be shocked how little your music can sound: Monster website, n.d.) Is it then so surprising that 'many young people believe music is enhanced when played very loudly', and have done so for decades (Daniel, 2007, 229)? Even the playing of some (non-amplified) folk forms can lead to hearing loss: studies of the percussive/melodic combination of music practised by steelband orchestras ('pannists'), for example,

> [...] demonstrate the potential for the intensity of noise generated in a steelband to cause sensorineural hearing loss [...] The noise level at the core of the band is consistently above 100 dB(A). This is comparable to

the level 2 to 4 meters from center stage of a rock and roll band [...] [S]teelband players are at a high risk of developing hearing losses, which is directly dependent on the length of time of exposure. (Juman et al., 2004, 464)

According to research on hearing disorders – that is, not simply hearing loss, but *other* disorders too – among musicians by Kim Kähäri et al., 'a large number of rock/jazz musicians suffered from different hearing disorders (74%). Hearing loss, tinnitus and hyperacusis were the most common disorders and were significantly more frequent in comparison with different reference populations' (Kähäri et al., 2004, 627). Rock and jazz musicians experienced greater hearing disorders than the other musicians looked at, classical players. In terms of gender, male musicians had worse hearing than female ones, not infeasibly because 'more men than women played the loudest instruments such as woodwinds, brass winds and percussions' (Kähäri et al., 2004, 629). The gendering of potential music-induced hearing loss is confirmed in Vogel et al.'s survey of young people, where

Males were found to have more social noise exposure, and were more interested in noisy sports, home tools, and shooting, and in playing in a band. They also used and preferred higher music levels, used their portable music players for a longer average time, expressed less worry about the presence of hearing-related symptoms, had more positive attitudes toward noise, showed lower levels of desired behavior change, and were less likely to use hearing protection. (Vogel et al., 2007, 127)

Social class, smoking and diet are all factors in the onset of hearing loss – so much so that one of *Rolling Stone* magazine's recommended 'five ways to save your ears' is 'Quit smoking: it doubles the risk of noise-induced hearing loss' (Ringen, 2005, n.p.). Yet in very recent years the place of the personal stereo as source of both diversion and motivation in contemporary exercise or gym culture has led to the ironic situation that, 'whereas participating in physical activity is generally seen as part of a healthy lifestyle, doing this in combination with high-intensity music could constitute a risk for hearing loss' (Vogel et al., 2007, 129).

Let us consider each of these cases of popular music-induced hearing loss in a little more detail, looking at, in turn, the rock aesthetic of loud volume, and the impact of the use of personal stereos.[3] In recent years there has been a slew of journalistic and academic articles about, as one put it, 'music making fans deaf', and making musicians deaf too. These writings have been prompted by the hearing loss experiences of the aging rock generation, combined with new concerns about young people's encounters with loudness via personal stereos. Writing in *Rolling Stone* in 2005, Jonathan Ringen maps out the affected male generation: '[i]n

1989, Pete Townshend admitted that he had sustained "very severe hearing damage". Since then, Neil Young, Beatles producer George Martin, Sting, Ted Nugent, [Fleetwood Mac drummer Mick Fleetwood] and Jeff Beck have all discussed their hearing problems' (Ringen, 2005, n.p). An advice booklet produced by Hearing Education and Awareness for Rockers quotes the following statistic: '60% of inductees into the Rock and Roll Hall of Fame are hearing impaired' (HEAR, 2004, 5). (The sheer loudness of much amplified popular music, particularly in the enclosed space of the indoors venue, has made hearing disorders an occupational hazard for musicians and fans alike – one could go 'deaf forever', as the English heavy rock band Mötorhead sang on a 1986 single of the same name.) In rock music, sheer loudness is woven into the excessive aesthetic, alongside other perhaps potentially precarious practices of music performance and consumption. One such – like 'the world wide phenomenon of head banging' – is a dance form soberly (or drily) defined in the *British Medical Journal* as 'a violent activity associated with hard rock and various subgenres of heavy metal ... [the] violent and rhythmic movement of the head synchronous with music' (though originating, apparently, at a Led Zeppelin concert in the late 1960s, in the indisputably dangerous practice of fans banging their heads on the stage in time to the band [Patton and McIntosh, 2008, n.p.]).[4] To be a head banger is to be a member of a subculture centred on rock music, the movement of the body and the potential (at least) for physical damage. Other rock fans ('short for fanatics', as Theodor Adorno has reminded us [quoted in McKay, 2005, 31]) would position themselves by or with their heads actually in the speaker boxes at gigs. As well as being a display of extreme fandom via excessive consumption to less committed adherents of the music in the crowd, this is also obviously a potentially disabling action.

In rock, then, loudness is part of the package: this is seen clearly in album titles like Nazareth's *Loud 'N' Proud* (2010) and Ozzy Osbourne's *Live & Loud* (1993), or song titles such as Kiss's 'I Love it Loud' and 'Shout It Out Loud' (on the 2009 album *Sonic Boom*). The career of British glam rocker chart-toppers Slade exemplifies the aesthetic: their 1970 album, their first with the name Slade, is called *Play It Loud*, and their final album, in 1987, is *You Boyz Make Big Noize*. The first of their three singles to enter the British charts at number one was 'Cum on Feel the Noize' (1973), later covered by Quiet Riot and by Oasis; intriguingly the effect of the group's characteristic mis-spelling of song titles works only in, in Lennard J. Davis's term, deafened mode. But it is Slade's 1981 album *Till Deaf Do Us Part*, their most heavy rock- rather than pop-oriented record, which is particularly notable. Guitarist Dave Hill claimed responsibility for the album title, explaining the curious thought behind the 'twist on words': 'What would separate you from your fans, what would it be if they went deaf?' (quoted in Ingham, 2007, 5). The original album front cover featured an image of an ear with a large nail penetrating the ear canal. The delicate pencil-style drawing and shading contrasts with, and accentuates, the violence of the image. The nail is bent – force has been applied – and its point protrudes from the *back* cover. The ear can only be profoundly damaged, the head well and truly banged. The lyrics of the title song connect heavy rock, live performance, masculinity, extreme volume, and the infliction of pain and death on the audience via the loudness of the music: 'Coming over to slaughter you [...]/Do you want us to torture you?' (The employment in recent years of rock music as instrument of torture or military intimidation provides a graphic illustration of the extent to which loudness in certain forms of music can be damaging; see Johnson and Cloonan, 2009.) Although there is an element of self-caricature within Slade's culture, of course – singer Noddy Holder opens the album with a mock 'rock and roll preach' promising an 'earholy catastrophe' to follow – at the time of its release some record stores refused to stock the album because of the 'offensive' cover (Heslam, 1992, 364).

The American heavy rock guitarist Ted Nugent was notorious for his use of extreme volume in live performances – an apocryphal but still much-repeated story from his 1970s heyday told of one outdoors gig where a pigeon was killed in mid-air by one of his power chords. Like Slade, Nugent used volume as part of his marketing strategy, and it inspired his repertoire too. His most famous slogan was 'If it's too loud, you're too old' – which challenged as well as defined his (non-avian) audience, by their youth. That is, generational difference in popular music is also articulated through the possibility of impairment, with its implication that hearing loss is for older people, not cool youth.[5] Because it is commonly associated with aging (presbyacusis), the state or onset of impaired hearing bears further anxious traces within the youth-oriented cultural zone of pop – this may help explain American rapper Foxy Brown's bewilderment with and initial denial of the public discovery of her own sudden and severe sensorineural hearing loss in 2005. Indeed, studies have shown that young people still reject protection from the potential damage to hearing of loud music because of 'cultural pressures to conform to stylistic norms and *youthful* images of attractiveness and healthy bodies' (Vogel et al., 2007, 129; emphasis added). Nugent's 1976 song 'Turn It Up' encapsulates the aesthetic practice of heavy rock, with lyrics such as:

> Turn it up, turn it up, make it louder than hell
> Turn it up, turn it up, make it ring like a bell ...
> Turn it up, turn it up, turn it up, louder, louder, yeah!

The song title, repeated lyrics, the bulk of the chorus, and even the fade-out coda (when the volume of the recorded music is actually, of course, decreasing) all instruct us to 'turn it up' – and it is essential to make the effect endure: the ear must 'ring like a bell', making the experience of tinnitus a central experience as well as a reminder of the gig. In fact, Nugent himself began to wear earplugs onstage, and has experienced hearing loss since his thirties (Gosch, 1984). In rock, then, loudness is part of the pleasure, and its effects on hearing accepted, even celebrated, by fans and musicians alike, as Mike Barnes has explained:

> [...] that ringing in your ears could be likened to a bonding experience, recounted with the same sort of jocularity-in-adversity with which you might discuss a hangover with fellow sufferers. But if the inner ear is damaged, the next-day ringing – temporary threshold shift – may become tinnitus, a hissing or whistling sound in the ear which can be permanent. One guitarist and DJ who has tinnitus reckoned that it was as much 'a badge of rock'n'roll honour as my Chelsea boot-squished toes or impaired liver functions.' (Barnes, 2009, 3)

The proudly damaged male body of the rock'n'roll wreck, wrecked from head to toe, self-presents as an authentic figure who has so far survived the culture's excess, as well as presumably the passing deaths of the less fortunate or the more appetitive. Sporting his 'badge of [...] honour', he has attempted to cheat the ageing process and its natural infirmities (though remember Tobin Siebers: 'there are no survivors' [2008, 7]) by enthusiastically embracing the disabling opportunities his culture has tempted him with before life did it anyway. Very rock and roll.[6]

## Headphones, earphones, earbuds, personal stereos

How does what Michael Bull (2005, 344) has called the 'privatised auditory bubble' public listeners create for themselves by their use of personal stereos in urban environments function less as a secure, closed experience, and more as a disabling potentiality? There is at least one link with the consumption of rock music, since, among users of portable headphones, research has shown that, of different music genres, 'rock and heavy metal was played the loudest by both males and females' (Daniel, 2007, 227). Otologists and medical academics confirm each other's findings about the dangers to hearing of popular music consumption in the new loud, mobile era, in particular around the impact of Walkman and iPod technologies on young people. Writing in a survey of recent research in the field in the *Journal of School Health* in 2007, Eileen Daniel found that,

> [w]hile age and hearing loss is linked, there appears to be a rise in hearing impairment among children and teenagers, usually related to

recreational noise exposure. Unlike industrial contact, many young people voluntarily expose themselves to loud noise via headphones, car sound systems, loud concerts, and nightclubs. (Daniel, 2007, 229)

The micro-technology of personal music consumption – in this instance, the ear- or headphone – is important: 'the actual sound level at the eardrum is [...] influenced by the insertion depth of the ear-bud in the ear canal. It is possible to obtain sound level of about 120 dB(A) in the worst case scenario [...] Furthermore, using software available on the internet enables to exceed these levels and reach values of 130 dB(A)'. Also the development in personal stereos of 'high-performance digital players' – as opposed to the older cassette Walkman, for example – 'with an increased dynamic range, has facilitated the listening to music at high levels due to reduced distortion at these levels' (SCENIHR, 2008, 9, 11 n. 7, 42).

Another survey of recent research on '[y]oung people's exposure to loud music', covering over 30 articles in the field, published the same year, opens with the observation that,

[...] with the massive growth in popularity of portable MP3 players, exposure to high noise levels has increased dramatically, and millions of young people are potentially putting themselves at risk for permanent hearing loss every time they listen to their favorite music. Music-induced hearing loss may evolve into a significant social and public health problem. (Vogel et al., 2007, 124)

While Vogel et al. qualify their understanding, projecting music-induced hearing loss into a future scenario, Oliver Sacks seems in less doubt. His present is replete with dangers for those musicophiliacs who are

[...] plugged into iPods, immersed in daylong concerts of our own choosing, virtually oblivious to the environment [...] This barrage of music puts a certain strain on our exquisitely sensitive auditory systems, which cannot be overloaded without dire consequences. One such consequence is the ever-increasing prevalence of serious hearing loss, even among young people, and particularly among musicians. (Sacks, 2007, 48)

Sacks's future is more bleak, while the present is deafening enough: 'problems can be expected to increase exponentially for people who play iPods or other music at too-loud levels. It is said that more than fifteen percent of young people now have significant hearing impairments' (Sacks, 2007, 132n. 1).

Yet it is possible that innovations of personal stereos are the pleasureful prosthetic for auditory culturalists like music fans. Walkman earphones and, even more, iPod buds, as well as the wires connecting them to their players, have arguably removed the stigma of unsightliness associated with hearing aids that, say, hearing-impaired singer Johnnie Ray's 1950s generation felt so powerfully, and which Ray directly confronted, not least with his coloured devices. Personal stereo earphones are now constructed as an icon of coolness. For instance, the advertising copy for one product line, Heartbeats earphones, reads: 'The incredibly unique style of Heartbeats came straight from Lady Gaga herself. Who needs earrings when you've got head-turners like Heartbeats?' Wearing pop celebrity-designed earphones 'make[s] on-lookers do a double take' – which is a quite different reaction from the 'double-take' regularly experienced by Ray's generation of ear device users (Heartbeats website; on Ray, see Herr, 2009 and McKay, 2013).

The cultural cachet of Apple products, the technology of choice of the world's creatives, touches the ears. In the past, hearing aids have been attached and therefore disguised on the earframes of spectacles, for instance – the discussion now is of them as an integrated technology with the personal stereo itself. The development of, for instance, Apple personal device applications (apps) into medical and disability fields has seen assistive technology apps produced for the iPhone and similar Apple products that mean it has the potential to function as a hearing aid. One hearing-impaired blogger, responding to the discussion thread about a new hearing aid app called soundAMP, writes of 'the irony of the iPod, with the hearing damage caused by its loud, long playing ability, and nearly universal use, now coming to the aid (pun intended) of the hearing impaired, is music to my ears!' (quoted in Berke, 2009). Others have criticized Apple for not ensuring that the iPhone is hearing aid-compatible (see comments thread to Kincaid, 2009). Among other available medical apps for hearing is one called Hearing Check, developed by the leading British charity the Royal National Institute for Deaf People, which is 'designed to be the best method of checking for sensorineural hearing loss (due to age or noise exposure[,] for instance) without seeing a medical professional' (RNID website, n.d.). Developments like these may be employed to enable personal music device producers – elsewhere, as we have seen, the target of criticism from academics, journalists and health professionals for the disabling possibilities of their modes of consumption by some, especially younger, users – to counteract the deafening negativity lined up against them.

This chapter has explored the fundamental and seemingly dichotomous relationship between popular music as a sonic art and the incapacity on the part of musicians and fans to hear it by looking at the causative place of popular music in hearing impairment – the terrible irony of music-induced hearing loss for rock musicians and pop fans. Here is some concluding advice for you from a man – a lifelong fan of jazz, rock, blues, pop, and a musician for 35 years, a teacher of music studies for 25 years – in his fifties: *turn it down!*

## Acknowledgement

The research for this chapter was made possible by an Arts and Humanities Research Council research leave award in 2009–10 for a project entitled 'Spasticus: popular music and disability'. This provided a matched sabbatical to one awarded by the University of Salford for the same project. I am extremely grateful to the AHRC and my university for their continued support. An extended version of the chapter will be available in my book *Shakin' All Over: Popular Music and Disability*.

PART TWO

# Punk Noise: Prehistories and Continuums

# CHAPTER FIVE

# Sounds Incorporated: Dissonant Sorties into Popular Culture

*Stephen Mallinder*

### Fade in ...

The place of the unexpected, the discordant, and the directly confrontational sound remains fundamental to our relationship not only with music but also with the worlds that we inhabit. Academic perspectives on noise, dissonance and atonal forms have frequently acknowledged their relationship with a wider popular culture, albeit at some distance and often with a level of knowing that can, at times, slip into superciliousness. Aside from cases such as Gershwin's, who unapologetically imported the energy and rhythms of the street and train tracks into his *Rhapsody in Blue* (1924), we maintain a sensitivity to the high-art/low-art divide in artistic discourses. And yet these boundaries have become increasingly blurred, so that there is now no value in polarizing the debate, however valid the conception of this divide remains. The noise narrative, and its corollary silence (or, in practice, ambience) is inevitably canonical in the domain of modern composition. It is a narrative that comes fully prepared with chapter markers and revered exponents: its precedents (Stravinsky and Schoenberg), its provocateurs (Russolo), its poster boys (Cage, Stockhausen, Schaeffer, Varèse), its range of more populist protagonists (Merzbow, the Haters, Sonic Youth), its naturalist and ambient kings (Alan Lamb, Chris Watson) and, in contrast, a retinue of bangers and crashers (Einstürzende Neubauten and Test Department most notably). In their wake followed the digital inheritors (Richard James, Autechre) and a growing army of glitch warriors. As this brief roll call suggests, the assimilation of the discordant, the dissonant and the downright cacophonous into mainstream popular music has been all but completed, and in the wake of this assimilation has come a loosening of the patrician's grip.

However, noise's encroachments into our everyday listening, and understanding of our surroundings, has been aided by a whole range of artists, and forms of media that fall outside acknowledged music grandees. Although the pioneers, avant-garde theorists, composers and general experimenters were conscientiously laying the foundations of modern music, both intellectual and popular (see Stubbs, 2009, 45), they have been aided by another tradition of popular but iconoclastic creators. A multitude of sound-recordists, writers, artists, filmmakers and television producers have filtered unconventional and elemental sounds through more popular modalities. For example, producers such as George Martin (the Beatles), Brian Wilson (the Beach Boys), Shadow Morton (the Shangri-Las), and Arthur Lyman, writers such as J. G. Ballard and William Burroughs, film directors such as Werner Herzog, David Lynch and Stanley Kubrick, have all contributed to how we listen and hear.

Starting from a position of a music practitioner, a number of these contributions have been drawn in to acknowledge the extent to which the embedding of non-musical sounds in popular forms has helped inform the recording process and – as a result of this – how we all, perhaps unconsciously, listen. Taken in the context of the consumption of popular culture in Britain, this assimilation of sounds, which is more readily associated with 'modern' composition, has been aided in part by easy access to a wealth of popular forms and the familiarities that come with this access. Cultures of continental European and North American films, television and music, which were presented without request to the post-war consumer, were also widely propagated in the British sphere by the rapid interactions of, and connections to, the national media of print, radio, and the moving image. The cultural congestion that characterizes British media, where everything is in seeing, hearing and touching distance, has helped to shape individual comprehensions of the resultant wide-ranging cultural landscape. This effective 'artistic hive' promotes a rapid dissemination of ideas and, in contrast to continental Europe and North America, engenders a less fraught relationship between 'modern' music and the more populist tropes of music.[1] Indeed as boundaries continue to blur, the question of that which could be said to constitute noise, irrespective of what cultural or aesthetic barometer determines popular, becomes increasingly problematic. The earlier taxonomy of significant creators also fails to acknowledge how other media, the visual and textual, have helped shape our understanding of sound. On the other side of these mergings and marryings of media – through television, cinema, science-fiction literature, and the popular press – audiences have developed meaningful relationships with sound and enabled more sophisticated auditory worlds to be created.

As a producer and performer myself, such a perspective has been consciously developed. It is perhaps apposite at this point to acknowledge that as a founder member of the group Cabaret Voltaire, my own sonic story is very much informed by these considerations. Over a 30-plus year period, through my own productions and performances, I have been conscious of how dissonant elements marry effectively with populist constructions, and how our understandings of sound are shaped by such collisions. Nevertheless it is as a critical reader, a watcher and a listener, that such worlds are more clearly understood. A familiarity with recording and performing perhaps gives some understanding of this acculturation, but it is important to address the context in which this cultural involvement occurred: to consider the time and the place, spaces in which music was both created and consumed, and the actual tools that shaped this engagement with a world of sound.

In the post-1945 'First World', the domestication of sound technology, which was ever more affordable, functional and available, had accelerated this assimilation of the experimental, and marginal, into the popular sphere. The proliferations of technologies have not only blurred the boundaries between noise and music (see, for example, Frith, 1996, 100) but also sanctioned noise's place in our listening. Mass production, mass media, wireless technologies and, more recently, programming software have immersed us all in a world of sound. These shifts, impacting all corners of the actual and virtual worlds, mark what may be the most significant reconfiguration in auditory history, as Taylor declares:

> The advent of digital technology in the early 1980s marks the beginning of what may be the most fundamental change in the history of Western music since the invention of music notation in the ninth century. (Taylor, 2001, 3)

Popular music has found itself sharing in the spoils of innovation, has found itself engaging new producers and communicating with new consumers and, consequently, breaking the canonical grip on 'challenging listening' exerted by modern compositional music. The online ecology has opened up global (if invisible) audiences to once-unfamiliar artists. It has focused spotlights on the liminal spaces where noisy subcultures once happily bashed around. File-sharing, streaming and social networking have all given new meaning to (if such terms should now be considered or utilized at all) centre and edge. However, this process of wearing away, completed in digital space, has been a century's work – with the occasional accelerant via more recent populist forms of music. The Velvet Underground's drone, punk's nose to noise confrontation, and techno's nocturnal emissions have, in turn, rescued pop from the shimmering excesses that all but drowned it in a sea of mediocrity. It is these heretics who challenged the rules of audience engagement, and what actually constituted popular sound, and so came to shape our listening.

## In the Beginning there was ...

Anyone who has had to roll up their sleeves and get dirty in all this auditory mulch is usually required to answer to the question: 'what did you do in the noise wars daddy?' Well, where did it begin? In designating for myself the vaguest descriptors – producer, mixer, DJ, and general sonic charlatan – how these roles and relationships have developed, from a personal perspective, inevitably comes under scrutiny. What drives the process of recording, or performing? When questioned by others (perhaps to confirm their suspicions that there never was a plan), the inquisition exposes, for myself, less of a sat-nav of connectivity but, rather, a Jackson Pollockesque confusion of associations.

From a personal perspective, as an inquisitive but untrained music mischief-maker, questions of how noise has infiltrated this timeline are understandably complex and multiple. Perhaps the most significant stage in the creative process is to acknowledge first and foremost that we are listeners and, as listeners, we have increasingly accommodated the unpredictable into our collective sonic worlds. By fortune, good or bad, this relationship to music-making has mapped a journey, in the broadest terms, from shiny vinyl pop culture to the splintering of our tangible world into a myriad parallel online universes. As the name Cabaret Voltaire sought to suggest, a key catalyst was how the spirit of Dada resonated within the stagnation of 1970s music and art. David Stubbs summarized it in this way:

> [...] the parallels between it [Dada] and the punk movement have proven irresistible to some – its explosive iconoclasm, its insolence in the face of authority, its primal aesthetic revolt and its liberation of ideas from the stifling over-dominance of technique. (Stubbs, 2009, 24)

Across this timeline it has to be said that the trajectory was always one that embodied a populist sensibility. And, although a listener brought up on a diet of soul, ska, and the more dysfunctional end of glam, this diet would subsequently allow for, as a music-maker, a harnessing of aspects of pre- and post-punk, electro and techno, and points beyond.

Popular culture has always been more accommodating to those unschooled in 'proper' music. As an unequivocal primitive in such things – and someone who placed expression over mastery of form – my influences and inspirations made for the broadest of palettes, and prompted an adoption of the most utilitarian of approaches. Put simply: if it worked, and had an effect, it was worthwhile. From the earliest moments of listening there was no immediate conflict between the popular and other, more cryptic, outpourings. Mine was merely a fascination with newness, the unconventional, and often bizarre. Inspiration came from the screen, the record, in the written word, from the streets outside. Sound was not rationalized, nor compartmentalized, by the untutored ear. This perception was perhaps rooted in an inclination to artifice, and self-deprecating humour and irony, rather than a blunt realism. It is, at times, a very English characteristic: a fascination with the darker, more satirical take on life – one that filtered through to the art-school-drenched popular music which was predominant during the late 1960s and 1970s. In particular, this sensibility exhibits a general tendency to conceptualize and theorise the popular, from Monty Python to Ray Davies, and all points in between. This trait appears to be something that persisted through the decades, in the stark contrast, for example, between the artifice of Britpop to the 'authentic' naturalism of American grunge of the same period. The British avant-garde has been more frequently positioned within popular music pursuits, and championed by more widely known artists, than its European and American avant-garde counterparts.

Attali's critical position on noise (albeit a position in which he casts himself as both judge and jury) – where noise is read as a tool of understanding power relationships and constructing cultural geography – explains the necessity of noise and, by extension, why noise has become a necessary part of the sounds incorporated into my own recordings. However, in regards to the actual forms of that cultural production, I probably then fall short of expectations. The mass-produced carriers of repetitive sound and the media through which I developed my understandings were, as Attali upholds, '[the] future forms of the repressive channelling of desire' (Attali, 1985, 6). As a product of popular culture myself, my environment was one of television, cinema, and 7" vinyl, and my earliest mentors were chintzy TV shows, seaside jukeboxes and, in time, the inky music press. In a hazy memory Radio Luxembourg carried a cachet of otherness: when listened to through a fuzz of white noise that was inseparable from the productions that crackled across its airwaves, it seemed to me to be beamed from a distant galaxy. Although they may choose not to admit it, I, like many contemporary producers, artists and non-musicians (terms that don't sit easily so I will allow others to tick their appropriate box) began a journey into sound whose first faltering steps came not through Pierre Schaeffer's noise experiments or La Monte Young's drone techniques. These steps were, rather, from more prosaic sources: Shadow Morton's motorbike screeches in the Shangri Las' 'Leader of the Pack' (1965), or the nightmarish memories of subterranean sounds emanating from the black and white television. I had a fascination with Brian Wilson's celery-munching rhythms recorded for the 'Vegetables' track on *Smiley Smile* (1967) which, much later, made perfect sense of why the languid cocktail ambience drifting through 'Re-Make/Re-Model' on the debut *Roxy Music* LP (1972) seemed wholly appropriate. This was a record that proved inspirational for a whole generation of experimenters and music-makers in the following years. Knowing that Maureen Tucker played telephone directories and used mallets as drumsticks on the Velvet Underground's 'Heroin' (see Budofsky, 2011) was very reassuring, although I haven't dared delve into my infantile cravings for old Spike Jones 78s, or *Sparky's Magic Piano*, that suggested surreal and somewhat eerie visions to accompany my first sonic steps. Sounds displaced or perhaps misplaced within a record gave unexpected narratives to what would have otherwise been rock for the discerningly stylish adult, quirky pop songs and a kitchen sink musical, respectively. Indeed it wasn't the workmanlike drums and bass on Roxy Music that attracted, but rather the sound of socialites, dandies and exquisites that exert seductive powers, as Bracewell argues (2007, 6). This would, in turn, open up a Pandora's Box of alternative sounds, in the form of Can, Faust, Captain Beefheart, Sun Ra, Ornette Coleman and Jimi Hendrix, to name but a few.

For an enquiring listener with a minimal music background there was no way in which such tangential sounds could be readily configured. Importantly, there was no real desire to separate the ambience or cacophony from the music structures which carried the songs themselves on the part of these music-makers. I was later to discover, and find explanations through, John Cage's modus operandi: one which held together extreme disparities, much then as one finds them held together in the natural world (see Ross, 2009, 389). My entry point was naïve and somewhat prosaic but the rationale, for me, was convincing: this was all part of the whole – it was all sound, after all. As much as I was a working-class anti-intellectual with an enquiring mind, I was also an untrained musician with a passion for a racket. I can offer a confirmation of this status: I was a person whose first instruments were, if we don't count the well-loved guitar which I tuned with a set of pliers, a hand-me-down Grundig tape recorder, with which I fashioned tape-loops from Beatles songs, and a glockenspiel – metal on metal. Looking at the space where music ends and noise begins has little meaning when technique is abandoned or, in this case, not even applicable. All sound was permissible; all space contested. Why shouldn't a motorcycle crash sit comfortably inside a four-minute slab of kitsch, honey-dripping teenage angst? Who said car horns and raw vegetables weren't percussion? And *musique concrète*? Perhaps this is all tacit knowledge now, but at the time it required some rapid reverse engineering on behalf of the youthful listener. Such sonic gems stood out from the pop crowd for their application of the everyday. They lent a sense of drama and of place, and so were sonic signifiers that could be readily understood. Popular culture is a gateway through which many enter in order to discover how the rules that govern majority tastes can be undone, to subversive effect.

The aforementioned tape loop experiments were, in consideration of the source, not without irony. Growing up in a household where the Beatles were inescapable, there was a certain devilment at the time in savaging their work – a payback of sorts. However, if some of the group's music was a little too kitsch and familiar, and so was permissible to cut up, then other tracks did give a thumbnail sketch of where to find the doors of perception. The period's growing fascination with all things (not actually) 'Occidental' brought with it a mixed sonic bag. The popularization and influence of Eastern musics, Indian raga in particular, enabled improvization to be increasingly incorporated into Western music. Although Martin Denny (with *Exotica* of 1957) and Arthur Lyman (with *Taboo* of 1957) had, for many, weirded out American cocktail suburbia a decade earlier, with the first contact with drones and sustained tonal parts, unusual instrumentation and the questionably exotic came through the Beatles. This was largely driven by the more widespread use of imaginative drugs, acid and cannabis, and such musical tropes became a common motif during the mid- to late sixties. Put politely, it was all very ersatz or, frankly, 'cod-Indian'. However one good thing emerged through these drones and harmonic styles: the 1966 Beatles track 'Tomorrow Never Knows', which delivered the unexpected to a mass audience fed mostly on a diet of bubblegum pop. The track predominantly consisted of five tape loops, as augmented by effects and delays (see MacDonald, 2005, 190–1). It absorbed the ideas and techniques of *musique concrète* to present them to a largely unversed popular audience. Here a series of interlocking and somewhat arbitrary loops collided, and to great effect, so that (and not for the first time) the popular and the experimental colluded. Of significance was the group's awareness of the developments in American and European avant-garde art. While Schaeffer and Stockhausen were perhaps more conspicuous in such circles, Paul McCartney, in particular, was *au fait* with La Monte Young, Cage and Fluxus. Although arguably catering largely to their own caprices, the Beatles, perhaps more than any other group during pop's apogee, had turned many on to other sonic possibilities. Although John Lennon would later begin to indulge himself, and the group, in further sound experiments ('Revolution 9' of 1968, for example), it was the earlier 'Tomorrow Never Knows', dropped on the unsuspecting consumer and found in the more commercial context of the *Revolver* LP, which arguably had a greater effect.

## Sound in words and pictures

All day the derelict walls and ceiling of the sound stage had reverberated with the endless din of traffic accelerating across the mid-town flyover which arched fifty feet above the studio's roof, a frenzied hypermanic babel of jostling horns, shrilling tyres, plunging brakes and engines that hammered down the empty corridors and stairways to the sound stage on the second floor, making the faded air feel leaden and angry.

'The Sound Sweep', J. G. Ballard ([1960] 2006, 142)

If popular music was for many an important entry point into a more esoteric world where noise could be readily accommodated, then the printed word, and moving image, provided the means to help contextualize such an entry. Sound could infiltrate these constructed worlds to great effect. The genre of science fiction exemplified the potential of sound to disturb readers and viewers. From the accelerated worlds of Phillip K. Dick to the dystopian vision of near-future Britain of Anthony Burgess's *A Clockwork Orange* (1962), sounds hummed through the pages. Jim Ballard's early stories presented strange exotic visions of futuristic worlds that sparkled with sound sculptures, sonic flora and oblique references to Stockhausen and John Cage (see, for example, Ballard's 'Venus Smiles' [(1957) 2006, 52]). The visions of Vermillion Sands conjured by Ballard evoked images that strangely echoed the exotica of Martin Denny's music of the same time, with its 'seductive, lingering shimmer – like a burnished aluminium UFO hovering in a desert heat haze' (Toop, 1999, 124). Darker sonic worlds were available within literature, where others, such as William Burroughs, harnessed the subversive power of sound and recording. Burroughs, adept at his own tape-montages, drenched his writings with a world of sound, from the slave-controlling tape recordings of *The Soft Machine* (1961) and the Master Musicians of Joujouka in *Nova Express* (1964) to the cinematic style of juxtaposing fractured narrative with whistles, street sounds and the 'clickerty clack' of train wheels in *The Last Words of Dutch Schultz* (Burroughs, 1961, 46).

These oblique sonic references in the texts of popular culture exerted untold influences on how music was made and heard. During the 1960s and 1970s group nomenclature was typically itself an acknowledgment of the word becoming sound. Soft Machine, Steely Dan, Moloko, Clock DVA, Comsat Angels, the Normal ('Warm Leatherette' of 1978) and, much later in the piece, Empire of the Sun have quite literally (and numerous others more figuratively) acknowledged the influence of visionary, and sonically attuned, writers. We were not alone in this marrying of media and noise; Throbbing Gristle, 23 Skidoo (the 'Final Academy' tour of 1982)[2] and Joy Division,[3] for example, not only toyed with collage, film, live projections, graphics and publications, but also appeared with writers like William Burroughs. A generation of artists, immersed in words and film, were attaining a keen sense of sound's role in the development of style and technique. In a world where popular culture became an important lingua franca, books, magazines and the music press became the media by which such ideas and influences could be shared and disseminated. Where the actual music failed to deliver, words can shape not merely the obvious (lyrical imagery) but also the ways in which sound connects with the listener on a purely visceral level.

The capacity to juxtapose sound with image in television and cinema provided alternative ways of hearing. Here, unrestrained by the format of the single, sound could be unleashed. Reruns from television's embryonic days, in fuzzy black and white, of the *Quatermass Experiment* series (1953–5) left a deep impression. This was a dark and foreboding slab of post-war paranoia, whose title music (composed by Trevor Duncan) belatedly seems to have been a gem of John Barry-esque arrangements. Television proved to be a fertile ground for sonic weirdness and one which came to partially fulfil Cage's prophecy, that

> [...] the use of noise to make music will continue and increase until we reach a music produced through the aid of electrical instruments which will make available for musical purposes any and all sounds that can be heard. (Cage, 1937)

Crucially, at a time of scant surplus income, television, like radio, was an important source of new sounds, as with the work of the BBC's Radiophonic Workshop and, in time, via British broadcasts of *The Outer Limits* (1963–5) and *Lost in Space* (1965–8). Such programmes were matched by the radical recordings of Raymond Scott, whose sound experiments during the 1950s and 1960s (compiled in 2000 as *Manhattan Research Inc.*), which had accompanied a multitude of American advertisements and cartoons, seemed

Forbidden Planet *(Wise, 1951)*.

to shape the popular perceptions of a future world. These unconventional but popular and widely consumed productions, together with Bernard Hermann's use of them for *The Day the Earth Stood Still* (Robert Wise, 1951) and Lois and Bebe Barron's exhilarating score for *Forbidden Planet* (Fred M. Wilcox, 1956), fed into a belief in the transformative qualities of electronic sounds. A drive to all things noisy, futuristic and rather outré, I suspected, came to us all instinctively. At a pivotal point in my own music-making one film harnessed the emotive power of noise. David Lynch's debut feature *Eraserhead* (1977) utilized the skills of sound designer Alan R. Spelt to construct a rather dystopian vision of industrial decay. The world that the film's characters occupied was bleak, surreal and unsettling, due in large part to the accompanying soundtrack.

A fictional character who prickled with Burroughs-like sensibilities, Harry Caul (as played by Gene Hackman for Francis Ford Coppola's 1974 film *The Conversation*) was a surveillance expert and melancholic operative, and brought paranoia, through sound, to the cinema. Caul reified the more forensic approaches to unravelling sound, as existing in a world in which noise signifies pure materiality – a culture beyond the realms of sound waves and audio frequencies.[4] Hence, as he notes of his modus operandi: 'I don't care what they're talking about all I want is a nice fat recording.' Doing for audio what Michelangelo Antonioni had done for the photographic image twelve years earlier in *Blow-Up* (1966), *The Conversation* painstakingly unpicks the salient individual parts which make up the mystery in order to present a series of conspiratorial possibilities. Coppola updates Antonioni's backdrop of London's free-spirited 1960s to that of San Francisco and Nixon's 1970s, and technology-induced paranoia. Here, the film's central character is dropped into the uncertainty of real events. As a technician, an outsider and an acoustic obsessive, Caul elevates the manipulation of sound waves to a truly aesthetic pursuit, and one that is now recognisable in the Logic Audio and Pro-Tools-enabled bedroom warriors. As a study of recording technology *The Conversation* shows the capacity of process to become a voyeuristic, and at times fetishistic, exercise in the laying bare of the intimacy of ambient recordings. In the invasion of the privacy of a largely unknown couple, the film exposes the arcane world of field recording to expose a world of intrigue that rang strangely true through Watergate-era America. The film perfectly illustrated the attraction of pure sound but it also highlighted a collision of senses in the twin helix of image and sound that is impossible to divide. As sound producers, the medium of film had come to shape much of the material created in the studio – just as the performances became an opportunity to present a visual racket to match the sonic onslaught. Again, the catalyst was drawn from the popular shelf as much as the darker drawers of cinematic illusion – from Wendy (or was it Walter?) Carlos's switched-on Beethoven in Stanley Kubrick's adaptation of *A Clockwork Orange* (1971), Popol Vuh

*Technologies for listening:* The Conversation *(Coppola, 1974).*

in Werner Herzog's *Aguirre, Wrath of God* (1972) and Orson Welles's *noir* classic *A Touch of Evil* (1958), whose Henry Mancini soundtrack provoked an unequivocal homage on the Cabaret Voltaire *Red Mecca* album of 1981.

One of the last acts undertaken, in 1993 and in the guise of Cabaret Voltaire, was to create a piece around unedited street recordings, captured with a discretely positioned DAT machine: a simplistic exercise in wrestling with the rhythms and organization of urban space (a subject which later formed the basis for analysis in Lefebvre, 2004). Clocking in at almost an hour, *Project 80* comprised virtually one disc of the final release: *The Conversation* (1993). The track was not only an appropriate way to find some closure on a long period of collaborative recording for the two remaining members, Richard Kirk and myself, but also an undisguised paean to the remarkable Coppola film – the movie itself but, perhaps more importantly, as a meta-reference to the centrality of film to music-making processes. If recorded music, in all its forms, had been a central part of this story, then sound in film had been an equally guiding influence. The media had informed not only what was, but also how we went about, our business – for years we had recorded with the television and a video recorder permanently plugged into the 24-channel mixing desk: it had its own channel, its own plug-in effects, a fifth Beatle. Not only did this afford us the possibility of dub mixes with snippets of gunshots, porn, or some abstract dialogue, but also the potential to bear witness to events as they happened. Well, you didn't want to miss anything did you? As a result it was possible to capture Pope John Paul II being shot, the aftermath of the Iranian revolution, and the Challenger Space Shuttle disaster, live and direct, in this way. The capacity to boilerplate or manipulate words and sounds directly from the natural world, as well as from film, television and video, enabled the direct embedding of popular forms into the recording process.

*Back cover of Cabaret Voltaire's* Seconds Too Late.

## Fade out ...

As a music producer one is first and foremost a listener. The capacity to contextualize sounds filtered through different media plays a significant role in the phenomena of hearing and subsequent recording. David Toop's continuing dissection of this ambiguous auditory world helps us to acknowledge how sound, often demoted in the hierarchy of senses, needs to be addressed through visual and textual media (see Toop, 2010). The often seemingly silent world of literature and compositional painting are, in effect, repositories of a whole range of auditory fragments. The pages of T. S. Eliot and Thomas Hardy are rich with attendant sound, Toop argues (2010, 7) and the voyeuristic compositions of Dutch painter Nicolaes Maes capture the granular auditory context in which the everyday activities depicted took place (Toop, 2010, 76). Toop's observations maintain the assertion that we exist in overlapping sensory worlds rather than experiencing compartmentalized sensations. Our capacity to cognitively render sounds and visions as we engage with literary texts and representative art is matched by the profound influence sound has on how the moving image is reconstructed by the viewer. Our rebuilding and understanding is most at work through popular cultural products, where consumers, often subconsciously, engage with the complexities of our auditory world.

From a personal perspective, the use of tangential sounds in recording remains strangely alluring. The 'moment' can be captured in the recording process most effectively both through the voice, as imprinting the emotive, human component, and also through the mechanism of noise. Such noise is the interjection of natural ambient sounds, or more mediated forms from film, television and other broadcast media, that filter through our consciousness, and the inclusion of these elements effectively help anchor the recording in its time and place. Such sounds also challenge the listener. To confront the listener through more conventional or popular modalities can heighten this effect. From the position of producer, contextualizing the peculiar with the prosaic is potentially more transgressive than when this operation is delivered in purely intellectual form. Either subliminal or overt, this contextualization suggests more lines could be crossed: subversion becomes potentially more powerful when attached to the *lingua franca* of popular culture. In delving into the iconoclastic world of Dadaism, Duchamp has taught us all that the natural world was, itself, littered with the detritus of a ready-made world. Duchamp was dismissive of Pop Art on its arrival, finding it difficult to support the aesthetics of such mundane objects, but for those born of the commodity age it was all part of the toolkit. Similarly, it became critical that music should find currency by locating itself within its immediate context and build in the everyday. By drawing upon such found sounds, the memories of time and place could function as a form of watermark running through the music. It is these sonic fragments, the often-overlooked incorporated sounds, which in fact help capture the tensions that exist at specific moments, and shape our understandings.

# CHAPTER SIX

# Stairwells of Abjection and Screaming Bodies: Einstürzende Neubauten's Artaudian Noise Music

*Jennifer Shryane*

## Introduction

This chapter is set within the context of Antonin Artaud's little-known influence on contemporary music. It focuses on the Berlin music collective, Einstürzende Neubauten, as a working example of Artaudian performers, through a selection of their music of collapse from 1980 to the present day. It aims to demonstrate the frequent and effective use of Artaudian themes, as well as the compositional and performance strategies employed by the group, particularly in their depiction of abject landscapes and organless, screaming bodies. The music selected from Neubauten's diverse oeuvre for this discussion includes two early experimental sound collages, later compositions for radio, theatre and film, and finally some recent work including the *Musterhaus* series.

The Berlin-based music collective, Einstürzende Neubauten, who have been organizing sound and performing noise music since 1980, invite study from a rich variety of perspectives. For example, their work can be philosophically examined through Walter Benjamin's concepts of the cheerful Destructive Character, his urban rag-pickers, and his Angel of History, while John Cage's boundary-breaking ideas on what constitutes music as instrumentation, score and performance offer a more musically orientated approach. Joseph Beuys's use of hybrid materials, his idiosyncratic enactments and social sculptures provide a milieu for the exploration of Neubauten's social art, and Jacques Attali's fourth phase of music, 'Composition', as discussed in his *Noise: The Political Economy of Music* (1985, 133–48) can be utilized to analyze their own cottage-industry structures of independence. In differing ways, Pierre Schaeffer's *musique concrète* explorations and his strivings to evade 'do-re-mi', along with the radical orchestration and semantic-free vocalization of Iannis Xenakis, who wanted the untutored 'listener to be gripped – whether he likes it or not' (Xenakis, 2009, 12), also offer fruitful investigative approaches. Both provide practical working and performance models from which to assess the influences on the work of Neubauten and their multifarious developments. With equally differing schemas, William Blake, Friedrich Nietzsche and Heiner Müller provide reference points for Neubauten's textual structures and thematic concerns with interims and opposites, apocalypse and myth, fire and flight. However, from such a plethora of potential perspectives, I have selected Antonin Artaud's articulation of the 'Theatre of Cruelty' (as discussed in his *The Theatre and its Double*, 1938) as a lens through which to explore a selection of Neubauten's music of collapse.

## Artaud's infection

Artaud's philosophy of theatre has been widely discussed in particular within Western theatre and performance art discourse. This encompasses his ideas of theatre as contagion, his breaking of both the textual domination over the body in performance, the necessity for all performative aspects to complement each other, and his foregrounding of non-linguistic extreme vocals, the scream and highly stylized choreography. But Douglas Kahn in *Noise, Water, Meat* (2001) has drawn attention to a more neglected area: Artaud's influence on Beat Poetry, Fluxus and, importantly, on the Black Mountain musicians, David Tudor and John Cage – particularly in connection with Artaud's ideas for freeing music from conventional instruments as well as from the constraints of time and continuity. In acknowledgement of this readily available existing literature, I have provided only the briefest of comments on Artaud's performance philosophy as it is relevant to Neubauten's music. Likewise, as I have already argued that Einstürzende Neubauten are one of the most effective examples of working Artaudian artists within contemporary music (Shryane, 2010, 323), this otherwise necessary supporting context is given here only the following short summary. My earlier argument for Neubauten's Artaudian status considered their performance of destruction as a version of Artaud's theatre of the plague. It was intended to 'infect' and collapse (as their name implies) West Germany's *Wirtschaftswunder* (Economic Miracle) in the 1980s and its accompanying architecture and culture, much as Artaud had hoped his plague would eradicate the stultifying, text-bound theatre of his day. I particularly focused on two areas: first, Neubauten's use of found and self-built instrumentation rag-picked from Berlin's *Narbengelände* (scar-faced terrain) in response to Artaud's proposal for 'utterly unusual sound properties and vibrations' (Artaud, 1970, 73); secondly, Blixa Bargeld's non-linguistic vocalization and use of the scream – as a 'material' voice (Hegarty, 2007, 31) which brings with it pain (*hör mit schmerzen*/ listen with pain) for both the expeller and the receiver. This was linked to Artaud's model for a new performance language 'somewhere between gesture and thought ... a spatial language' (Artaud, 1970, 68–9).

Previously, I also argued that the group, as *Nachgeborenen* (future/ post-Second World War generation) artists,[1] shared a desire to reject their parents' tainted past and present consumerism, as well as their contemporaries' various responses (from political action to making music of cosmic escape) in order to reinvent their own distinct, guilt-free sound. Here my intention is to concentrate on some of the outcomes of this philosophy of, and approach to, sound organization in order to present evidence of Neubauten's interpretations of Artaud's performance ideas and concerns.

Artaud's *Pour en finir avec le jugement de dieu* (To Have Done with the Judgement of God, 1947)[2] is the linchpin here with its aural assault of percussion and the screaming (organless, genderless) body plus, particularly in *My Cry in the Stairwell,* its distinctive visceral metal noise. These are the mainstay features of Neubauten's idiosyncratic sonic quality; hence, *Pour en finir* provides a useful starting point and throughline. In the Sub Rosa recording of the work's aborted radio broadcast (it was banned by Wladimir Porche, head of the French radio the day before its scheduled broadcast on 2 February 1948), Artaud emits a polyphony of tortured screams, from high-pitched utterances, hoarse croaks and shouts to shrill bird-like screeches. These are overlaid and spliced with percussion, metal bangs, xylophonic noises, invented language, apocalyptic laughter and vitriolic text. There is a sense of randomness and unrepeatability but, in fact, the performance and co-performers were carefully orchestrated by Artaud. Neubauten's *Stahlmusik, aufgenommen am 1.6.80, in einer Autobahnbrücke* (Steelmusic, recorded inside an autobahn flyover) owes a striking debt to this still most disturbing work but it also transcends it with variety and surprising lyricism.[3]

## Collages of collapse

In June 1980, Neubauten's quest for new tonal territories within the topography of their half-city took them to a steel cavity under an autobahn flyover in Friednau-Schöneberg in which Bargeld used to play as a youth with Andrew Unruh. The project was to create sounds from the steel walls of the enclosed space along with a guitar, some metal percussion and a few bits of battery-powered equipment which they could squeeze into the small cavity. Pocket torches were used for illumination, a Telefunken Bajazzo transistor radio as an amplifier, candles as indicators of oxygen levels and a cassette recorder to capture the work as *Stahlmusik*.

The result is a remarkably radical and varied field recording which retains its attractive yet startlingly primitive quality. As with Artaud's composition, it is simultaneously random, ritualistic and unrepeatable while being orchestrated, carefully planned and disciplined. The sounds one hears are muted, hollow and strangely remote; there is an echoing, vibrating metal drumming of the interior walls, higher persistent metallic chimes, low rumbles of the passing traffic bleeding in, a sawing, gnawing noise which hurts, a guitar which drones and cries on its battery power and toward the end, as the final noise of closure, a slamming, as if from huge metal doors. A solitary clap follows which provides a touch of destructive, anarchic humour (as invoked by Artaud, 1970, 31). This clap marks what is missing, for Unruh explained that he and Bargeld were totally alone from midnight to 6 am, working on the cassette recording (personal interview, Berlin, 14 February 2007). Then, of course, amidst this orchestra of surprisingly controlled noise, there is Bargeld's voice which ranges from the intoning of different vowel sounds through varied pitches and tempos, elongated yells, rasping screams, drones of non-phonemic sounds, and at one point – in Dadaist fashion – the German alphabet which is shouted amidst sharp yelps. Unlike Artaud's angry, accusing text, this voice offers no logos (apart from the alphabet snatches), no literal meaning is ensconced in its musicality; it is heavy with another language – the ur-language for which Artaud also strove – his 'spatial poetry' (1970, 50–4) intoned in a place which feels as equally abject as Artaud's hollow stairwell.[4]

This sonic representation of an alienating, possibly post-apocalyptic space where 'draussen ist feinlich' ([the] outside is hostile) is present in a range of Neubauten's work; for example, the first two albums, *Kollaps* (1981), from where the above statement comes, and *Zeichnungen des Patienten O.T.* (The Drawings of Patient O.T., 1983), as well as work composed for Heiner Müller during the late 1980s and early 1990s and later, *Berlin Babylon* (2000) and *Anarchitekur* (Anarchitecture) and *Unglaubliche Lärm* (Unbelievable Noise) of the *Musterhaus* experiment (2005–7). In performance, the intricate and potentially dangerous industrial playground of chunks of machinery, metal, fire, water, found materials and self-constructed sound objects visually reinforces this terrain and illustrates Artaud's wish that '[Musical instruments] will be used as objects, as part of the set. Moreover they need to act deeply and directly on our sensibility through the senses' (Artaud, 1970, 73–4).

*Zeichnungen des Patienten O.T.* is probably Neubauten's most completely Artaudian work and, hence, will be considered in more detail. The album creates a sonic world which suggests a state out of joint, primeval, without buildings or people, perhaps after Artaud's plague; it is an abject space filled with noises heavy with subterranean darkness, bubbling mud, smouldering fires and blundering, groaning beasts, all constantly threatened with being sucked into a swirling vortex of noise or smothered by the pounding muffled beat of the taut spring or metal sheet. Alexander Hacke's blowing of a five-foot length of drainpipe results in an unnerving, horn-like drone which suggests both the call of a wounded animal and a human cry for contact. Unruh's 'found' vibrator provides the fragile humming opening of both 'Armenia' and 'Die genaue Zeit' (The Exact Time). With 'Armenia' this hum opens out into the vastness above ground of an empty space which contains Bargeld's hoarse, broken whispers and tortured cries. Fragments of extraneous noise are included on several tracks: a recording of a hospitalized child singing and chattering, snippets of broadcasts, a drill against metal, a looped police phone-in helpline concerning a kidnapping, smashing glass, a howling dog, a finger click against a tooth, the sampling of an Armenian folksong and water dripping on a hot stove. These shards ebb and flow in the sound frame and are frequently cut through by icy, swirling reverberations of falling metal ('Vanadium-i-ching') and by Bargeld's extreme, ever-surprising voice which often is hardly articulated or appears strangled by weight, as in 'Die genaue Zeit'. In terms of textual

*In performance at Columbiahalle, Berlin, 23 October 2010.*

*Jochen Arbeit manipulating effects for his guitar at Relentless Garage, London, 17 October 2010. Taken by Kieran Shryane for the author.*

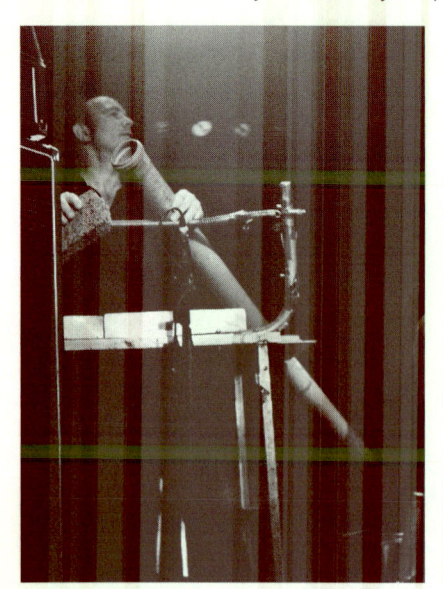

*Andrew Unruh creating noise at Columbiahalle, Berlin, 23 October 2010.*

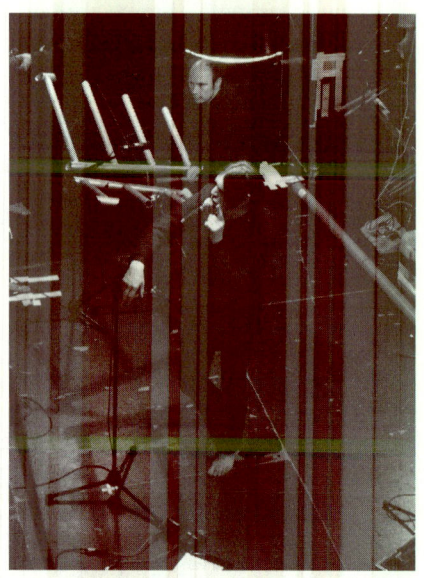

*Blixa Bargeld creating noise by tapping his mouth (with Unruh on the pipes) at Ancienne Belgique, Brussels, 21 May 2008.*

content there is an abundance of Artaudian concerns: vultures hover, lead burns, souls are invited to be torched along with towns in order to free both of fungi and carrion, cadavers dance, God's testicles go up in flames, the protagonist develops nine Kafkaesque arms and easy-listening *musak* is ridiculed as painless, caught between the telling times of 33 and 45 and fit only for mortuaries and new buildings because it cannot create chord scars on the face or ears as wounds. Release comes from the prison of 'sameness' and 'exact time' as the stylus 'skips'.[5] Threaded through the complex, ponderous textures and the celebratory incitements of destruction, there is a sense of urgency as tracks seem to collide into each other, similar to the energized call for immediate action in *Pour en finir* and previously focused in 'Kollaps' as 'Bis zum Kollaps ist nicht viel Zeit, drei Jahre noch' ('Not much time until the collapse, only three years').

## Müller terrain: noise and word

The collaborations with Heiner Müller had a profound effect on Neubauten's development during the 1990s and resulted in several extraordinary pieces of 'apocalyptic landscape' noise. Müller initiated the first project with Neubauten in 1988 and during his lifetime there were four more, plus other unfulfilled proposals based on Artaud's and Jean Paul's writings.[6] The finished works included two radio plays by Müller: *Bildbeschreibung* (Description of a Picture, 1988) and *Hamletmaschine* (Hamlet-Machine, 1990) for Berliner Rundfunk, and the use of tracks from Neubauten's first two albums for Müller's radio adaptation of Brecht's *Fatzer* (1987).[7] The music which Neubauten composed for *Bildbeschreibung* was reworked to underscore Müller's eight-hour staging of *Hamlet/Hamletmaschine* at the Deutsches Schauspielhaus in 1989. It is *Bildeschreibung* and *Hamletmaschine* which are discussed here as Artaudian examples of the use of noise with the spoken word as in *Pour en finir*.

*Bildeschriebung* opens with the unnerving cry of crows, recalling the desolate atmosphere of *Patentien O.T.* When these bird noises reoccur toward the end of the work they uncannily suggest a child in distress. The opening repetition of the title and author sets up a distancing effect in suggesting 'an error' – a technique frequently employed by Müller and adopted by Neubauten.[8] An ominous low, slurred grumble can be discerned alongside the voices which are immediately recognizable as man, woman and child, unlike in *Pour en finir* where gender and age in the excessive vocalizations are irrelevant. The noise mass steadily advances as if oozing from a subterranean home; gradually, disturbingly it pushes forward. At times a single rogue noise occurs – a plucked spring or a high metallic twang, as if these have shaken loose only to be quickly re-engaged with the main body mass. The voices continue dispassionately and steadily to expound the text. The elements, as Artaud wanted, work separately.[9] The sonic shape, like a primeval monster-sloth or mud-laden war machine, dully rattles forward with its occasional flash cry or distant creak; this latter sound suggests less of the former accidental utterance and more of an achieved deliberate breach. Eventually the voice fades as if enveloped, leaving only the final soft beats of the noise's arrival and bedding in. The above almost-narrative description, however, could be misleading, for Neubauten's composition refuses to be naturalized in the sense of being an interpretative soundtrack; as Kruger said of the use of *Kollaps* and *Patentien O.T.* for Muller's radio interpretation of Brecht's fragment, *Der Untergang des egoisten Fatzer* (1987), '[the music's] abstract minimalism keeps it one remove from the mimetic' (Kruger, 2004, 156–7).

The Wende (Velvet Revolution)[10] interrupted further work between Müller and Neubauten as East German Radio was reorganized but, in 1990, Neubauten were invited to work with Wolfgang Rindfleisch (who had been involved with *Fatzer*) on Müller's *Hamletmaschine*. In this 32-minute radio version there were four actors: Bargeld (who also co-directed) as Hamlet/Actor, Gudrun Gut as Ophelia, Hans-Werner Krösinger reading the intertitles and Müller himself reading the stage directions. The outcome again suggests the petrified, inhuman landscapes of *Patienten O.T.* with the cruel, threatening sound of metal smashed on metal, shrill drones, scratches, vibrating springs, repetitive jarring piano notes, falling debris, modulating moans and sustained strangulated screams. At points there is a medley of frantic whispering, gossiping voices through which Bargeld declaims Hamlet's text as if pontificating at a political rally; this delivery creates an alienating, robotic effect, whereas Gut's vulnerable, overtly feminine confessing voice coming out of a softly intoned 'religious' hum and framed by smashing glass heightens the ghastly content of her monologues – thus the two voices, sandwiched between the confidentially shared stage directions and intertitles, effectively polarize the two roles.

## Playable landscapes of abjection

The work with Müller (whom Kalb labels in *The Theatre of Heiner Müller*, 1998, as an Artaudian practitioner) deepened Bargeld's understanding of being a performer, writer and director. This new development is evident in his lyric writing from *Tabula Rasa* (1993) onwards and in his direction of Maria Zinfert's stage version of J. M. Coetzee's *Warten auf die Barbaren* (Waiting for the Barbarians, Salzburg Festival, 2005; Hamburg, 2006). Here he employed many Artaudian techniques in his use of a recorded sound collage of voices, screams and sounds which played a vital role in his *mise-en-scène* by representing the bodiless tongues of the tortured and the torturer. This sound collage, which included Bargeld's own whipping and slashing screams,[11] worked in conjunction with the knife-like, flashbulb sequences employed by Neubauten's lighting designer Lutz John. The synchronization of sound and light was so precise that it created for the spectator a painfully tangible cutting away visually and aurally, which was both sudden and yet sustained in its impact on the senses. While the brief moments of darkness offered relief from the over-exposed white light on the cruel white, empty space, the periods of silence roared. Bargeld had deliberately striven for Artaudian cruelty and wanted lighting like 'arrows of fire' (Eshleman and Bador, 1995, 10), and a performance which attacks not just the ears and eyes, but also the breast of the spectator in its depiction of the novel's story of 'Otherness' and 'Civilization'.[12]

An earlier work for the stage was *Faustmusik*, which is one of Neubauten's most fascinating Artaudian sound architectures created in 1994 for Werner Schwab's stage play, *Faust, meine Brustkorb, mein Helm* (Faust, my breastplate and my helmet) directed in Potsdam by Thomas Thieme (after Schwab's sudden death). Here Neubauten strove to create 'wooden' library music instead of the more familiar metal, concrete or fire-induced sounds. The stage set signified Faust's study which disintegrated during the performance; this was visually represented by an onstage conveyor belt constructed by Andrew Unruh which mixed wood, paper and water, pulped these into briquettes which were pushed through a funnel to fall on Faust. Unruh also built a huge music-box as a book-tearing machine (the Orchestrion) which had a fan to flutter book pages, a book catapult and a centrifuge. There were big folios used as bass drums and various sizes of books hollowed out and struck by oversized clappers. Tables with their tops sawed out in tongue shapes were used as percussion instruments and some tables were strung to create bass chords; one piled with books became a drum kit. The concept being explored was not of music composed for the theatre but music as produced from the physical effects of the theatre itself, as Artaud had proposed; Neubauten had constructed sound bodies which were also stage properties. Hence, the stage was transformed into a *musikalisch bespielbare Installation* (musical playable installation)[13] and the performance emulated much of what Artaud desired for his 'Total' theatre. Bargeld said:

> We needed an especially designed instrumentarium, a stage set to be played as an instrument [...] a wooden music [...] Einstürzende Neubauten in the laboratory of Faust. Bookdrums, hollow books, knocking, old volumes. Tables, manipulated tables, different tables strung with strings or wires, sawn out tables, kalimba tables, moving tables. Book-machines, pageturningmachines, a motorised book-hi-hat, a whole orchestrion put together out of different book machines. (Maeck, 1996, 128)

*Faustmusik*, as 'wooden library' music, consists of muffled, muted, internal sounds dominated by paper, wood and wind, within a small, confined space. 'Tische' ('Table') is a three-minute drone of a humming machine interwoven with rustling of papers while the muffled wood and metal beats of 'Besetzt' (Full) are interspersed with sparkings, fuzzy rustles and choric voices comprised of phonetic sounds. 'Das Orchestrion' suggests a roomful of machinery all slightly out of synchronization. Here papers rustle, doors slam and muffled thuds conjure up wading, then stamping, through thick piles of papers.

In contrast, Neubauten created expansive, outdoor sounds for Hubertus Siegert's television documentary, *Berlin Babylon* (2001), a critique on restitched Berlin's demolishing and rebuilding frenzy which transformed the city into a vast building site. Its title track consists of swirling, uncoordinated sounds sliced through with the rhythmic heavy pound of earth-moving machinery, the clang of metal, the clash of steel and the hum of scaffolding. Busy helicopters and walkie-talkies contrast with the delicate high-pitched vibrations of 'Glas 1 Sony-Center' (the huge glass-fronted skyscraper which dominates the redesigned Potsdamer Platz). The sound rises ethereally through amplified resonating wires with shrill, intermittent tremors and the tap of thin metal on metal. Together with its companion piece 'Glas 2 (Richtfest)', it offers a balance to the predominance of heavy pounding sounds, surging movements and a recurring motif of a circular noise which seems wearily to be going nowhere. Of particular relevance here is Neubauten's treatment of Angela Winkler's recitation of Benjamin's 'Angel of History'. As she speaks the iconic words, storm winds rush across an open, desolate space and seep through the ghostly cracks and future ruins to attack her voice. The winds rise and move forward, swamping the whole sonic frame, followed by waves of falling glass and disintegrating structures which submerge the prophetic language in swirling apocalyptic chaos.

## Twenty-first century: *Musterhaus* and *Empty at Last*

Sonically created abject places interlaced with screams and/or other vocalizations continue to feature in Neubauten's work. Some of their most recent Artaudian experiments can be found in their *Musterhaus* explorations, which Bargeld called 'the more experimental side of Neubauten'.[14] The first two albums are noted for the way in which the voice sometimes quits the landscape of noise or appears to be on the perceptual threshold as 'borderline' art.[15] In *Anarchitektur* it merely forms an occasional mantra from the title and seems to be attempting unsuccessfully to dismantle the growing acoustic architecture. In *Unglaublicher Lärm* it moves aside into the 'missed' zone. This work creates weave upon weave of sound which includes parodies of motorik musik, Classic FM and Radio Sunshine. All this is orchestrated into an ebb and flow effect of a slow, difficult journey indicative of much of Neubauten's work. Amidst this caravan of sounds, periodically, it is just possible to decipher a human voice, muffled, unobserved, slowed down like a yawn or a groan, a piece of swallowed text: '*Ohne Sie, im Garten, ein, zwei, drei*' ('without you, in the garden, one, two, three'), a breathy 'I', a rhythmic 'oh yeah', or some high squeaks of radio tuning or mechanical nonsense-speak. As the wall of noise moves on, these little hiccups are too distant and too brief to make a difference; even the trademark scream is absent. The brief presence of human utterance appears accidental, playfully suggesting that the voices are in error; they should not have been picked up.

Neubauten's experiments in the twenty-first century foregrounded a new aerial, ethereal lightness which is captured by the distinctive Aircake instrument, textual concerns of birds, flight and astronomy, and the use of plastic, polystyrene, dried leaves and air duct pipes. There seemed to be less desire to be 'cruel' to oneself and to the spectator, but although these new works were often not demonstratively painful to listen to, they were – like the multi-layered, fragile 'Ein seltener Vogel' (A Rare Bird, 2003) with its bells, humming voices, springs, plastic and mantras and the misleadingly gentle 'Compressors in the Dark' (2003) with its dada word lists, which dissolve into animalistic squeals, squeaks and gurgles – still unsettling and provoking.[16] The work continues to demonstrate what Eshleman and Bador called Artaud's 'steely rigor and dramatic intensity' (1995, 10) and to experiment with a range of sounds which include Artaud's 'booming pounding musical rhythm and sustained, hesitating fragile music which seems to grind the most precious metals, where springs of water bubble up' (Artaud, 1970, 41). They also continue to give language its 'full, physical shock potential, to split it up and distribute it actively in space' (Artaud, 1970, 35). The texts too, where present, still focus those concerns of Artaud for a 'revolution based on fire, magic and anatomical transformation' (Eshleman and Bador, 1995, 15).

I will close this discussion on some of Neubauten's Artaudian credentials with a brief look at two very Artaudian texts which are still performed in an overtly, choreographed physical manner: the first, 'Redukt' (Reduce) (2000) and the second, 'Unvollständigkeit' (Incompleteness) (2007).[17] Both works are concerned with Artaud's final thoughts in *Pour en finir* – the gravity-defying, dancing organless body and the ability to rid oneself of unnecessary, weighty ballast. 'Redukt' begins deceptively quiet and low with Unruh's steady strike of metal on metal and Bargeld's rhythmic list of body parts: 'gibt es überflüssiges oder Festgewordenes, das sich abstreifen lässt' ('is there anything redundant, solidified, that can be peeled off'). This restraint serves to emphasize the sheer aural assault of Bargeld's unanticipated invocation of 'Redukt!' The word is hurled at the audience as an imperative and the 'blow' is accompanied by the simultaneous swing of the bank of intelligent spotlights onto the faces of the audience, perhaps with the intent to achieve those earlier sought-for wounded ears and chord-scarred faces. A more conciliatory tone follows with 'lassen wir das Ganze einköcheln' ('let's reduce the lot on a slow flame') but it is the final statement before the closing explosive 'Redukt!' that encapsulates Neubauten's artistic milieu: 'Endlich, unendlich, in Ruhe gelassen, aber beweglich, frei zu lärmen, ohne Schuld' ('Finally, infinitely, left in peace, but moveable, free to make noise, without guilt').

'Unvollständigkeit' (Incompleteness) explores the same wish to free oneself from gravity's unnecessary baggage. It begins with a similar deceptively calm atmosphere created by Bargeld's quiet, idle vocalizing and a hardly discernible and equally soft rhythm on plastic pipes. This is unexpectedly interrupted as a whirlwind noise twists up like a rising sandstorm created from a mantra of the title word which translates as 'incompleteness'. The tempo builds as Bargeld enacts pulling from his throat all the ballast which he does not need ('wie einem Glückskettchen'/'like a charm bracelet'); behind him, on the higher stage level, Unruh tips from above his head a tray of aluminum sticks, then Bargeld screams. The closing section is quiet, almost polite, as the final satisfying emptiness is achieved: 'Ein letztes Gas, ein Flatus, Einlich leer, Ich: meine Hülle' ('A last gas, a flatus, Empty at last, Me: my shell').[18] The rendering of these two works during the Thirtieth Anniversary Tour, October-December 2010, demonstrated that Einstürzende Neubauten are still adhering to Artaud's proposals and are, as he desired, in both their creation and performance of their music, 'like those tortured at the stake, signaling through the flames' (Artaud, 1974, 6).

## Acknowledgements

Lyrics used with permission from Blixa Bargeld. Translations of the lyrics by Matthew Partridge. Special thanks to Andrea Schmid (manager of Neubauten's affairs between 2000 and 2010) for the generous use of the Neubauten Berlin Office Archives (NBOA). The members of Einstürzende Neubauten were Blixa Bargeld, Mark Chung, F. M. Einheit, Alexander Hacke and Andrew Unruh until the mid-1990s; when Chung and Einheit left, Jochen Arbeit and Rudi Moser became members.

# CHAPTER SEVEN

# Make a Joyous Noise: The Pentecostal Nature of American Noise Music

*Seb Roberts*

## In the Beginning

Despite being the first country officially to alienate church and state, the United States is a religious nation. This claim, made by everyone from politicians and pundits to theorists and comedians, is hardly controversial. Neither is it inaccurate: according to a global poll conducted by Gallup International (Carballo, 1999), Americans are twice as likely as Europeans to attend church on a weekly basis, and two-thirds of Americans believe in a personal God, compared to one-third of Europeans. It's no surprise, then, to see religious belief systems, social architecture and rituals reproduced throughout a variety of public contexts and cultural practices – at sports games, Hollywood premieres, but most precisely at live music events. The analogy between music and religion isn't merely a handy critical trope: the two echo each other as they structure how we experience and perceive our world. Jacques Attali argued that music and religion even grew from a single root:

> Thus, in most cultures, the theme of noise, its audition and endowment with form, lies at the origin of the religious idea. Before the world there was Chaos, the void and background noise ... Music, then, constitutes communication with this primordial, threatening noise – *prayer.* (Attali, 1985, 27; Attali's italics)

Therefore, music and prayer move closer towards a shared original purpose as they become less ornamental, less moderate, more elemental, more unhinged. A musical event more directly resembles a religious ceremony the wilder and more raucous it becomes, and some of the most wild and raucous Christian sects are also the most distinctly American in character. To that end, the most extreme American music – American noise music – is a categorical analogue of arguably the most extreme denomination in American Christendom: Pentecostalism. Operating within the context of a pious society, American noise music fulfils a role different than that which noise fulfils in more secular countries. Noise musicians from other nations may make similar sounds, employ similar gestures, and perform in front of similar audiences, but no other country's noise music shares American noise music's symbolic foundation, steeped in an atmosphere of faith and a routine of worship.

## The world without God

A discussion of American exceptionalism should (but does not always) start by examining that to which America is an exception – which, in this case, is the developed world's casual regard for God (Chaves, Hadaway and Marler, 1993, 741). A recent Eurobarometer poll (European Commission, 2005) showed 18 per cent of Europeans 'do not believe there is a spirit, God, nor life force'. Though a similar 15 per cent of Americans identify with no specific religion, a mere 1.6 per cent 'explicitly describe themselves as atheist or agnostic' (Keysar and Kosmin, 2009). And while 83 per cent of Americans claim God is among the most important figures in their lives, only 49 per cent of Europeans would agree with such a statement (Carballo, 1999). So if religion plays a comparatively minor role in European life, the concerns of European artists should be correspondingly secular.

Many of Europe's archetypal noise acts (Throbbing Gristle, Einstürzende Neubauten, Laibach, KMFDM, et al.) formed in the late 1970s and early 1980s. It was during that era that the first cracks in the Communist Bloc began to show, as economic stagnation plagued the 'satellite states' and the USSR's currency reserves became depleted. Meanwhile, Western nations – the United Kingdom in particular – suffered from waves of successive strikes and the consequent obliteration of organized labour power. Despite these differences in their respective tribulations, both the Warsaw Pact and NATO countries were undergoing the difficult transition from industry and manufacturing to a consumer- and service-oriented economy.

As such, Csaba Toth (2009) argues that 'the birth of Noise culture can only be understood in the context of the collapse of the industrial city'. Certainly, Western European noise music has been defined by its obsession with the factory and its machines, literal and metaphorical. Einstürzende Neubauten and Test Dept used the devices and detritus of industry to symbolize (and expedite) the grinding dissolution of Fordist society. Both bands employed power tools and found metal objects as instruments and staged concerts in unusual locations like train stations and decayed warehouses, incorporating the bleak, mechanized environments into the performance. Neubauten were also infamous for damaging venues with their berserk theatrics (see BBC, 2007; Jenkins, 1995; Kromhout, 2006). Other groups punctured and parodied the society-as-machine in both neoliberal and autocratic contexts. Throbbing Gristle attacked the bourgeois propriety of Thatcherite Britain by preaching an anarchic individualism in such songs as 'Don't Do As You're Told, Do As You Think' (Throbbing Gristle, *Heathen Earth*, 1980). Meanwhile, the Slovenian (then-Yugoslavian) band Laibach satirized nationalist authoritarianism by donning military uniforms and refashioning arena-rock hokum like Opus's 'Life Is Life' (Laibach, *Opus Dei*, 1987) into thunderous martial anthems. Their totalitarian role-play was so inscrutably deadpan that Laibach was extolled and disdained in equal measure by both leftist subversives and neo-fascists.

Fundamentally, what allied the above bands was their criticism and deconstruction of prescriptive morality, ideological coercion and dehumanization. Though religion could easily have been impugned upon these very grounds, rarely did Western European noise musicians specifically address religion, with the obvious exceptions of Cabaret Voltaire's *Red Mecca* (1981) and Public Image Ltd's infamous post-punk dirge 'Religion' (*First Issue*, 1978). But however valid it may have been to attack religion as a politically ambitious power structure, such a critique would not come to substantially bear on the founding tenets or spiritual function of faith.

Elsewhere in the post-industrial world, Japan has a buffet-style, syncretic approach to spirituality with few rigorous practitioners of any specific faith. Some estimates suggest as much as two-thirds of the country self-identifies as atheist or agnostic (Zuckerman, 2007). Consequently, Japanese noise music channels its transgressive potential from other sources and against other targets. Chief among these is the homogeneity and narcissism of Japan itself. To wit, the national census asks for nationality as opposed to ethnicity, thus semantically assimilating naturalized citizens and refusing the existence of a multi-ethnic Japan. According to Paul Hegarty, the 'messy and complex hybridity' of Japanese noise music works against this monocultural conceit:

> Noise works across globalization, neither in nor out, and exists in a marginal form of the world economy. Noise moves Japanese music beyond a hybridity of discrete forms becoming new discrete forms to an absence of form... (Hegarty, 2007, 138)

*Japanese street noise: performance and propaganda.*

Noise troubles the collective harmony of Japan in two ways: by introducing an alien interference, as above, and also by disrupting the communal identity with individuation. Sound is among the strongest tools for societal normalization, and the aural environment of urban Japan is an unending siege of instruction and intimidation. Chimes broadcast the beginning and end of business hours; androidal voices issue directives from ATMs, train ticketing machines, and pedestrian crosswalks; megaphone-toting politicians hector passers-by from moving vehicles and in front of train stations; commercial pitches blare from ubiquitous storefront PA systems; atop all this is the tidal roar of traffic and trains. The cumulative effect is that the Japanese are disciplined into a differentiated mass of semi-militarized consumers. Against this sonic totalitarianism, noise music works as a reclamation of autonomy within acoustic space. Sometimes, this personal insurrection is acted out, as in the hysterical physicality of a Masonna or Hanatarash show. But even immobile performers refuse cooperation and insist upon difference via disruption: the famously poker-faced Masami Akita, aka Merzbow, declared in a 1999 interview with Chad Hensley: 'Sometimes I would like to kill the much too noisy Japanese by my own Noise. The effects of Japanese culture are too much noise everywhere. I want to make silence by my noise' (Hensley, 1999).

This endowment of sound with purpose and power is what Attali saw as 'the origin of the religious idea' (Attali, 1985, 27). But while both music and religion are symbolic structures with a civilizing effect, their purpose and power are manifested differently. Religion is an ideological lens, through which an internal logic is built and maintained. Music is a relational affect, because 'ordering is the human intervention that creates music' (Hegarty, 2007, 34) and music therefore has no constitutional goal or meaning. As a structuring of sound, music is a symbolic expression of power, but it does only what power bids of it: music has no will of its own. Consequently, music can be mobilized in an endless variety of ways to satisfy whatever perverse demands power makes of it – including bullying the public into emptying their wallets.

## Moneylenders in the temple

A variety of criteria had to be met to commodify music effectively: a musical object appropriate to mass production, planned obsolescence, and broad market appeal; an efficient network of distribution; and a growth-oriented economy to produce stable (if not ever-expanding) demand. The convocation of precisely these factors occurred in the United States following the Second World War:

[...] the baby boom and the end of the post-war economic crisis produced an enormous demand on the part of white youth, coincident with the introduction of a syncretic product ready to respond to that demand by using black despair – carefully filtered – to express young white hopes: *rock*. (Attali, 1985, 105; Attali's italics)

Supported by such technological advances as the Magnetophon tape recorder, the long-playing vinylite record, and FM radio, rock music became the social fundament of young America by the mid-1950s. This was not by accident. According to Ian Svenonius, the US could only capitalize on its newly acquired post-war power and wealth by 'chang[ing] the population from fairly self-sufficient farmers and craftspeople with a "depression mentality" and "Christian work ethic," into perfectly efficient consumers. This required a conversion from the Christian doctrine of denial to a new capitalist religion of eating a lot' (Svenonius, 2006, 66).

This would reverse a centuries-old ethos ingrained in the cultural bedrock. Piety has propelled America since its very inception. Its earliest settlers were often escaping religious persecution in the Old World, as were the Puritans of the Massachusetts Bay colony. For colonists whose motives were more imperial, commercial and apostolic ambitions frequently went hand-in-hand: Sir Thomas Dale, governor of Virginia throughout the 1610s, was famous not only for shepherding the colony's growth as a leading tobacco exporter, but also for instituting capital punishment for failure to attend church. Throughout American history, there have been recurrent flurries of revivalist fervour: it was during the First Great Awakening of the 1730s that evangelicalism coalesced into a self-conscious movement, and the Second Great Awakening a century later birthed the millenarian and so-called 'holy-roller' movements that remain familiar to this day. ('Holy-roller' was originally a pejorative nickname for Pentecostals, who would experience convulsive fits during church services.) Christianity would enjoy its greatest modern rejuvenation thanks to the Cold War. Countering the Godless threat of international Communism, the United States became more declaratively pious in the immediate post-war period, as evidenced by the controversial insertion of the phrase 'under God' into the Pledge of Allegiance in 1954. The following year, church attendance hit an all-time high of 49 per cent (US Census Bureau, 1989, cited in Caplow et al., 1991, 287).

As a culture centred upon excess, instant gratification and earthly pleasures, rock 'n' roll would be a hard sell in a society of devout modesty. Consequently, it would have to resemble the Christian template – which it does uncannily. Elaborate ceremonies are routinely staged to seduce converts and reassure the faithful. Before the rapt congregants stand self-appointed proselytes who have given themselves, body and soul, to the cause. These ideologues all claim to be humble vessels of a higher power yet sole possessors of the truth, as they deride the apostasy of competing interpretations and the heresy of other forms. In fact, rock and Christianity mirror each other right down to their constituent sects. Svenonius elaborates:

> Nearly every sect that grew from rock 'n' roll was expressly interested in saving the medium's original mystic energy and promise from the perversions of later generations. [...] Work cults like indie rock resembled Seventh-day Adventists, garage and rockabilly purists resembled the Amish (for whom history has stopped at a certain moment) [...] Heavy metal people, being polygamist, arcane, and simultaneously conservative, resemble Mormons. (Svenonius, 2006, 74–6)

Following this comparative mode (which Svenonius extends between hip-hop and Islam), what would be the theological analogue of noise? Atheism would seem to make sense, in that it rejects tautological claims of authority, truth and beauty based on arbitrary criteria. Both noise and Atheism foreground the materiality of process, refusing ideological dogmatism in favour of a subjective appreciation of experience based upon a more fluid, adaptive epistemology.

An alternative analogy could be drawn to Zen Buddhism, as suggested by the work of John Cage: without requiring determinist intervention, music is immanent and omnipresent. The division of the divine and inspired from the profane and accidental is illusory and snobbish. The formlessness of noise is totalized, and the acoustic universe is at once musical and not. Sound simply is, unitarily.

This is why neither the Atheist nor Zen Buddhist analogy works. Though the latter is mystical and the former decidedly not, both advocate a uniform ontology whose contradictions are counterbalances wed to a whole: yin and yang, entropy and inertia. Abrahamic theology is not unitary but binary: it describes opposites not as symmetry, but as in violent contradiction. Thus, when speaking of either God or music, the tendency is not to witness it in all things, nor even to witness where it is not, but to witness both it and that which acts against it.

This Manicheanism demands a rockist framing of noise: as a combative expression of power, as formally excessive, as physically immersive, as contagiously ecstatic, as subjectively annihilative – in other words, as Pentecostal.

## The American Jerusalem

Pentecostalism is an offshoot of the holiness movement, as inspired by Methodist theologian John Wesley. The holiness movement teaches the doctrine of 'entire sanctification', a multi-stage process by which perfection can be achieved. First, the sinner must repent and accept Jesus Christ as their saviour; second, they are sanctified as their sins are forgiven; finally, their salvation is made manifest by baptism in the Holy Spirit, enacted through so-called gifts. One oft-cited Biblical list of gifts, Corinthians 12.8-11, includes prophecy, the power to heal, words of wisdom, discerning of spirits, speaking in tongues, and the working of miracles. Underlying the doctrine of 'entire sanctification' is the belief that grace can only be received directly from God. Faith alone is insufficient, sacraments are but formalities, and officiants act not as divine conduits but as spiritual coaches who steer their parishioners upon the path towards God. Grace is subjective, and communion with God is personal.

Pentecostalism became a discrete sect during a 1906 spiritual revival in Los Angeles, California. William J. Seymour had been conducting prayer services in a private residence for five weeks when, on April 9th, congregants began speaking in tongues. As the clamour inside the house grew, so did service attendance, prompting Seymour to relocate his flock to an old livestock shelter at 312 Azusa Street. For the next three years, church services were held three times a day, seven days a week, with as many as 1,300 participants at a time (Allen, 2006).

It's remarkable that, in the 'Jim Crow' era, Seymour was an African-American presiding over a diverse congregation of blacks, whites, Latinos and Asians from an array of socio-economic backgrounds. The new denomination's social practices were as radical as its religious ones. Consequently, while some traditional holiness churches admonished Azusa Street simply for its ecclesiastical unorthodoxy, the revival's harshest critics were explicitly racist in their attacks. Even Seymour's white mentor, Charles Fox Parham, was disturbed that 'white people were imitating unintelligent, crude negroisms of the Southland' (Pete, n.d.).

To Azusa Street parishioners, however, the riotous services were the prophesied manifestation of the Holy Spirit, anticipating Christ's return: 'And it shall come to pass afterward, that I will pour out my spirit upon all flesh; and your sons and daughters shall prophesy, your old men shall dream dreams, your young men shall see visions' (Joel 2.28, King James Version). If the gift of tongues was indeed the first evidence of Holy Spirit baptism, and if these were indeed the end times, then it was the burden of every saved soul – regardless of demographic peculiarity – to prepare in earnest for the Second Coming. As the Holy Spirit descended 'upon all flesh', upon 'sons and daughters' alike, Pentecostal missionary Frank Bartleman enthused, 'the "color line" was washed away in the blood' (Bartleman, 1909, cited in Allen, 2006).

The movement's name, Pentecostalism, referred to the Jewish Feast of Weeks ('Shavuot' in Hebrew, 'Pentecost' in Greek) celebrated shortly after the crucifixion. As the apostles ate together, their salvation was suddenly and dramatically evinced as 'they were all filled with the Holy Ghost, and began to speak with other tongues, as the Spirit gave them

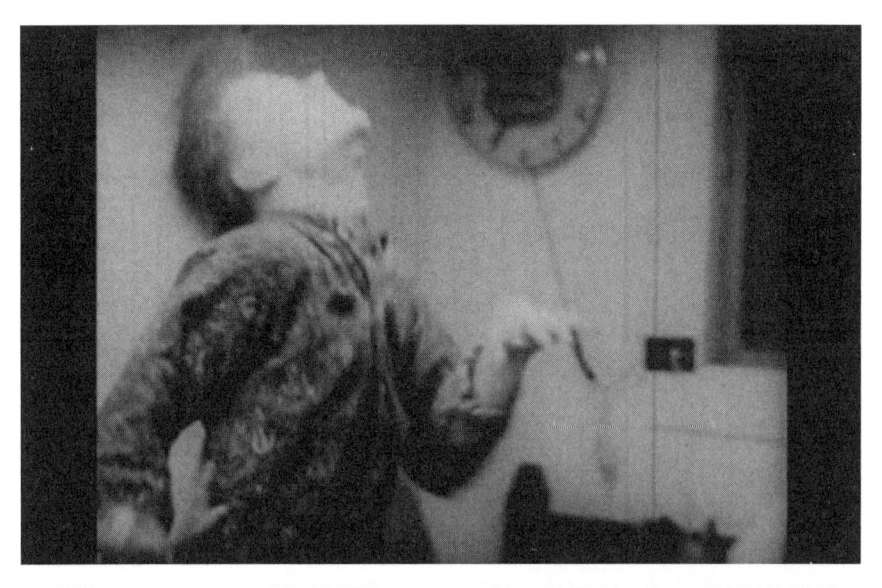

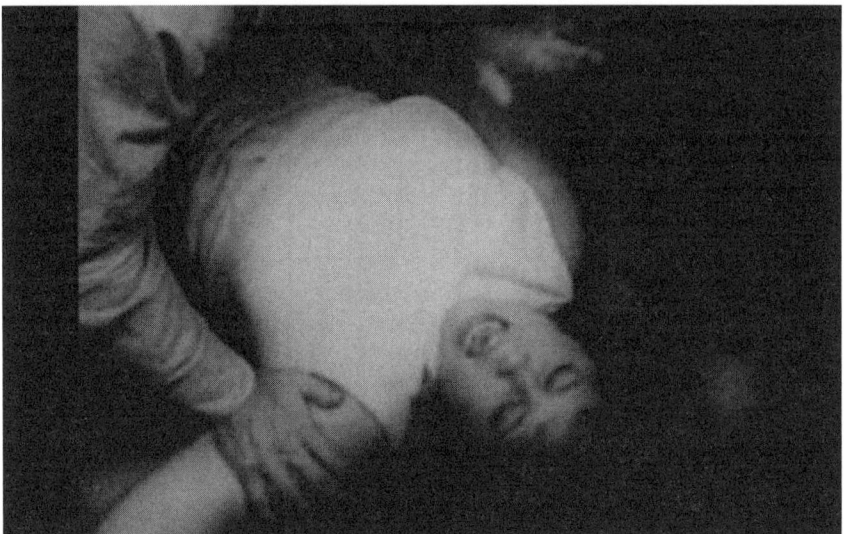

*Images from the documentary* Holy Ghost People *(Peter Adair, 1967).*

utterance' (Acts 2.4, King James Version). Such unmediated communion, free of history's distortions and embellishments, was Pentecostalism's goal, exceeding even the reductionist ambitions of the Protestant Reformation. 'The whole movement,' wrote preacher Batsell Barrett Baxter (1959), 'is designed to reproduce in contemporary times the church originally established on Pentecost, A.D. 30.'

## The ascension

New York in the late 1970s may have been far from heaven, but it too witnessed a movement that sought a return to primeval forms. The No Wave scene was where American noise music became recognizable as such. Previous excursions to the demilitarized zone between noise and music had been either politely academic or an avant-gardist extension of recognizable forms. No Wave's intentions were twofold: on one hand, to critique the stultifying self-consciousness of popular rebel music and the avant-garde; on the other, to behave as though it was antecedent to those very musical modes it attacked (see Hegarty, 2007, 100). As the scene's participants themselves described it in Scott Crary's 2004 documentary *Kill Your Idols*:

> Lydia Lunch: The intent behind Teenage Jesus [and the Jerks] was to disregard the influences that caused me to want to create in the first place [...] It was about making music that referenced nothing else, that reminded you of nothing else.
>
> Arto Lindsay: I thought about sort of rearranging the basic building blocks of music.

Punk had been a reformist movement, like Protestantism, intended to repeal the gaudy garnishes and tacked-on accoutrements that had accumulated over the years. Still, it obeyed structural and symbolic conventions – 'this blues-derived thing', as Glenn Branca (*Kill Your Idols*, 2004) sneeringly called it – that had become canonical in tandem with music's commodification. No Wave was so dogmatic in its primal reductivism that any growth or development whatsoever was superfluous perversion. 'It came out of the gate finished', explained Thurston Moore in an interview dated 2 June 2008 posted on Ben Sisario's blog: 'Where do you take it? You don't take it. It dies' (Moore, 2008).

Its unsustainability notwithstanding, the 'Year Zero' project of No Wave became consecrated as an ideal of unprescribed creation, and ironically some of its participants have since yielded massive influence over the American Underground. And arguably casting the longest shadow in this respect is Glenn Branca. His distinguishing musical features read like a diagnostic checklist for every 'unconventional' rock act since 1980: rhythmic regularity, dynamic restraint, effective tonality, relative and unresolved disharmony, non-linear formality, and physically arresting volume. This formula was successfully exploited by Branca's disciples – most prominently Thurston Moore and Lee Ranaldo of Sonic Youth, and Paige Hamilton of Helmet – to achieve nothing less than rock-star status. That their fame exceeds Branca's does not diminish his prevalence. Rather, the still-widening ripples of Branca's influence cast him as an apostolic figure in American noise music.

This would no doubt have horrified John Cage, who in 1982 gave Wim Mertens this famously defamatory assessment of Branca's *Indeterminate Activity of Resultant Masses* (1982):

> My feelings were disturbed [...] The Branca [piece] is an example of sheer determination, of one person to be followed by the others [...] Say it was good intentions he was expressing, with vehemence and power. It would be like one of those strange religious organizations that we hear about [...] If it was something political, it would resemble fascism. (Cage, 1982)

While this is unflattering, it is not unfair. As outlined by Hegarty, noise music of Branca's idiom can appear totalitarian:

> [...] giving yourself over into something beyond the individual, attaining some more authentic, lost sense of either body or mind, the notion of submitting, the control on the part of the noise producer, the power of a spectacle that is physically oppressive. (Hegarty, 2007, 124)

But however tempting the comparison, noise music – music that attempts noise, noise attempting to be musical – is not quite fascistic. Fascism's concern is the non-consensual imposition of arbitrary power in a vulgar way, which bears more in common with, say, Calvinism and Romantic classical music. Noise music, on the other hand, aspires to exceed human control, to become power expressing itself, to cross from the realm of the rational – that is, of beauty – into the sublime. Further, noise music is contractual in the same sense as Pentecostalism: submission is voluntary. Music and noise cannot interreact without the listener's consent, and the sinner cannot be saved unless he repents.

## Mutiny in heaven

Once sufferance is granted, the power of the spectacle is terrible and oppressive indeed. Few bands better demonstrated this than the thuggish New York troupe Swans. Their use of obscene volume and onerous repetition transformed power from abstract to embodied, physical, visceral. Anecdotes of audience members nauseated to the point of vomiting inevitably recall eyewitness descriptions of the Azusa Street revival, where 'strong men [lay] for hours under the mighty powers of God, cut down like grass' (Bartleman, 1909, cited in Pete, n.d.). Again quoting Hegarty,

*Swans in performance in 1986, from* Public Castration Is A Good Idea.

this is 'the normalization of the "state of exception", where the exercise of sovereign [...] power is no longer occasional or transgressive, but made into a new law' (Hegarty, 2007, 124). And indeed, what greater sovereign than God?

Such power – formless, sublime, total – defies perception or representation. Language as a relational medium becomes useless and decomposes into glossolalia. This desperate failure to correspond is not so much pre-linguistic as extralinguistic: above and beyond the capacities of human discourse. Speaking in tongues – the definitive proof of a Pentecostal's salvation – is a miraculous reversal of the Tower of Babel's linguistic diaspora; a divine pan-lingualism that paradoxically alienates the believer from vernacular society. Communication becomes similarly unfeasible in noise music. Gibby Haynes of Butthole Surfers makes extensive use of delay and pitch-shifting effects, re-tailoring his voice to the band's hallucinatory soundscape (Butthole Surfers, 'Sweet Loaf', *Locust Abortion Technician*, 1987). But moulded around such cartoonish cacophony, Haynes's vocals are too grotesque to be understood. Meaning is sacrificed in the mutation. Pointed speech is similarly impractical during Sonic Youth's most dissonant moments, substantiated by the band's preference for lengthy instrumental explorations over vocally led arrangements. On the rare occasion that Sonic Youth layer a human voice atop a markedly clangorous passage, the vocals are little more than imbecilic chanting (Sonic Youth, 'Death Valley '69', *Bad Moon Rising*, 1985) or bestial shrieking (Sonic Youth, 'Mildred Pierce', *Goo*, 1990). Even the most simplistic attempts to communicate amidst noise fail: as Swans smash their way through the grueling monotony of *Public Castration Is a Good Idea* (1986), Michael Gira's croaky incantations become more garbled and guttural with each iteration. Grinding over the same word or two *ad nauseum*, Gira gradually erodes both enunciation and meaning.

Language is the subject's means of representing itself and its relationship to the other, so with linguistic deconstruction comes a concomitant dissolution of identity. Self-understanding is further troubled as noise becomes physical through volume and vibration. Confronted by the material of noise, the body is made aware of itself, as a body but not as a self. This is the effect on all in noise's presence, audience and performer alike, forming a collectivity based on a mutual loss of discrete identity (see Hegarty, 2007, 125). In subjectivity's place is what Wim Mertens described in his 1982 interview with John Cage: 'an accumulation of energies without content, without dialectics in it. Without communication, without feedback' (Cage, 1982). The restoration of content, of meaning, can only come from and result in alienation – an awareness of the self as separate from the other. 'The sensual re-appropriation of alienation,' says Howard Slates, 'is having to stake a claim upon the "worst of ourselves" in a mutually supportive environment; one which allows for emotional intensities to be experienced in common' (Slates, 2009, 162). Such an environment, which allows for common confrontation of our own impure materials, can be found at a Pentecostal service. Because the officiant possesses no special authority and grace can only be received from God directly, it's a hierarchically flat space wherein differentiation is not made by social, rational, human criteria. All sinners are equally abject, and all sanctified equally saved before the divine sovereign.

Should a subject fail to reappropriate their individuality through alienation, the absence of meaning persists. Identity remains annihilated. Subjectivity is enthralled to an aggregation of energy that, by its very intensity, defies explanation, purpose, or even perception. But, again by its very intensity, this is not simply no meaning: it is 'any, all and no meaning' (Slates, 2009, 159), the totality of possibility – which, Ray Brassier tantalizingly posits, 'is a synonym for God' (Brassier, 2007, 65).

## Sound and fury signifying nothing

The ultimate likeness between Pentecostalism and noise music is that the same things threaten to extinguish them. The first is institutionalism. Practice has ossified, thanks to 'a rapid accumulation of stock gestures' (Brassier, 2007, 63) that signify 'authenticity' while betraying its opposite. Hackneyed pratfalls, nonsensical hollering and self-conscious convulsions have become commonplace in Pentecostalism. Deriding contemporary worship as a 'performance-oriented enterprise', evangelist Wolfgang Simson (1999) notes that 'formalized and institutionalized patterns developed quickly into rigid traditions'. Noise musicians equivalently employ laboured rock expressions that have not been fresh in thirty years; it is often possible to count down to the moments when the sound will explode 'out of control'. The very fact that 'noise' has become such a cloistered and conspicuous genre-tag to earn its own section in record stores is proof of its premature exhaustion. Ben Watson warns that 'any term accepted in the marketplace can quickly become a cover for inept simulacra and calculated fraudulence' (Watson, 2009, 119). If God or noise is rendered spuriously, if it is not suffered in common by both the active and passive participants, then it becomes the cynical infliction of sadistic power by arrogant performers upon a gullible audience. This has obvious and unpleasant parallels with fascism and neoliberal capitalism.

The second danger is external, as the world leaves less and less room for either God or noise. Advances in the sciences, soft and hard, increasingly relegate God to the position of a superstition. Certain studies suggest that educational achievement is inversely proportional to religious inclination (see Winseman, 2003; Paton, 2008). In any case, as the multifarious complexity of the human experience expands, and as developed nations become ever more culturally diverse, the number of Americans without faith is climbing to the highest levels on record (US Census Bureau, 2010). Meanwhile, many metropolitan centres have become as loud – sometimes louder – than a symphony orchestra (see Battles, 2008; Slackman, 2008). The ever-growing cacophony of the quotidian world makes maximalist styles of noise music sound redundant. Lester Bangs wryly identified this problem way back in 1981: 'Sounds great in midwestern suburbs, but kinda unnecessary in NYC' (Bangs, 1981).

If they are to avoid retreating into fundamentalism or disappearing altogether, God and noise cannot be the predetermined factor of an individual or collective abreaction, nor can they be the recognized outcome of a given routine. God and noise are a relational affect between forms. They are an abstraction that vanishes upon apprehension, as they only exist outside the rational, the definitive, the human. They are as they are not.

Perhaps the analogy to Zen Buddhism was too hastily dismissed.

# CHAPTER EIGHT

# Roars of Discontent: Noise and Disaffection in Two Cases of Russian Punk

*Yngvar B. Steinholt*

> In those years his angry face was cast in black bronze, and discernible in his voice was the iron howl of an approaching subway train. The voice sounded so dark, the train appeared to run in total darkness and never again would there be light. With fear in my trembling boyish cheeks I felt, that any moment now, within the blink of an eye, I would be crushed beneath this oncoming, cast-iron snout. I barely escaped until the end of the song, but then began the next, and again everything became just as joyous and sinister.
>
> Zakhar Prilepin (2010)

Sometimes we become inexplicably attracted to dirty, distorted, rough, overpowering sounds. As suggested in the epigraph, such encounters can have lasting impact on our lives, our worldviews and our aesthetic preferences. Not all such attractions are profound or long-lasting, but of interest here are those occasions where something causes a loss of affection with sound. Most of us have experienced how a favourite song by a favourite artist suddenly loses significance, how a source of great joy (re)turns to noise, its effect on us from affection to disaffection. The sounds have not changed, only our relationship with them. Music fans occasionally experience mass disenchantment with artists and songs. John Lennon's comparison of the Beatles' popularity with that of Jesus Christ made scores of fans burn their favorite albums; Bob Dylan's electric guitar at the Newport Folk Festival disgusted his folk-purist followers; for better or for worse, 'Helter Skelter' was never the same after Charles Manson. The topic of this chapter is not myth-building, star personalities or failed PR, however. Its central object of interest is noise. How do sounds and extra-sonic events combine to affect our distinction between pleasurable and unpleasurable noise?[1] Can extra-sonic events (that is, factors other than the strictly audible or musical) represent a form of noise in their own right? If so, how do they cause disaffection with a sound object?

## Punk, music, noise

Punk is all about the enchanting power of noise. It is about attitude, energy, anger, confrontation. It puts the manner of performance over what is performed. This means that virtually anything (from national anthems to lullabies) can be successfully performed as punk. To successfully perform punk as something other than punk is a lot more demanding.[2] I turn now to two cases of Russian punk. Both involve furious reactions to cultural hegemony. The first relates to the early 1990s and Russia's post-Soviet transition, the second to 2011–12 and the protests surrounding Vladimir Putin's return to presidency. Both involve a loss of pleasure from noisy music. Before turning to the concrete cases, however, a closer look at the concept of noise and its various uses and definitions is required.

The relationship between music and noise has been part of popular music discourse for centuries. Yet with the development of musical amplification and the spread of portable sound devices in public spaces, debates concerning music and noise have intensified further. Surely, as Bruce Johnson (2009a) notes, noise is subjective. What we regard as noise and what we regard as music varies with the situation, our role, and the degree of choice. A person who actively seeks exposure to loud sound easily gains pleasure from it, even as it reaches health-damaging levels. For, as Garret Keizer (2010) points out, noise may be subjective to our minds, but it is fundamentally objective to our bodies. It can reach levels that far exceed the capacities of the human ear. Noise is a physical force, which directly impacts upon the human organism. Loud sounds at low frequencies are known to create stress and nausea (see Wilson, 2012; Johnson, 2009b), biological responses that precede intellectual evaluation. Thus, before we value sound aesthetically, our bodies have already determined whether it is reassuring or threatening (Johnson, 2009c). Taken to its logical extreme, this turns sound into a military weapon and music into an instrument of torture. (See Johnson and Cloonan, 2009 for a disquieting account of noise and violence.)

The destructive potential of noise is not reduced by our desire for it. That we are unable to close our ears, and that noise can have quite sinister physical and psychological effects on the human body (exhaustion, stress, incontinence, fear, depression), strengthens the arguments of anti-noise activists and the defence of our rights to silent environments. More relevant to the current discussion is that similar anti-noise arguments are widely used for less honourable defensive purposes by cultural elites. Popular music has ritually been condemned as harmful and meaningless noise, from folk and jazz to rap and techno. As a rule, elitist notions of noisiness are grounded in norms of musical education and craftsmanship. New styles classify as noise partly because their musicians have failed to undergo monitored education and do not play in the traditional sense. Accusations of a lack of musicianship have accompanied virtually every technical novelty in music, from the piano to the sampler. The hostility of cultural establishments to innovation has helped infuse new styles with an aura of rebellion, in some cases encouraging further aesthetic provocations and foregrounding elements of noise. The question of noise, and who has the right to define it, is found at the centre of the power struggle between succeeding generations, between hegemony and innovation. What a hostile establishment perceives as noise is likely to be the very qualities that make the new music exciting to its creators and audiences, but in a cultural conflict no positions are absolutely stable. This opens the way for experiences of sudden enchantment or disenchantment. Sounds can sweep us away, but also let us down.

## Case 1: Grazhdanskaia Oborona go political

The case of punk rock in the USSR and post-Soviet Russia illustrates a number of connections between sonic and extra-sonic noise in the context of popular music. The corrosion of the old Soviet cultural elite that began with Gorbachev's reforms set the stage for a battle over cultural hegemony, which was to last well into the 1990s. This battle involved a wide range of loud and provocative initiatives, spanning art and literature, popular music and political movements. Although a marginal phenomenon beyond the realms of media broadcasts and record labels, the voice of punk nonetheless became a distinct feature in the socio-cultural cacophony that preceded the Soviet collapse. At the time Siberian punk was at the forefront of this marginal phenomenon and the most influential band in this respect were Grazhdanskaia Oborona (henceforth: GrOb) from remote Omsk, fronted by Egor Letov.[3] Despite all the commotion that characterized Russian culture during the post-Soviet transition, no dramatic shift took place in the ranks of the cultural establishment. A large, fractured and increasingly frustrated generation of younger artist and intellectuals remained on the margins. They responded noisily. Part of the noise came from Letov, whose political shock tactics won GrOb many new followers, but split the band's old fan base, of whom many turned away in disgust or disinterest. To them, GrOb's pleasurable noise had turned bland.

GrOb's esteem among rock fans in the USSR was meticulously built up through a steady stream of home-recorded punk albums, spanning the 1980s. Letov's songs brimmed over with everything Soviet ideologists despised: rage, spite, self-destructivity, violent anti-communism, and cascades of poetic swearing. The debate surrounding rock music in the USSR in the 1980s in many ways mirrored the fear of musical noise expressed in the West during the 1960s and 1970s: the alleged harmful psychological effects of amplified and distorted (guitar) sounds, uncivilizing and antisocial effects of rhythmic music, or destabilizing potentials of disharmony. On this background, it is perhaps not surprising to find early Russian punk quite melodious. Letov's early songs are indebted to musical styles as diverse as Soviet evergreens, psychedelic rock, reggae and punk. The musical noise of early GrOb songs comes from a rather crude DIY recording process, worsened by endless copying and recopying of the original tapes. Indeed, were the songs not melodious to begin with, it is hard to imagine how they would receive a following in such a format. Most listeners made their first acquaintance with Letov's band by listening to recordings scrambled beyond recognition by cumulative layers of tape-recorder hum. In the 1990s early GrOb songs were remastered and issued on more than forty CD albums. Although improved, the sound remained charmingly low-fidelity.

Initially Letov's lyrics contributed as much to his noisiness as his music. In the turmoil following the band's first live gig at the 1987 Novosibirsk rock festival, the local security apparatus tried to silence the band, but pressure from the KGB only fanned the flames of Letov's glowing anti-Soviet sentiments. It drove his music towards hardcore punk and his lyrics towards further provocative heights. His desecration of the sanctity of the memory of Lenin effectively warned of a coming ideological collapse. According to Alexei Yurchak (2006: 294), when the reformative deconstruction of authoritarian discourse began questioning its bearing principle – Lenin – the whole ideology deflated. The following lines are from the final verses of GrOb's 1989 'Pesnia o Lenine' from the album *Voiná* (War):

> Lenin is the bullet that heals us,
> Lenin is the fear that cripples us,
> Lenin is the arse in which we stink,
> Lenin is the blood we're sucking.
>
> Lenin is Hitler, Lenin is Stalin,
> Lenin is Kim Il Sung, Lenin is Mao,
> Ever young and ever with us,
> He shall always, always live.

Far less controversial songs were labeled 'fascist agitation' by Soviet cultural authorities. The height of GrOb's popularity lasted from 1987 to 1991 and saw the release of over twenty cassette albums. Without a trace of fascist sentiment, these albums cemented Letov's anarcho-punk image, a Siberian equivalent to Crass or Jello Biafra. As the Soviet Union faded away, Letov released acoustic solo albums of existing songs and founded another band, Egor i Opizdenevshchie. Here, his music returned towards psychedelic rock and 1960s Soviet pop. Songs such as 'Samootvod' ('Withdrawal'), about Mayakovsky's suicide, are characterized by a depressed, melancholic-ironic national romanticism. Letov's popularity peaked both among the mature urban rock intelligentsia and among wider circles of young rock and punk fans.

After President Yeltsin bombarded Russia's legally elected parliament in 1993, a new organization came into being. The scandalous fiction writer Eduard Limonov, recently returned from US emigration, and the nationalist ideologue Aleksandr Dugin founded the National Bolshevik Party (NBP). It rallied for the unification of extremist forces of right and left under a red flag with a black hammer and sickle in a white circle, replacing the Nazi swastika. The NBP has been explained as a highbrow ironical act of protest from a generation of marginalized artists and intellectuals. However, the political project soon developed far beyond the jocular. In its inception the project may have appeared deeply ironic, but this ironic dimension was not necessarily widely acknowledged. By inviting organizations such as the explicitly racist Russian National Union as collaborators, the NBP soon attracted massive support, predominantly among young men from rural and suburban Russia (see Gabowitsch, 2009; Laruelle, 2009; Shenfield, 2001; Sokolov, 2006). As the NBP effectively grew to become the country's largest non-government youth organization, its common ranks largely consisted of people who took the party's programme literally.

In early 1994, Egor Letov and the St Petersburg avant-garde musician Sergei Kurekhin formed an organization for Russian musicians called Russkii Proryv (Russian Breakthrough). It collectively joined the NBP. Thus it was that Letov first appeared at a political rally, the so-called 'Unification of Leftist Forces' in Moscow. Here the Siberian with his long hair, thick glasses and modest stature was seated between NBPs Dugin and Limonov and alongside prominent Russian fascists, racists and Neo-Nazis. He declared:

> A new proletarian revolution is brewing, a righteous and final revolution, and I believe that if we – extremists, radical nationalists, and radical communists – unite our forces, victory will be ours! [Russkii Proryv] consists of [...] those young guys, and people of all different ages, who resist the very principle of the Babylonian civilization that rules our world, and also resist the rules of the game and the very stasis of life imposed on them by the powers.[4]

To fully understand the impact of this declaration we have to think back to the decade of irony, where political involvement was unfashionable and unrestricted irony the epitome of cool. In Russia these trends of the 1990s came on top of a strong general disillusionment with politics. Already during Perestroika, as old members of the *nomenklatura* tightened their grip on political and cultural life, the democratically minded intelligentsia had become disgusted with the crude dishonesty of political life. The intelligentsia's withdrawal from active political involvement left the country in the hands of entrepreneurs from the old party elite. For the general public, the collapse of the Soviet Union meant a new freedom from politics and ideology as such. To be apolitical had become a right worth celebrating. Anything that tasted of the over-politicized discourse of the past was shunned. The new nationalism, which scores of Russians would find so appealing, was almost exclusively allowed to reap the benefits of these sentiments.

Arguably, political art in post-Soviet Russia has never been more out of sync with contemporary sentiments than during the traumatic first half of the 1990s. Despite its tint of hyperbolic irony, Letov's message returned to the language of Soviet ideology at a time when Soviet nostalgia had yet to catch on. More than a mere provocation, Letov's views were rooted in the feelings of the provincial population. Rural Russia was hard hit by Yeltsin's reforms. In the provinces the word 'democracy' soon came to signify chaos and uncertainty, yet the intellectuals of Moscow or St Petersburg failed to fully comprehend this. Despite having cultivated leftist sentiments since the 1840s, the cultured Russian intelligentsia has surprisingly little knowledge of the lives and ideas of common provincial people.

Thus, rather than create an unwelcome racket among the urban cultural elites, events such as the 'Unification of Leftist Forces' were either met with short-term roars of laughter followed by long-term disinterest, or they prompted people to turn away in disgust. The playing of political games was instrumental to this moment, and more so than any connection with racist organizations. Nonetheless, the fate of GrOb was to be denounced as fascist again, and this time by democratically minded critics, while thousands of devoted fans simply became disenchanted with the band. New fans attracted by the formation of Russkii Proryv were different from the mature audience of Russian rock bands and the more unruly elements among them soon brought the band trouble. That Letov broke with the NBP and supported the Communists in the 1996 elections did little to improve matters. GrOb's gigs of the late 1990s became prone to cancellations, rioting and hooliganism. The situation hardly motivated old fans to return to the fold.

Egor Letov died from heart failure in February 2008, aged forty-one. By then he had long since declared himself apolitical. Even the NBP had become less threatening following a leftist, alter-globalist turn and a government ban. In obituaries, memorabilia and portraits, the emphasis is firmly placed on Letov's anarcho-punk years before Russkii Proryv. It appears the distortion of Letov's political stunts is losing its grip on GrOb songs. As the causes of dissatisfaction have retreated into recent history and the controversies have become subject of retrospective reinterpretation, the noise of these songs has once again become pleasurable to the contemporary Russian listener.

## Case 2: Pussy Riot vs. State and Church

Unlike the case of GrOb, a band that became associated with politics after the peak of their popularity, our second case was founded as a political art project. The Moscow project Pussy Riot formed in early November 2011, partly as a reaction to Putin's announcement that he would be running for a third term of presidency. At the time of editing this chapter, debate is still raging in Russia and abroad following their most controversial performance to date, a performance for which three key members of the group were sentenced on 17 August 2012 to two years in prison (in addition to six months of custody). Other members are under investigation and two of these are reported to have left Russia. The jailed band members Tolokonnikova, Alekhina and Samutsevich began serving their sentences on 3 September 2012. They have signalled their intention to appeal. Inspired by the Riot Grrl movement, but insisting on occupying their chosen venues rather than hiring them, Pussy Riot perform un-sanctioned hit-and-run gigs in public places. Their agenda is:

> [...] feminism; resistance to organs of social control; the rights of gays, lesbians, bisexuals, and transsexuals; anti-Putinism and the radical decentralization of the organs of power; preservation of the Khimkin forest; and the relocation of the Russian capital to Eastern Siberia. (Pussy Riot, 2011a)

Although they sympathize with the cause of the wider protests accompanying the presidential elections, Pussy Riot are convinced only widespread illegal demonstrations can achieve lasting change. Key members of the group are former participants in the performance collective Voiná [War] (see Gololobov, 2011), which also valued the importance of hiding the identities of their members. The young women that make up Pussy Riot wear brightly coloured balaclavas during performances and interviews. All their statements are made unanimously.

Pussy Riot's actions have received notable press exposure both in Russia and abroad. True to tradition, our Western media have been most concerned with the macro-political context of the performances, rather than their aesthetic side. Whilst this may be in perfect line with the activists' artistic intention – Pussy Riot explicitly value activist performance over music – their sounds remain meaningful and worth a closer examination. When some classify the group's performances as disturbance of public order and acts of (cultural) terrorism, sound is a main basis for their verdict. The same goes for those who enjoy the show and feel that Pussy Riot give voice to an increasing frustration with the current Russian government. To stand forth as a feminist in contemporary Russia is, in itself, courageous (those in doubt need only skim the pages of hate responses to Pussy Riot's web postings). Pussy Riot's open support of gay activism, the risks they take when staging the performances, and the fierce government reactions they have brought upon themselves further emphasize the courageous nature of their project. Certainly, the acknowledgment of this courage is connected to the pleasurable effect of the performances on a sympathetic audience. Interestingly, though, the ability of Russians to rejoice in this noise receded somewhat as performances began taking place in locations of higher symbolical importance.[5] As I turn to the five performance documents posted by Pussy Riot up until the arrests and detention of the key members in late February 2012, I will give considerable attention to the soundtracks. Presently available information about Pussy Riot's sound barely amounts to a couple of lines. The band classifies their music as punk, inspired by feminist bands such as Bikini Kill. The choice of shouts and screams over singing is partly a generic feature of punk, and partly related to the demands of flash demonstrations, and the imperative of message. Sound quality is limited by the need for portability and speedy retreats: battery-powered mini-amplifiers, one or two guitars, and wireless microphones. The live performance is documented, edited and posted on YouTube with a pre-recorded track with added bass-and-drum backline, sometimes synthesizer and various sound effects. Sounds from the live performances are occasionally included in the mix. Each video posting is linked to a detailed and richly commented photographic report on LiveJournal.

'Free the Cobblestone'[6] was documented on video and published on Revolution Day, 7 November 2011, compiling several performances in Moscow metro stations and on bus and trolleybus roofs.[7] The instruments visible in the footage are a guitar on mini-amp, a microphone, a whip, and a flare gun. There are three band members performing, giving vocals to one part each, whilst the band's favourite lyric couplet is sung in unison. It translates:

Egyptian air is good for your lungs
Make a Tahrir on the Red Square
Spend a wild day among strong women
Search the terrace for a crowbar, free the cobblestone
Tahrir! Tahrir! Tahrir! Benghazi!

(Pussy Riot, 2011a)

The guitar centres on a single-chord drone, punctuated at regular intervals by a brief, three-note scale that allows the singers to catch some air in their stream of dactylic lines. The shouts give priority to diction, audibility and volume over any kind of vocal effect, noisy or otherwise. The sound of the pre-recorded song mimics the spontaneity of the performance and the qualities of the live instruments – tiny amplifiers, vocal domination, single-take recording – but the production is more elaborate than one might first think. It opens with the sound of a metro train followed by guitar and drum roll. A second drum roll introduces vocals barely seven seconds into the song. The singer launches straight into the first couplet. The bassline follows the guitar and stands out only occasionally. Sparse ornamentation includes an elaborate drum roll followed by a single-note bass drone. Car horns feature during one of the outdoor shots. The whip cracks and signal-gun shot are in perfect sync with the footage, and the final drum roll is cross-mixed into the sound of the metro train doors clapping shut.

The actual live sound in the acoustic space of Vorobitskaia metro station or from the bus roofs can only be guessed at. However, shots of affection and disaffection in the faces of passers-by suggest that a message comes across. Ultimately, *the* message is reinforced and the noise aestheticized for the benefit of the main audience on the Web. The production replaces the spontaneity and surprise of the live performances with an edited version, better suited for repeated home viewing. Thus, crude as it may be, the song far from abolishes listening pleasure.

'Kropotkin-vodka' documents a second batch of performances. The video was released online on the day of the parliamentary elections, 4 December 2011.[8] From the LiveJournal entry: 'The concerts were held in places where rich Putinists gather: in the capital's boutiques, in fashion shows, on exclusive cars, and on the roofs of bars in the vicinity of the Kremlin' (Pussy Riot, 2011b). The performance includes the use of fire extinguishers and a somewhat perilous pyro show on the occupied catwalk. Again, there are three performers in the footage, sporting two microphones and one or two guitars on mini-amps. This time the three women perform a catchy punk song in line with familiar Riot Grrl conventions. The vocals still dominate the mix, if slightly less than in the first video.

> Kropotkin-vodka flows in your guts
> You feel fine, but the Kremlin villains
> Face loo riots and deadly poisonings
> Blue flashing lights won't help – Kennedy's meeting them
> (Pussy Riot, 2011b)

The movements in the many snippets of footage are carefully synchronized with the soundtrack, but instruments seen and heard do not correspond. The unseen instruments are more distinct than before, especially the distorted bass. The guitars are tuned low. The opening shot of a powder-gushing fire extinguisher is accompanied by a hissing sound. In the second half of the song there is a two-tone guitar solo, which ends in an ascending slide. It is followed by what may be feedback buzz or a synth drone. A police siren is added shortly before a final punchline sung in unison, before the song ends in a bass slide. Perhaps unsurprisingly, when they target the material wealth of the privileged elite, Pussy Riot win wide acclaim. Repeated shots of a distressed male celebrity at the fashion show contribute to this. This is a DIY music video, with a wide appeal, and it will have boosted Pussy Riot's following.

The next documented performance, dated 14 December 2011, further increased Pussy Riot's popularity and respect among and beyond Moscow's citizens. They climbed the roof of a garage facing Detention Centre Number One, where arrested demonstrators were held following protests against the flawed Duma elections. Here, three band members armed with a guitar, a microphone with stand, and Bengal flares performed 'Death to Prison, Freedom to Protest' for the inmates.[9] The song calls Russian people to peacefully take to the streets and demand the release of all political prisoners. The sonic qualities of the one-minute flash gig follow the now-established pattern. Background shouts and cheers of male voices form part of the recording, evolving briefly into slogan shouting. If these have been edited in, the cheers and shouts of 'thank you!' following the final chord are clearly the voices of inmates. The urgency of the action has left less time for editing, hence this video's relative simplicity. The rough soundtrack enhances the feeling of risk and urgency conveyed by the visuals, increasing their appeal.

In 2012, prior to the presidential elections, Pussy Riot made its two most (in)famous performances, attracting the attentions of the international media, including the UK press.[10] The first took place on the Red Square's Lobnoe mesto, a platform from which the Tsar's declarations were read out in pre-revolutionary times (see Chernov, 2012). Eight masked Pussy Riot members climbed the podium with two electric guitars, a purple feminist flag and purple stage smoke, performing 'Putin Pissed Himself'.[11] All performing band members were arrested following the gig, were held in detention for five hours and fined 500 roubles each. The sound of this video differs from the former by mixing the voices even louder, to a point where they occasionally drown out the accompaniment altogether. The three-chord composition is among the band's more advanced, but is reduced to a background-noise foundation for the shouts.

Public reactions to this performance were more ambivalent. The reason might be found in a number of factors or combinations of factors. Importantly, the arrests secured higher media exposure, disseminating the event to a wider, less sympathetic audience. A coordinated response from Putin-loyal youth groupings (e.g. the remnants of the semi-official youth organisation, Nashi) could also have played a role. The high symbolic value of Red Square combined with the song's provocative call for riots is another possible key factor. Moreover, when Western media take interest in a controversial event in Russia, it is known to arouse suspicion and conspiracy theories, further fuelling antagonism.

On top of all this, the sound itself is significant. A consequence of sacrificing the minimal aestheticizing of the musical sound is a reduced potential for listening pleasure. The shouting voices are allowed to break free from the accompaniment, limiting the carnevalesque aspects of the sound and enhancing the aggressiveness of the shouted slogans. To first-time listeners this disruption of balance between lyrical message and aesthetic whole may well have limited the video's appeal. Returning to Johnson (2009b, 2009c), our instinctive, pre-contextual interpretation is that angrily shouting human voices signify danger. In order to feel safe, we need to falsify the threat by establishing that we agree with what these specific voices are shouting. It is far more demanding to conduct such an analysis without the reassuring effect of musical sound, because our starting point is one of fear and uncertainty. Of course, other contextual factors may limit such an effect: the visuals, or receiving the link in an email from someone trusted, for instance. My point is that, sound-wise, the Red Square video is less likely to trigger a positive first response than the soundtracks to the first three Pussy Riot clips. In order to fully disenchant the converted, however, a more powerful kind of noise is required – such as that of desecration.

The last of the first quintet of Pussy Riot performances took place in front of the altar of Christ the Saviour Cathedral in Moscow,[12] and was uploaded on 21 February 2012.[13] The footage testifies to a chaotic performance with several interruptions and it is difficult to determine how much of the song was actually performed live. Presented as a 'punk prayer', the song 'Mother of God, Chase Putin Away' was performed with the usual vigour. It created a roar of indignation and lasting, heated debates, and ultimately became the public cause for arrest and prosecution. The initial reaction of the Russian Orthodox Church was split between advocates for forgiveness and hardliners calling for severe civic punishment for the 'feminist demons'. The latter won through and two women, Mariia Alekhina and Nadezhda Tolokonnikova, suspected of being the organizing members of Pussy Riot, were detained pending investigation. Shortly after, a third suspected band member, Ekaterina Samutsevich, was arrested. Charged with hooliganism, the three women could in principle face prison sentences up to seven years, and could be held in detention for up to 18 months, pending police investigations, before even beginning to serve such a sentence (see Omel'chenko and Min'kova, 2012a, 2012b). The August 2012 court sentence of two years' imprisonment, after six months of detention, has been described by some hardliners as lenient. Many of Pussy Riot's high-profile supporters initially denounced the punk prayer as deeply insulting and stupid, whilst continuing to petition for their release. Joint actions first took place in Russian, European and US cities on 8 March, demanding the release of Alekhina and Tolokonnikova. Following the sentence on 17 August, an ever-increasing number of international celebrities and free speech activists have demanded the release of the Pussy Riot Three. The advocates for forgiveness and release underline that the Russian Orthodox Church is responsible for bringing political protest into the churches, with Patriarch Kirill having openly propagated for the re-election of Putin. Even so, few other than the artists themselves, and their closest supporters, go as far as to argue that this has made the churches, including their sacred altars, legitimate sites of protest. Nonetheless, the support for Pussy Riot is on the rise within the Russian cultural establishment and the voices within Russia demanding their release have grown louder (see Elder, 2012). The court verdict has not altered this trend, and even voices from within the Russian Orthodox Church have objected to the long prison sentences, noting that two of the women are mothers of young children.

The soundtrack to the 'punk prayer' goes beyond the established format of Pussy Riot punk by including a church choir theme in the beginning, middle and end of the composition. The choir mimics Russian Orthodox liturgical song, but features an additional synth piano accompaniment. The vocal arrangement is performed according to generic demands with clear voices, carrying no audible spite or ironic sneers. This enhances the effect of the prayer's words, which echo the title of the song. In the second and third choir parts, the line is extended to 'Mother of God, become a feminist and chase Putin away'. Each choir component lasts for about fifteen seconds. In the first, a distorted electric bass falls in, gently mocking the religious melody and introducing the song's first punk component. The punk parts follow the established Pussy Riot standard with drums, distorted bass and guitar on mini-amps, and shouted vocal lines. The parts consist of two four-chord couplets, separated by two-chord breaks. The breaks are highlighted by the four repeated shouts of 'Sran' gospodnia!' ('Shit of the Lord!'), directed at Putin and his retinue. The voices directed at the Virgin Mary sound earnest and respectful; spite and aggression only comes forth in the punk parts, where the lyrics address Putin and his government. One can hardly expect offended believers to pay notice to the finer nuances of the performance, yet the soundtrack does offer an opportunity for closer analysis of the message, intention and main target of the performance. However, these features are lost in the deafening noise of desecration.

Pussy Riot have succeeded in raising an important debate of ties between the Kremlin and the Russian Orthodox Church. Warnings have been issued against the forces that strive for 'Iranian conditions' in Russia.[14] Time will show if Pussy Riot's project has been killed in the process, or whether their sounds still bring pleasure to a sufficient number of followers.

## And?

We have looked at two cases of Russian punk that involve loss of listening pleasure. While both cases demand the inclusion of substantial qualitative material in order to properly address the problem of noise and listening pleasure, the cases of GrOb and Pussy Riot have proved helpful in illustrating the interaction between sound and extra-sonic factors in the creation and loss of listening enjoyment. The noise of Egor Letov's involvement with extremist politics disturbed listening pleasure because it contradicted the anarcho-punk aesthetics associated with the band. Pussy Riot's audience appeal was undermined by the extra-sonic noise generated by the act of desecration of Russia's perhaps most prominent place of worship; it drowned out more subtle messages from their 'punk prayer'. Both cases demonstrate that extra-sonic events may well be regarded as a form of noise, provided that the actual sounds are also considered. Further study is required in order to establish a fully-fledged approach to these issues. We should keep in mind, however, how easily we are seduced by extra-sonic contexts – visual, social, or political – to a point where we ignore the sound itself along with its physiological and psychological impacts. In analysing music and noise in a scopocentric world, we must constantly remind ourselves of the fundamental significance of sound. What we embrace as pleasurable noise and what we discard as harmful or uninteresting noise does to a large degree rely on this extra-sonic context. However, lest we include the sounds themselves, we can never fully grasp the size and importance of that degree.

# CHAPTER NINE

# Noise from Nowhere: Exploring 'Noisyland's' Dark, Noisy and Experimental Music

*Michael Goddard*

### Introduction

This chapter will examine some of the industrial, experimental and noise music that emerged in New Zealand from the 1980s onwards. While there has been some critical work done on the more 1960s-oriented melodic rock groups associated with the Flying Nun independent record label (Bannister, 1999; Mitchell, 1996; Unterberger, 1998), the noisier, more artistically daring and experimental groups such as the Gordons/Bailter Space, the Dead C. and This Kind of Punishment have received considerably less attention. This chapter will examine the aesthetics of some of these groups, in particular their breaking down of conventional musical structures and embrace of the chaotic energies of noise, to argue that they constituted a unique form of innovative cultural production, fully engaged with the situation of New Zealand as a marginal location in the transnational economy of global popular music. This is not only through the well-known DIY attitude as a response to New Zealand's cultural isolation from global trends that can be said to characterize Flying Nun groups in general, but also through a more radical interface between transnational aesthetic practices and popular music. The results of this transnational appropriation were unique and varied musical recordings and performances that constitute a form of vital and dislocating 'noise' in relation to the history of New Zealand popular music and culture more generally. Furthermore, two distinct tendencies can be heard in these groups, namely a search for alternative structures and modes of sonic composition and organization in the cases of This Kind of Punishment and the Gordons/Bailter Space, as opposed to the embrace of chaotic, deliberately disorganized and spontaneous noise on the part of the Dead C. and related projects. This chapter will attempt to contextualize and analyse these examples of antipodean sonic expression in proximity to concepts of psychogeography and (dis)utopia.

## The emergence of the Flying Nun media ecology

To understand the aesthetics of this music, it is necessary to give some historical context. It emerged directly out of the first wave of New Zealand punk music which, as in other countries, was an expression of youth dissatisfaction with both social conformity and conventional rock music, in the case of New Zealand as epitomized by 'NZ Rock' groups such as Split Enz or Dragon, both of which had found some success internationally. While New Zealand had its fair share of standard punk groups, merely imitating British styles, very early on a number of other groups emerged who saw in punk an impetus towards experimentation rather than a pre-existing model to be followed, tending towards the formation of alternative and autonomous forms of culture. Many strange groups emerged following this tendency, for example, Wellington's Shoes This High, whose multiple changing rhythms, enigmatic lyrics and bursts of guitar noise were almost certain to be appreciated only by a minority audience, and who left behind only one recording of a four-track EP.[1] (Ultimately their singer, Brent Hayward, under the name of Smelly Feet, and subsequently the Kiwi Animal, left the band and electric instruments altogether, and instead performed only with acoustic guitar and even more enigmatic lyrics, whose inaccessibility was only emphasized by the fact that they were read out from scraps of paper attached to classical musical stands.)

What were the conditions for this autonomy? Apart from an adoption of the punk ethos of DIY and autonomy, the cultural conditions of New Zealand in the 1980s had a lot to do with the emergence of this autonomous music culture for a number of reasons. First, influences from the UK and the USA, the countries at the centre of global popular music, were relatively indirect since very few international groups ever came to New Zealand, especially the newer punk or alternative ones, and even their recordings might only have a relatively limited availability, despite there being a lively trade in even the most obscure imported records.[2] Secondly, the possibilities of commercial success for any even mildly innovative group were incredibly remote – the only really domestically successful music at this time was country music and anything else had to find success overseas, at least in Australia and preferably in England and Europe. Unlike in Australia, the idea of any kind of success in the United States was generally not even considered, even if ultimately Flying Nun music would experience a delayed popularity on American College radio, partly facilitated by high-profile 'fans' like Byron Coley of *Forced Exposure*, Gerard Cosloy of *Conflict* zine and Homestead records and later Stephen Malkmus of Pavement. But few bands had the resources or record company backing to make international touring possible, so while some still tried to adapt to and follow foreign trends, many others took the attitude that if there was no chance of international success, then you might as well follow your own path. Thirdly, there was a kind of cultural vacuum in which there really was little or no autonomous culture, whether artistic or popular, to speak of; many people were just very bored with their conformist and unimaginative cultural surroundings. It was clear that if there was to be any interesting culture in New Zealand it would have to be created, but the question was how?[3]

The first, production side of the equation was relatively straightforward, that is, coming up with some idiosyncratic or challenging music, but how then was it possible to reach an audience? Many groups at this time simply didn't record anything, or if they did, it was only a track on a compilation possibly organized by a music venue or an alternative/student radio station (which were also just starting to develop). Another interesting possibility was through cassette-only releases; these could be produced at minimal expense and then be made available through mail order (such as through Industrial Tapes or later Dunedin's Xpressway), as well as at gigs and record shops, particularly second-hand ones, that were not so dominated by the mainstream music industry. However, these recordings were often of a very low quality and the minimal expense invested even in their packaging meant that few people would risk purchasing them unless they already had personal experience of the groups through attending gigs. The problem was therefore one of how to maintain autonomy while still having some effective distribution beyond an entirely micro local market – a problem to which the response was the formation of small independent record labels, usually formed by either musicians themselves or their fans, which would at the same time allow artistic freedom and provide the minimal capital necessary for at least nationwide distribution and marketing (for example, through the new medium of music videos), not to mention at least the potential for improved audio quality (lo-fi is OK but you should at least be able to hear the music). The most successful of these micro labels, which in the end became quite big, was Flying Nun, and eventually many of the more well-known groups, whether relatively mainstream or experimental, had something to do with this label, including the main examples I will be referring to. Ironically enough, given its subsequent association with the 'Dunedin sound', Flying Nun was originally created by Roger Shepherd to give exposure and recording time to the decidedly post-punk scene of his native Christchurch, and the first Flying Nun recording was in fact of the decidedly early Velvet Underground and Joy Division-influenced Pin Group's first single, 'Ambivalence'.

It is at this point that questions of music and place need to be addressed, especially since most of the writing on alternative New Zealand music, usually seen in its entirety in relation to Flying Nun, tends to be discussed reductively in terms of the 'Dunedin sound' (see Mitchell, 1996, 224–8; Connell and Gibson, 2003, 96–7).[4] Like other similar geographical constructions such as the Mersey sound, or Seattle grunge, such a conception is highly limiting and distorting in numerous respects. First, a good deal of Flying Nun music did not originate in Dunedin but in more northern cities like Christchurch and Auckland, and even the music that did come from Dunedin was often the result of a considerable north-south traffic of musicians and producers between these locations. Chris Knox, for example, started out in one of the first Dunedin punk groups, the Enemy, relocated to Auckland where he was a key member of the groups Toy Love and Tall Dwarfs before, as a creative director of Flying Nun, returning to the South Island with a TEAC four-track to record some of the first Flying Nun releases.[5] This did not prevent, however, the development of a mythology centred around Dunedin. As Connell and Gibson put it, 'a sense of local uniqueness, of remoteness and distance from capital cities and centres of mainstream music production was central to the growth and "mythology" of a distinct sound' (2003, 96–7). Nevertheless, the extent to which the Dunedin sound expresses musically anything related to the specific space of New Zealand or, more precisely, Dunedin is debatable; according to Tony Mitchell, the pure pop melodies and jangly guitars that are the most frequent signifiers of the Dunedin sound are generic components of transnational rock music and similar qualities have been used to describe music from various other cities such as Liverpool, and indeed Beatles and 1960s-influenced rock music worldwide (Mitchell, 1996, 225). Conversely, some writers have attempted to make such geographical linkages. David Eggleston, for example, writing of the Bats, claims that '[t]heir sweet sticky pop songs are suffused with the tang of something wild and strange ... capturing a sense of the South Island Landscape – the slow turn of the seasons, and of what it's like to live in that landscape ... they are nothing if not tribal' (Eggleston, cited in Mitchell, 1996, 227). Given that Eggleston is a performance poet of Maori descent, and the music of the Bats is probably the 'whitest', least funky music imaginable, the use of the word tribal here is perhaps intended ironically, but even so, such associations of a direct link between musical qualities and geography are common, even if they are almost impossible to maintain coherently.[6]

Nevertheless, the myth of the Dunedin sound is a resilient one, and one that Flying Nun are inadvertently responsible for originating – one of their earliest releases being the double EP known as the 'Dunedin Double', of which one side each was allotted to four Dunedin bands: the Chills, the

Verlaines, Sneaky Feelings and the Stones, the latter named parodically after the famous international rock group. However, even listening to this originary artefact of the Dunedin sound is enough to dispel or at least trouble this mythology; if the Chills and Sneaky Feelings' sides do indeed abound in jangly guitars and pop melodies, things get decidedly more post-punk on the Verlaines side with its more complex song structures and tendencies towards sudden time changes, while the Stones are a Stooges-like lost garage punk band, who conclude their alienated, repetitive rock dirges with a parodic surf music track, 'Surf's Up'.[7] Ultimately, if anything is shared between the four sides of this release, it is less a common musical aesthetic (even in the case of the first two sides, the reworked 1960s influences are as distinct as US psychedelia and mid-period Beatles pop) than the lo-fi effect of being recorded on the same four-track tape recorder, which would also characterize many other early Flying Nun releases, and was both an economic necessity and a deliberate aesthetic choice on the part of Chris Knox, the prolific producer of many of these releases.[8] Of course, many of these releases, including the work of Knox himself, and the seminal the Clean, showed as much a (post-)punk as a purely 1960s sensibility, while others were decidedly darker, more experimental and noisier. Nevertheless, the myth of the Dunedin sound has effectively marginalized these other musical practices from discussions of Flying Nun, in which they tend either to be barely mentioned, if at all (Mitchell, 1996; Connell and Gibson, 2003), or disparaged (Bannister, 2006, 54, 86–8).[9]

Even so, there is a strange sense that regardless of any validity to the Dunedin sound, Dunedin itself in the 1980s definitely took on utopian resonances, so much so that many emergent bands and musicians in the more urbanized North Island cities of New Zealand actually relocated to this small, southernmost city of New Zealand, as if hoping to be touched by the mythic local pop genius, located in the very atmosphere of the town; or more prosaically hoping to participate in the active and supportive music scene already underway. While at first glance there would seem to be little to support such a utopian view of Dunedin, given its punishing climate and its relatively parochial, conservative and monocultural population (relative to more cosmopolitan cities like Auckland or Wellington), however modified by the influence of the large university, its utopic dimensions actually have quite a long history. Tony Mitchell has claimed that Samuel Butler's nineteenth-century utopian novel *Erewhon* was based on this part of New Zealand, where Butler himself had lived (Mitchell, 1996, 224), although more accurately this was Christchurch and inland Canterbury. Nevertheless, the idea of New Zealand in general and Dunedin in particular being 'nowhere' or a 'non-place' was expressive of a widely felt cultural dislocation, ultimately derivative of the colonial construction of New Zealand as a giant farm serving the needs of England, only to be coolly abandoned when the United Kingdom joined the EEC in the 1970s. It must be remembered that it was only after the Second World War that New Zealand ceased to be a dominion, effectively administered from England, and became an independent state, and it is common in (white) New Zealand literature of the 1940s and 1950s to hear England referred to unambiguously as 'home' even by people who had never been there. This was given another twist in Dunedin due to its large proportion of Scottish immigrants, whose legacy was not only the naming of the town after the Gaelic name for Edinburgh, and most of its streets after streets in that city, but also persistent traditions of pipers, tartan and other elements of Scottish culture; however anomalous it might seem, it was still a common occurrence to run into a piper in the Octagon on most important occasions and several quite random ones. Beyond this, the geography and psychogeography of Dunedin was itself generative of the sense of being a non-place, one of the main suburban areas of the hilly port city being simply called 'North East Valley', while the large peninsula featuring many secluded and inaccessible bays and coves was popularly known simply as 'the peninsula'. Whether it was the legacy of the gold rush and its ensuant economic decline, meaning that students and musicians could easily find themselves sharing Georgian mansions, or the persistent myth of a buried pyramid and converging leylines in the peninsula, or the more banal claim to possessing New Zealand's and possibly the southern hemisphere's steepest street, Dunedin was a space highly amenable to mythologization; already a culturally displaced, isolated 'nowhere', the etymological meaning of utopia. It was therefore ready to assume a distinctive place on the map of global independent music that would ultimately be picked up on by various international lo-fi luminaries in groups like Pavement and Sonic Youth. As Tony Mitchell suggests, 'the "Dunedin Sound" was generated through a cultural geography of isolation, which produced […] a mythology of place assembled by fans, artists, critics, promoters, and industry personnel [that] made Dunedin a metonym for Aotearoa/New Zealand music as a whole' (Mitchell, 1996, 224).

However, not all alternative music made in Dunedin can be characterized in terms of the Dunedin sound, not all of even Flying Nun music was made in Dunedin, and some of the local independent music was not released on Flying Nun but on more obscure and short-lived yet influential labels like Bruce Russell's cassette and vinyl label Xpressway, although the latter had a close relationship with the former, releasing recordings by many of the Flying Nun bands considered to have less commercial potential. The sense of Dunedin and New Zealand generated by some of these more marginal recordings is far more urban and alienated, as well as being expressive of the darker aspects of cultural dislocation and isolation; if there are musical influences they are decidedly post-punk imprints of groups like Joy Division or the Fall rather than 1960s psychedelia, unless it is the drony, art psychedelia of the first two Velvet Underground albums.[10] The rest of this chapter will focus on three examples of this darker, more dystopian music;

combining these two aspects of New Zealand as both a lo-fi utopia and a post-punk dystopia, it is perhaps justified to refer to New Zealand and its music as a 'disutopia', to use Antonio Negri's term:[11] both prison and escape, both paradise and cultural purgatory, leading to an unmistakable intensity in both these musical tendencies.

## Standing on the edge of the world: from the Gordons to Bailter Space

The first example I want to mention of this NZ noise music is the Gordons (originally just 'Gordons', no 'the'), who later mutated into the group Bailter Space (after a brief period with a different line-up as Nelsh Bailter Space), relocating in the 1990s to Hoboken, New Jersey. Emerging out of the Christchurch punk scene, this group was among the earlier post-punk artists to release an entire album, and subsequently their EP and first album were re-released via Flying Nun, as was their now unavailable second album. This group was striking for having from the beginning a fully formed vision, expressed by both the music and its accompanying artwork, a vision expressing a dystopian futurism embodied by the cyborg figure of the 'Gordonaut'. Several key features of the Gordons were immediately apparent on their first recording: a tendency towards musical repetition and variation accompanied by equally repetitive lyrics; a tight musical structure composed of aggressive and distorted sonic components; and a heaviness that never sounds like heavy rock but rather seems directly expressive of the sonic overload of technological urban environments (aspects of which would appear in many of the lyrics). The band seemed to intuit from the beginning that by pushing rock, including its punk variations, to a level of abstraction, it was possible to generate a sonic equivalent of the future itself. This explains why the band felt no necessity to subscribe to the punk insistence on speed; many Gordons tracks are rather ponderously slow in order to generate a structure around which multiple layers of noise could be articulated and multiple variations could be developed – take for example 'Machine Song' from the first Gordons *Future Shock* EP. The track begins with an almost formalist two-line bass riff on the top of which an irregular guitar line pursues a range of variations to a simple drum beat before giving way to waves of distorted noise. The lyrics of the song are also about a type of machine-mediated existence that is directly confronted: 'You walk around like machines/You go to work in your dreams/Your mother's telephonics made you mad/Oh what to do is in your head' (Gordons, 'Machine Song'). These lyrics seem quite ambiguous in at once denouncing a type of schizo-inducing submission to work and technologies, a human programming, while suggesting a possible escape, if only an imaginary one;

in a sense it is through the type of composed or organized noise that the Gordons perform that an escape from technological submission is at least implicitly suggested. Even more abstract was the 'Future Shock' track itself, whose bursts of guitar and other noises become organized in an aggressive rhythmic assemblage whose only lyrical content is a constantly repeated warning of Future Shock, the famous concept of Alvin Toffler.[12]

If New Zealand alternative music in general had a strong influence from the Velvet Underground, in the case of the Gordons this was from their noisiest and most radical experiments, such as on *White Light, White Heat*, rather than their later melodic music which would influence many other Flying Nun groups. There is also a strong resonance with other noise groups including industrial bands such as Throbbing Gristle, or guitar bands like Chrome (who share a similarly dystopian futurist vision) or Sonic Youth, but in these cases resonance is a much more accurate term than influence, since the Gordons actually preceded Sonic Youth (Sonic Youth on a tour to New Zealand expressed their admiration for the Gordons, by saying 'we've got a Gordon too!'). What was clear in their music was a strong relationship between the industrial, technological landscape they were exploring thematically, namely the destructive impact of developing technologies on the future of human life, and the musical forms they were deploying which injected the maximum degree of noisiness into still-recognizable musical structures. This dynamic of noise and music, of chaos and structure can be said to characterize many forms of music and can reveal a lot about the social context in which it is produced. In the case of the Gordons, the music was a direct assault on the senses, but one that was absolutely distinct from other contemporary loud musics of the time such as heavy metal or even conventional punk music. This is because the Gordons' use of noise not only tended to dissolve individual identity and therefore the kind of macho posturing evident in these other musics, but was also seeking out what was beautiful or transformative in noise itself – this aim anticipating the later development of groups ranging from Sonic Youth in the mid- to late 1980s to so-called British shoegaze music of the late 1980s and early 1990s. If this aim was less apparent in the relatively punk *Future Shock* EP, some of the songs on their first album, simply entitled *The Gordons*, clearly demonstrated this poetics of noise – something that would continue to animate the later recordings of Bailter Space. Furthermore, this music was distinguished by having a critical politics; most of the songs not only presented a dystopic future world but critiqued certain elements of it, especially social conditioning, whether of a generational or technological nature, as well as the potential for military and ecological catastrophe, an obsessive theme of the Gordons' second album.[13] While Alister Parker was creating a new band in Christchurch called Nelsh Bailter Space, originally with Hamish Kilgour from the Clean, John Halvorsen and drummer Brent McLaughlin were both playing in another seminal experimental noise band, Palmerston North's Skeptics, while also setting up the Writhe recording studios in Wellington. Ultimately, all three were reunited in the now-renamed Bailter Space, which continued to record and tour for another decade, first in Wellington and then in New York.

Names of bands function as impersonal concepts that take on and also lose meaning over the lifetimes of the groups they name; while the Gordons is a typical punk name that seems to revel in the ordinary and the everyday, Bailter Space has a much more cosmic resonance, as if it were the name of some alternate universe accessible via a certain mastery of patterns of noise. There are probably two related elements of the Bailter Space concept that make it distinct yet related to that of the Gordons: one is an idea of 'the orbital' and the second is a technical process that can be described as a form of sonic sculpture. The orbital can be understood in terms of the movement of a satellite, spaceship or planetary body encountering different forces of gravitational attraction in different cosmic contexts, the metaphorics of which were fully explored by Jean Baudrillard in *The Ecstasy of Communication* (Baudrillard, 1988). More straightforwardly, the orbital simply references the outsider position of coming from such a marginal location as NZ to somewhere like New York, as Bailter Space have done – when Bailter Space sing about 'standing on the edge of the world' it has both these geographical and cosmic resonances. As far as sonic sculpture goes, there is an extension of the already intensive use of repetition in the Gordons into new realms of layered construction of songs as sonic sculptural artefacts; while Bailter Space construct everything from melodic layered pop songs to aggressively experimental slabs of structured noise, all of their work has this sculptural dimension based on the super-imposition of multiple layers of sound. Sometimes the result of this process can be deceptively simple; for example, the song 'Shine', while on the surface a simple pop song, superimposes layers of differently textured and distorted guitars which generate a unique sense of spatiality. At the same time the formerly strident aggressive vocals of the Gordons have become murmuring, even whispering, incorporated into the sonic construction of the track as semiotic fragments more of affect than of meaning. But in case one was under the impression that the punk stridency of the Gordons had been entirely abandoned, it is only necessary to listen to a track like 'Projects' off the powerful *Vortura* album, which is every bit as hard-edged and aggressive as anything the Gordons ever did. Again the song at once speaks both to present realities and articulates a sci-fi dystopia – the 'people in projects' referred to in the song, no doubt both a response to the band's encounter with high-rise housing conditions in New York City and the latter's architecturally sharp divisions between the rich and the poor, as well as being a dystopian vision of the future. In this song the progressive rock 'hey you!' aggressively interpolates the inhabitant of the top of some Ballardian tower block, if not Phillip K. Dick's *Man in the High Castle* himself: 'Hey you in your ivory tower/There's going to be some day/When you come down to the street below' – all of this accompanied by one of Bailter Space's most attacking riffs and repetitive, atonal self-sampling.

This is where the relations between Bailter Space and the avant-garde movement of futurism could be addressed, seeing as the album *Vortura* seems to reference both Futurism and Vorticism, or at least the future and vortices. In contrast with both historical futurism and its techno- or neo- varieties, Bailter Space acknowledge the radical technological transformation of human life as absolutely central without celebrating it.[14] Instead their music is a type of immanent participatory critique of technological processes, the selection of what technological processes might actually be useful for enhancing survival and the rejection and critique of the destructive potentials of some technologies as well as the military-industrial complex (which pursues its interests by putting human life at risk whether from nuclear, military or ecological destruction). However, this critique rarely takes the form of denouncing forms of power, with the exception of a few songs about nuclear reactors, but rather is a micropolitical affirmation of desire expressed as much through the fabrication of uniquely beautiful and powerful sonic forms as it is through any lyrical content, which often tends toward repetitive minimalist mantras. Nevertheless it is this drive toward the auto-valorization of technically mediated micropolitical desire that make Bailter Space much closer to Sonic Youth rather than apparently similar post-rock bands like My Bloody Valentine or Mogwai; whereas these latter bands share a desire for the fabrication of affectively intense sonic forms, Bailter Space and Sonic Youth both discern and articulate critical relations with the future tendencies of the present. Both groups oppose technological fetishism with a real machinism, the expression of desires, intensities and affects via the human-machine interfaces of noisemaking instruments. For all the future orientation on technology, Bailter Space have always been an affirmation of the possibilities of human survival and desire in an increasingly technically mediated universe, even if this desire can only be articulated via technical, noise-producing machines constituting an 'autopoiesis', or in Guattari's terms a 'machinic heterogenesis' of mutant cyborg subjectivities.[15]

## 'In the Same Room': the aesthetic strategies of This Kind of Punishment

Another experimental group worth mentioning is This Kind of Punishment. Beginning as Nocturnal Projections, a kind of Joy Division-like depressive but powerful post-punk band from New Plymouth, the Jeffries brothers, the key animators of this group, soon became bored with the limitations of this format and instead started experimenting with different ways of producing music collectively, using the name This Kind of Punishment. As with Chris Knox's Tall Dwarfs, this was also in some respects the adoption of a more lo-fi aesthetic – not least because they were borrowing Knox's four-track – but more importantly, it involved questioning the ways in which rock music is produced. This was both on the organizational level of what exactly constitutes a rock group, and on the level of musical form itself, as well as on the level of the different ways that music might be distributed (they were later very closely linked to the Xpressway label, for example, as well as producing all and distributing some of their recordings themselves). In terms of the first point, this group operated more as the organizers of a series of artistic projects rather than as a fixed rock group, encouraging audience identification with and of their personalities. Apart from the Jeffries brothers, the personnel on their various recordings would often change and involve people from various other alternative groups (often associated with Flying Nun) including Chris Matthews, Shayne Carter and Michael Morley, while the two brothers simultaneously pursued other solo and collaborative projects. This also meant that different albums would have extremely different aesthetics and, more specifically, abandoned the idea that a group needs to be identifiable by a particular sound. So while some of their recordings involved a lot of guitar noise and feedback, others, especially on their second, self-produced album, *A Beard of Bees*, were largely composed of minimal acoustic guitar and piano chords, accompanied by enigmatic, abstract and at times barely comprehensible lyrics. In fact minimalism, in its full artistic sense, can be said to characterize several of their musical projects, without losing all relationship to contemporary rock music; they seem to have been exploring what happens when you strip rock music down to a bare skeleton of just a few chords and refrains, suspending not only beats and rhythms but also clear meanings. However, in this enterprise I would argue that they remained no less a noise band than the Gordons; not because some of their recordings were still characterized by a noise aesthetic, but rather because the removal of conventional rock noise, and especially the use of silence as a compositional element, is itself a form of noise in relation to the norms of contemporary rock music and even of popular culture more generally. Through these kinds of modernist, formalist experiments, This Kind of Punishment were examining rock music as a form and one that could be modified and deconstructed into a few key elements, in a practice highly resonant with that of the UK post-punk group Wire. In a different way to Bailter Space, much of the music of This Kind of Punishment also aims at generating affective intensities, most evident in some of the tracks from their *In the Same Room* album, especially 'Immigration Song', with its account of the alienated perspective of being a stranger in a strange town, and the truly searing account of a relationship break-down, 'Don't Go', every bit as cathartic an exorcism of relationship trauma as Joy Division's 'I Remember Nothing'. This is music that poses questions not only about conventional musical forms and modes of organization, but also about forms of sensibility and sociality, a questioning of sonic and social forms that was taken up in a markedly different way by the Dead C.

## 'Vain, erudite and stupid': approaching the music of the Dead C.

The Dead C. is inseparable from the figure of Bruce Russell, one of the most forceful and polemical characters in Antipodean music. Nevertheless, the Dead C., also featuring Michael Morley and Robbie Yeats, are very much an ensemble in an almost free jazz sense, since their performances and recordings feature a collective improvisatory approach in which apparent errors become woven into the process of sonic elaboration. Russell has recounted the anecdote that during one of the first Dead C. recordings, after a visit to the bathroom during which the other band members had decided to play a different track to the one previously planned, he happily played the wrong track and marvelled at how interesting the results were, after which he never looked back. Unlike the sonic layering of either Bailter Space or This Kind of Punishment, the Dead C. and other related projects like A Handful of Dust or Gate are based on precisely incorporating this kind of radical contingency, even if in some cases their work seems to result in recognizable musical structures. While there was at certain times a proximity between the Dead C. and more mainstream New Zealand indie music, expressed by the release of their *Eusa Kills* album on Flying Nun, they nevertheless were for some time the most hated noise group in the country due to their uncompromising and unpredictable performances (for example, when asked to support Sonic Youth's *Dirty* tour, their noisy improvisation was met with indifference, contempt and confusion on the part of audiences largely there for Sonic Youth's most grunge period rock; an ironic reaction given that this was just the kind of noisy chaos that marked Sonic Youth's emergence out of New York No Wave). Russell not only performs with his two groups but also works as a sound artist and is a prolific writer, contributing to both the recent *Noise and Capitalism* (Mattin and Iles, 2011) and *Reverberations* (Goddard, Hegarty and Halligan, 2012) collections, co-editing a collection on experimental music in Australia and New Zealand, *Erewhon Calling* (2012), and producing a book collection of his writings, *Left-Handed Blows*, many of which previously appeared in obscure publications, including ones also produced by Russell himself. These writings on sound, which would be worthy of a presentation in themselves, are at once engaging and hermetic, referring to familiar and unfamiliar reference points; the context of NZ cultural history and music is highly present, as are the writings of the Situationists, Karl Marx and Walter Benjamin, alongside the occult texts of Robert Fludd and Giordarno Bruno. Even the style of some of the chapters, where, for example, a free noise manifesto against the harmony of the spheres is accompanied by footnotes that take up 90 per cent of the page, seems to be structured in such a way as to be overrun by (textual) noise.

The music of the Dead C. is much more difficult to describe than that of the other bands mentioned, precisely because it eschews even alternative forms of compositional structure in favour of a free play in which noise, feedback, errors and other chaotic elements are freely incorporated. Relative to the Dead C., these other noisy groups come across as quite conventional in their production of often melodic, clearly structured songs of a generally reasonable length. A typical Dead C. album, in contrast, frequently involves tracks of over ten minutes, and conversely of around one minute, which may or may not incorporate recognizable rock or even musical elements such as rhythms, vocals or tunes (melodies being too strong a word here). *Tusk*, for example, begins with a track, 'Plane', composed of repetitive scraping and other percussive loops of sound, by no means recognizable as music, which is followed by 'Head', an extreme lo-fi but more recognizably rock-related drone track featuring shifting rhythms and extensive guitar feedback, and after around six minutes some typically drone-like vocals. The next track, 'Tuba', however, sounds like a heavy rock track heard through a cassette recording in a duffel bag, and lasts only a minute and a half. Nevertheless, there are at least moments of the Dead C. that are song-like enough to feature on Flying Nun compilations, although this tends to be their earlier work from the Flying Nun-released *Eusa Kills* album like '3 Years' or 'Scarey Nest' which, like the Gordons' 'Coal Miner's Song', have somehow been able to be incorporated into the Flying Nun canon.

One of the ways in which this music has tended to be approached is as a form of 'head music'. Adapting Simon Reynolds' earlier characterization of different forms of UK indie music ranging from the Smiths to the Jesus and Mary Chain as a head rather than a body music (Reynolds, 2007, 13–19), Mitchell applies this not only to jangly Flying Nun pop bands but also – and especially – to the bands associated with the Xpressway label, who were also described as 'head music' by Erik Davis. However, what Davis had in mind was more affinities with the drug-related, experimental, improvisational groups associated with Krautrock like Can or Faust, where 'head' is more a reference to marijuana than an opposition to the body, as it is in Reynolds' account of indie music. Mitchell's disparaging description of the 'avant-garde, experimental and often self-indulgently left-field orientation of Xpressway bands' (Mitchell, 1996, 236), is also echoed by Matthew Bannister's relative aversion to 'drone' as opposed to 'jangle' tendencies in indie guitar music, albeit referring to bands like Bailter Space rather than the Dead C. According to Bannister:

> I hear indie sound (white noise drone) as representing a synthesis of folk and modern attitudes to technology ... Mediation through technology is ubiquitous in popular music ... [but w]hereas pop music aims to hide the effects of its mediation by positing a direct, intimate relation between singer/song and listener, in indie guitar rock, this relationship is always in some way being questioned ... Perhaps the buzz of distortion can be seen as analagous to the continual background noise of an overcrowded, industrialised, mediated society. (Bannister, 2006, 121)

Bannister's formulations are more interesting than Mitchell's due to the formal attention they play to sound and noise and the fact that, while privileging the more commercial, 'jangly' pole of independent music, he nevertheless articulates what precisely is interesting in more drony and noisy forms of this music, namely a foregrounding of technological mediation in which 'a multitude of possible, possibly phatasmagorical voices' (Bannister, 2007, 121) can be heard. His objection to noise, when taken to what he describes as an extreme (references here ranging from the Gordons and Big Black to Dinosaur Jr. and My Bloody Valentine) is that the 'wall of sound' they produce reinforces the very forms of rockist, masculinist power and authority that they would most want to oppose, even in the absence or dissolution of any rock machismo: 'Noise ends up confirming male autonomy and power, because its power can be equally used for subversive or conservative ends' (Bannister, 2007, 160).

Returning to the Dead C. and Xpressway, it is difficult to see how this masculinist critique of noise can be maintained. While it is possible, if inaccurate, to make such an argument about the 'sheet metal' loudness of the Gordons, the sheer chaos and radical contingency of the Dead C. disallows the affirmation of any such power structures, and this is even more the case with some of the other Xpressway groups ranging from the fragile electric violin playing of Alistair Galbraith to the Nico-esque sonic poetry of Sandra Bell. If it is true that performing noise affirms power, in the context of Xpressway this is no longer the power of a white male or any other stable subject but a power of expression, rejecting in advance any identification with both hierarchically and capitalist-defined social structures, just as their work rejects predefined sonic structures.

Such, at any rate, are the terms in which Russell theorizes what he calls 'free music' or 'improvised sound work' (Russell, 2009, 21–4ff.). While this conception draws on the modern legacy of attempts at escaping the strictures and rules of classical composition (La Monte Young, Cage, Xenakis), it is not uncritical of the limitations of these escape attempts, and aims to go further. In particular, Russell advocates the use of low-tech 'amplified electrical instruments' (Russell, 2009, 24) as a means of expanding the audible frequency spectrum and thereby exceeding the experiments of classical minimalism: 'Free music which utilises rock instrumentation and aesthetics as its jumping-off point can harness a noise more purely random and less limited by subjective considerations than that of any but the most determined acoustic musicians' (Russell, 2009, 24). The reasons for this potential are, however, not only sonic, but social, as improvised sound-work is, for Russell, a form of critical praxis, gaining power from the outmoded potential of analogue rock instruments in the digital era. Without going into all the complexities of this argument (Russell, 2009, 11–16; 2012a, 248–52 ff.), the Benjaminian concept of the revolutionary potential of outmoded forms and technologies is deployed by Russell to assert the radicality of improvised sound-work using analogue instruments like the guitar, as constituting 'the most perfectly autonomous sector of cultural production' (Russell, 2012a, 247). As such, the praxis of the Dead C. and related groups provides a more complex and coherent articulation of the concept of *disutopia* which, as in Negri's account of Spinoza, dispenses with imaginary, idealist constructions such as the 'Dunedin sound', or even Dunedin/New Zealand as a psychogeographical utopia, in favour of a materialist *disutopia* founded on concrete practices of noisemaking on the margins of independent music in New Zealand.

## Conclusion

This chapter has attempted to explore some of the noisier, more aberrant independent musical practices taking place in New Zealand from the 1980s. As such it has necessarily set up distinctions between musical tendencies, in order to highlight divergences, both conceptual and practical, between different practices of independent music in New Zealand. In the first place this has been between the melodic 1960s-inflected rock most usually associated with Flying Nun and often reduced to the 'Dunedin sound', and a range of noisier, more experimental practices; but it has also involved making distinctions within these noisier New Zealand musics, between alternative forms of structured composition, still strongly related to those of independent rock music (the Gordons/Bailter Space, This Kind of Punishment) and improvised sound practices with more affinity to free, improvised musics, albeit conducted with rock rather than classical/acoustic or digital technologies. Nevertheless, none of these divergences are absolute distinctions, and the fact that members of the Dead C. have also had significant roles within Flying Nun (Russell as a publicist and curator, Robbie Yeats as drummer for the Verlaines) indicates that all these groups exist on the same spectrum, even if this spectrum involves radically divergent practices. In this respect it is interesting that alongside the latest of a slew of retrospective Flying Nun compilations, most of which attempt in some way to be representative of the diversity of the groups involved, Russell has recently 'curated' a collection of (mostly) Flying Nun music from the period 1981–6, entitled *Time to Go: The Southern Psychedelic Moment*. While not without its relatively obscure contributors such as Max Block, the Shallows, or Michael Morley's pre-Dead C. band, the wonderfully entitled Wreck Small Speakers on Expensive Stereos, it also features such canonical Flying Nun groups as the Clean and the Chills recontextualized as so many varieties of (neo-)psychedelia. In the words of Russell's liner notes:

> Taking off from the blank slate of punk's year zero, adding-in a massive dose of disrespect for authority born out of the contemporary and very urgent struggle for social justice, and looking forward to a new New Zealand that was not going to be all about white bread and white men playing rugby – the new music dug deep into its own independent and international tradition, and got very widely, very weirdly, and very seriously psychedelic. (Russell, 2012b).

For Russell, this turn towards psychedelia constituted at once a derangement of the senses and a channel for countercultural rebellion that enabled shared, if diverse, modes of musical expression in the specific time and place of South Island New Zealand in the early to mid-1980s. While the inclusion of some groups in this psychedelic rubric seems at first counterintuitive (situating the Gordons and Sneaky Feelings in this way seems somewhat forced), it nevertheless provides a more consistent – and inclusive – way of getting at what was singular about the spectrum of music produced in this particular time and place, without reducing it to terms of banality and cliché: 'a collection of tracks that depict a reality that was obvious at the time but has been rather lost to subsequent history' (Russell, 2012b). This chapter has also aimed, in a different way, to attest to and recall this singular disutopic reality.

# Acknowledgements

I would like to acknowledge the invaluable input of Bruce Russell into the writing of this chapter that ranged from correction of historical detail to incisive and very humorous critical commentary.

# Archive

# Indestructible Energy: Seeing Noise

## *Julie R. Kane*

To me, noise gigs illustrate Carl Jung's concept of synchronicity, the relationship between seemingly random events that develops into an expression of a deeper order, creating an Indestructible Energy.

PentaxK10D.  'By tracing "noise" to its etymological roots [...] The concept of "taste" is intrinsically linked to "nausea".' (Jackson and Jeffrey, 2008)

18–55mm.   I have always tried to document what is happening as well as capturing the emotions of the band and the audience.

10–17mm.   I aim to capture the visual events, lighting, smoke and projections in a way that the viewer can hear the music by taking in the image.

## Image List

Damo Suzuki – The Windmill, Brixton – February 2011
Filthy Turd – The Grosvenor, Stockwell– November 2010
Gnod – Supersonic Festival, Birmingham – October 2010
Gum Takes Tooth – This is DIY, London – June 2012
Gun Cleaner – This is DIY, London – July 2012
Lash Frenzy – Supersonic Festival, Birmingham – October 2010
Mutual Extermination Club – Amersham Arms, London – February 2012
Skullflower – The Grosvenor, Stockwell – April 2011
The Telescopes/Infinite Suns – The King's Arms, Salford – July 2010
Twilit Grotto – This is DIY, London – July 2012
Voltiegers – The Grosvenor, Stockwell – November 2010
Chris and Cosey – ICA, London – February 2011
FulangchangandI – The Dream Machine, London – August 2012
Fushitsusha – St Johns at Hackney, London – October 2012
I Polly Touch – The King's Arms, Salford – July 2010
Keiji Heino – Cafe Oto, London – April 2011
Noble, Ward, Moore – Cafe Oto, London – March 2012
One Unique Signal – Rip This Joint, London – January 2011
Rohame – The Pig and Whistle, Shepherd's Bush – September 2011
Safe (Paul Hegarty) – The King's Arms, Salford – July 2010
Sly and the Family Drone – Supernormal, Oxfordshire – August 2012
Swans – Alexandra Palace, London – July 2011
The Telescopes – Amersham Arms, London – February 2012
The Telescopes/Infinite Suns – The Miller, London – October 2008
Throbbing Gristle – Tramway, Glasgow – June 2009

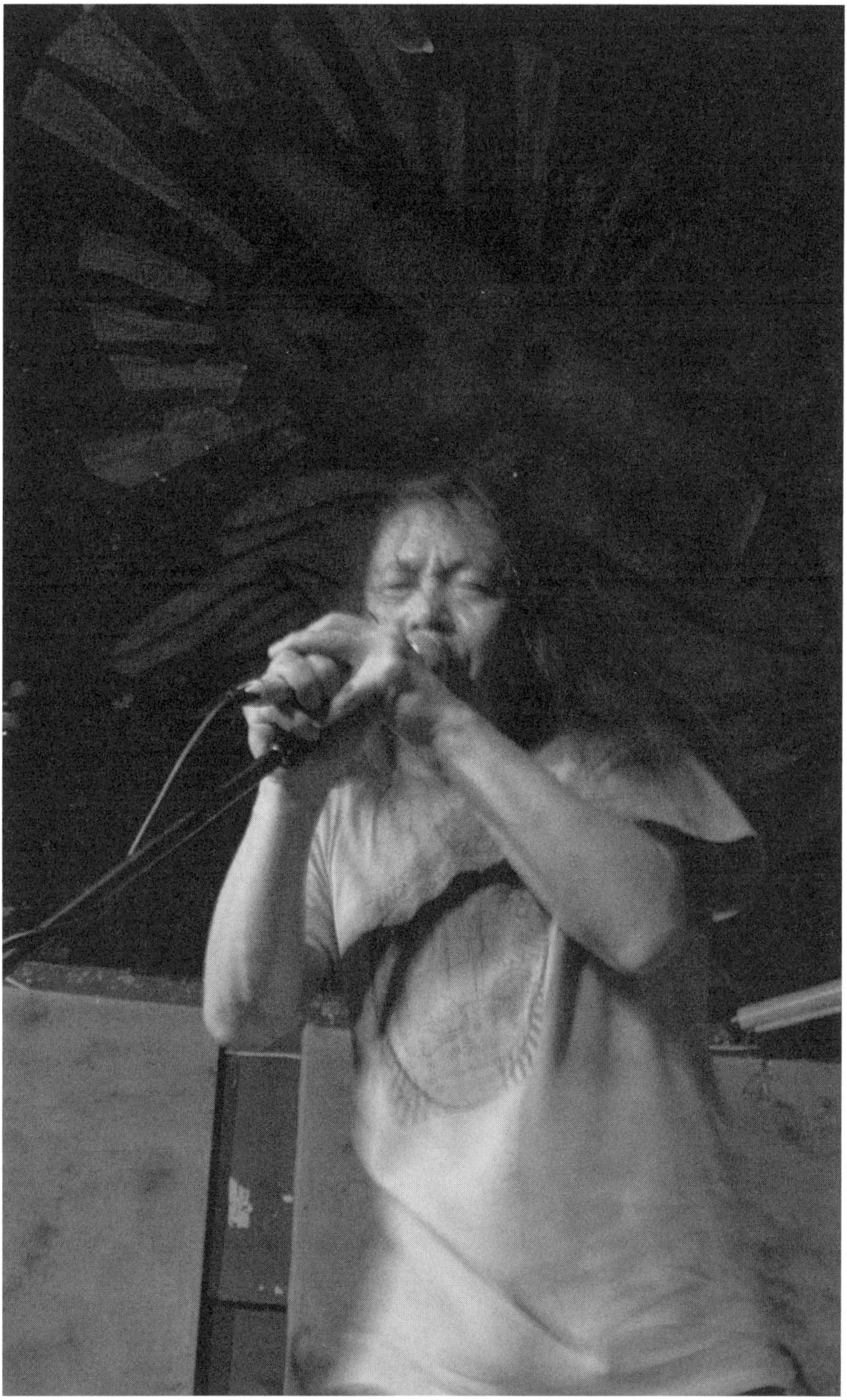

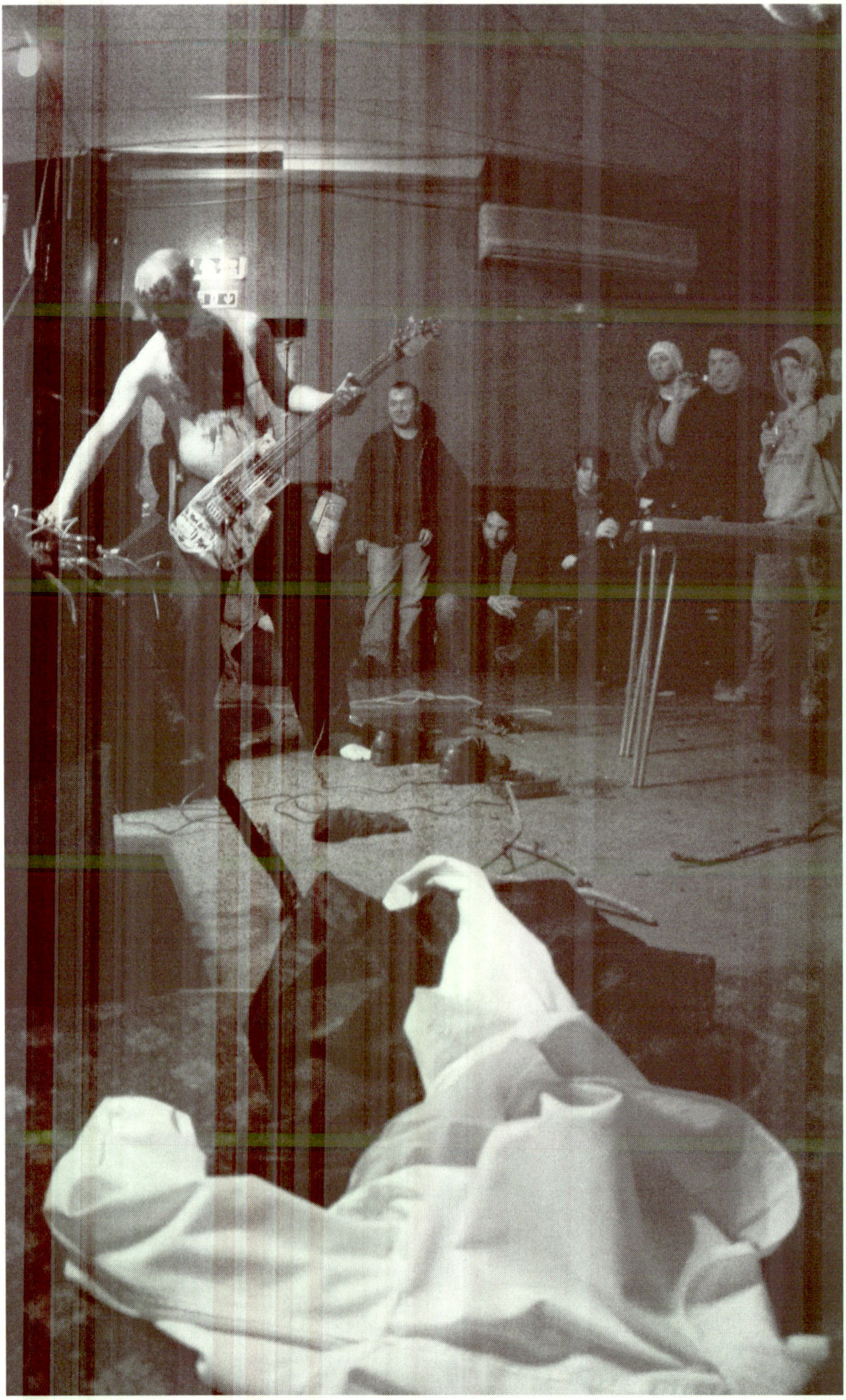

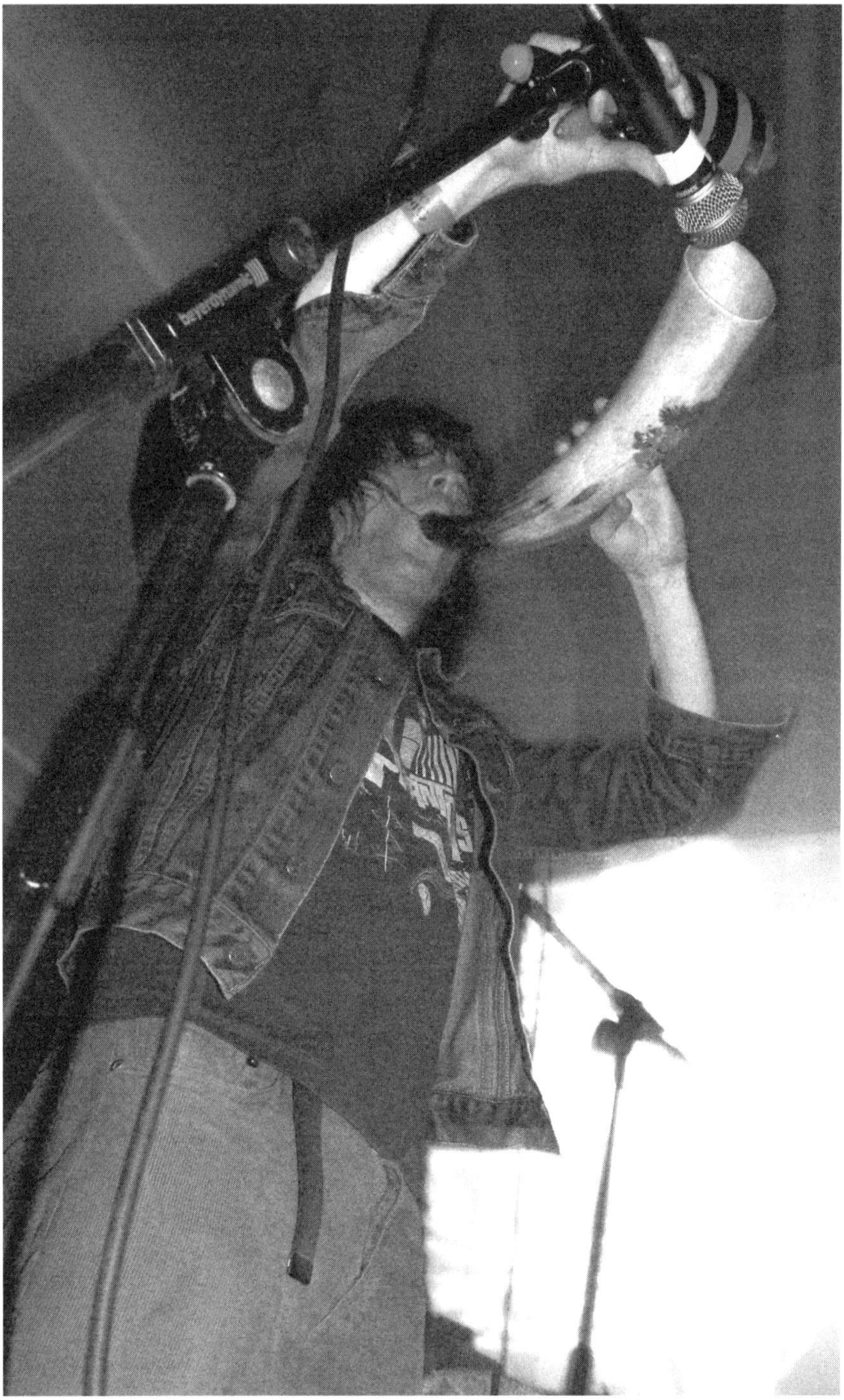

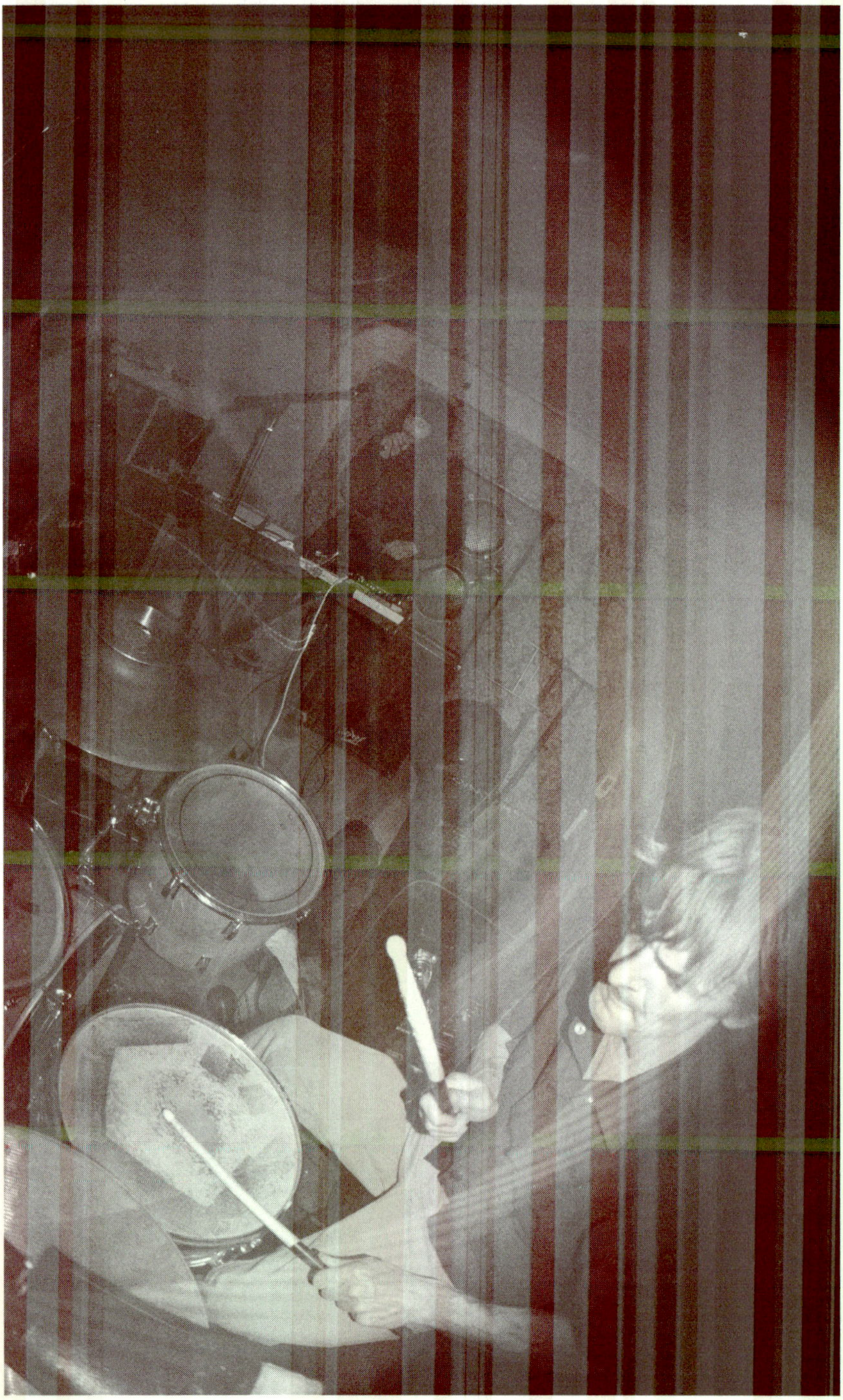

## INDESTRUCTIBLE ENERGY: SEEING NOISE

160 RESONANCES

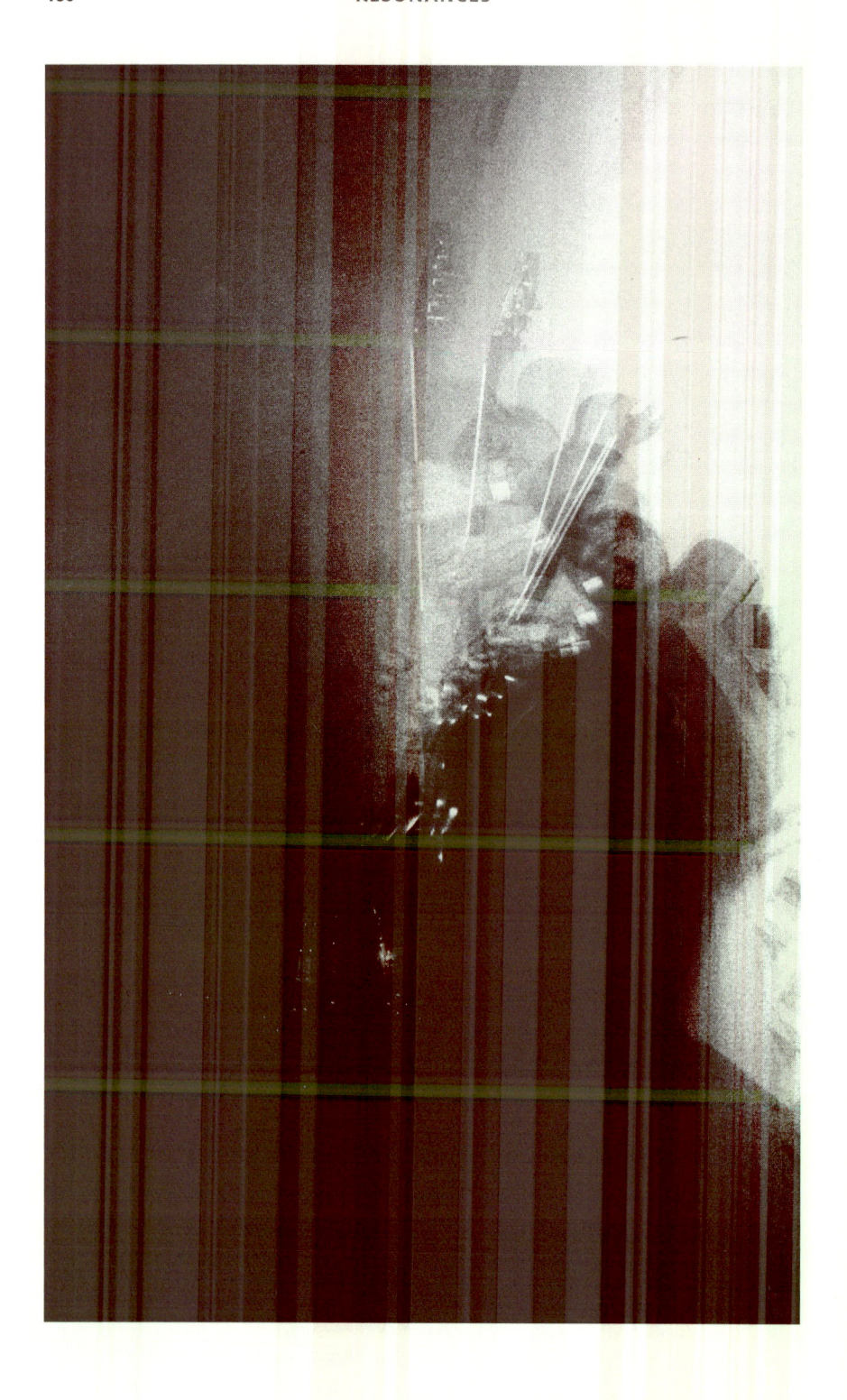

# INDESTRUCTIBLE ENERGY: SEEING NOISE

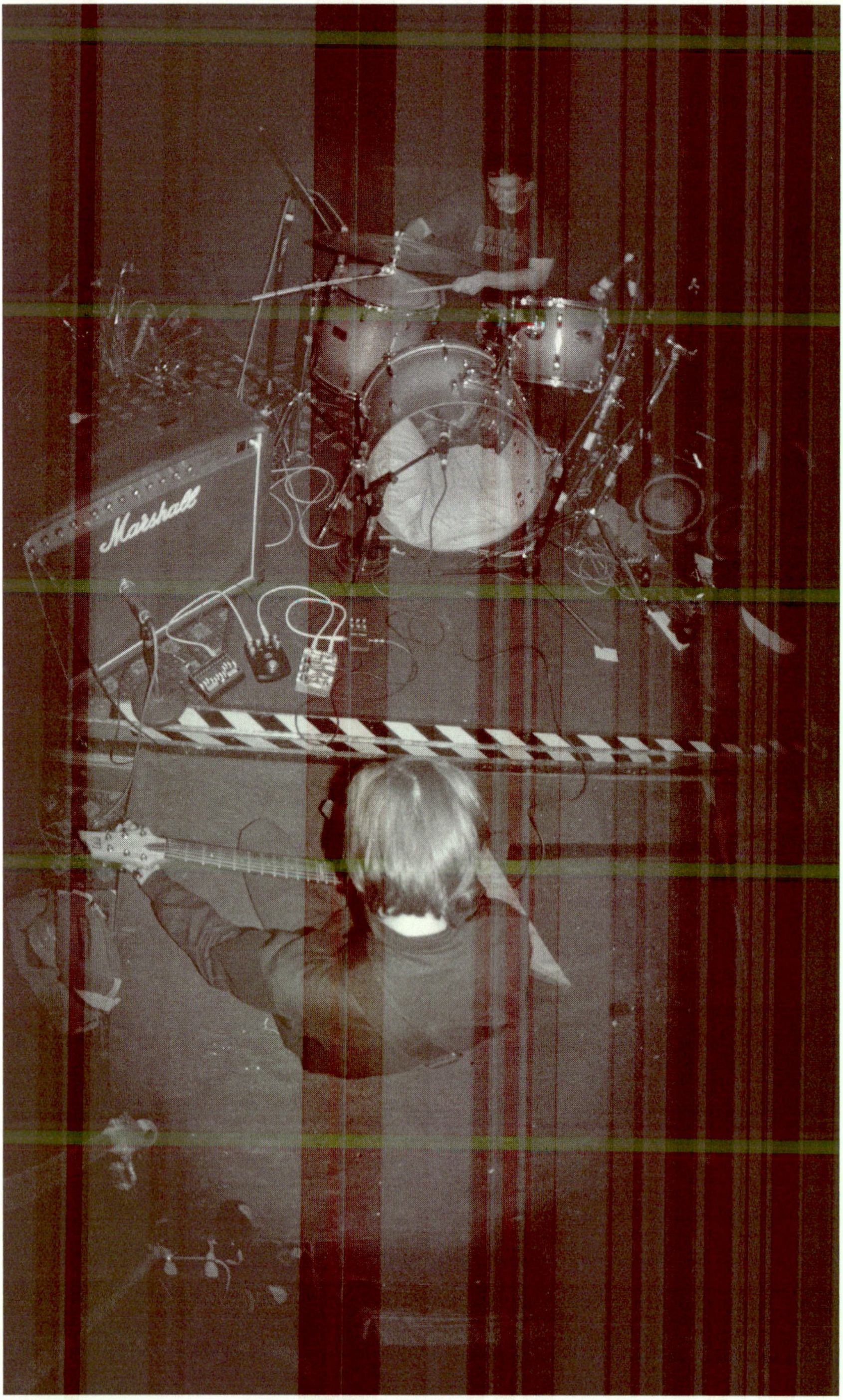
Marshall

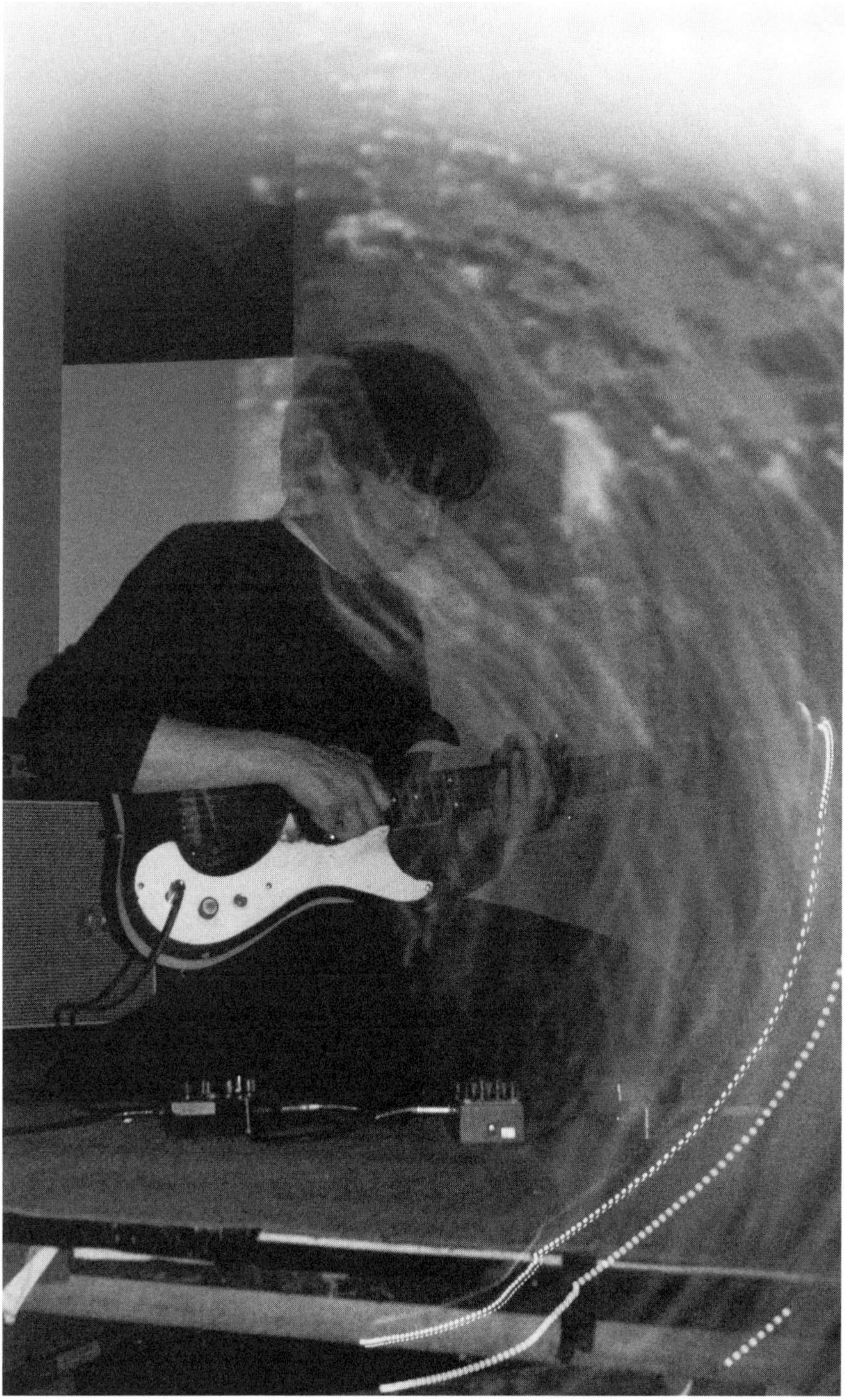

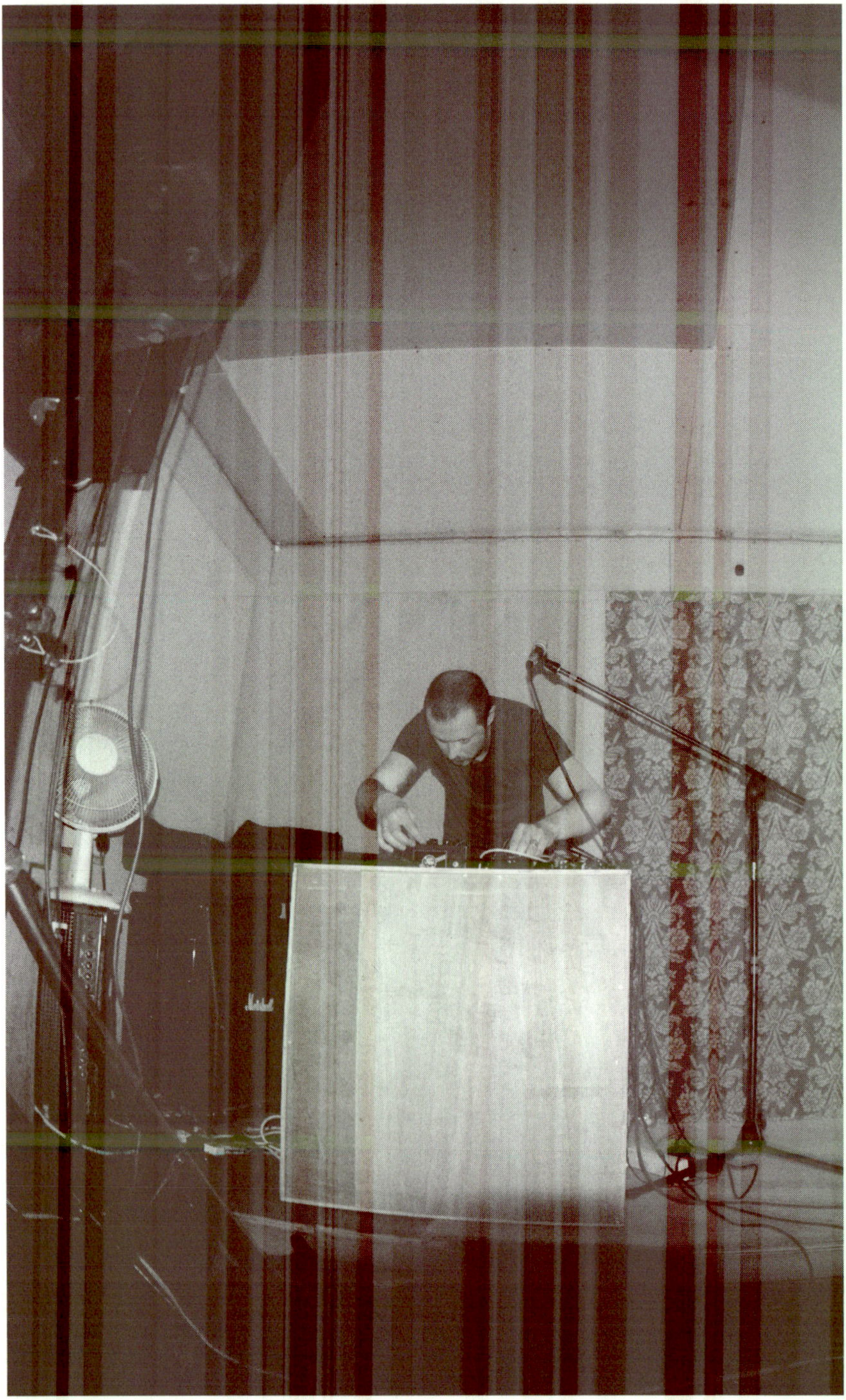

## INDESTRUCTIBLE ENERGY: SEEING NOISE

RESONANCES

# INDESTRUCTIBLE ENERGY: SEEING NOISE 167

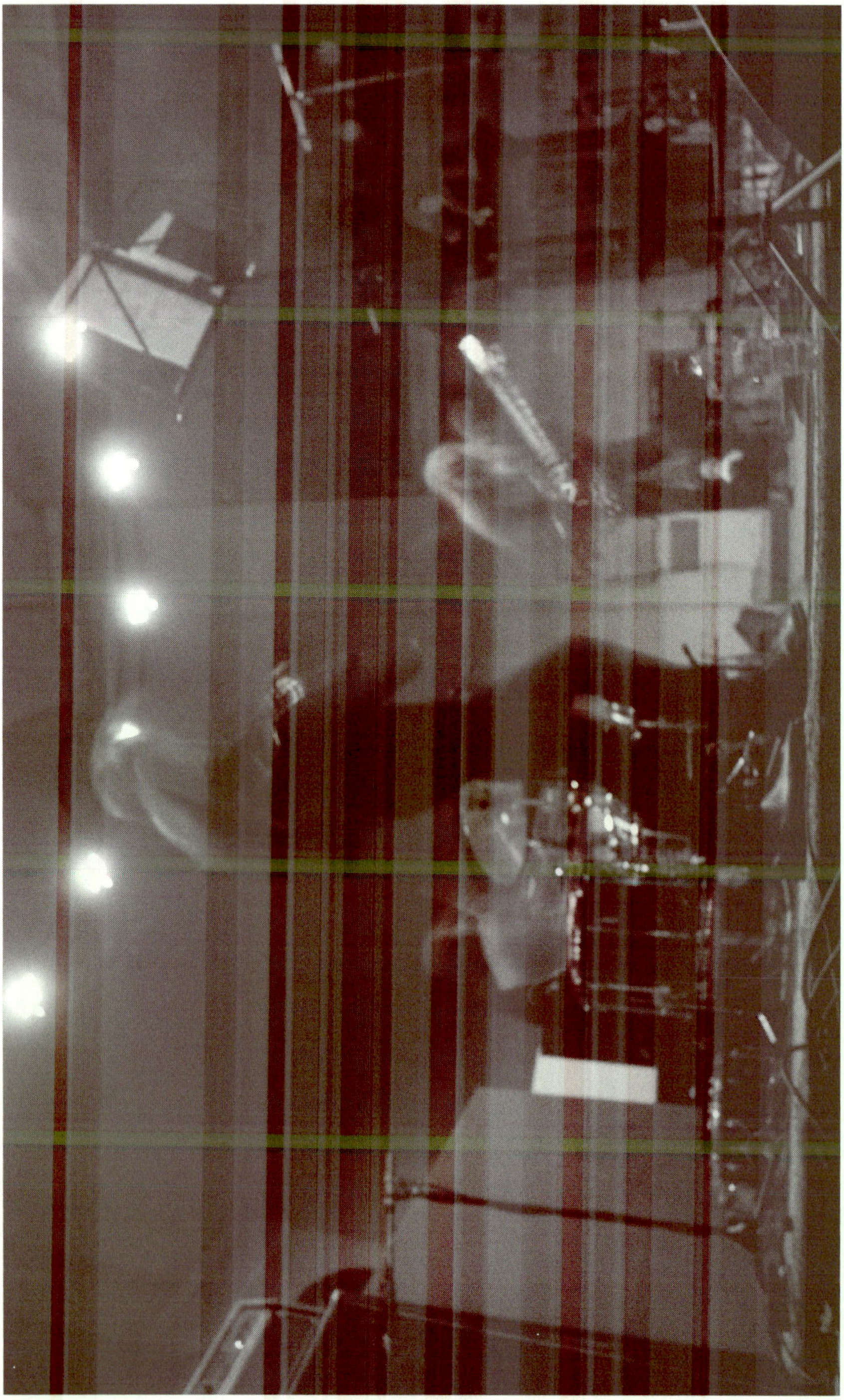

## INDESTRUCTIBLE ENERGY: SEEING NOISE

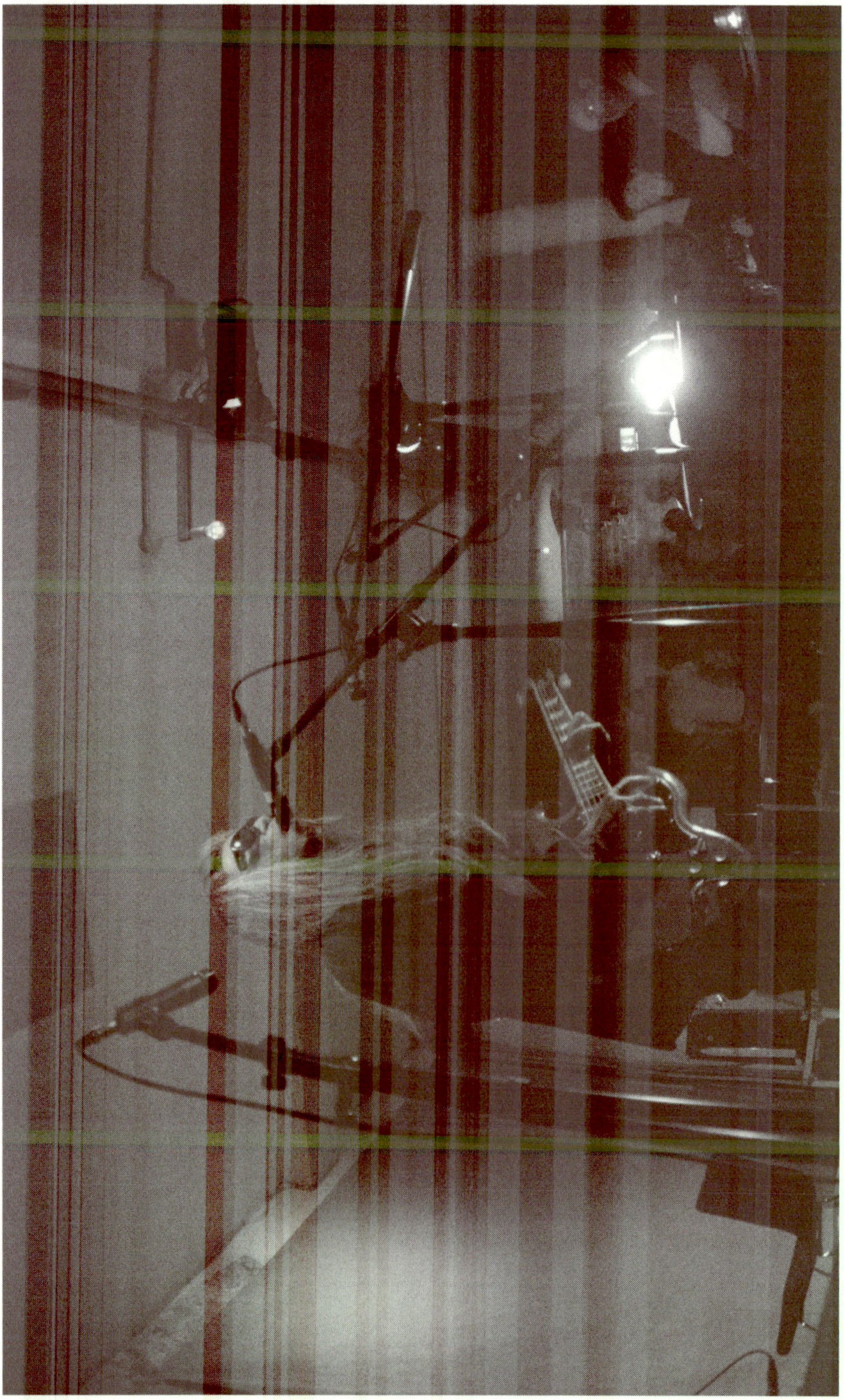

## INDESTRUCTIBLE ENERGY: SEEING NOISE 171

172 RESONANCES

# INDESTRUCTIBLE ENERGY: SEEING NOISE

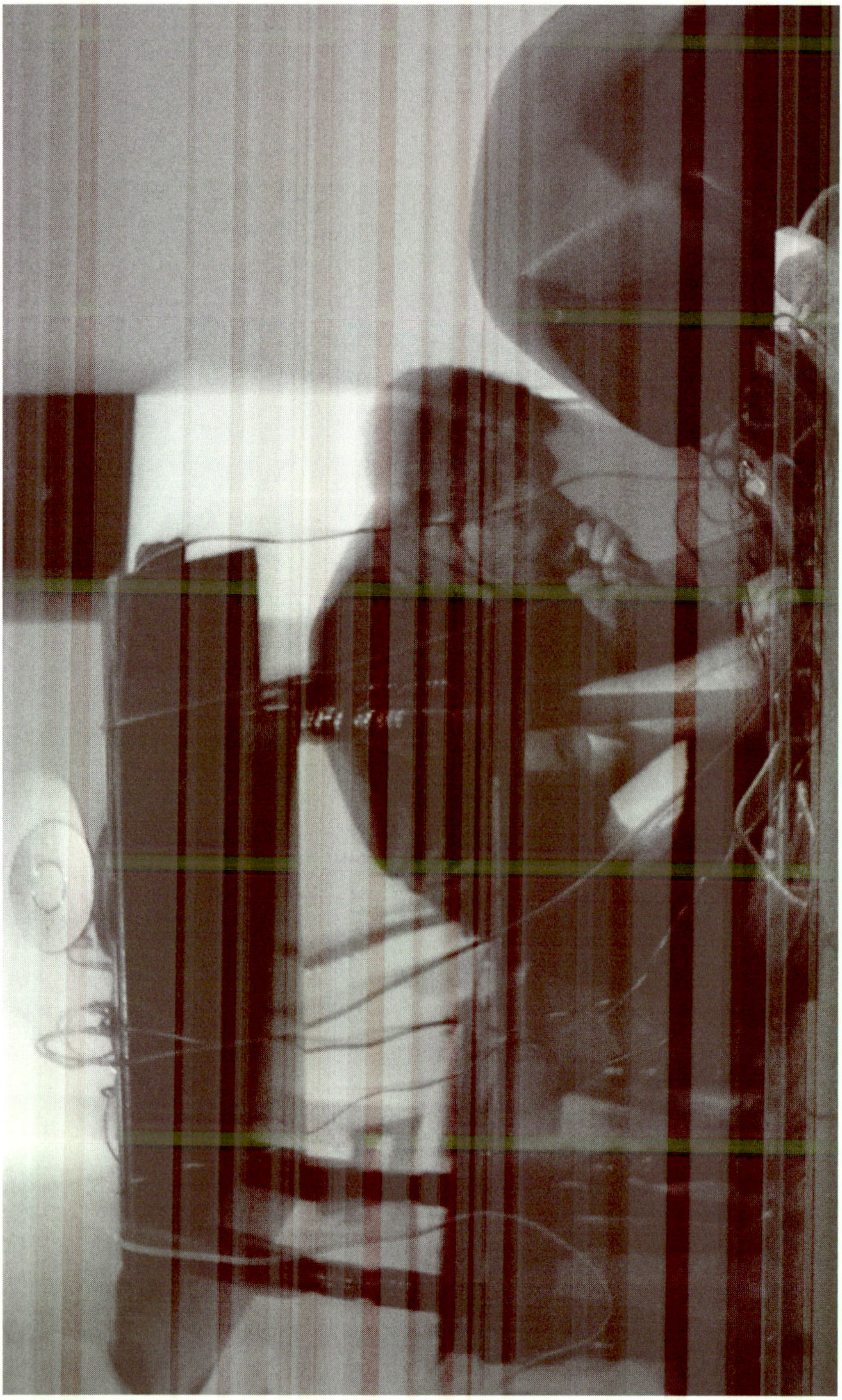

# INDESTRUCTIBLE ENERGY: SEEING NOISE

176 RESONANCES

# INDESTRUCTIBLE ENERGY: SEEING NOISE

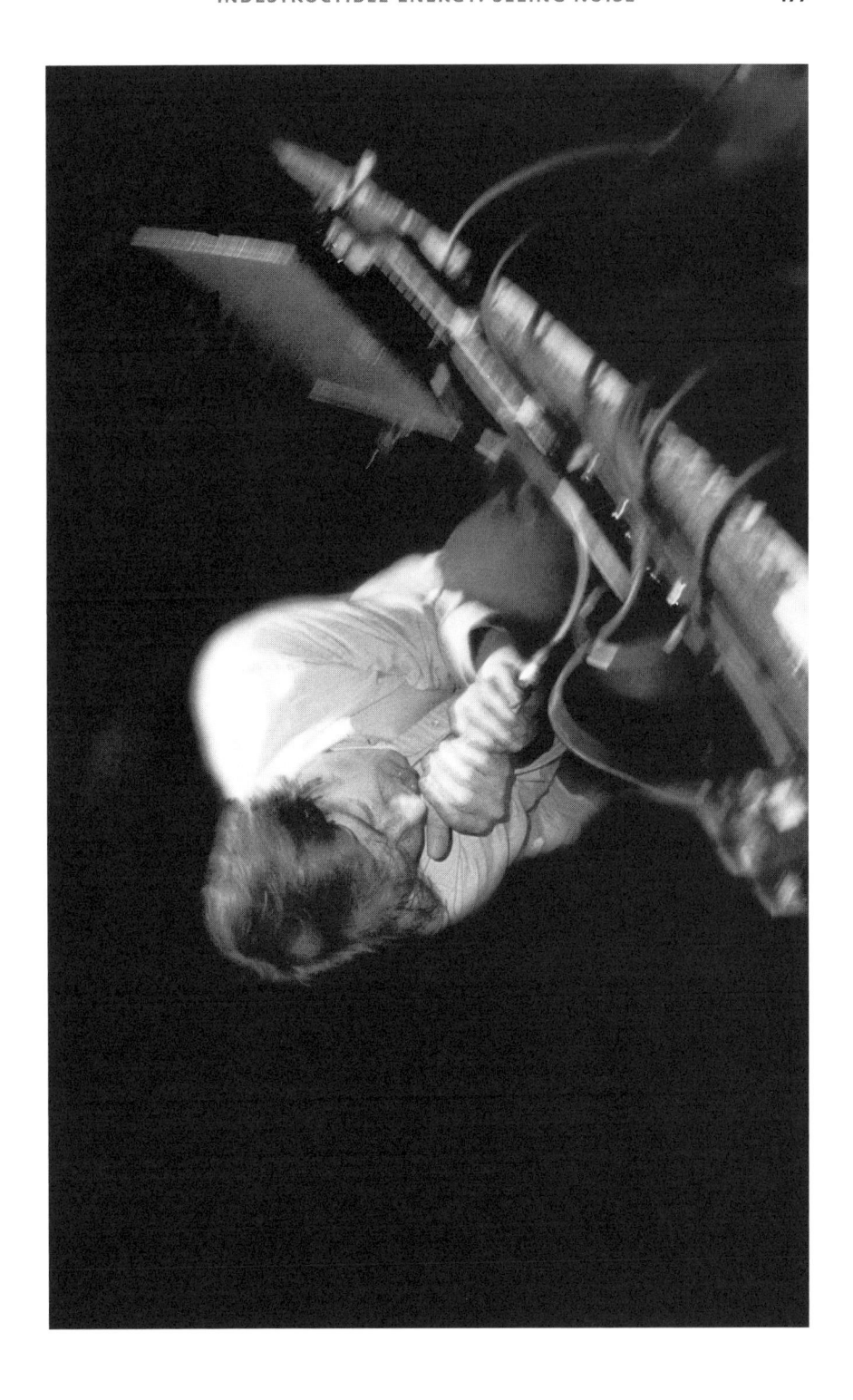

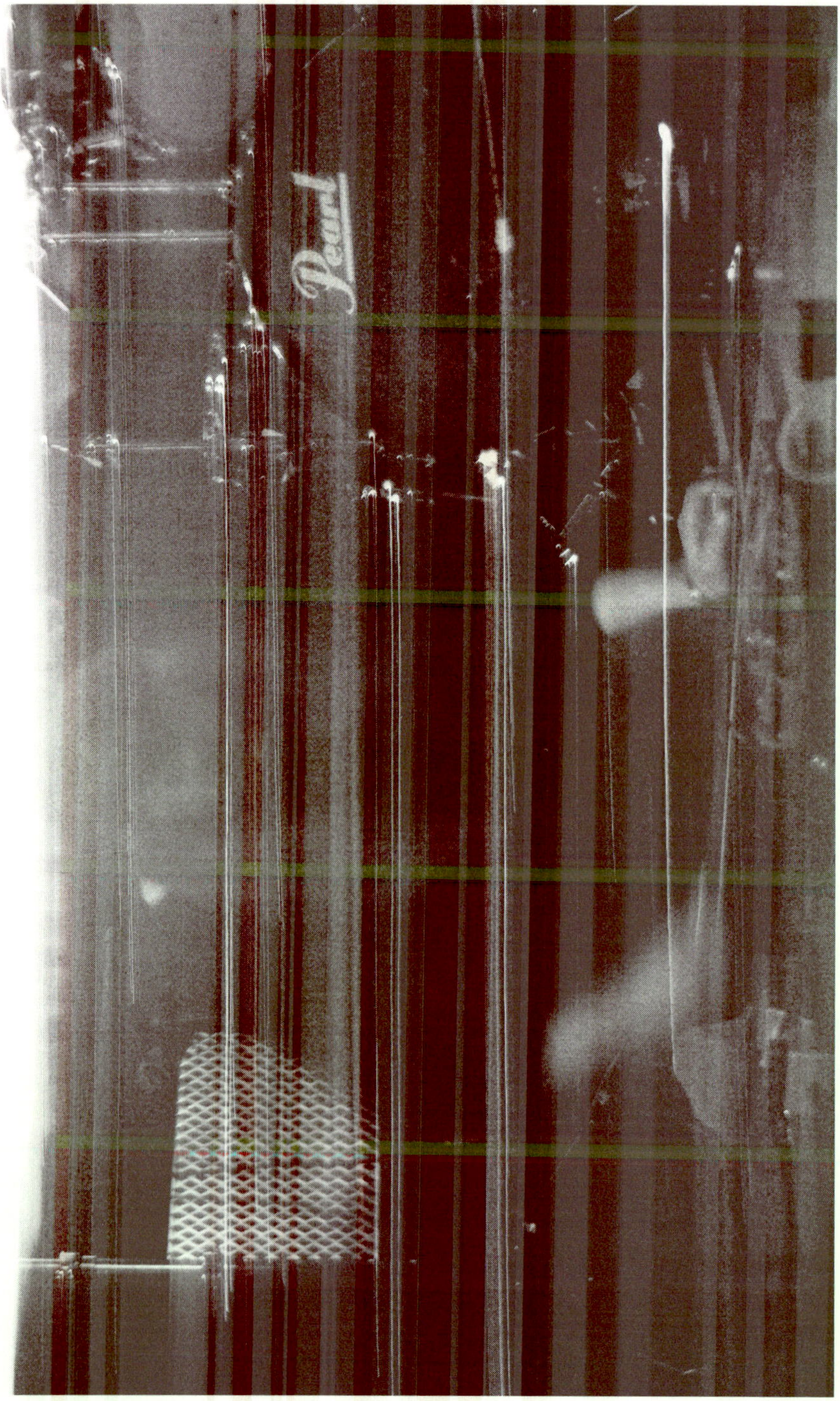
Pearl

# INDESTRUCTIBLE ENERGY: SEEING NOISE

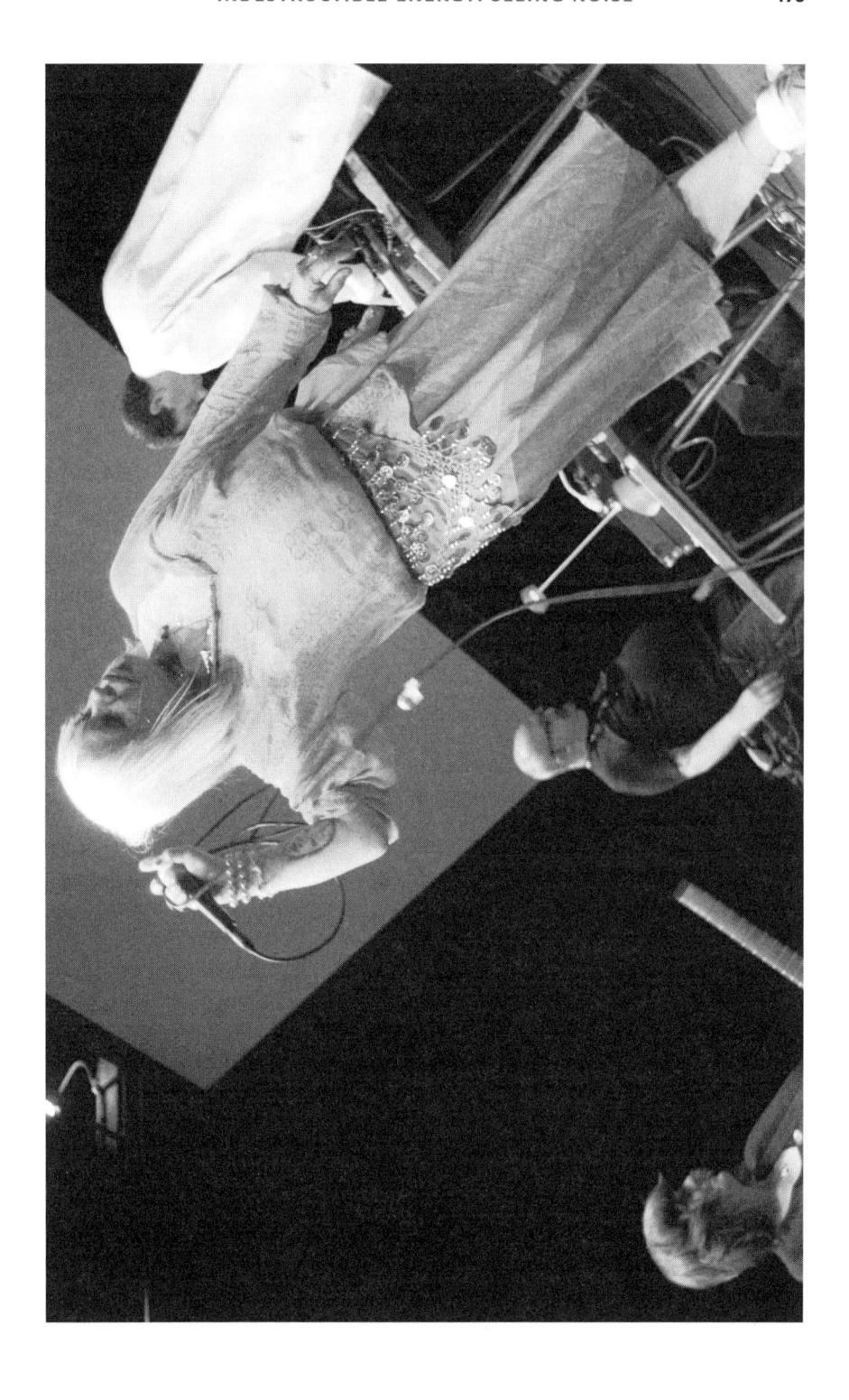

# PART THREE
# Noise, Composition and Improvisation

# CHAPTER TEN

# Xenakian Sound Synthesis: Its Aesthetics and Influence on 'Extreme' Computer Music

*Christopher Haworth*

## Introduction

This chapter presents a genealogy of the noise music offshoot known variously as 'extreme', or 'radical' computer music, as well as 'computer noise'. But the musicological typologies of offshoots and sub-genres that we customarily employ are called into question when it is not music but 'noise' that presupposes them. So the chapter is also an attempt to identify what qualities a sub-genre would honour were it to belong to this family. I argue that every appearance of noise must grapple with this question anew, and further, that this struggle with the fixed classification of genre is a part of noise's aesthetics. As such, the question of what noise is, and how it works in music, is implicit throughout. The chapter works through such issues as noise and genre, noise and influence, and noise and the digital, before moving on to a close examination of the relationship between institutional electronic music and bedroom techno, particularly as it plays out in the work of Florian Hecker and Iannis Xenakis.

## Genealogy

Attempts to historicize and classify noise as genre, sound strategy or object in our everyday sonic environment are complicated by its notorious undecidability. Signal or judgment, absence of meaning or even the condition upon which meaning is made possible,[1] attempts at such a thing as a genealogy of noise must be sensitive to its multifaceted ontological status, its mutability in time and between subjects. As an autonomous entity, noise isn't ever there: it always arises in relation to something else, denying, exceeding, distorting it; and as a single moment in musical history it is as though it never happened. Each showing is a simultaneous withdrawal from view, as what was called 'noise' becomes 'just music' alongside everything else no sooner than it has been recognized. Paul Hegarty (Hegarty, 2008, 13) has argued that noise poses a similar problem of definition as the notion of the avant-garde, for just as the 'announcement of the new' is constrained by its temporal definition, so noise, cacophony and formlessness has the uncanny effect of sounding not so noisy, cacophonous or formless once it has become familiar. And this constitutive undecidability is further complicated by the fact that noise very much *is* a genre, no different from any other. There are noise music festivals, noise music fans, and, like other genres, noise music has its defining figure in the Japanese artist Merzbow. More importantly, we know noise music when we hear it, or at least we think we do: it is loud, aggressive, often distorted, and generally falls far from what we might class as 'organized sound'. Most genre names are conceptually tenuous yet don't elicit the same semantic anxiety: 'avant-pop', for instance, is perfectly oxymoronic. Yet, rather than refuting noise's alterity, 'noise music' actually confirms it, as surplus excess born of the cancelling operation: noise/music. Ray Brassier (2007) has noted a tendency for artists classed as 'noise' to reject the label, and, for different reasons, those to whom I refer in this article do similarly. The contradiction is not trivial. It is the foundation upon which noise, as a positive negation, is built, and to take a single component of noise practice as an object of study requires sensitivity to that. So, rather than talk of 'offshoots' and 'trajectories' when considering the relationship of noise to its constituent parts, we might imagine something like a fractal structure: a self-similar part that the whole is derived from, but which it, at the same time, is contained within. Because while all genres are but names that achieve their identification only within a system of differences, noise never fully owns up to its own. As potential it stands before genre, but as actuality it retreats to the spaces between them: 'between electro-acoustic investigation, free improvisation, avant-garde experiment, and sound art [...] between post-punk and free jazz; between musique concrète and folk; [...] stochastic composition and art brut' (Brassier, 2007, 61).

## Unhearing Led Zeppelin

In 'Just What Is It That Makes Today's Noise Music so Different, so Appealing?' (Hegarty, 2008), Paul Hegarty explores the 'noisiness' of influence as it plays out in the surrealist noise music of Nurse with Wound (NWW) and the New Blockaders (TNB). Hegarty argues that NWW present the 'exhaustion' of influence, the surreal list of seemingly unrelated artists that accompanies *Chance Meeting on a Dissecting Table of a Sewing Machine and Umbrella* (1978) acting to self-reflexively foreground their own historically contingent formation, whilst TNB's vehement 'anti-anti-art' aesthetic represents the 'extinction' of influence. Influence is a system no art escapes but that noise can never sit comfortably within. As with genre, it is both within and without, simultaneously accepting and refusing it. This means that, to all intents and purposes, noise music plays the game of influence in no more exotic a way than it is played in other genres; it *is* exotic, and, as David Keenan (Keenan, 2009) notes, has led to a retroactive shake-up of the canon of British and American rock music, whereby overlooked heavy psychedelic rock bands such as Blue Cheer suddenly receive the acclaim that has been denied them. But this is a familiar pattern of identity formation in music. That the new announces itself in the present by staking its claim on the past is one of the signature emblems of rock music's infinite regress: white blues and American folk are born of similar processes, which is to say nothing of the cultural refurbishment of critically maligned 1980s pop music that recent genres such as 'chillwave' and 'Hypnagogic pop' enact. What distinguishes the reterritorialization of Western rock music that Fushitsusha and other Japanese Improv and noise bands perform, then, is the peculiarly 'noisy' way by which it comes about. Keenan reports:

> I remember a musician that briefly played in Fushitsusha [...] once told me that, growing up in Japan, it was really difficult to get any information on Western rock groups, to actually hear the music. So they would read about it a lot in magazines [...] and [Led Zeppelin] would be described as, like, the loudest rock band ever, monolithic walls of amps [...] But they'd never heard it; they never knew what it sounded like, *so they began to make a music that was based on their idea of what that music would sound like*. And so the Japanese underground in the late 90s evolved out of that, and it became a massively exaggerated, mutant version of rock music. They focused in on specifics and exaggerated them to the nth degree. And this exaggeration, this focus on accidentals – the things that weren't supposed to happen – they focused on these aspects. (Keenan, 2009, my italics)

Keenan emphasizes the fetishization of failure these bands display, but no doubt the most captivating feature in his (possibly apocryphal) tale is the blissful mishearing/unhearing that their geographical remoteness permits. The clean, linear evolution of the Western rock music canon that recursively reinforces itself year on year becomes garbled in its translation across hemispheres: poor distribution forming a blockage in the given channels (or 'noise in the system', if you will). What results, to manoeuvre Seth Kim Cohen (2009) somewhat, is a peculiarly 'non-cochlear' transformation, whereby a mistranslation 'sounds out' an alternative path rock music might have taken. And that the story seems so dubious, so romanticized even, is no doubt because it plays out a fantasy common amongst record collectors. Few rock music enthusiasts can deny the disappointment-ridden path canonically influenced record collecting leads one down. Music journalism that emphasizes the spectacle and awe of rock music can produce expectations entirely at odds with what comes out of the speakers; to put it bluntly – and Keenan's example is as good as any – Led Zeppelin don't sound anything like as good as they're supposed to. Rehearing the past, curating it, isolating the 'good bits' and leaving the remainder, might be *the* modern aesthetic, into which Fushitsusha's amplification of the noisy elements of heavy rock bands feeds directly. But less than isolation and curation, what makes this noise is that it actualizes a latent potential, giving voice to the unvocalized, affective force of rock music history, something that is made possible through a 'noisy' intervention, through a glitch in the self-perpetuating feedback loop of influence. So on the one hand there is a reading of this as a partly humorous hesitation between a romanticized aesthetic of the beautiful and a romanticized aesthetic of noise, evoking 'unheard melodies' of the soul (or Led Zeppelin) and the wrecking of history, progress and canonization; and on the other, a notion of noise as a non-agential, destabilizing force, which, in discarding the message, makes room for the Other, allowing it to be heard.

## Error

Fetishization of failure and error is one of the transcendent aspects of noise music: it crosses the analogue and the digital, the 'harsh' and the 'lower case'. In 2000, Kim Cascone suggested a new genre name based upon the failure tendency as it appeared in the then-modern digital forms of glitch and microsound music. The so-called 'post-digital' aesthetic

> was developed in part as a result of the immersive experience of working in environments suffused with digital technology: computer fans whirring, laser printers churning out documents, the sonification of user-interfaces, and the muffled noise of hard drives. But more specifically, it is from the 'failure' of digital technology that this new work has emerged: glitches,

bugs, application errors, system crashes, clipping, aliasing, distortion, quantization noise, and even the noise floor of computer sound cards are the raw materials composers seek to incorporate into their music. (Cascone, 2000, 12–13)

Ideologically this is a version of noise, since it takes digital to be the pinnacle of audio fidelity (technology driven by the ultimate desire for perfect clarity and the elimination of noise) and situates itself after: after the revolution, amidst the rediscovery of noise through digital malfunction. But where it differs from a more general theory of noise is that, for most of the artists he cites, 'failure' merely describes another technical method whereby electronic musicians can generate new sounds; only in a few cases is it conceptually driven. The distinction might be made clearer if we compare the glitch music of Oval, who Cascone cites in his article, with the noise music of Yasunao Tone. Both make use of similar sound strategies, using 'prepared' CDs that cause the playback technology to 'fail' as the laser misinterprets the information stored therein. But whereas, for Tone, the unpredictability of this technique generates both sound and structure – each performance of *Solo for Wounded CD* (1997) is different because the prepared CD cannot produce the same result on different playings (and this in itself is an undermining of the promise of 'same every time' digital technology) – Oval, despite a lot of obfuscating rhetoric to the contrary,[2] uses the results as 'noises' with which to arrange compositions, and usually with a keen melodic and rhythmic sense.

The distinction sketched here, between a 'noise' indicative of improvisation, unpredictability and technological failure, and a 'tamed' noise, or 'composition using noises', which redirects the practice straight back into a well-established continuum of electroacoustic music derivations, is pertinent when we come to consider the possibility of a 'computer noise'. Indeed, besides the oft-invoked concerns about their physicality and 'liveness', it is one of the chief reasons a great many improvisers have been steadily rejecting laptops over the past decade.[3] Where once the figure of the solo laptop performer was a staple of experimental music performances, in recent years the figure has remained the same but the instrument has changed. Chaotic, idiosyncratic setups using junkshop equipment, DIY analogue synthesizers, dozens of effects pedals, cheap keyboards, microphones etc. tend to preside in modern live electronics performance – a 'post-digital' turn, perhaps, but not in the way Cascone imagined it. What follows can in part be read as a critique of this tendency, which harbours a quiet mistrust of all-digital performance, as though it were not live, not noisy enough. Through the example of extreme computer music (ECM) we will see that noise defines itself outside of the physical/non-physical, analogue/digital prejudgements that underwrite these trends.

## 'Computer music'

A post-techno offshoot, ECM came to prominence in the early 2000s to denote noisy, laptop-based music informed by 1990s techno, ambient, glitch, DJ-ing, industrial, Japanese noise, as well as the 'academic' electronic music styles such as electroacoustic and acousmatic music. Many of the artists linked to ECM have had recordings released on Austria's Mego (latterly Editions Mego) label, but more recently Allon Kaye's Entr'acte and Roc Jiménez de Cisneros' Alku label have been associated with the name. And whereas in the early incarnations these subtle genealogies were more or less implicit, there has been a recent tendency among artists associated with the genre to emphasize them, sometimes to the point of absurdity.

The title to Florian Hecker's *Acid in the Style of David Tudor* (2009) plays on Art and Language's '... in the Style of' series, in which the group ironically delivered portraits of world leaders painted in the formalist, non-representational style of Jackson Pollock. But although the 'acid' to which Hecker's title refers is rendered similarly unrecognizable when channelled through the 'neural synthesis' algorithms of David Tudor,[4] here the juxtaposition serves a very different purpose to that which it references. Less indicating a dry postmodern exercise in appropriation, or even a surreal clash of arbitrary connections akin to NWW's exhaustion of influence, *Acid* voices the very real connections that had emerged between the ostensibly disparate domains of 'institutional' and 'amateur' electronic music. For, due to the new circuit opened up by the internet in the mid- to late 1990s, sound synthesis and signal processing techniques that were being developed in research institutes and published for academic music periodicals such as *Computer Music Journal* were freely circulating amongst musicians who would previously have had little or no access to them – a demographic that could account for the entire roster of the Mego label circa the early 2000s. Cascone had already identified the tendency in his post-digital article, where he praised the new dissemination of knowledge but lamented the fact that the music it makes possible 'rarely makes it back to the ivory towers' (Cascone, 2000, 12). He noted that the post-digital practitioners put the techniques to different uses than they would likely enjoy in the research centres:

> Because the tools used in this style of music embody advanced concepts of digital signal processing, their usage by glitch artists tends to be based on experimentation rather than empirical investigation. In this fashion, unintended usage has become the second permission granted. (Cascone, 2000, 16)

Clearly one could be drawn to see another 'noisy' intervention here. Like Fushitsusha's mistranslation of British and American rock music, the tools and techniques of academic computer music are 'misused' through their being put to unanticipated ends – David Tudor's neural network research 'becoming' acid techno in the journey from the ivory towers to the bedroom studio, perhaps. But when these links are made explicit, as they are with *Acid*, the question arises as to whether Cascone's notion of intended and unintended usages still holds. I want to suggest that ECM is less a product of the crossbreeding of different histories as it is a self-reflexive comment on the situation whereby such hybridization can take place. That is to say, its 'rehearing' is altogether more curatorial than the post-digital aesthetic can encompass.

Cascone's reference to 'permission' implicitly draws a comparison between glitch artists' use of advanced signal processing techniques and sampling etiquette. While the former isn't disrespectful in the sense that sampling is, there is nevertheless a utilitarian attitude to the materials used: those techniques that 'work' are used all the time (FM synthesis, granular processing, or the 'Amen' break etc.), whereas those that don't are dropped, streamlining the range of techniques in circulation by way of natural selection. ECM, on the other hand, has developed into a genre that is almost respectful towards the sources it draws from. Indeed, the very use of 'computer music' over 'electronic', 'electroacoustic' or 'acousmatic' music is itself a form of selective curation, a simultaneously associative and dissociative gesture respective to electronic music histories.

Although there is much debate over what defines these categories, and many artists and musicologists use them interchangeably, the ECM of such artists as Hecker, Marcus Schmickler and Roc Jiménez de Cisneros is characterized by what I would consider to be an ideological preference for sound synthesis over pre-recorded sound, and for algorithmic sound organization over the 'sound sculpting' that might define such forms as electroacoustic/acousmatic composition. This strategy fits a taxonomic definition of 'computer music', which Eric Lyon has given as 'any music in which computation is essential to its production' (Lyon, 2008, 209). But ECM plays equally on the cultural associations of the term, which pertain to the early experimental period of sound creation via computer, when perception, cognition and music research was often conducted in the same centres and by the same people (cf. David Wessel, John Chowning and Max Mathews). This pedigree has bestowed upon 'computer music' an indistinct, slightly dated quality, which has led to attempts to discard the term. Leigh Landy writes:

> Of all the terms here, this is the only one I would like to see disappear in the not too distant future. Computer Music is a term relating to many disparate communities ranging from electroacoustic music to audio engineering to cognition [...] to people creating analyses, traditionally notated scores and computer-based compositions for instruments. (Landy, 2006, 5)

While not strictly speaking an act of reappropriation – computer music has never to my knowledge been used as a disparaging term, at least not popularly[5] – there is nevertheless an 'underdog' claim being made here, an attempt to stake out 'minor' territory in the densely populated sphere of digital music creation. This 'minor praxis', to use Deleuze and Guattari's term (1987), also extends to the appropriative use of sound synthesis and compositional systems.

## Dynamic Stochastic Synthesis

As already indicated, Florian Hecker's work embodies many of the practices discussed so far. He uses complex computer music techniques, 'improving' (in his own words)[6] on various compositional strategies of modernity, such as those of Iannis Xenakis and David Tudor, so as to produce sound works that exaggerate their radical abstractness, often to the point of absurdity. Recently his work has focused on live events such as diffusions and gallery presentations, but his 2003 record *Sun Pandemonium* was crucial in defining an ECM sound. Its centrepiece is a 21-minute epic entitled 'Stocha Acid Vlook'. Though more cryptic than 'Acid', this title again reinforces a 'clash of styles'. Here, acid house meets 'Stocha', or 'Dynamic Stochastic Synthesis' (DSS) – the obscure computer music technique that is used abundantly on the track.[7] DSS is a microsound synthesis technique devised by Iannis Xenakis. Developed from the late 1960s to the end of his life in 2001, it is used in a handful of his published compositions: *La Legende D'er* (1977), *Gendy3* (1991), and *S.709* (1994). DSS is one of a family of 'non-standard' synthesis techniques, so called because they are based on non-imitative, abstract or intuitive models for producing pressure waves, as opposed to the 'standard' synthesis approach whereby sound is simulated 'given a description in terms of some acoustic model' (Holtzman, 1978, 1). Its technical implementation is closely tied to Xenakis's own aesthetic philosophy, and one of the outcomes of this is that the sound it produces undoubtedly bears the aesthetic stamp of its creator. It is 'Xenakian' in a way that other, more utilitarian techniques are not.[8] For this reason, an explanatory digression is required before we can progress further.

Xenakis's model for sound construction was theorized in opposition to the presiding ideologies that drove the work of the major computer music centres during the 1970s and 1980s, namely the focus on the simulation of sound as it is produced (acoustic models) or as it is heard (perceptual models). He singled out in particular the reproduction of musical sounds by way of Fourier analysis, which he saw to be both sonically and ideologically flawed, the use of a technology to recreate existing sounds rather than create new ones. But this is not the simple dismissal it appears to be, an unyielding modernism set only on progress beyond the limited range of orchestral sounds available to music. It is because synthesis using Fourier analysis does *not* approach the complexity of musical sounds that Xenakis is primarily inspired to reject it. For Xenakis, sounds realized in this way are marked by a 'simplistic sonority, which resembles radio atmospherics or heterodyning', and this is due to the fact that 'synthesis by finite juxtaposed elements' (to use his own terminology) cannot, by nature, address the non-periodic, micro-fluctuations in amplitude and pitch that are present in all acoustic sounds. He writes:

> Meyer-Eppler's studies have shown that the spectral analysis of even the simplest orchestral sounds [...] presents variations of spectral lines in frequency as well as in amplitude. But these tiny (second order) variations are among those that make the difference between a lifeless sound made up of a sum of harmonics produced by a frequency generator and a sound of the same sum of harmonics played on an orchestral instrument. These tiny variations, which take place in the permanent, stationary part of a sound, would certainly require new theories of approach, using another functional basis and a harmonic analysis on a higher level, e.g., stochastic processes, Markov chains, correlated or autocorrelated relations, or theses of pattern and form recognition. (Xenakis, 1992, 244)

We can see Xenakis's 'second order variations' as analogous to the way communications theory has come to conceive of noise: not as parasitic upon clear transmission of a message, but as a constitutive element that makes communication possible. Sound synthesis by the summation of static harmonics would therefore be something like the signal sans 'noise', a lifeless, unmusical simulacrum. But when Xenakis invokes the microscopic variations observable in Meyer Eppler's spectral analyses, he is not thinking in terms of more accurate reproduction, and whether the new sounds will be able to perform the concert repertoire. Rather, he proposes that the construction of new sounds follow acoustic principles without imitating acoustic sound. That way they may be novel in the way electronic and noise sounds are, but also complex and pleasing to listen to in the way musical sounds are. To put it in the language of ecological psychology, Xenakis covets 'ecologically validity' – sounds that the auditory system has developed to be able to hear, but that do not necessarily mimic natural sound. The ear's thresholds and limitations, and more controversially, its 'requirements', map out the 'composition space' of DSS.[9] 'The intelligent ear is infinitely demanding,' he writes, adding 'and its voracity for information is far from having been satisfied' (Xenakis, 1992, 244). It is for this reason that we should be careful about proposing Xenakis as a 'noise artist', at least for the time being, even though his compositions may be listened to as though they were noise. DSS was one solution to a technical and aesthetic problem – the creation of 'living' electronic sounds in a computationally efficient way. At its simplest, it can be modelled as an oscillation between two different types of perceptual inertia: the inertia of too little information, as represented by a simple sine wave, and that of too much, as represented by white noise.[10] In this way, the first rule of musical form – namely, that one find 'a successful mean between the opposite extremes of unrelieved repetition and unrelieved alteration' (Scholes, 1970) – is applied to the sounds themselves. So, for all it has proven popular with 'noise' artists, we could equally see DSS's continual fluctuation between the two poles of 'too little' and 'too much' as an attempt to *dodge* noise: the noise of static, 'lifeless', 'not as good as music' sounds.

## Stocha Acid Vlook

Let us now turn to what happens when all this collides with acid house, as is promised by the title of 'Stocha Acid Vlook'. The track is built around a near-static, sawtooth wave drone that gradually changes in spectrum as different harmonics are emphasized, either by a low-pass filter or additive-synthesis technique of some sort. Into this meditative hum is introduced layer upon layer of very chaotic 'voices' that change timbre very rapidly, from near-white noise to buzzing tone. This noisiness is relative to a voice's position in the mix; very noisy voices 'hover' round the edges until they are rather abruptly drawn into focus at ever-decreasing temporal intervals as the piece gains in intensity. The sudden ramp in a voice's loudness is synchronized with a decrease in its rate of timbral flux, so that an individual voice becomes more 'stable' as a consequence of its being brought into focus. During the short time in which it takes precedence the voice has an almost hummable pitch, which is shattered into noise as the timbre becomes aperiodic. It returns 'away' from centre to merge with the other voices, producing an accumulative noise at the back of the stereo image.

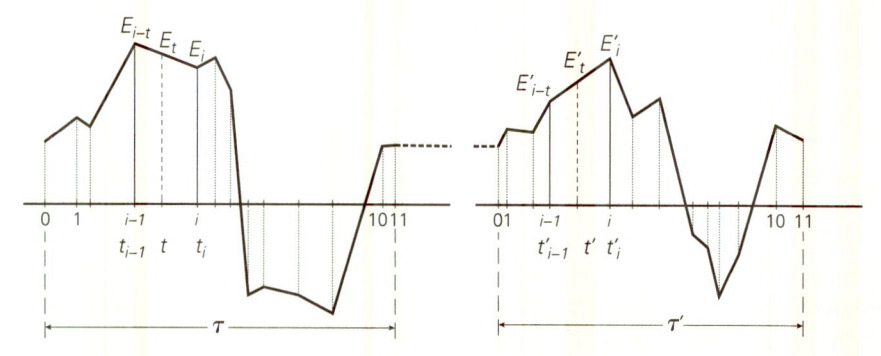

*Abscissa of the polygon's summits (Xenakis, 1992, 290).*

This unstable timbre gives the piece, and the DSS sound in general, its particular quality. Xenakis used Brownian motion to define variable time and amplitude positions of a constantly fluctuating waveform (although an abstract mathematical model devised to describe the movement of particles in gases, it nevertheless turns out to be particularly very well suited to the creation of periodic, yet changing waveforms). Each new value is constrained in terms of how much it can jump from the last value, and it is the amount of constraint that defines the relative smoothness or noisiness of the resulting timbre. When the pitch is hummable it sounds rather like Brownian motion looks: a wavy, drunken line with no tonal centre of attraction.

The spatial movement is the piece's most novel characteristic, since it creates a depth of field not normally achieved in noise-related music. For instance, as a voice that has been rendered into the centre of the image declares itself and then rapidly moves away, it has a three-dimensionality more reminiscent of commercial sound-design. This effect is emphasized by the material, which over time begins to resemble tropical environments. Screeching, banshee-like wails amass rapidly into a whirlwind of noise, suggestive of field recordings of rainforest sounds: bats, birds, monkeys, and so on. The voices continue to accumulate until there is nowhere else to go, and at 9' 0" the underlying drone shifts down in frequency until it becomes inaudible, masked by the din. Having lost its 'floor', inertia sets in as the next ten minutes or so of sound comprises a cascade of hundreds of independently synthesized DSS voices, each oscillating wildly between the front and back of field, white noise and near-stable tone. At around 16' 0" these chaotic sounds are gradually stripped away until the piece quickly fades to silence two minutes later, whereupon there is a short, eight-second 'false' ending. The harsh, rectified sounds are then abruptly resumed and allowed to continue for three more minutes.

Although the piece flirts with the institutional computer music of composers like Agostino Di Scipio in its material, as well as electroacoustic music and drone in form, it is in this 'coda' more than anything else that 'Stocha Acid Vlook' betrays its relation to noise. The false ending functions like a wink to the listener, to acknowledge the unrelenting nature of what we have heard so far. Very abrupt and unpredictable silences are common in the work of 'harsh noise' artists such as Prurient and Russell Haswell, and we might even see it as a reference to the 'drop' in electronic dance music. But in 'Stocha' the drop does not function as a tension-building device; it is more humorous, at most a nod to the excessive, punishing tendencies of some Japanese noise music. It underlines, in a somewhat juvenile way, an already obvious absurdity whereby what, in electroacoustic music, is usually a softer, more subtle mimetic quality takes on elements of the grotesque. If we follow Simon Emmerson's division of electroacoustic music into language and syntax (Emmerson, 1986), then we might say that Stocha

Acid Vlook represents a monstrous example of his 'combination of aural and mimetic discourse with abstract syntax' category. Mostly abstract, over time the cartoon-like chatter of abstract sounds sharply advancing and retreating starts to invoke horror films, an alternatively soundtracked, surround-sound version of Alfred Hitchcock's *The Birds* (1963), perhaps.

## Total composition/anti-noise

We have arrived at an understanding of 'Stocha Acid Vlook' as a kind of simulation, noise as a final aesthetic rather than as process. Where Oval's careful organization of sounds derived from noisy processes coalesces into shimmering, bouncy pop, here the outcome, conversely, is noise – noise simulacra. In the brief discussion of the technical implementation of the DSS technique necessary to study the piece, we touched upon a method of composition already far removed from any conception of noise, or so it seemed. Now we need to examine this further, for although in histories of twentieth-century music the discovery of noise and electronic sound tend to go hand-in-hand, driven as they are by the same progressive urge for new sounds beyond the range of the orchestra, their implications for composition are diametrically opposed. Cage's 'let sounds be themselves' was a call to freedom from intentional organization, offering a music more like natural sound; with nothing to express, sound-in-itself promised a music that just 'is'. But microsound composition allows the composer's intention to stretch further than it ever could previously, all but enabling the ultimate goal of *Elektronische Musik*: the 'real musical control of nature'.[11] On the working processes of Horacio Vaggione, Curtis Roads writes:

> Micro-montage is what Horacio Vaggione does. [...] He will load about a hundred sounds. Then he picks one out, and puts the mouse down there on the timeline. And then he picks another one out, and puts the mouse down there. And he does that seven days a week, for six weeks, and then he has one of his compositions – and it is essentially all composed by hand – tens of thousands of sound particles, like brush-strokes in a Pointillist landscape. (Roads, 2010, 6)

Microsound composition makes something like 'total composition' conceivable, whereby every aspect of music right down to the atomic level is released to precise, intimate control. Timbre, once the 'final frontier' of music composition, need no longer be given from without; it becomes *form*, a temporal structure that can be designed like any other. The perennial gap between idea and realization is further closed, prompting Xenakis to adopt near-revolutionary rhetoric in his 1991 ICMC paper, where he likened composition of new works using DSS to the big bang: musical composition can begin *ex-nihilo* (Xenakis, 1992, 295).

But noise works against all forms of control, especially the control of the creative act itself. This is why, where the musician traditionally tries to master his instrument so as to draw sound ever closer to intention, we find that the 'noisician' often deliberately unlearns or unplays his. In the common recourse to extreme, sometimes violent improvisatory practices, noise pursues a pure spontaneous action unrestrained by forethought or a rewriting that would return the object closer to a preconceived idea, however subconscious. (We could say that this return is inevitable anyway, but noise acts as if this isn't so.) So where, to sketch out a broad schematic, the performer employs improvisation as a tool with which to bring about surprise at what she herself produces, thus forcing her to be *present*, listening and responding here and now, in noise this can become a masochist desire to induce humiliation, self-disgust or altered states. Justice Yeldham uses volatile, dangerous media to intensify the critical moment of improvisation – most notably, a pane of glass fitted with amplified contact mics which he sucks, blows and mauls until it breaks, usually lacerating his skin:

> It's also quite cathartic experience for me, if I can say such a word without being taken for a wanker. When I play I get into an ecstatic state, lost in the music, almost so much that the pain simply doesn't register. I honestly don't perceive the pain while playing. I'm more likely to wince when cleaning up afterwards and get a small shard stuck in my figure [sic] even though earlier I was shoving its parent piece down my gob! (Weingarten, 2005)

This kind of noise performance echoes the extreme performance/body art of artists such as Chris Burden, whose works become ritual exercises in self-transcendence that anticipate ecstatic states bordering on unconsciousness. Noise is created as the by-product of a transgressive act, the 'accidental' outcome of this physical disruption. Cast alongside this, then, would it not be more appropriate to propose works using micro-to-macro sound design as a heroic form of *anti-noise*, whereby potentially no aspect is left open to indeterminacy?

## S.709

Let us now consider the question of total composition as it pertains to one of Xenakis's own works using DSS, *S.709* (1994). After 'Stocha Acid Vlook', one could almost be persuaded one were listening to the same piece, with two or three voices soloed in the mix. But this seven-minute work is aesthetically the most unforgiving and raw of any created using DSS. In the earlier *Gendy3* (1991), Xenakis had used post-production cuts and edits to create high-level form, 'crafting' a sense of development out of what was essentially a series of immobile, formless sections. *Gendy3* is characterized by crude juxtapositions of static electronic atmospheres, which vary in colour from being very noisy to almost consonant. The 'noise' of stasis is again circumvented, this time by the creation of an illusory 'form-giving' forward movement. *S.709,* on the other hand, is stark and uncultivated. It sounds like the straight-to-file output of his GENDYN software.[12] A formally static piece, the few DSS voices perpetually oscillate between variable, descending tones and chaotic, arrhythmic behaviour, with no real development beyond these binary positions. The descending tone has a piercing, tinny whine that resembles something like a wasp or buzzing insect, and this organic quality is mirrored by its repetitive behaviour. As it emerges from broadband noise and descends each time to the same ticking, arrhythmic loop, it appears to be responding to some force of attraction, like a moth going towards the light.

Since the high-level formal development of *Gendy3* is never attempted in this piece, we have access to what feels like an earlier 'moment' of composition. It is as though we hear it in the same state as Xenakis himself first did, and what clear, global authorial decisions can be discerned serve only to strengthen this radical disconnect between sound and form, or authorial agency. There is little in the way of development during the 7' 4" duration, and the final sound is cut off midway towards its irregular descent. These operations are performed *on* the form rather than in correspondence with it; it is as though the sound itself is starkly ambivalent, a constant becoming with neither origin nor destination. To quote Gerard Pape, 'here we have Xenakis's view of death: death is no grand finale ... and at some point, we just stop being' (Pape, 2002, 19).

## Conclusion

In *S.709* we hear the sound of micro-level instruction being rendered audible, sound and form becoming indistinguishable. As compositional 'decisions' pass too quickly for them to be heard as such, high-level structure emerges all by itself; 'intention' is translated as timbre, and form becomes a kind of noise. An obvious correlation suggests itself, between sample-by-sample composition of sound and the frame-by-frame description of movement we see in animation. *S.709* is an audible rendering of the same effect we notice in the Claymation cinema of Ray Harryhausen, where a 'false movement' emerges as a consequence of a static form becoming dynamic.

Gilles Deleuze considered animated movement to be 'foreign to cinema' because the individual instants from which it is comprised are themselves 'privileged' (i.e. composed). For Deleuze, true cinematic movement could only arise if the individual moments were each inconsequential; he called this the 'any-instant-whatever' (Deleuze, 2002, 3). The 'foreign' movement of animation that the succession of privileged instants produces could equally be called uncanny, since what comes forward is the almost-human, the almost-natural, the feeling of the Other in the same. There is a famous anecdote about the painters Hans Hofmann and Jackson Pollock's first meeting that is pertinent here: Hofmann said of Pollock's work, 'Ach! You work by heart, not from nature', to which Pollock replied, 'I am nature' (Friedel et al., 1998, 82).

Noise, in such 'total composition' paradigms as dynamic stochastic synthesis, would be what is produced from the breakdown of this operation, from the failure to convincingly produce a second nature. It is where we can say that non-standard synthesis techniques come into contact with the self-transcending techniques of anti-instrument practitioners, such as in the early Merzbow. For while the desire for artistic agency to 'get outside of itself', trip itself up, and speak with the voice of the Other is a common artistic goal, it is in its failure that we discover something particular to noise; a 'genre characteristic', perhaps …

# CHAPTER ELEVEN

# Sound Barriers: The Framing Functions of Noise and Silence

## *Alexis Paterson*

The framing function pervades our daily lives. The ways in which frames define boundaries and barriers between a thing and its other are visible in both our language and our behaviour: time*frames*; window or door frames that provide portals between inside and out; the structural frame that supports or shapes an object (a bed, a playground attraction, a computer network), and the action of 'framing' itself (when taking a photo, articulating a concept, or a 'frame of mind', for example). Each of these instances demonstrates the commonplace nature of the frame, a feature that is just as easily overlooked in the field of cultural consumption: the frames of pictures, films, music and sculpture. This article seeks to explore the commonplace nature of the frame, and then to ask what general effect twentieth- and twenty-first-century artistic developments might have had on this function, and specifically, to explore the way in which 'noise' (and the concurrent reconceptualization of 'silence') has contributed to a blurring of the traditional boundaries between a performance event and the space that surrounds it. To do this, a particular emphasis will be placed on the development of so-called minimalist works, particularly those that bear a direct inheritance from the experimental practices of John Cage. Since La Monte Young's drone pieces focused on 'getting inside the sound', the durational extremes of minimalism have challenged classical notions of teleology and form. Applied to the wider context of noise composition, the same elements of minimalist music that led Tim Page (1981) to describe it as an exercise in 'framing the river' raise questions about how music that defies traditional framing functions through the blurring of boundaries between work and space can be dealt with in musicological discourse.

Richard Littlefield (1998), in his article 'The Silence of the Frames', examines the various ways in which frames function across the arts. He sets out four qualities of the frame, which, he argues, are universal. First, he suggests that the purpose of the frame is to identify an object as 'art'. Littlefield writes: 'the frame separates the work from its context. In doing so, the frame enshrines an object, thereby bringing it to our attention as beautiful form or "art". The frame provides us with an object that can have intrinsic content' (Littlefield, 1998, 217). Secondly, he argues that the function of a frame is only made possible by virtue of the fact that we understand its purpose: the frame must be recognized as such. Littlefield explains:

> the frame must not be considered part of the art work, even though physically attached to it. Thus, the frame also separates the work from the frame itself. [...] in relation to the work, the frame seems to disappear into the general context (such as a museum wall); in relation to the general context, the frame disappears into the work. Therefore the frame belongs fully to neither work nor external context. (Littlefield, 1998, 217)

Thirdly, Littlefield suggests that the frame should be viewed as 'contingent': the frame is only recognized as such because of the work it contains. This third characteristic reveals the symbiotic relationship of frame and content that is implied in the first quality of Littlefield's description, and leads him, in his fourth and final criteria, to a contradiction of sorts, since the frame, he insists, is also *necessary*. He explains this contradiction thus:

> the frame *defines* the work by *confining* it. This is a paradox in the rigorous sense; the frame is not contingent *or* necessary, but both contingent *and* necessary at one and the same time. It is impossible to decide logically where the borders of the frame stop and the work begins or where the borders of the work stop and the frame begins. (Littlefield, 1998, 218)

While, to a certain extent, Littlefield is talking figuratively in this final criteria (since, in once sense, it is a simple enough task to identify the varnished or painted batons of wood, or the crisp edges of a photograph's mount, and describe the physical dimensions of a frame), the point he is making about the difficulty of separating the experience of viewing 'the painting' from 'the frame' is an important one. It is easy, when you recall any gallery full of Rembrandts or Cezannes, to see how these criteria describe the way the frame works very well. No matter how uniform the frame around one's contemplative subject(s), it not only signifies an artwork while remaining 'apart' from that work, but it regulates the experience of viewing – the frame acts as a marker at which to set one's peripheral vision (for a large painting) or a definitive area on which to focus (for a smaller one). In a room full of paintings, this division draws our attention to the status of the single artwork: to the masterpiece. Yet Littlefield pays little attention to what the actual *placement* of the works (with their frames) *inside* the gallery or museum might mean in terms of a kind of 'secondary' frame. Do we look at artworks on the decorated walls of stately homes in the same way as we do in the more clinical surroundings of most galleries, for example? In the ballroom of an eighteenth-century Regency home, where decorative wallpaper or ornate panelling behind a series of portraits draws the eye across the patterned expanses of these rooms, does it encourage the viewer to see these successive frames as a series? As ancestry writ large across walls that accumulate the status of history and heritage with every successive tourist's footfalls? And how do these hallowed halls relate to music? How – from such relics – do we reach noise?

To answer such questions, the fundamental changes to the qualities of the frame that took place in the visual arts during the twentieth century must be addressed, and it is here that minimalism comes to the fore as the clearest expression of the changing nature of the frame. Consider Barnett Newman's 1949 painting *Onement IV*. This, as the title suggests, is the fourth in a series of six paintings that Newman began in 1948 and finished in 1953. The paintings all consist of a saturated colour field, intersected by a vertical stripe – or 'zip', as Newman called them – but *Onement IV* is particularly striking due to the monochrome contrasts of black background and white stripe and the perfect uniformity of the lines (the first *Onement* is a more ragged-edged and colourful affair, with a burnt orange strip against a deep red block of colour). And importantly, the impact of *Onement IV* is enhanced by the absence of a physical, external frame. Hanging on the white, sanitized walls of the Metropolitan Museum of Art in New York,[1] *Onement IV* gives the viewer an impression of peculiar rupture; on the one hand, it is easy to see where the dimensions of the painting begin and end, easy to point to the material edges of the painting. But on the other, the wall that it hangs on – the space around it – seems to be somehow altered. It's almost as though this 'zip' draws the surrounding wall *into* the field of the painting. Yet the 'framing function' – the fourfold action that is marking the work as 'art', that is identifying the object 'frame' as separate, and that is making that object contingent and necessary – must surely be present (if Littlefield is correct) for the work to function as 'artwork'. If this is the case, then what might be taking the place of this physical frame? The shadows cast on the gallery wall from a deep canvas standing proud of the plasterwork? Perhaps the submerged frame: the rough batons that shape the canvas and give depth to the depthless surface through the extension of the block colour onto the painting's edges? Or is it simply the placement of the painting: the decision to situate it in a gallery, to assign a title, a small explanatory placard, and an eagle-eyed gallery steward? Perhaps even the memory of this context – the photograph of the gallery, the postcard, the description – simply the *fact* of having been assigned the status 'artwork', provides a conceptual frame in which *Onement IV* demands to be contemplated.

It is Newman's first work of the series, *Onement I*, that Edward Strickland singles out to mark the beginning of minimalism across the arts (2000). Strickland's book, *Minimalism*, remains one of the most comprehensive surveys of this emerging trend (the use of the term 'movement' is avoided precisely because of the lack of genuine interdisciplinary aesthetic motivations that Strickland and other commentators demonstrate so frequently). In music, Strickland argues that minimalism only emerges a decade later, with that crystalline stasis of Young's *Trio for Strings* in 1958, while in sculpture, film and dance, he dates minimalism still later, to various activities taking place in the run-up to 1961, at which point he argues that they become a coherently minimalist trend. However (and importantly when considering the place of the frame, or, where 'art' begins and 'reality', or 'life', ends), Strickland also firmly places the roots of minimalism in the Cageian experimental tradition: 'Minimal dance [...] is foreshadowed by Merce Cunningham's work from the late 1940s onwards to roughly the same degree as the work of Cunningham's comrade John Cage adumbrated developments in Minimal music' (Strickland, 2000, 10). That Strickland chooses to highlight Cage's and Cunningham's activities as a root of much minimal exploration is significant, given Cage's interest in the sonic environment, for it is this blurring of the boundaries between 'music' and 'sound' that Cage explores (and indeed, the blurring between modes of performance and visual arts that are so evident in Cage/Cunningham collaborations)[2] which plays an important part in the changing nature of the musical frame.

So when considering music – or indeed, any art form that exists in time as well as space – how does Littlefield envisage the frame? For him, the presence of *silence* is the key parameter of the musical frame: music is marked as such by an absence of auditory stimulation, which, he argues, is present before the commencement of a performance. To understand Littlefield's assertion, one need look no further than a traditional concert setting. Imagine that you have, first of all, much of the activity that could be described as 'secondary' framing (in the same way that Littlefield does not consider the secondary frame of the gallery wall, the secondary frame of the performance space is not discussed in his article): an audience member goes to the 'concert' hall; has a pre-concert drink, or perhaps orders one for the interval (an action that reinforces an expectation of the *form* the event will take); perhaps the concert-goer buys a programme. It is at this point that secondary framing experiences become more personal and subjective: if the purchase is made, one might read the programme before the concert begins, thereby gaining a structural knowledge of the work, and introducing a cognitive 'frame' that comprehends the repertoire's musical dimensions[3]. If the programme is read after the event, the experience may be to add detail, or to give structural coherence, to the mental space that is the memory of the performance.

As the start time of the concert approaches, the secondary framing experiences of the audience once again begin to coalesce. Seven-thirty approaches; a tannoy or bell announces a final call for the audience to take their seats; fixed entry points to the hall, often with particular doors assigned depending on the region of the chosen seat; a steward may assist in locating the audience member's place; each ('passive') participant is now orientated towards the stage. Imagine this event is orchestral: some of the wind and brass are on stage warming up (that *physical* frame – the stage – is set); people turn off their phones (again, another part of this secondary frame is visible in that barrier you erect to the outside world); a few conversations fall to whispers and tail off as the lights dim, and the orchestra takes their seats. The co-leader stands; an oboe 'A', the almost-cacophonous almost-unison of the fine-tune that fades to a pause. The audience applauds as the leader takes their place and the conductor takes the podium. And then ...

*silence*

It is this pause – this suspense and anticipation, the *silence* before the music begins – that Littlefield considers the real *essence* of music's frame: not just at the beginning of a piece, but in the space between movements, and those fleeting moments after melancholic close and before applause. Littlefield says of this silence:

> it is hard to imagine something more non-signifying, more meaningless that the silent frame. It is less meaningful, in the representational and propositional sense, than absolute music, which has proven itself quite susceptible to verbal description; it is much easier to coax a clear meaning from a piece of sound than from a piece of non-sound. [...] Music [...] is a virtual world of another temporal quality – a world we could not access without the silence(s) of the frames. For a musical work to exist, the frame is necessary, perhaps more so than the 'music itself', which always requires a frame to make itself understood as music. (Littlefield, 1998, 227)

Silence, states Littlefield, is 'meaningless' – a 'piece of non-sound'. But then there was Cage. And because of Cage, we all know that that vast, pregnant pause as the conductor's hands hang motionless in the air – summoning the audience's attention and completing that time-honoured pre-performance ritual – is not silent at all. Stifled coughs; shuffling programmes and people; whispered comments; perhaps a snatch of noise front-of-house as a door closes a little too late; the rustle of last-minute, 'did I switch my phone off' anxiety: all this 'silence' is full of sound. Berio, too, has pointed out that the distinction we make between the music and non-music is based primarily upon our expectations, rather than the actual presence (or absence) of sound. For Berio, music is (only) *everything* we listen to with the intention of listening to music. So when silence is nothing more, nor less, than the absence of organized sound, and the absence of organized sound may, or may not, be intended as music, where does this leave the frame? Where, despite the fact that Littlefield pays scant attention to any of the habits outlined above, does the fullness of silence leave the secondary frames of convention? In an interview from 1987, Cage tells Peter Dickinson that 4'33" is his favourite creation (Dickinson, 2006, 41). 'Why?' Dickinson asks. And Cage, amidst what Dickinson annotates as 'extended laughs', replies: 'Well, I listen to it all the time!' Recalling Berio's comments about *intending* to hear, Cage hammers home the realization that it is not silence at all that acts as the frame, but the social conventions – the concert etiquette – that we attach to it.

Just *where* is the frame in contemporary art? It is easy to say that in painting, ornate woodworking is replaced by shadows cast by canvas edges standing proud of monochrome walls; that podiums are discarded as sculpture makes its presence felt by sheer magnitude and physical disruption of space. But perhaps this is only half the story. Because aren't those secondary framing functions still there? The intention of seeing – the intention of hearing – art? This intention is still latent in the decision to visit the art gallery, to pay for admission, to anticipate the act of viewing. It is *intention* that marks the true frame of artistic experience. Of course, this is not to contradict Littlefield's assessment of the frame. His enquiries address a physical object. They explore the way this seemingly mundane object (and its musical counterpart) plays a particular and important role in centuries of cultural history. Yet in the same way that intention identifies art in the way the physical frame or window of silence does for Littlefield's traditional settings, his remaining criteria find parallels in contemporary art. Littlefield argues that it seems 'impossible to formalize quantitatively the interactions of frame and work' (Littlefield, 1998, 228). Therefore, if silence is to be discounted as the quality that meets these criteria, what instead might appear both separate, contingent and necessary to the work of art? What functions only in relation to a work without which it would be meaningless? The answer might lie in all those associated items that are both part of a work and absent from its material presence: titles, programme notes and composer manifestos or interviews. But if we admit these peripheral devices to the orbit of the framing function, then what about recordings? Are they work or frame (or does it depend on *who* has created the recording)? How about part of a recording? A snippet on the radio? What about a postcard of a painting? A blueprint of a sculpture? Of course, these questions apply not only to contemporary art, but to all art that is reproduced in our time. All of our experiences as consumers of culture are coloured by the postmodern condition: the emphasis on intertext and on the (*re*)creative act of interpretation. This transformation of our *attitude* towards artistic experience is crucial to understanding the changing nature of the frame, and here minimalism plays an important role in understanding the transition in the framing function that allows experimental musics to exist as 'art'. Minimalism is a phenomenon that develops alongside this emerging postmodernity, and as a result, its transformation (from a final high modernist, dogmatic impulse to a heterogeneous, plural, multifaceted field) mirrors conceptually many of the features of postmodern artistic development that influence the changing nature of the frame.

A significant feature of minimal music has been the lengthy duration of works, most notably La Monte Young's interest in sustained drones. From the *Compositions 1960* ('Draw a straight line and follow it', 'to be held for a long time') to the Drift Studies (1969) (a continuous tone that, in Young's words, invites the listener to 'get inside the sound'), the idea that a brief period of silence could signal the temporal dimension of his music seems nonsensical: performances in Young's Theater of Eternal Music could last hours, or even days. When Young's drones are replaced with the rhythmic vitality of Philip Glass or Steve Reich, that sense of stasis still remains, and many commentators have pointed to the anti-teleological nature of minimal music precisely due to its lack of harmonic direction.[4] However, the actualities of start and finish (even if they are not witnessed) and the fact that it is possible in this early minimalism to identify a process or concept that dictates the development of the overall work, point to a sense of progression throughout the duration of the piece. A contemporary critic of these composers, Tim Page, tries to introduce minimalism to a wider audience in 1981, in an article where he urges his readers to 'imagine trying to impose a frame on a running river – making it a finite, enclosed work of art and yet leaving both ends open and free, leaving its kinetic qualities unsullied. Minimalist composers are framing the river' (Page, 1981, 65). This metaphor of the river – the idea of something that can be summed up, be *witnessed*, while at the same time conceived of as something that stretches to the edges of our imagination – is the very essence of minimalism.

The duration of minimal works challenges Littlefield's notion of a convenient, silent frame. Instead of silence, these extended durations invite the audience to choose their starting point, either through the context of their presentation, or through extreme duration. Early performances by Reich and Glass, for example, took place not in concert halls, but in lofts and art galleries, where audiences were free to come and go, to enter or leave the work at any point in its performance, and where there could often be more than one performance taking place simultaneously. There was also an expectation that the audience would wander freely in and out of an event, thereby not experiencing the work as a 'framed event' such as Littlefield describes. Traditional teleological notions are thwarted as these experiences become potentially 'unending' (because there is no indication of how far into a performance you have entered, and whether you will leave before it ends). Similarly, when works were performed in traditional concert venues, those such as Glass's opera *Einstein on the Beach* confronted the audience with a work already-in-progress as they entered the auditorium ('Knee Play #1' began before the public were admitted), and actively encouraged them to leave and return as they pleased. Not only do such decisions on the part of the composer thwart the initial sense of beginning, they also undermine the notion that what is contained within the 'frame' constitutes some unified whole that must be received in its entirety. Glass points out that *Einstein* 'was never intended to be seen as a whole, narrative piece. Its "wholeness" comes from its consistency of subject matter and overall structure and becomes the theatrical equivalent of an "act of faith" for the audience' (Glass, 1987, 57). Where, then, does the 'frame' of *Einstein* exist?

Despite Glass's resistance to the idea of unity within *Einstein*, what all early minimal music has in common is *audible process* (the clear 'phase shifting' between the two performers in Reich's *Clapping Music* [1972], or the evident additive structure in Glass's *1+1* [1967]). The same identifiable process exists in minimal sculpture, painting, film and dance. In the words of Reich, 'once the process is set up and loaded, it runs by itself' (Reich, 2002, 34). And this simplicity of process reveals itself to the audience. Minimal music gives no 'privileged' position or higher knowledge to the composer; its composition is laid bare. With regard to the frame, the implication is that once identified, knowledge of this process (be it through a programme note, a score, or hearing a section of the music) makes the *whole* of the work known to us. While experiencing it might be a very different thing, we enter into that experience with a concrete notion of how unity is exhibited throughout the work. Each work is framed not by any external factors, but by *our understanding of what that work is.* Is it possible, therefore, that the essence of the work's frame that Littlefield requires is to be found not in the work's temporal existence, but in its conceptualization? Jonathan W. Bernard, in a critique of Wim Mertens's work on minimal music, argues that 'Mertens has (seemingly inadvertently) identified a paradox: that on the one hand the minimal piece cannot be regarded as finished until the listener "actively participates in its construction"; but on the other, that this same listener "is reduced to a passive role, merely submitting to the process"' (Bernard, 1993, 123).[5] Yet postmodernity revels in paradox, in the contradiction. If we now compare Littlefield's original criteria, and our 'altered' frame, we see that what Bernard and Mertens describe fulfils those remaining criteria of Littlefield's: the *listener* is passive *and* active. It is the *listener* who fulfils this contingent *and* necessary role; the listener's experience and response operates on two distinct yet interactive planes.

On the one hand, the physical participation in the process of listening (which demands the listener be subject to the playing-out of process) is a passive one. For as Bernard observes, minimal music 'more than depends on time as a medium of presentation; it is devoted to making the listener keenly aware of the passage of time. Not clock time as a rule, for the rate of passage of time certainly varies from piece to piece, and even, often, within the same piece. But there is something about this sense of the passage of time that is *enforced*' (Bernard, 1993, 122 [my italics]). On the other hand, there is an engagement by the listener with the *conceptual* existence of the work. A knowledge or expectation that a process is indeed being iterated allows the listener to assume an active role, thereby maintaining a conceptual framework that compensates for the absence of beginning, or indeed, end. In summary, our ability to conceptualize – to understand the work *outside* the mere passage of time – frames the work. Silence, for Littlefield, functions as a temporal marker of start and finish. When start and finish become somewhat superfluous notions, the silences of the frame are once again those busy, bustling moments of non-organized sound that Cage describes.

Of course, not all minimal works begin before the audience expects, nor do they last so long that it is impracticable for an audience to hear a work in its entirety. However, the existence of this conceptual framing device provides a substitute for the traditional teleological function; the logic of the piece allows the listener to identify and respond to the subtleties of a gradually evolving work without the need for climax, release and thematic development. It is, finally, this shared knowledge of a process that subverts the traditional framing function, and along with it, the privileged distinction between creator and receiver. Thomas DeLio, in a survey of new works performed at Kitchen (by Glass, Reich, Lucier and others), noted a 'reevaluation of those attitudes that support the traditional boundaries separating composer and listener [...] Of paramount importance to much of this work are those qualities that lead the perceiver to experience the discovery of relationships, and the emergence of form, from a vantage point once reserved for the composer alone' (DeLio, 1981, 271). By allowing the listener to sample a section of a work, or anticipate development, framing becomes not the work's separation from its context, but the contextualization of the work. While audible process provides an insight into the way that *conceptualization* of music alters our perception of it, the *intention* to hear music – to perceive sound as organized or not – is a universal function of the frame.

If we accept this premise, then it also follows that the conceptual framework that one places around an individual work also has a bearing on the way in which we frame ideas of genre and style. Although tongue-in-cheek, when Michael Fried argues that minimalism is a difficult movement to define because 'there exists no agreed-upon point of formal and image complexity which is Enough' (Fried, 1998, 95), he highlights the role that the secondary frames referred to throughout this article come to bear on our conceptualization of a work. In minimalism, it is this intangible boundary between the 'enough' and the 'not-enough-to-be-recognized-as-art' that generates some of the aesthetic interest. It is almost impossible to point to a work that contains an absolute 'minimum of means', but there are countless examples of works that express an economy of compositional device and a concentrated presentation of single ideas. Consider, for example, more recent extreme forms of electronic minimalism that have stretched the perceived limits of minimization to breaking point. JLIAT's 'anti-musical ideology' has led him to create works such as the *Still Life Series, 'Six Types of Silence'* (all JLIAT's works are undated and made available copyright free), which comprises various forms of digital 'silence', where audio data exists on each CD, but in practice is either inaudible or unplayable by most standard equipment. Similarly, the Onement record label also presents an interesting extension to the minimalist aesthetic, producing records with so few pressings (and no master) that the works recorded are unavailable even to the composers and performers themselves. Onement's first release was five realizations of *4'33"*, the fourth track being pure digital silence: the label presents an interesting aesthetic question, but such projects bring yet more questions to the concept of the frame. Does severe restriction of availability – rarity value – enhance the 'frameable' qualities of an object as art? If so, one wonders how events such as the campaign to make *4'33"* Christmas number one in the UK charts fit alongside such ideas. This campaign is not the only example of these minimalist roots breaking through into popular culture and challenging the *status quo*. While the links between rock music and minimalism are often heralded as the 'breakthrough' between high and low (for example, John Cale's move from the Theater of Eternal Music to Velvet Underground, or Eno's collaborations with both Gavin Bryars and Tom Waits), it is also blamed for the anodyne of the commercial, the generic 'background' music, and the dreaded 'muzak'. But if we accept that contextualization and conceptualization are the key parameters of the framing function, then it has to be recognized that *spaces* will create frames, and the objects that are made 'art' within them will be contingent on that framing space: the 'lift music', the 'iPod bubble' – these are all spaces that are framed by a mixture of personal expectation and public convention.

So finally, where might the future of the frame lie? In our postmodern culture, we should be self-consciously aware that what we consider 'music' or 'performance' changes over time, just as collectively we have multiple notions within society of what might constitute art: our frames are flexible. However, secondary framing (those behavioural responses to context) still take place, and we must also recognize how much our sense of performance is culturally conditioned. How many people, for example, walk around Carl Andre's bronze pavement, *Venus Forge*, at Tate Modern? Should we be walking on it? If *Einstein* were to be staged at the Royal Opera House next season, how many people would come and go freely throughout the performance? Are those traditional concert hall conventions stronger than any invitation a work makes to subvert them? What if, like Wagner at Glastonbury,[6] it were performed in the open air, as opposed to in an arena where even the physical space you occupy for the work is clearly delineated and framed in advance? It is too easy to equate minimalism's crossing of boundaries to a 'popular music' ethos (although such claims are made all the time); most minimalist works are still recognizable as concert works, albeit in altered frames. And even then, it is too facile to suggest that pop and rock gigs are free of conventions. They inherit norms, some that are just as recognizable in a concert hall – how many times have you stood in a crowd and cursed that person who chats through every song? The frames of modern cultural consumption are altered, but they are nevertheless still frames. Several years ago, Classic FM tried to take chamber music into pubs (a more common venture now than it was then), with the aim of reaching new audiences, and removing the 'stuffy' image of the concert hall. A conversation with one of the organizers at a conference not long after the project had finished its pilot sessions revealed what was (to him) an unexpected finding. 'It was great', he said. 'We went in, set up, the place was packed, everyone was talking and doing regular pub things.' He paused, and then added: 'then the string quartet started playing, and everyone shut up.'

The conventions of the concert hall, even for those who rarely or never attend, constitute very strong frames indeed. And so, to return to Littlefield, frames are necessary and contingent. What has changed is the way in which we recognize *ourselves* as an integral part of that framing function. It is not the silence that builds the boundary; it is us as consumers, our knowledge, our expectation and our conceptualization, that allows art to exist as 'art'. Yet without that art, our frame would not exist to be conditioned.

# CHAPTER TWELVE

# Listening Aside: An Aesthetics of Distraction in Contemporary Music

*David Cecchetto and eldritch Priest*

In this chapter, we discuss distraction as a key aesthetic vector – both witting and unwitting – of contemporary concert music, and moreover one that places the tangibility of the latter in a persistent feedback relation with broader cultural shifts in listening practices that are regularly attributed to the proliferation of recorded music.[1] To this end, we begin by characterizing the concert music paradigm as a 'concentration machine', which serves as a synecdoche for music whose experience is organized around the perception of its internal formal relations. From here, we argue that one way to narrate post-1945 music is by locating its reflexivity in this field of concentration as a tendency to collapse this formal concentration into the content proper of music. A corollary to this, we argue, is that by insisting on the protocols of concentration, composers as varied as Cage and Lachenmann mobilize a catachrestic materiality of music that involuntarily (and paradoxically) teaches us to be bored and to listen away from music. In this boredom, we conclude, a listener's *inattention is forcefully directed towards the affective content of music*, a situation exemplified in composer Martin Arnold's *Burrow Out; Burrow In; Burrow Music* (1995). In short, we suggest that *Burrow Music* retains the alibi of music as an object of attention that coincides with concert music's idealized materiality, while also palpating a broader cultural tendency – amplified by recording technologies – to listen to the side of music.

## The Machine in the Ghost: music as concentration machine

A predicate of this essay is that concert music has at least the potential to *matter*. Indeed, this is the case in two – co-implicated – senses: first, the argument at hand depends on concert music bearing the capacity to be involved in the generation of something like a musical materiality, which is to say some sort of object of study. In short, the deterritorializing vectors of an aesthetics of distraction depend on a territorializing movement within music itself, not as the opposite of distracted listening but rather as that which ensures the specificity of any instance of distraction. Put simply, the distraction that we find in the music of Canadian composer Martin Arnold is to be found *there* specifically – in its relation to a particular idea of music as a something-to-be-listened-to – and this specificity offers broader insights into listening more generally for precisely this reason (i.e. its 'innovation' – a hesitant term – is *material*, rather than simply perspectival).

This material mattering conditions our argument throughout, but at this stage it is perhaps more pressing to focus on the second sense of the term 'matter'. If we are to make an argument about listening that starts from concert music, it is necessary for the latter to bear some relation to the former. This assumption is not as obvious as it may seem to those deeply invested in the concert tradition. In addition to the almost total absence of contemporary concert music from the largest economies of music (radio, digital music sales, advertising), even when it is found in these settings it exists precisely in the absence of exactly that which defines it, namely the set of rituals, affordances and listening practices performed in and by the concert hall. That is, it is entirely reasonable to suggest that on the rare occasion that one hears a contemporary work for string quartet on the radio (for example), one is not actually hearing a version of something conceived for the concert hall and subsequently transposed to a new setting, but rather something that is 'recording native'. Indeed, one of the reasons that musical synthesizers haven't entirely liquidated musical practices of analogue instruments is that many of the former's promises – total performance control, virtually unlimited virtuosity, nuanced timbral modifications, and the general absence of 'noise' – are achieved in advance through recording techniques. In sum, it is at least arguable that the concert hall exerts its greatest influence today as an alibi for something like musical authenticity rather than as a literal space. In this sense, concert music relies heavily on a sense of its own virtuality, its reality as an abstraction.

At the same time, it is precisely this virtuality that suggests that the relevance of concert music is not quite as anachronistic as those many music lovers who have never set foot inside a concert hall proper might presume. It's not that concert music has special significance because it is 'high art', or that it exerts hidden influence as some kind of musical Rosetta Stone; instead, the concert paradigm positions concert music as a synecdoche for music in general, i.e. 'concert music' stands in for the construction of a musical object that is taken to be separate from the listening subject, and by corollary, a subject who engages this object through direct and focused attention. This is to say that music conceived of as an object of attention remains active in contemporary listening, but the summons – whether achieved through social pressure, education, or regimes of taste – no longer dominates audition.

If this much is true, then (paradoxically) it follows that to listen to a piece of music, to listen to the set of relations for which the idea of the concert performance stands in, is simultaneously to listen away from specific elements that co-construct the performance as something that one may engage (or not) as an object of attention.[2] Concert conditions are an enchantment ritual, a procedure for conjuring daemons of sound. This ritual requires spells to dampen the affectivity of the body's non-aural senses, and spells to turn attention away from the rebarbative din of everyday life. To realize this form of musical superstition demands that the participant listen away from the 'accompanying circumstances of the concert institution that contradicts its idea' (Heister, 1992, 51). That is, to realize music as an autonomous activity – an activity wholly separated from the heterogeneous interests of life's clamorous desires and strident demands – one has to actively exercise a practice that 'excludes or annuls the "un-artistic"', or more reasonably, 'makes it relative' (Heister, 1992, 51). The concert ritual does this, of course, through its well-developed ideological summons that invokes the fiction of aesthetic autonomy. However, the ritual is aided by a spatial layout that not only enforces a separation between the site of music's production and its consumption, but also cultivates competing forms of self-consciousness. On stage the musician's sense of self is mediated by acts that compose her as a performer and empower her as an hieratic figure of attention. The listener, on the other hand, is delivered a self through scripted performances of non-acting – namely, acts of shutting-up and staying still that establish her as an appendant. This formulary for *listening to* the liturgical spectacle is also a formulary for *listening away* from the noise of necessity, away from the racket of socio-economic complexities that both underwrites the concert's autonomy and contradicts its ideals.

Put more simply, concert music matters because its suppositions lend crucial insight into the means through which the act of listening that constitutes music as a sonic event distinct from sound, noise, or even speech, entails an act of *not* listening; or, more accurately, a distracted listening that is figured as non-listening. In short, both concert music and background sounds (including backgrounded music) share the same sense: listening.[3] In its concerted mode listening is not hearing the 'ambient din', while in its more distributed mode what is listened-away-to (what is not being heard) is the 'musicky' bit. Concert music and background sounds are privative aspects of the same sense of listening, which is why, for example, one can do virtually anything on a concert stage (or even in the proximity of the stage) and 'concert music' will still result, provided that the protocols which satisfy the ritual and its routines are all (or mostly) present and properly executed.

Indeed, this is how – apart from its historical importance – Cage's 4'33" matters: its deterritorialization of music's concentration techniques, premediated by precisely the 'structural listening' that it is mobilized against, reveals the virtuality of music. That is, 4'33" (and the myriad pieces that follow from it, directly or obliquely) relies not only on the performative dimension of concentration as an assemblage of behaviours and dispositions, but specifically on concentration as a coupling technique whereby the 'specifically aesthetic [formal] potential' of sound becomes the 'distinctive characteristic of music's realization' (Heister, 1992, 53). This reliance on concentration and the recognition of such aesthetic elements as 'form' or 'structure' perceived *via* the variations that play across and as certain objects, phenomena and processes, is telling of a thoroughgoing mediation that undermines music's apparent actuality. In contrast to a painting whose object status is expressive of a dualism between its actual materials through which manifests its virtual image, music makes no such actual/virtual distinction. As sociologist Antione Hennion points out, whereas the materiality of visual works of art retain a relative stability that secures debate around its idea (its virtuality), 'Music is in the reverse situation: its object is elusive; social interpretations just take it as the expression of a social group (ethnic trance, rock concert), aesthetic studies as a nonverbal language of immediacy. Music has nothing but mediations to show: instruments, musicians, scores, stages, records' (Hennion, 2003, 83). This is to suggest that music is the expression of certain mediations such that its reality wholly coincides with the activity of its medial couplings. Music is thus a completely virtual reality that acquires a material profile through the concentration – assembly – of those processes and ideas that posit its mattering.[4]

This heightened virtuality of music is perhaps most clear when we consider the relation between music and sound. We could say that in musical discourses sound is often associated with a chaotic matter against which music is expressed as a principle of mastery. Music in this model is taken to be made from sounds, and thus constitutes a claim to evolutionary superordination (as evidenced, for example, in the meaning we might attach to the observation that monkeys cannot hear music). However, this opposition entails the continuous displacement of sound from the scene of music proper, for when sound is described within musical discourses it becomes a substitution for the music on whose behalf it supposedly speaks. Or inversely, when and where sound is represented within the discursive economy of music is precisely the site of its erasure. As a result, sound is that which can never be sounded as music proper but whose exclusion from that propriety is music's enabling condition. But the inverse is not true; music is not sound's enabling condition. We may say, then, that music only hears sound in catachresis, that is, in sounds that function improperly, musical figures that are not music, for example, as when one listens to a canonical work and notices the inadvertent harmonies of partials emitted from an overpressed bow, or the rhythmic squeaks of fingers on a fingerboard.

To the extent that music only hears sound as errors within its rhetoric, this catachrestic nature is captured precisely by the music of composer Helmut Lachenmann, whose soi-disant *musique concrète instrumentale* professes to haunt and co-opt the musical material-semiotics from which sound is excluded.[5] Lachenmann's work is apposite to this discourse because it stands in for a tendency in contemporary composition to regard music as a practice that combines the raw dynamism of performance with the actual materials and forces of instruments. For example, whereby serialism is understood as an approach oriented towards the abstraction of pitch class as a primary site of manipulation, Lachenmann shifts attention towards instruments themselves as sites that locate energetic processes. In this there is an explicit movement away from the parametrical formalism of serial composition towards an approach that attends to sound as a dynamic matter.

Indeed, we can understand each sub-term of *musique concrète instrumentale* as a functioning under erasure. Firstly, his compositions are 'music' insofar as their performance executes a negation of their performance as music. Lachenmann likes to think of his work in the form of the question that solicits the reversibility of dialectical reasoning: 'If it is not music, I would say it is a situation of perception, which provokes you to wonder, "What is music?"' (Lachenmann, in Steenhuisen, 2004, 11). As such, his music is decidedly an occasion that is not what it is. Secondly, his work is 'concrete' or 'real' to the extent that it marshals and harnesses certain physical and kinetic processes in the construction of sonic events. But this sonic ontology arises from an understanding of sound whose materiality is precisely what is contested. It is for this reason that Lachenmann has not simply produced electronic compositions: he is working with the 'energetic aspect of sounds' because 'even the most exciting sounds are no longer exciting when projected through a loudspeaker' (Lachenmann, in Steenhuisen, 2004, 9). Finally, Lachenmann's work is typically 'instrumental' in that it tends to be scored for ensembles of (relatively traditional) instruments. However, these instruments are not used in a way that their sounds can be taken independent of their own materiality (i.e. they are not used instrumentally); the instruments themselves, rather than the tones that they produce, are mined in a way as to invent a living materiality of the orchestra.

These considerations combine to perform a materiality of music that is catachrestic in the sense that the sound/music (or noise/music) opposition it assumes complicates itself through the inclusion of 'excluded' sounds, sounds that cannot function within music's rhetoric; they cannot be musical *per se*. To the extent that music itself is constructed in opposition to sound, Lachenmann's (and Cage's) approach deconstructs it. Rather than opposing, revolutionizing, or correcting music's oversights or exclusivity, this deconstructive reflexivity is available to show how extramusical elements are simultaneously essential to music. In both Cage and Lachenmann (whose practices are in many respects anathema to one another, and whose combined influence is almost impossible to overstate), we understand that that which guarantees a piece of music as 'music' – namely, the exclusion of sound as such – simultaneously precludes it from its self-causation, its aseity.

That music is subject to deconstruction is not particularly remarkable, and has already been amply remarked on and demonstrated in any case. What is worth noting here, though, is the mechanism that links Cage's and Lachenmann's work, since their practices would appear to be so opposed. That is, if music is always under erasure, its fiction as a sonic matter nevertheless persists through the alibi that music and sound coincide – they are made of the same stuff. However, by keeping the listener's attention oriented towards the sweeping rhetoric that the practice of music is, both composers unwittingly reiterate this alibi of coincidence. Their performance of music's deconstruction through traditional concert conditions effectively obscures the genetic difference that underwrites music and sound. And despite how their praxes diverge, Cage's and Lachenmann's accounts – being as they are dialectically expressed – ultimately converge in a kind of second-order listening that may be described as another form of attention wherein one attends to one's self-attending: hyper-attention. Taken this way, what was initially described as the movement of form into content can instead be thought of as an expansion of the attentional field to include the activity of attention itself, which, by virtue of attention's always being supplemented by inattention, is also to include the impossibility of attention's full attention.

What this all amounts to, then, is understanding the concert ritual itself as a kind of technology, one whose several parts together function as a concentration machine to actualize the idea (virtuality) of music as a pure aesthetic object. Or said differently, concentration is the invariant effect of music realized in its mode of being something relative to which all manner of sounds can be folded into, obscured, and/or recombined without threatening its constitution. In both its actual and conceptual space, virtually anything can be added, altered, or removed from this machine without threatening the idea that it expresses – everything perhaps except concentration itself. In short, concerted music and the virtual musicality immanent to every actual instance of it can feint and bob, disappoint or mislead one's attention in any number of ways so long as attention is concentrated. As such, when listening itself is distracted from its attentive obligations, the musicality that supposedly inheres in any object of concentration – any sound – risks becoming what is not it.

But what happens when there is nothing to impinge upon this concentration? If concentration entails listening away from certain sounds, noises and activities in order to realize music as something-to-be-listened-to, which in turn realizes these sounds, noises and activities as elements of distraction, then what results when there is no 'outside' element to draw attention away from its expressions of concentration? That is, what constitutes 'music' if nothing can be listened away from; if, in short, nothing distracts?

## The Ghost in the Machine in the Ghost: reflexive (in)attention

Logically it follows from the question posed above that 'everything' is music. But as we've argued, music (not only, but especially, in its concert(ed) form) is only possible when *not* everything is music. At issue here is not just the sense of music's mattering but the matter of inattention – distraction – as it relates to concentrated listening.

Consider, then, Martin Arnold's *Burrow Music*, a one-hour ten-minute acoustic piece in two movements composed to be listened to as a recording.[6] Like the anonymous and nondescript music you might hear at a cocktail lounge drifting quietly in the background, *Burrow Music* aimlessly meanders with seeming indifference to whether it's being listened to or not. This is not to say that there is no sense or character to *Burrow Music*, but rather that its occasion of listening is conducted otherwise and away from the facts that typically organize musical audition. The *faits accomplis* of musical listening here are intentionally deficient in order to promote a form of listening that delights in the elaboration of local details without concern for the latter's structural implications or formal significance. Oddly, to listen in this way is also to listen away from the rhetorical force that music circulates in its insistence on comprehension (in the broadest possible sense) over mere apprehension. In this mode of listening it is the appearing itself – the *appearancing* of the music – that matters; the fact of things happening is sufficiently interesting and amusing, independent of what happens or even why and how they happen.

To a large extent, the listener's powers of concentration have to be considered here, specifically insofar as they have been altered by contemporary culture's varieties of corybantic distraction that encourage a form of continuous partial attention.[7] This means that *Burrow Music* (a composition that assumes many of the attentional conceits of concert music) concerns the way music-to-be-listened-to indirectly engages the kind of penumbral audition that characterizes how backgrounded music is heard and how the latter, operationalized under the sign of the former, converts the perceptual aberrations (noises) of subliminal listening into aesthetic 'wonders' that transfigure the image of music-to-be-listened-to into something grotesque, something weird.

If Arnold's music is able to leverage the listening techniques that are called forth in realizing music as a dimension of the background, this is in large part because the backgrounding music has become habitual since the advent of recording technologies. Indeed, the conventional musical mode of realization – one that elevates certain structures shared by all musical phenomena to the level of autonomy – has been in decline since sounds became something that could be recorded and effectively re-presented. While it is undeniable that the concert(ed) mode of realization informs the address of recorded music, insofar as the latter is typically presented in a way that asks the listener to take what is playbacked as an object of attention, it's also clear that recorded music has produced its own set of affordances and protocols that skew the matter of music as something-to-be-listened-to.

For Arnold (and for this essay) the most significant of these reconfigured affordances is the way recorded music, unlike concert music, gives tacit permission to ignore music. This is not to say that music as a something-to-be-listened-to disappears from the listener's purview, but rather that its imperative does. The sense of summons that pressures all occasions of audition, a sense the concert hall isolates and raises to an aesthetic level, does not have the same force in recorded music owing to the technical and social economies that are specific to recordings.[8]

Arnold explicitly places a lien on this condition in *Burrow Music*, which he describes as taking its impetus from his observation that his 'fundamental experience of listening to music was through recording' (Arnold, 1995, 18). To the extent that recorded music does not simply represent but in fact reconfigures the order of its constitutive mediations, to express this fundamental experience of music-as-it-is-recorded *Burrow Music* is sensitive not only to the way it will sound and be heard as projected from a stereo, but how 'production techniques are significant, distinct, and active contributors to the resultant recorded music' (Arnold, 1995, 18). In short, *Burrow Music* takes the mediations introduced by recording technology and recording techniques as an essential part of recorded music's potential. Beyond traditional elements such as 'pitches, rhythms, textures and sonorities (and their histories outside of the piece)' (Arnold, 1995, 27) are ambient elements that Arnold believes are 'latently audible' in the final recording. Things such as

> the dimensions of the room (including sills; ledges; outcroppings; trim; smooth or angled corners); all the materials involved in the walls

(plaster/stipple/paper/kind of paint); the amount of furnishing...and the placement, shapes, and material make-up of the furnishing; the floor surface and covering; the number of windows, the number of curtains, and the number of curtains drawn or not; the difference between the street noise from the third floor, the second floor, and the ground floor, (Arnold, 1995, 7)

as well as the kind of microphone used; the placement of said microphone relative to an instrument; the amount of gain applied to the microphone; and, as legions of informed and not-so-informed musicians will attest to, whether these sounds are recorded in a digital or analogue format. For Arnold, 'how a piece is recorded is a part of the music, as much as all the other aspects of interpretation – dynamics, phrasing, articulation, *rubato*, etc.' (Arnold, 1995, 18).

In order to understand how this is accomplished in *Burrow Music*, a more detailed description of the work is in order. Basically, one can hear *Burrow Music* as a timbrally rich, extremely long, and very weird work of slow-moving modal counterpoint. The first movement (at sixty-eight minutes) is the longer of the two, and is essentially composed of three-part modal counterpoint with an accompanying punctuating line that activates (opens/closes) a gated tape part on which is recorded an improvised organ and string performance (both instruments being played by the composer). Each of the voices is recorded separately and independently of one another on a cassette four-track recorder, and throughout the piece, the melodic lines are performed at different times by one of twelve different instruments,[9] each of which have been recorded in different ambient spaces using different recording techniques to create, in a sense, a second and third order counterpoint based on instrument timbre and ambient resonance. The strategies that Arnold uses for ordering the parameters of pitch and rhythm are many and multilayered and require too much space to detail here in depth, except perhaps to note that much of the material was generated using different applications of Danish composer Per Nørgård's 'Infinity Series', a recursive algorithm with fractal-like properties whose self-similar 'wavelengths' or 'refractions' are audibly related to the originary series that gives its constantly expanding row the semblance of hierarchical order.[10]

The second movement, which times at forty-two minutes, is a representation of the same scored material that comprises the first movement. However, for this movement a MIDI-realization of the score is made and recorded to cassettes that are then listened to through headphones by performers who either whistle or hum along with one of the three principal melodic lines. Additionally, the MIDI-recording of the score is gated (turned on and off) and projected through speakers by a signal that comes from the microphone into which the performer whistles/hums. What's heard on the recording then is an extremely murky blend of whistling, humming and

MIDI pianos. As Arnold writes: 'This movement celebrates the non-expert pastime of humming and whistling-along and all the sonic anomalies that go with this activity' (Arnold, 1995, 13).

Aside from his underlying taste for medieval polyphony, Scottish Piobaireachd, 1970s Prog Rock, and jazz-lounge, Arnold cites an interest in experimental film and video, particularly those reflexive works that 'take on some kind of investigation into various aspects of various kinds of apparatus set in motion for the[ir] production and consumption' (Arnold, 1995, 20). Though citing the work of Michael Snow, Ernie Gehr and Peter Gidal as influential, it is film-maker/theorist Trinh T. Minh-ha whose work Arnold feels particularly indebted to. In Trinh, Arnold discerns what he calls a 'non-demonstrative' approach, where the 'unsettling [of] various conventions and preconditionings' are present in such a way that their 'subversions are not lucid enough or consistent enough or pervasive enough or dramatic enough to take on another [alien] authority' (Arnold, 1995, 20). The expressive ambiguity Arnold sees in Trinh's *Naked Spaces* (1985), for example, parallels his desire for *Burrow Music* to both exploit and subvert conventions while never presuming mastery or control of his creative strategies or the effects that they condition.

Like Trinh, Arnold seeks to keep the affects – the abstract but perceivable force of change immanent to and expressive of an experiential modification – of convention and subversion in play without isolating or classifying which artistic effect belongs to which affect. Arnold describes this as 'a condition where the dialectic line that can be cut between the two disappears and they become unknowable as categories' (Arnold, 1995, 27). Describing his ideal reception of *Burrow Music* and the kind of experience he aims to cultivate in listening to the work, Arnold explains:

> I want the array of elements that make up my hybrid material to be as capable of being (mis)apprehended as all context and content [...] I want a situation in which any given element in any given moment might seem familiar (and maybe beautiful or sentimental or comfortable) but in which there is *no real sense of what is going on*; no solid indication or even implication of what my agenda or intent as a composer might be. (Arnold, 1995, 27)

In short, *Burrow Music* aims at a reflexivity that avoids the quotation marks that so often cling to the term; Arnold is less interested in a kind of attentional navel-gazing than he is in perverting the navel-gazing that has always-already taken place as the ground of (in)attention.

But much of what Arnold describes in *Burrow Music* are its internal formal details. While details such as the unusually long duration, the otiose melodic drifts, and a veritable absence of dynamic variety are necessary elements that help *Burrow Music* sidestep the expectations that mediate the way a listener takes account of a musical event, these alone are not sufficient conditions to render 'the strangeness of its existence so disorienting' (Arnold, 1995, 100). If they were, one should expect *Burrow Music* to relinquish some of its unsettling effects with successive hearings. Its being recorded would presumably give the listener a degree of control that would countervail *Burrow Music*'s troubling affect by giving one the opportunity to develop the kind of attention that evolves from multiple listenings, an attention presumably informed by the totality of its repetitions.

But the fact is that as many times as one listens to *Burrow Music*, and as well as the objectives of the piece can be understood, it remains enormously difficult to grasp what's going on in the work at any given moment. This suggests that the capacity to listen plays a key role in determining what Arnold says is *Burrow Music*'s 'insidiously disorienting instability' (Arnold, 1995, 101). Thus, while treating the mediations of audio technology in a way that addresses how 'production techniques are significant, distinct, and active contributors to the resultant recorded music' (Arnold, 1995, 18), it should also be considered how listening to recorded music affects the way one attends to music. This is again to insist that attention – to or away – actively contributes to the way music sounds, to the resultant experienced music. Arnold is right that 'there is nothing neutral about the recording process' (Arnold, 1995, 18), but there is also nothing neutral about the circumstances of listening, and certainly there is nothing neutral about what sound technology has done to these circumstances. Simon Frith puts it this way: 'As we have taken power over music on records, as they have become ubiquitous [...] so the musical work has ceased to command respectful, structural attention' (Frith, 1996, 242). As a consequence, he contends that 'All music is more often heard now in fragments than completely' and 'because *all* our experiences of time are now fragmented and multilinear, fragmented music is also realistic music' (Frith, 1996, 242, 243).

Production techniques are therefore not only active contributors to the way music is heard through recordings, but active contributors to the way even non-recorded music is heard. For the majority of the population of industrialized cultures whose primary experience of music is circumscribed to that of listening (to recordings), the peculiarities of recording's mediations are no longer exceptional. Thus, in addition to affecting what is or is not audible, as, say, the way a microphone position alters the amount of perceived finger noise made when playing a guitar, recordings have taught us how to listen in moments as well as indifferently, and thereby to orient 'the listener's attention to "sound"' such that 'perception of the sound is more important than consideration of the "composition" as an entity in and of itself' (Hosokawa, in Frith, 1996, 243). Pausing, turning down, rewinding, skipping ahead, stopping a song in the middle of playback, and simply forgetting about it are behaviours that develop around the way recordings allow one to affect recorded musical sounds. But these behaviours also adjust the importance of the music downwards so that they become something grasped or appropriated unconsciously and no longer something to be taken as catachrestic figures.

In this way, *Burrow Music*'s 'insidiously disorienting instability' is as much a function of how recorded music and a media-rich environment – an environment that it helps create – invite us to listen distractedly. What this means is that part of *Burrow Music*'s strangeness derives from the fact that a highly mechanized information-saturated culture of hybrid bio-petrol-geo-electric-social networks already teaches its subjects how to listen 'rhizomatically', how 'any point [of listening] can be connected to anything other, and must be'; how an act of listening 'may be broken, shattered at a given spot, but [...] will start up again on one of its old lines, or on new lines' (Deleuze and Guattari, 1987, 7, 9). Because listening to music through recordings is central to contemporary culture at large, its members already pay a certain inattention to music in general. The parts that one tunes in and out of when listening to *Burrow Music* never survey the piece and so never compose an image of the work that would dominate hearing and organize its expressions into signifying regularities. Or in Deleuze and Guattari's language, *Burrow Music* has no face to 'define zones of frequency or probability, [to] delimit a field that neutralizes in advance any expressions or connections unamenable to the appropriate significations' (Deleuze and Guattari, 1987, 168). In a sense, *Burrow Music* borrows from distraction its ramifying capacity and its cognitive sleights, and transposes these into a stationary context (the context of listening through headphones) to perform a 'fractal deformation', a process in which listening lives on bites of what Paul Mann defines as 'increasingly fragmented gestures, features, images, that never add up, never amount to a whole body' (Mann, 1999, 154), or, a face.

\* \* \*

As Walter Benjamin notes, habits that develop around the way an individual uses things (or the way things mediate one's use of them) impinge on how these things figure into one's perception and influence the significance they can have.[11] So as well as affording a separation of performer and audience, recordings encourage us to regard music as something that can be wilfully tuned in and out of: the sound of music becomes something alternately neglected or cherished according to a nebulous set of continuously shifting priorities that are becoming increasingly multiple and superficial. Additionally, and coupled with the fact that recorded music's ubiquity makes this almost universal, the scission between performing and listening spaces gives musical sounds an impropriety that allows them to circulate limitlessly as impersonal environmental qualities that one learns to listen away from. Or, like architecture, which is rarely perceived apart from the lived economy of its spatial array, music (especially as it has become increasingly omnipresent) serves as a felt background from which one's attention can be detached and given rein to drift towards more obscure perceptions and sublimated tropes.

Put differently, 'attention' is no longer captured by a conscious subjective agent, but is expanded to include the various affective registers in which autonomic couplings constantly form, morph, modulate and break. That is, the habitual reception of musical sounds is an effect of the way music has, largely as a consequence of its mechanized mediatization, become an agentless feature of the environment such that it comes to be heard the way streetcars and lawnmowers outside of one's house are heard – always to the side of another activity. In thus becoming a ubiquitous part of everyday life, music loses some of its formal significance while enhancing what Ian Cross calls its 'floating intentionality', a drifting aboutness that refers to the way music 'can be thought of as gathering meaning from the contexts within which it happens and in turn contributing meaning to those contexts' (Cross, 2005, 30). If much of contemporary music listens attentively to the paradoxes that result from the way that music bespeaks its fictive self – to the fissures of its folded materiality – Arnold's music suggests that things might be otherwise if we listen away instead. In this, the matter of music might matter anew, but only insofar as this way of mattering can never matter as such.

# CHAPTER THIRTEEN

# Using Noise Techniques to Destabilize Composition and Improvisation

*Eric Lyon*

## Twentieth-century noise

Noise played a distinguished role in the evolution of pan-European classical music throughout the twentieth century. Early examples may be found in the works of the Futurists, notably represented by Luigi Russolo's *The Art of Noises* (Russolo, [1913] 1986); Edgard Varèse, whose music explored noise-spectrum percussion with the intention of liberating sound; and John Cage, who valorized noise and electronically produced sounds in *The Future of Music: Credo* (Cage, [1937] 1961). To these traditional avatars of noise we might also add Arnold Schoenberg and others who championed atonality, leaving behind a harmonic detritus as the grammar of tonality collapsed of its own weight toward the end of the nineteenth century. Experiments in microtonality by Alois Hába further subvert the 12-tone scale substrate of both tonality and atonality, and in the composed-out noise of Charles Ives, marching bands or other extraneous sounds heard in the distance crash against each other in works such as *Central Park in the Dark* (1906) and *Symphony no. 4* (1910–16).

Iannis Xenakis is widely recognized as being a key innovator in the post-Second World War use of noise. His stochastic music is highly technical, applying mathematics along with an early use of computers to assist in the task of composing with masses of musical events. Xenakis's work ranges over acoustic, electroacoustic and computer music, and multimedia art, making essential contributions with works such as *Metastasis* (1953–4), *Concret PH* (1958), *Gendy3* (1991) and the *Polytopes* (1960s–1970s). Perhaps more than any other composer of his time, Xenakis demonstrated the startling range of possibilities for the application of noise techniques to music.

## Total randomness vs. total organization

John Cage is of particular interest as a composer whose sustained use of noise-based musical techniques crosses the Second World War boundary. Cage discusses the historical inevitability of the full entry of noise to music in his 1937 speech 'Credo' (Cage, 1961, 3–6), stating: 'I believe that the use of noise to make music will continue and increase until we reach a music produced with the aid of electrical instruments.' Equally intriguing is his correspondence with the young Pierre Boulez, who, along with Karlheinz Stockhausen, was exploring a seemingly opposite approach to the late 1940s integral serial music. It was later suggested by Iannis Xenakis that total serial music sounded just as random as random music (Xenakis, 1992, 8). But the dialogue between Cage and Boulez, focused on techniques and musical innovations, reveals clear ideological divisions (Nattiez, 1993). For Cage, the dialectic between randomness and compositional control can be broken, since the structures, after all, result from coin tosses. For Boulez, however, compositional control can never be safely relinquished, stating in a 1954 letter to Cage: '… I will never admit – chance as a component of a completed work. I am widening the possibilities of *strict* or *free* music (constrained or not). But as for chance – the thought of it is unbearable!' (Nattiez, 1993, 150). It may be argued that collectively, Cage and Boulez metaphorically killed their shared father, Schoenberg, by eliminating from their music the final stylistic remnants of tonality that pervade the rhythmically conservative textures of his later 12-tone works. For Boulez, 'Schoenberg est Mort' (Boulez, 1968, 268–75) and for Cage, the serial idea yields to noise, and then beyond, to indeterminacy.

The highly mechanized approach of total serialism quickly lost its appeal, and the automated nature of Boulez's *Structures* (1952 and 1961) yielded to more fluid approaches to rhythm and articulation. Cage, meanwhile, moved toward the less mechanically structured, more improvisational approaches of indeterminacy in an effort to fulfil the following aims: to free the composer from aesthetic bias; to direct the listener's attention beyond the proximate sound art object to the surrounding acoustic environment; to use the mechanism of improvisation to motivate discoveries.

## Articulating noise

In late 2007 I began a compositional project with the intention of creating music constituted primarily of noise. I was already quite experienced working with noise in various ways for computer music applications (small amounts of noise are essential to give life to digitally synthesized sounds, and random choices underlie many aspects of algorithmic music). However, my explicit plan here was to maximize the presence of noise in the compositions, without having the resulting music necessarily sound like noise. The idea I formulated is what I now term 'articulated noise' – an approach in which decisions at larger time-scale structures are completely random, and as the process moves closer to the compositional surface, more composer prerogatives are engaged (Lyon, 2008). The surface details of the composition thus arise from a negotiation between aesthetic choices, and totally random choices.

The potential for novelty through stochastic processes was recognized early on by information theorists. John Pierce, discussing various results of experiments in stochastically generated text, writes: 'Poor poets endlessly rhyme love with dove, and they are constrained by their highly trained mediocrity never to produce a good line. In some sense, a stochastic process can do better; at least it has a chance. I wish I had hit on *deamy* but I never would have' (Pierce, 1980, 263–4). Such a view has an evident bearing upon my own work, for when I began to compose articulated noise scores, the main attraction with regards the use of noise was its incoherence. Each new value in a white noise sequence has no correlation to any previous value in the sequence. When noise techniques are deployed, moving from any musical event to any other becomes frictionless. The goal was not to produce incoherent music, but rather to destabilize aspects of musical structure that might otherwise tend toward the conventional by default. To further illustrate this premise, the following section describes several recent noise compositions in terms of their compositional templates, code implementation, and implications for further compositional work.

## *Three Noises for Violin and Piano*

A key element in my first articulated noise composition, *Three Noises for Violin and Piano* (2007), is the random choice of rhythmic configurations. In order to foster maximum variety, metric levels are allowed to interact in ways that potentially produce score segments which are impossible to perform at the notated tempo. Such segments, when allowed into the final composition, are marked 'impossible' in the score. The essential rhythmic

FIGURE 13.1 *Noise-controlled rhythmic elements of the first movement of* Three Noises.

manipulations for the first movement can be seen in the opening bars of the violin part as shown in Figure 13.1.

Each beat is broken up by a basic subdivision. The individual subdivided attack points are then grouped into some portion of the entire beat and these subgroupings are further subdivided. For example, in the fourth beat of bar 1, the beat is first divided into three parts, then the first two-eighths of the triplet are grouped together into a quarter note, and finally that quarter note is subdivided into another three parts. The integer values for all three operations are chosen at random, and in some cases, successive operations cancel one another out. The time signatures are also randomly selected, as are all tempo indications. In bar 4, at 107 beats per minute, the time interval between each articulation is approximately 15 milliseconds, corresponding to a speed of approximately 68 attacks per second, which is far beyond the human motor performance capabilities. This bar is thus marked 'impossible'.

FIGURE 13.2 *Scalar passages in the first movement of* Three Noises.

The pitch materials for the violin fall into three categories: minor third patterns, scalar patterns and random pitch-class selection. A minor third pattern is seen in the first three beats of the first bar as shown in Figure 13.1. Scalar violin passages are apparent in bars 11–13 as shown in Figure 13.2. The piano part generally follows a simpler rhythmic template, with only one layer of subdivision, as seen in the quintuplets on the first two beats of bar 11. Occasionally, random stretches of the violin music are assigned to unison doubling with the piano as evident in beats 4 and 5 of bar 11.

## Musical template code

Small snippets of code were written in SuperCollider according to specially constructed musical templates, to assist with the compositional process. The code to generate tempo changes and time signatures is shown in Figure 13.3.

```
(
var barcount = 15, segment_count = 2;
var num, denom;
var ds = #[4,8,16];

segment_count.do({
      var tempo, barseg = rrand(1,8);
      tempo = rrand(50,150);
      ("tempo is" + tempo + "for" + barseg + "bars").postln;
      barcount = barcount + barseg;
});
barcount.do({
      num = rrand(1,13);
      denom = ds[3.rand];
      ("time signature:" + num + "/" + denom).postln
});
)
```

**FIGURE 13.3** SuperCollider *code to generate a series of tempo markings and time signatures.*

In this example, only two segments are generated. The actual number of segments, defining the duration and metric structure for the entire movement, was selected at random. Typical output from this code is shown in Figure 13.4.

Once the rhythms have been generated, the choice of materials is also selected at random (SuperCollider code to make these choices is shown in Figure 13.5). In this case the choices are weighted so that, for example, a random texture is three times as likely as silence (tacet). Based on the material selected, a type of transformation is assigned, along with the

```
tempo is 101 for 8 bars
tempo is 64 for 2 bars
time signature: 13 / 8
time signature: 5 / 16
time signature: 12 / 16
time signature: 2 / 16
time signature: 7 / 16
time signature: 5 / 4
time signature: 4 / 16
time signature: 7 / 4
time signature: 11 / 8
time signature: 6 / 4
time signature: 12 / 4
time signature: 13 / 16
time signature: 3 / 16
time signature: 10 / 8
time signature: 6 / 8
time signature: 10 / 4
time signature: 5 / 16
time signature: 7 / 16
time signature: 11 / 16
time signature: 9 / 4
```

**FIGURE 13.4** *Output from the random tempo and time signature generation code.*

duration in beats for the segment. Given the constantly changing time signatures and tempos, the number of beats contributes to, but does not directly determine, the duration of a particular section.

The random scrambling of materials and transformation promotes considerable variety in the resulting musical textures. The minor third (m3) material is deployed either at a fixed pitch level, with an interval other than a minor third (deformation), or in the case of permanent transposition, the reference level itself is transposed to a new level.

Typical output from the materials code is shown in Figure 13.6.

```
{
var mytype, transform, beats;
var types = #[tacet,m3,scales,random];
var m3transform = ["none","large transposition","deform interval","permanent transposition"];
var sctransform = ["none","repeat attacks","reverse","scramble order"];
var rtransform = ["none","no final subdivision","tight middle octave","extremes only"];
10.do({
        mytype = types.wchoose([1,2,1,3].normalizeSum);
        transform = rrand(1,4);
        beats = rrand(1,11);
        transform = switch(mytype,
            \tacet, "none", \m3, {m3transform.choose},
            \scales,{sctransform.choose},\random,{rtransform.choose}
        );
        ("type:"+mytype + ":" + transform + ".. beats:" + beats).postln;
});
}
```

**FIGURE 13.5** *Random selection of musical materials for* Three Noises.

```
type: scales : reverse .. beats: 2
type: tacet : none .. beats: 6
type: random : no final subdivision .. beats: 9
type: m3 : none .. beats: 10
type: tacet : none .. beats: 6
type: scales : repeat attacks .. beats: 8
type: m3 : none .. beats: 11
type: random : extremes only .. beats: 2
type: random : no final subdivision .. beats: 4
type: m3 : large transposition .. beats: 10
```

**FIGURE 13.6** *Output from the material generation algorithm.*

## Second movement of *Three Noises*

The second movement explores a completely different texture in which slow chords in the piano part are articulated melodically with violin harmonics (unless otherwise marked, all violin notes in this movement are played as harmonics). The first piano chord is randomly assembled as a pitch-class set with instructions for registration. Subsequent chords constitute either successive transformations of the chord, or substitution with a newly constructed pitch-class set. Interstitial violin melodies separate the piano chords, while the piano chords themselves are occasionally embellished with introductory grace notes. A characteristic passage is shown in Figure 13.7.

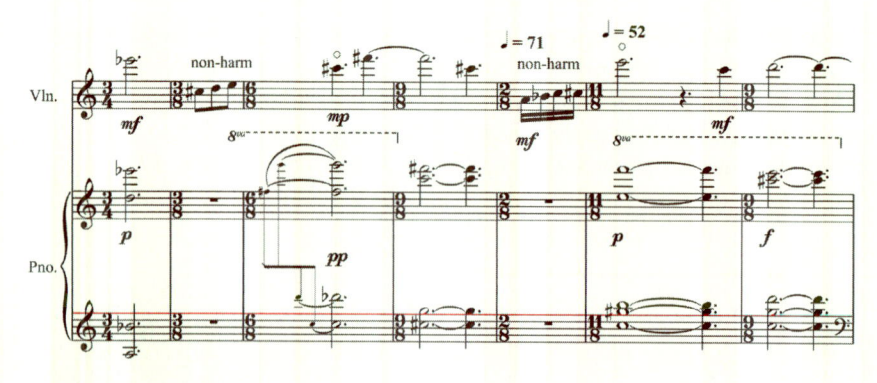

**FIGURE 13.7** *Excerpt from the second movement of* Three Noises.

Later in the movement, extremely fast piano arpeggios undermine the predominantly slow character of the work (see the final bar of the movement, shown in Figure 13.8).

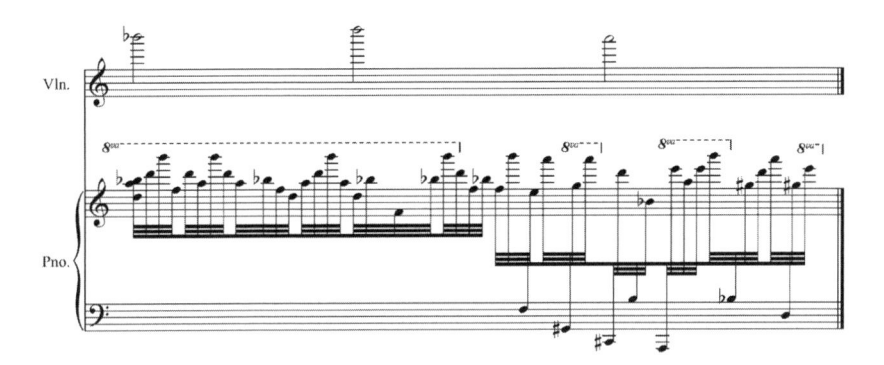

**FIGURE 13.8** *Rapid piano arpeggiation of a chord with random deviations.*

Each note of the piano arpeggiation is randomly subject to constraint by pitch, pitch-class, or alternatively, a totally free note. The extremely fast piano arpeggiations mirror the violin arpeggiations, which are presented throughout as slow melodies.

## Third movement of *Three Noises*

The third and final movement is a toccata of sorts. Most of the violin writing consists of a propulsive stream of sixteenth notes punctuated by percussive low register piano chords. The tempo is constant throughout the movement, but the time signatures are randomly selected for each bar. The violin lines are conditioned by random selection from the following melodic profiles: totally random selection of specific notes; upwards or downwards trajectory; focus on a single randomly generated tetrad; variation on what was just played; a completely out-of-character motion. The piano chords are randomly assembled, based on a prototype chord, and each attack is a transposition, re-registration, or randomly controlled deformation of this prototype. The attack time-points are also randomly selected. A characteristic passage is shown in Figure 13.9.

The examples from *Three Noises* shown here demonstrate that strikingly different musical textures can be produced using extremely similar noise techniques; the approach is highly adaptable to nearly any musical context one can imagine. In the design of the code, there is an ongoing balancing process between what will be randomly determined and what is to be left as a compositional prerogative. As a passage evolves, very similar parts side-by-side may have been arrived at with very different degrees of compositional freedom. Essentially there are two composers working together: the human composer and a stream of computer-generated white noise.

**FIGURE 13.9** *Passage from the third movement of* Three Noises.

Large-scale structural decisions such as the length of sections, length of the complete piece, tempos, and the selection of materials are generally made completely at random. However, decisions concerning what materials will be subject to random distribution, which effectively determine the 'language' of the composition, are largely left to the composer. Consequently, at the surface level of musical detail, the composer has considerable freedom, but that freedom is constrained by the outcome of purely random decisions. For example, in a series of four notes that have been rhythmically fixed, the pitch of the first note may be specified, leaving the composer no freedom; the second note might be specified as a pitch-class, leaving the composer the choice of registration; the third note might be chosen at will from a randomly generated pitch or pitch-class set; and the fourth note might be chosen freely by the composer without any interference from the noise-generated constraints. The previously noted tendency toward extreme or even impossible musical configurations is largely because the rhythmic structure is a result of random decisions about tempo, time signature and tuplet subdivisions, with no expert knowledge or 'error-checking' built into the generating programs. This effect could be avoided by testing the resulting speeds, then 'limiting' them to humanly playable speeds. More simply, one could discard any random decisions that produce unplayable musical results.

While there are some striking semblances between the results of random processes and deterministic serial processes, one very clear distinction is that with serial procedures, no matter how remote from the surface, one can still believe in a certain unity resulting from the consistent application of a single structure, a unity that would be damaged if one were to discard the results and substitute other notes in place of serially determined ones. In working with noise, that possibility of structural unity does not exist even in theory – one random run is as incoherent as the next. And yet, in practice, I almost never discard a random result. And I certainly never do so in order to produce a more 'reasonable' result. Impossible situations are viewed as a residue of the 'unreasonable' random processes that collaborate with the human composer to produce the final composition.

## Recombinant structure

Consistent application of the aforementioned noise techniques leads to some interesting paradoxes. Despite the largely uncorrelated decisions used to assemble large-scale structure, the resulting music doesn't sound particularly random. This is due in part to the large amount of compositional effort directed toward polishing the musical surface materials. Another factor is apophenia – the human tendency to see patterns in random or meaningless data. The two seem to be mutually reinforcing; the presence of clear surface patterns suggests the plausibility of larger-scale musical structure as well. Of course, once all of the elements are fixed, there is a resulting form; since it is random, the emergent form is sometimes classically balanced, other times extremely eccentric.

The articulated noise approach rebalances the compositional effort, resulting in a primary focus on surface elements, almost to the exclusion of everything else. Once the basic templates for a composition are in place, the general tenor of the piece does not change much, and moment-to-moment changes tend to sound tactical rather than strategic. It would be easy enough to alter this dynamic by building irrevocable, large-scale changes into the structure of the generating code. However, I have not yet felt the need to do so. The play with surfaces seems an important aspect of what the technique has to offer; adjusting the balance of effort would undercut that emphasis. There is also an agreeable association with the compositional emphasis found in certain pieces of techno music, notably early 1990s Aphex Twin tracks such as '73 Yips' and 'Xepha' (Aphex Twin, 1993). Such works present a fully formed sonic vocabulary from the outset, and the unfolding of the piece primarily involves ingenious combinations of repeated elements. Like such techno works, articulated noise pieces are inherently recombinant, the main difference being that the recombined elements are not fixed materials, but rather the constituent parts of potential pieces of material. Both approaches seem to avoid overarching musical narratives in favour of drifting (if somewhat aggressively) through possibilities.

## More recent articulated noise compositions

Since *Three Noises*, I have composed several more articulated noise pieces, and currently consider this approach to be my central compositional direction. In *Diagonal Noise* for solo piano (2008) the entire tempo and metric structure for the composition was generated in a single run with the SuperCollider code shown in Figure 13.10.

```
(
var tempo=100, curTempo, trats, now=0, beatdur;
var tmax=180, tmin=40;
var barstretch, bardur, num, denom, tbars, tfactor;
trats = [2/3, 3/4, 4/5, 5/4, 4/3, 3/2];
beatdur = 60.0 / tempo;
while({now < 360},{
    barstretch=1;
    denom = [16,8,4].wchoose([0.2,0.5,0.3]);
    num = rrand(3,13);
    tbars = rrand(1,7);
    barstretch = tbars * (num/denom) * beatdur;
    post("tempo:" + tempo.trunc(1.0) + "time sig:" + num + denom + "bar count:" + tbars);
    postln(" (realtime):" + now.trunc(0.1) ++ ")");
    now = now + barstretch;
    tempo = tempo * trats.choose;
    if(tempo < tmin, {tempo = tempo * 2});
    if(tempo > tmax, {tempo = tempo / 2});
    beatdur = 60.0 / tempo;
});
)
```

**FIGURE 13.10** *Code to generate the large-scale time structure for* Diagonal Noise.

In this piece, all adjacent tempos are related by simple ratios contained in the 'trats' array. The application of these ratios is completely random; the result is a wide variety of tempos both quite slow and quite fast, interspersed throughout the piece, sometimes in close succession. An excerpt from the output from this code is shown in Figure 13.11.

```
tempo: 100 time sig: 6 8 bar count: 7 (realtime): 0)
tempo: 75 time sig: 13 8 bar count: 2 (realtime): 3.1)
tempo: 56 time sig: 5 4 bar count: 4 (realtime): 5.7)
tempo: 45 time sig: 8 8 bar count: 5 (realtime): 11)
tempo: 72 time sig: 11 16 bar count: 3 (realtime): 17.7)
tempo: 57 time sig: 6 8 bar count: 4 (realtime): 19.4)
tempo: 46 time sig: 10 8 bar count: 3 (realtime): 22.5)
tempo: 61 time sig: 10 8 bar count: 6 (realtime): 27.4)
tempo: 46 time sig: 10 8 bar count: 1 (realtime): 34.8)
```

**FIGURE 13.11** *Tempo, time signature and bar count data for* Diagonal Noise.

A further technique in *Diagonal Noise* treats the two hands as independent rhythmic voices and distributes a rhythmic division scheme over a given number of beats. The code is shown in Figure 13.12 and characteristic output is shown in Figure 13.13. The code determines a pattern of rests (characterized by a zero) and monads, dyads and triads. In the musical templates for *Diagonal Noise*, pitch attributes are never specified; the attack types determine how many notes should be played on an attack, but the actual choice of notes is left entirely to the discretion of the composer (an excerpt from *Diagonal Noise* is shown in Figure 13.14).

```
~handpair = {|beats, mindiv=3, maxdiv=9|
    var hits = [\dyad,\triad,\monad];
    var atks, subdiv,odds;
    odds = [4,2,10].normalizeSum;
    2.do({|hand|
            hand.switch(0, {"** left hand **\n".postln}, 1, {"\n** right hand **\n".postln});
            beats.do({|i|
                atks = nil;
                subdiv = rrand(mindiv, maxdiv);
                ("beat" + (i+1) + "subdiv:" + subdiv).postln;
                subdiv.do({
                    if(0.66.coin,{atks = atks.add(hits.wchoose(odds))},{atks = atks.add(0)});
                });
                atks.postln;
            });
    });
};
```

**FIGURE 13.12** *Code for independent hand rhythmic configurations.*

```
** left hand **

beat 1 subdiv: 4
[ monad, triad, dyad, dyad ]
beat 2 subdiv: 3
[ dyad, 0, 0 ]
beat 3 subdiv: 3
[ monad, monad, monad ]

** right hand **

beat 1 subdiv: 5
[ 0, 0, monad, 0, monad ]
beat 2 subdiv: 3
[ dyad, monad, monad ]
beat 3 subdiv: 8
[ dyad, 0, monad, monad, triad, 0, monad, monad ]
```

**FIGURE 13.13** *Characteristic output for independent hand rhythms.*

FIGURE 13.14 *Excerpt from* Diagonal Noise.

## Performer perspectives

Presenting a score with several passages marked 'impossible' can be off-putting to musicians, and indeed my first few articulated noise compositions, including *Three Noises*, have never been performed. However, there are musicians such as Cory Bracken and Daan Vandewalle who relish the challenges posed by articulated noise scores. They understand that passages marked 'impossible' to perform simply represent a particular interpretative challenge, and their interpretations reflect their own musical personalities. Bracken, when performing my *Three Melodies for Vibraphone*, hurls out impossible passages with an intensely physical onslaught. Vandewalle, by contrast, when performing my *Diagonal Noise* for solo piano, maintains a controlled state of calm throughout, despite the constant changes in speed, style, density and dynamics throughout the piece. The interpretations of these two musicians are near opposites, yet both please me very much as a composer and seem to go over well with audiences too. Interestingly, both musicians found it perfectly reasonable to perform scores that contain completely impossible situations. As Bracken mentioned during a rehearsal of *Three Melodies*: 'the notation achieves a specific effect which could not be achieved without it. Therefore it makes perfect sense within our traditions of notated music.'

## Noise-driven improvisation

In 2008 Paul Stapleton invited me to compose a new work for his modular sound sculpture MiSS to be premiered at the 2008 Sonorities Festival. The MiSS is a large bowed and struck instrument with built-in resonators, which was designed to inhibit instrumental mastery. It struck me that it might be interesting to write a concerto for an instrument that cannot be mastered, and given Paul's preference for improvisation, I decided to make the work in the form of a guided improvisation. It was at this point that I realized it might be possible to redeploy some concepts from articulated noise in an improvisational context. The compositional articulation (all of the score-based surface detailing) would go away, but the key concept (utilizing noise to destabilize musical processes) would remain. The *Noise Concerto* was designed as an improvisational structure that would be composed in real time during performance with all structural decisions driven by computer-generated white noise. One stream of instructions is sent to the MiSS soloist, and another set is sent to the 'orchestra' comprising an ensemble of any number of players of indeterminate instrumentation.

The mechanism for transmitting instructions to the performers is a Max patch receiving its instructions by Open Sound Control (OSC) messages over a local WiFi network. Performers receive a performance directive displayed in a *umenu* object and a countdown displayed in a *number* object. Consequently they always have guidance on what to play at any given moment, and how much time is left to play it, but they have no idea what performance directive is coming next. Neither the soloist nor ensemble members know which performance directive the other is currently assigned, and the segments for both are uncorrelated. Durations of each section are also random and

- Imitate Ensemble
- Focus on one sound
- Lyrical
- Super Fast
- Develop Material Already Played
- Build Patterns
- Play Extremely Sparsely
- Play with Directionality
- Play Aimlessly
- Play in Limited Space
- Play in Full Space

**FIGURE 13.15** *Soloist directives for the* Noise Concerto.

- Support Soloist
- Imitate Soloist
- Play Louder than Soloist
- Tacet
- Build Intensity
- All Play The Same Pitch
- Play Non-Pitched Sounds
- Play One Note of a Chord
- Ensemble Plays the Same Melody
- Play Very Sparsely
- Play Complex Music
- Play Simple Music
- Play Entirely from Internal Motivation
- Gradually Play Faster
- Gradually Thin the Texture
- Get Into a Groove

**FIGURE 13.16** *Ensemble directives for the* Noise Concerto.

independent of the particular directive (directives available to the soloist and ensemble are shown in Figures 13.15 and 13.16 respectively).

Given the relatively large number of directives, there is considerable variety in the possible combinations between soloist and ensemble; in a heterogeneous ensemble the same directive might simultaneously be interpreted in several ways. Moreover, some sequences or combinations of directives prove paradoxical or impossible to perform literally (for example, the ensemble might be told to imitate the soloist while the soloist is told to imitate the ensemble; the ensemble might gradually play faster, reaching a very fast speed, only to receive another directive to gradually play faster – there is no prohibition on the repetition of directives).

Using improvisation as the main generator of material leads to a very different dynamic than in articulated noise scores, since the surface vocabulary is now dependent on the musical inclinations of the performer. Following its premiere by Paul Stapleton and members of the QUBe Ensemble, the *Noise Concerto* has received several performances with soloists on instruments other than the MiSS. Despite the variety of stylistic approaches in these successive performances, the concerto seems to maintain its structural profile, with a key element being the unusual juxtaposition of performance directives, and often, the lack of correlation between any piece of material and the timing allocated to perform that material. At the same time, each performance is heavily conditioned by the stylistic preferences of the improvising performers. As with articulated noise, the energy of the system comes from a collision between randomness and human aesthetics; but with noise-driven improvisation the aesthetic is an emergent, collective one.

## The Noise Quartet

Despite the enthusiastic energy that players brought to performances of the *Noise Concerto*, and the fun of being able to quickly assemble and harness large ensembles for the piece, each performance was, for the players, something of a one-off. I next wanted to explore noise-driven improvisation in a context where pieces would be rehearsed repeatedly over a period of

- Choose another player and imitate what they are playing
- Choose another player and augment/support what they are playing
- Choose another player and only play when they are not playing
- Be the soloist
- Play almost nothing
- Choose one sound and stick to it
- Play only what someone else is already playing
- Gradually increase your tempo
- Gradually decrease your tempo
- Choose three different sounds and use only them
- Go Crazy!
- Play a simple pulse with no regard for what anyone else is playing
- Work a groove. Join up with any currently active grooves
- Play like how you feel right now
- Play with intense concern for every sonic property of every sound you make
- Play without any goal in mind
- Provide barely noticeable textural support
- Play as fast as possible
- Put out a rapid stream of sonic information with little concern for the details
- Harmonically support everything that is going on around you
- Play very disjunctly
- Play with very smooth connections
- Play glissandi
- Work with the lowest sounds on your instrument
- Work with the highest sounds on your instrument
- Focus on your midrange
- Play a beautiful melody
- Grab a motif that someone else just played and develop it
- Play something that you played earlier in this performance, as accurately as possible
- Massive dynamic range
- Play with high density and very low volume
- Completely avoid repetition

**FIGURE 13.17** *The directive pool for* Noise Quartet #1.

time by expert musicians. I also wanted to take part in the performance in order to fully experience the noise-driven improvisation from the perspective of a performer, and this led me to form the Noise Quartet. The Noise Quartet consists of Franziska Schroeder, saxophone, Paul Stapleton, electric guitar, Steve Davis, drums, and myself on piano. To date I have composed twelve noise quartets for this ensemble. *Noise Quartet #1* drew directives from a generic pool of instructions that were not idiomatic to any particular instrument. Section durations were made at random during performance, and all instruments received a different, randomly chosen directive at the start of a new section (the directives pool is shown in Figure 13.17).

## Visual presentation of the quartets

The temporal structure of each quartet is randomly created anew for each performance in a Max patch, with most of the coding done in an embedded JavaScript patch. A local WiFi network is created, and the performers each connect their computer to this network. The quartet is driven from a master patch, which shows the current directive for each performer. Each individual performer sees only his or her directive, along with a countdown, and a progress bar showing the current time within the total duration of the current quartet. Since the programming is mainly done in JavaScript, the same Max patch can be used to drive every quartet. That way, a concert can be given without requiring performers to load a new patch between pieces. A snapshot of the master patch performing the first noise quartet is shown in Figure 13.18.

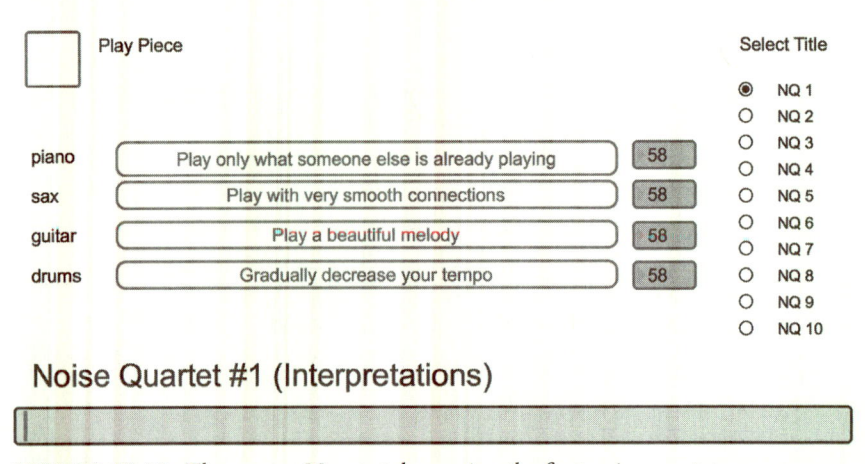

**FIGURE 13.18** *The master Max patch running the first noise quartet.*

## Performer reaction to the quartets

In response to the first quartet, performers particularly liked directives that gave them a large degree of interpretative freedom. I therefore took this idea to extremes in the second quartet, with each section choosing from one of four directives: 'slow', 'fast', 'loud', and 'quiet'. Unfortunately this was a complete failure; the performers were unsure what to play, and how to react to each other, especially since there was no correlation in duration or content across the four independent lines of directives. In the third quartet, I thus returned to the more specific directives performers had appreciated in the first, but with the added variation that each section could be either a solo with only one performer playing, or an accompanied solo in which the randomly selected soloist had a 'soloist' directive and the other three performers were assigned an 'accompaniment' directive. Performers responded favourably to the greater textural variety afforded by this approach.

The fourth quartet called for a steady stream of sixteenth notes with players changing their mode of play according to various directives. For example, one may be playing within a small registral bandwidth while another played over the full range of their instrument. At first, the performers did not care for the quartet; it was technically difficult to maintain the fast notes over the course of the piece and it was hard to keep a steady tempo while following the various directives. I therefore made some adjustments, adding directives in which performers played sparsely, or used slower subdivisions such as triplets, eight notes or quarter notes, and greatly shortened the duration to less than a minute. The resulting piece still required the most rehearsal, but in the end proved rather striking.

Noise quartets five through eight each focus on a single performer as soloist, and were the first to include instrument-specific directives. In addition, the four solo quartets use different formal structures. For example, the saxophone quartet is a set of theme and variations, where the saxophonist invents a theme at the outset of the quartet, and then succeeding directives request specific forms of variation (for example, 'play the melodic phrase backwards' or 'gradually deconstruct the melodic phrase'). The drum quartet constructs a long drum solo over the course of the piece with directives such as 'focus only on cymbals or other high register instruments' and 'hang in the grey zone between a groove and a texture'. The other instruments either support the drums or drop out of the texture altogether.

The remaining four noise quartets returned to more general directives, and focused on collaborative production of materials. Noise quartet nine focuses on shapes, assigning one of the performers to create a shape, followed by a sequence of transformational segments. The shape creation

- Make an angular shape
- Make a shape with only two sounds
- Make a shape with trills
- Make a shape with much repetition
- Make a shape with a single varying sound
- Make a shape varying only in dynamic level
- Make a shape surrounded by much silence
- Make a motivic shape
- Make a shape with a prominent pitch trajectory
- Make a shape with streams of rapid notes
- Make a shape with much timbre variation

**FIGURE 13.19** *Shape creation directives for* Noise Quartet #9.

directives are shown in Figure 13.19, while the transformational directives are shown in Figure 13.20.

In some cases all four performers receive the same transformation directive, and in others, each receives a different, randomly selected directive. The tenth noise quartet focuses on dynamics exclusively, albeit with more variety than the second quartet, but once again, dynamic guidance alone proved insufficient and this quartet was abandoned. The eleventh quartet focuses on harmonic content, randomly generating a combination of key, mode and articulation mode (the drummer, working with non-pitched instruments, is assigned an accompaniment role in this quartet). This was a fun quartet to play since it generated passages where all pitched instruments played in the same key, in addition to ones where the harmonic textures were polytonal. The twelfth quartet is quiet throughout, and focused on slowly evolving timbres, centred on a low, saxophone

- Keep the shape in its current form
- Gradually move to a higher tessitura
- Gradually move to a lower tessitura
- Gradually get quieter
- Gradually get louder
- Gradually become more complex
- Gradually become simpler
- Gradually lose its character
- Gradually transform to a different shape

**FIGURE 13.20** *Transformational directives for* Noise Quartet #9.

multiphonic. The ninth and twelfth quartets were the most successful from this group, spurring the ensemble to explore modes of playing that had not arisen in our earlier work.

## Conclusions and future work

Future Noise Quartet projects will exploit more detailed knowledge of individual performer preferences, and will attempt to make ever more precise directives, while not impacting the fluency of the improvisations. Generating greater structural variety will be another area for exploration. We will incorporate randomly configured live DSP into future performances.

The first set of articulated noise scores focused on the usefulness of random techniques to bring about intensity and instability. The 'impossibility' of the scores, which serves as a marker of these goals, no longer seems necessary. I now plan to apply articulated noise techniques to music that is much simpler on the surface. I also intend to develop articulated noise methods that will interfere much more directly with the compositional process.

The applications of noise described in this chapter have proved useful for orchestrating compositional and improvisational behaviours that might otherwise be difficult to achieve. The use of noise as a stimulus to creative activity long predates the work described here. However, both articulated noise and noise-driven improvisation techniques bring about a particularly useful balance between randomness and musical intentionality, providing engaging challenges to both composer and performer.

# CHAPTER FOURTEEN

# Noise as Mediation: Adorno and the Turntablism of Philip Jeck

## Erich Hertz

There are several reasons not to consider Philip Jeck's work with vinyl as very musical. The sounds that he places in juxtaposition to one another were never created to be played together; as a turntablist, he uses turntables as the primary instrument through which he composes his work; the pieces themselves don't establish or conclude any melodic arcs; many of the collisions of sounds occur by arrhythmic accident; and the turntables and vinyl that he uses are not of the highest quality or in the best shape. The result: his pieces make a lot of noise. In fact, it is this noisiness that is one of the primal facets of all of his pieces. It is not noise in the sense of something loud, but in terms of a work that makes something new out of the limitations of technological reproduction. His piece 'Now You Can Let Go' from his 2004 album 7 builds a very subtle percussive track by looping the pops and crackles that are often the result of bad needles on worse vinyl. He overlays this with other snippets from other looping turntables: three notes of a old jazz band, the drone of a lathe coming in and out throughout the piece, randomly occurring slices of solo jazz guitar and, on top of these, other sounds that have been sped up or slowed down so much that their original source is impossible to identify. Of course, the use of sound in the creation of music is far from revolutionary in the first decade of the twenty-first century. As Paul Hegarty has recently demonstrated, the history of bringing noise into music and what gets called musical was a contestation waged at the beginning of the last century by Futurists like Luigi Russolo.[1] What interests me in specific here, though, is how to make sense of noise in relationship to the technological reproduction that is the source of exploration for many of the turntablists or sound artists of the late twentieth century. The issue of noise in music is a particularly Modernist question that I think is best understood through an analysis of Adorno's writings on the development of music in the twentieth century and how technology influences and mediates our relationship to music. If discussions of noise in contemporary music can too often result in affective or emotional description, putting Adorno's work in contact with Jeck's pieces serves two purposes: to more clearly articulate a concept of noise in Adorno's critical theory and simultaneously to give noise music some of the theoretical heft it deserves in its role in the development of music history.

Adorno's confrontation with the technological reproducibility of art came early in his career when he wrote essays on the gramophone for journals based in Vienna. As Thomas Y. Levin (1990) argues, these early interrogations of the gramophone do not yield the picture of Adorno that we might expect. If readers of the History of Ideas know one thing about Adorno, it would be his disdain for the culture industry and its products. The last few decades have seen both simplistic attacks and generous apologists for Adorno's analysis of the products of culture. My own reading of Adorno would focus on his dissection of the industry of cultural production – that is, not taking him to task for rejecting the products as such, but focusing on the ideological forces that name such a product as cultural to begin with, and the ways that those same ideological forces reify art, turning the consumable products into things that substitute, to nefarious effect, our experience. While Adorno's position on the products of culture is important and is a point to which I will return, it is his early focus on the use of recording devices that begins to give us a good vocabulary to contextualize Philip Jeck's work within the development of the cultural and musical history that Adorno spent so much of his career consumed with.

In a 1934 essay entitled 'The Form of the Phonograph Record', Adorno makes a provocative claim: 'If at some later point, instead of doing "history of ideas" [*Geistesgeshichte*], one were to read the state of the cultural spirit [*Geist*] off of the sundial of human technology, then the prehistory of the gramophone could take on an importance that might eclipse that of many a famous composer' (Adorno, 2002a, 279). For Adorno, the appearance of technological devices that capture sound is more worthy of our attention for an analysis of 'cultural spirit' than the focus on the intervention of individual composers in the narrative of musical history. For readers of critical theory, we are immediately reminded of Adorno's close association with Walter Benjamin and how the two would exchange ideas and critiques over the next decade.[2] Benjamin makes a very similar case as Adorno in his famous essay 'The Work of Art in the Age of Its Technological Reproducibility' (also translated as 'The Work of Art in the Age of Mechanical Reproduction'). Although Benjamin partly focuses on film in this essay, there is nevertheless an interesting correlation between film and music (and one that Adorno will make as well). Benjamin makes the case that original works of art have a certain aura about them that is lost when those works are reproduced. For example, when *Macbeth* is performed there is an aura from the performer, perceived by the witnesses of the event. That aura, however, is dispelled when that performance is viewed in its film version, since that performance is now reproduced – 'removed' from its original, historical context. The claim that Benjamin wants to make is that even though one, when encountering the reproduced work of art, then loses this auratic experience through this loss of aura, what is gained is a new revolutionary capacity for collective aesthetic experience. So, for Benjamin there is something fundamental lost in the process of technological transmission. All objects that collect and hold a version of the original, either the celluloid film or the vinyl record, are nonetheless marked by this loss. It already has embedded in it our inability to experience the aura of the actual thing. What the reproduction offers us is mediation between ourselves and the art object that we cannot experience in its totality. And this mediation is noisy; we are endlessly reminded of the lack of its fidelity to the original source – even when this mediation might appear to be an enhanced or more aesthetically pleasing version of the original object lost.[3]

Benjamin's main argument about this loss is that we gain the possibility of communal, and therefore revolutionary, experience. However, he makes a subtler point important for thinking about the additional advantages of reproduced objects. He claims:

> First, technological reproduction is more independent of the original than is manual reproduction. For example, in photography it can bring out aspects of the original that are accessible only to the lens (which is adjustable and can easily change viewpoint) but not to the human eye; or it can use certain processes, such as enlargement or slow motion, to record images which escape natural optics altogether. (Benjamin, 2002, 103).

For Benjamin, our recompense from the loss of the original aura is the ability to experience the work in ways that would not normally occur. Reproductive technologies can manipulate our sense of what we perceive as natural, grant us new, and for Benjamin revolutionary, access to experience the world in wholly new ways. Or, as in Eadweard Muybridge's famous series of pictures from 1887 showing a horse galloping, they can provide us with a medium to see the world as it really is (it turns out that at some point all four of the horse's legs are off the ground). Even though Benjamin mentions the gramophone in the same essay, he does not consider it in these terms. For Benjamin, the gramophone only has this register of expanding the experience of music outside of the concert hall and into people's homes. I would like to suggest here, and come back to later, that what Benjamin suggests as one of the revolutionary registers of photography and film has a corollary in the way that Jeck uses vinyl – that is, as a way of manipulating and recontextualizing sound that provides an experience of noise by using the object of mediation (in this case the vinyl) to explore facets of noises unheard.

To square Adorno, though, with a concept of noise is a tricky manoeuvre. Adorno is quite well known as a philosopher of dissonance. He was trained as both a musician and a philosopher, and wrote extensively on the idea of dissonance. His thinking has itself been described as dissonant.[4] For Adorno the trained musician, though, dissonance and noise are not at all conflatable. Dissonance has a very precise meaning and it is grounded in the history of the development of harmony in Western music. Traditional classical music, or what Adorno would call 'serious' music, depends upon the establishment of a key and the rules of harmony to stipulate what tone of notes conform to our aesthetic standard of beauty. So, dissonance is not just noise; it is a very specific relationship of a series of tones in relation to an established key. Adorno made much of the appearance of the dissonant flat-fifth in Beethoven, but he made even more out of the attempts of Schoenberg, Webern and Berg to shift toward atonal music: an attempt to create music phrasing unfettered by its relation to an established key. Adorno would then have much to say about the pitfalls of Schoenberg's later nearly mathematical serial compositions, but his lionizing and demonizing remained dependent upon the grounds of the historical development of harmony. One of the problems with Adorno's ideas is that he confines himself only to harmony as such and this limited focus therefore disallows any recognition of the progressive nature of music outside of that which Adorno calls serious music. As David Cunningham aptly notes,

> This has the effect of either marginalizing other forms of experimentation, in the spheres, for example, of rhythm or timbre, or, as in total serialism, presuming that such spheres can be assimilated to the same essential procedures as those underlying the negation of tonality. The most obvious result of this is a complete dismissal of the possibility of avant-garde work and experience in relation to forms like rock or funk music – which are far more driven by timbral and rhythmic innovations than by harmonic ones – as well as the difficulty one would have in extending Adorno's precise theories to account for that radical twentieth-century art music which does not follow on from the broadly Schoenbergian path of development and the experimental priorities it implies. (Cunningham, 2003, 67)

Cunningham's distinction between dissonance and noise is an important one. He wants to create an opening to explore the importance of many kinds of twentieth-century art by making a distinction between arguments based on tone and arguments based on the kinds of instruments that make up the production of music. For example, we might note the emphasis on rhythmic complexity in the percussive works of Steve Reich or the ways in which funk developed as a genre that explored the percussive and rhythmic qualities of all the instruments in the band (so that the guitar was not often used for its usual role as a tonal instrument, but instead deployed the wah pedal and other picking effects to generate percussive noises).[5] While I'm sure that Cunningham might not foreclose this possibility, this delineation doesn't quite capture the 'noise' of Philip Jeck's work or others whose sounds escape the bounds of tonality and rhythm.

Jeck's noise is a kind of sound built around discordance and chance and the juxtaposition of sounds that constellate against each other – without key, often without established rhythm, and outside the language of music altogether. Simon Reynolds makes some overarching assertions about the importance of such kinds of noise in *Blissed Out* about the use of noise in rave music:

> Noise is about fascination, the antithesis of meaning. If music is a language, communicating moods and feelings, then noise is like an eruption within the material out which language is shaped. We are arrested, fascinated, by a convulsion of sound to which we are unable to assign a meaning. We are mesmerized by the materiality of music. (Reynolds, 1990, 57)

This might be a relatively good description of Jeck's work and a productive way to think about the importance of noise in late twentieth-century music; indeed, it would be difficult to find many people who would take umbrage with a description that categorized the value of noise in this way. However, Adorno would have to immediately point out that noise in itself, especially any pleasure taken in being 'unable to assign meaning', would be a mistake; this kind of noisiness forgoes any participation in the dialectical movement of musical history. Adorno, having lived into the late 1960s, had ample opportunity to digest and react to the music that deployed noise as one of the fundamental elements of composition. He heard Stockhausen's early experiments and he responded to *musique concrète* works dismissively. Even if we account for how Adorno's commitment to tonality and harmony disallows any consideration of rhythmic nuance, he argues in 'The Aging of New Music' (2002b) that the attempt to find tones outside of the musical tradition of classical music is a return to a kind of retrograde primitivism; to completely dismiss the inherited rules of tones is a fallacious attempt to recover a pre-musical world and an attempt to bury the critical capacity of music. Hegarty, in his discussion of the role of noise in relation to Adorno, tarries over an important passage from Adorno's essay 'Music and Technique' (1999) on the issue of technique:

> The work of art without content, the epitome of a mere sensuous presence, would be nothing more than a slice of empirical reality, the opposite of which would be a work of art consisting of mere rationality devoid of all enchantment. The unmediated identity of content and appearances would annul the idea of art. (Adorno, 1999, 197)

Many of Adorno's central ideas about art are packed into these few sentences. The first to hone in on, for our purposes, is the idea of a work of art without content. For Adorno, the idea of including noises, as opposed to dissonance, in composition is that noise is dehistoricized in relation to the composition.[6] Tones and their harmonization carry with them centuries of development and their use can indicate a particular historical moment. Dehistoricizing the music in this way, by reaching outside the boundaries of tonal harmony, elides a critical capacity: its ability to serve as mediator between subject and world. Noise, on the other hand, is not an experience of history and therefore, as Adorno puts it, is a 'mere sensuous presence'. The moment that music jettisons its deployment within harmony, it forgoes its critical capacity to be art. To use noise directly in composition is not art for Adorno, because it does not perform any function of mediation. Art must be an aesthetic experience which allows us to understand the world at one remove, since we cannot understand it directly.

For Adorno, whether it is in the form of Kafka's writing or Schoenberg's early work, art must carry the fundamental brokenness of Modernity.[7] This is its 'seriousness':

> What can, without stirring up the musty odors of idealism, justly be called *serious* in art is the pathos of an objectivity that confronts the individual with what is more and other than he is in his historical imperative insufficiency. The risk taken by artworks participates in their seriousness; it is the image of death in their own sphere. This seriousness is relativized, however, in that aesthetic autonomy remains external to suffering, of which the work is an image and from which the work draws its seriousness. The artwork is not only the echo of suffering, it diminishes it; form, the organon of its seriousness, is at the same time the organon of the neutralization of suffering. (Adorno, 1997a, 39; Adorno's italics)

The work of art is a marker of suffering for two reasons. First, it needs to, on the level of form, contain the contradictions and alienation of existence in Modernity. Second, the artwork is an 'echo', its very existence is a mediation of the real thing that it can only approximate. A work of art is regressive if it forgoes or attempts to cover over its own role as an object of mediation that carries with it both the congealed history of its medium and its role as a medium through which suffering becomes visible. As we have seen, this regressive character of artworks should easily apply to noise understood as this attempt to bring in merely sensual sounds from the world – sounds that either directly resemble themselves as they are in the world (like the Futurists shooting a gun in a composition) or sounds which attempt to circumvent the tonal history of classical harmony. In this regard, the sound sculptures that Philip Jeck produces seem like they are incommensurable with the strictures that Adorno places on the autonomy of Modern artworks. Jeck's works are much too noisy to participate in Modern music as understood this way. But, as Douglas Kahn points out, there are many different ways to parse what we mean by noise and different kinds of noises have different registers depending on their historical manifestation. I would like to suggest that Jeck deploys a specific kind of noise here than the one with which Adorno takes such issue (grounded in his later years as a riposte to the experiments of composers like Stockhausen and Boulez).[8] Indeed, when we return once more to the issues of technological reproducibility, we find in Jeck's noise participation in the question of what is at stake, in terms of what counts as music in respect to this fundamentally Modernist way of looking at the world.

Vinyl Requiem.

The kind of turntable sound art that Philip Jeck creates has several important forbearers in the avant-garde. John Cage had experimented with turntables as a sound source in and of itself as early as *Imaginary Landscapes* in 1939. And the way that he manipulates the vinyl by cutting or taping grooves had given rise to further experimentation by Christian Marclay on his *Record without a Cover* in 1985. Simultaneously, Jeck was profoundly influenced by the early hip-hop scratching and mixing techniques of New York DJ Walter Gibbons. But I will make the case that Jeck's deployment of these experiments with turntables actually participates in and elaborates the history of Modern music, and in a way that allows us to both introduce a more specific sense of noise into Adorno's theorizing and more fully enunciate what kind of work Jeck's pieces perform.

Jeck (born 1952) began his artistic career by first focusing on visual arts at Dartington College in Devon, in the United Kingdom. He first attracted attention in 1993 for a work entitled *Vinyl Requiem*, which was an installation involving 180 turntables, 12 slide projectors and two film projectors, and for which he and his partner in the project, Lol Sargent, received the *Time Out* Performance of the Year Award. Already encoded in Jeck's work is this sense of capturing a history which is no longer directly accessible. He and Sargent staged the piece about what they felt was a specific transitional moment in technological reproducibility – that is, the moment when vinyl was being supplanted by the CD as the primary object to contain audio. Their point in naming the performance a requiem, in the immediate and most obvious sense, was to mark this moment of the end of vinyl. But – and less immediately – the requiem aspect also extends to the history of the culture that produced them. As Peter Shapiro argues, 'turntablism recognizes that the best music is a complete triumph of style over substance; everything's been said already, so why bother listening unless the speaker's got some serious chutzpah?' (Shapiro, 2002, 164). While Shapiro emphasizes the early turntablist's desire to make something new out of a sense of all good stuff having already been iterated, Jeck's work reveals more about how decades of information are stored on this medium, and to hear the performance of *Vinyl Requiem* is to hear the congealed fragments of the history of recorded music being restirred: all those splinters from across decades lofted out to register their ghostly presence – the presence of something already irretrievably lost, yet still contained in this remainder. And Jeck didn't just put into play these moments from the vinyl, but also the very mode in which the vinyl is transmitted; those imperfections which Adorno complained about in the 1920s, that thing which so thoroughly marked the gramophone as a flawed mediation of the real world, is the very thing that Jeck foregrounds throughout his career: the pops and cracks that can occur when a dirty and imprecise needle comes in contact with imperfect or dirty vinyl.[9]

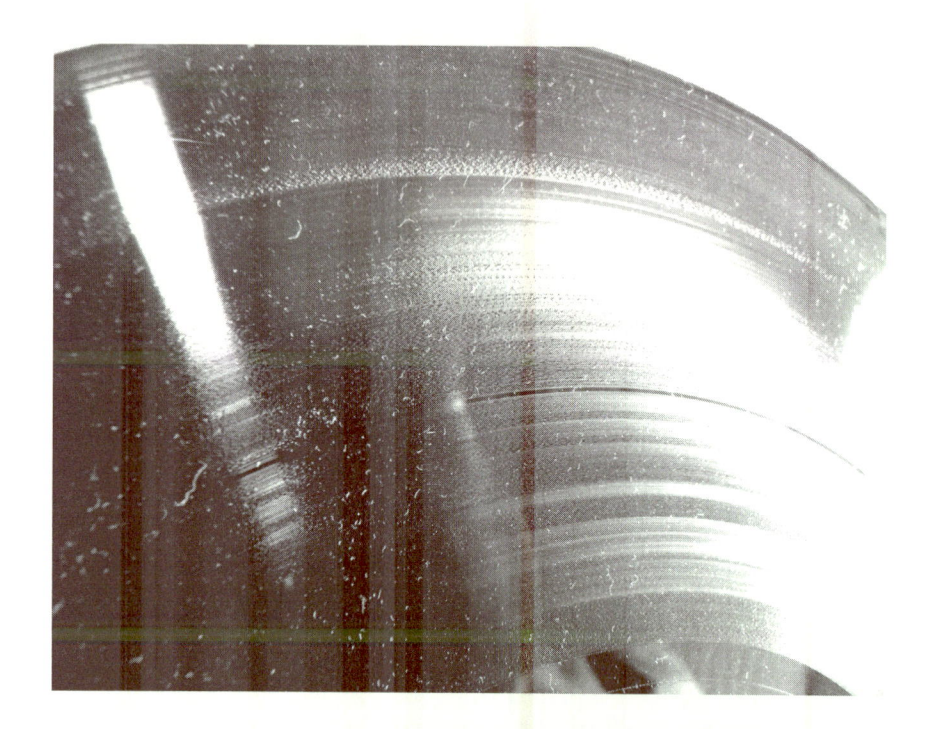

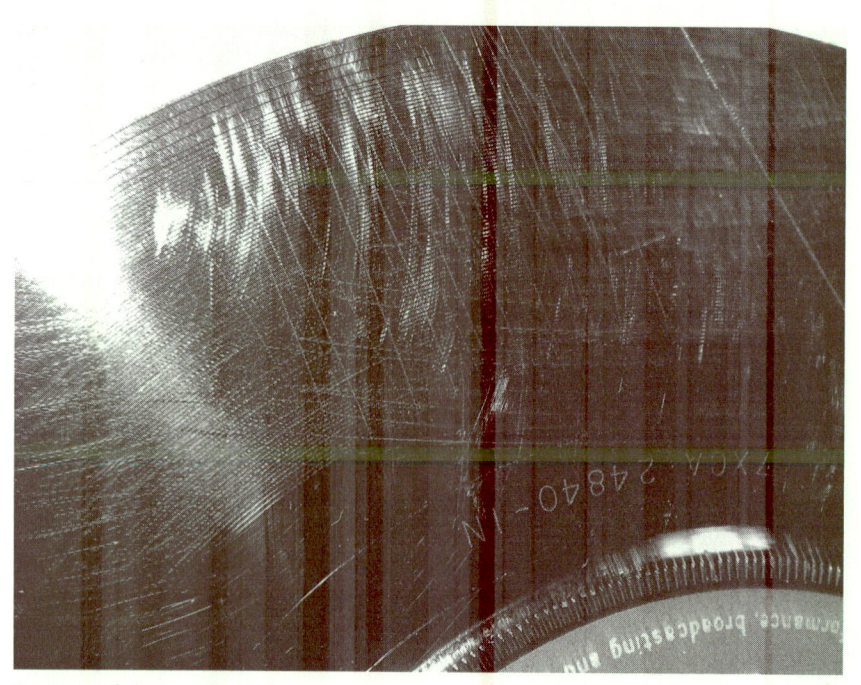

*Dusty and damaged vinyl.*

From this performance, Jeck found an aesthetic that matched how he wanted to create art and he released his first album, *Loopholes*, in 1995. Since his 1999 release, *Surf*, he has released a solo album nearly every year: like *Vinyl Codas I-IV* (2000–1), *7* (2003), *Stoke* (2004), *Sand* (2008), and *An Ark for the Listener* (2010). Writing on Jeck often stresses the nostalgia his work performs without conceptualizing why that is so. In a profile for *Wire* magazine from 2002, this claim is made about Jeck's work: 'Call it nostalgia, history or memory, Jeck's music is redolent of it. There's the half-remembered echo of some musical passage on a record, distorted to a greater or lesser extent by his manipulations' (Bell, 2002, 30–1). It is certainly true that the major force of Jeck's work is the way the splices of cultural memory seem to float in and out of his pieces, and this is certainly one form of the nostalgia that his work iterates. It is no wonder that Jeck in that very same interview talks about the litter that vexes him in his native Liverpool. The connection is never made in the profile, but it doesn't seem too much to stress that Jeck's work is constantly repurposing 'litter'. In one sense, we can take this literally. Without even considering the excessive record collection plundering that comes from being a vinyl obsessive influenced by early hip-hop records, Jeck freely admits to decades'-worth of searching for record players that have been discarded and prizing them specifically because they are old and foreground their age by how noisy they are. Indeed, one track on *7* (2003), entitled 'Bush Hum', builds an entire piece with loops and feedback out of the hum that his Bush record player makes when it is ungrounded. That hum is the sole source for the entire piece that unfolds slowly and seems to envelop itself as the overtones collide with each other. But this also gets us to the other sense of nostalgia that remains difficult to ignore: Jeck's music appears nostalgic precisely because it foregrounds the flaws of the transmission of reproduced music. It is its inherent, and amplified and manipulated, noisiness that registers this nostalgia for decades of listeners who, despite all of our intentions to keep our vinyl and needles in the best condition possible, still recognize in that noise a time that theoretically belongs to the past.[10] These noisy indicators highlight the ways that vinyl records are mediators between our current historical moment in the world and the world of the past that is embedded within not just their historical content, but the history which is apparent through the quality of the fidelity. It is this noisy fidelity that Jeck wants to foreground. He freely admits to treating his vinyl poorly, not putting the records away carefully, leaving them out to collect dirt.[11] For Jeck, those sounds should register a historical distance even as they are being combined into something new.

As noisy as such an idea is, this position echoes sentiments that Adorno explores in his essays on the vinyl record:

> There is no doubt that, as music is removed by the phonograph record from the realm of live production and from the imperative of artistic

activity and becomes petrified, it absorbs into itself, in this process of petrifaction, the very life that would otherwise vanish. The dead art rescues the ephemeral and perishing art as the only one alive. Therein may lie the phonograph record's most profound justification, which cannot be impugned by an aesthetic objection to its reification. For this justification reestablishes by the very means of reification an age-old, submerged and yet warranted relationship: that between music and writing. (Adorno, 2002a, 279)

First, this inaugurates a position that Adorno would further elaborate in much later essays like 'Opera and the Long Playing Record' (1969). There, Adorno would go on to reflect on and mirror what Benjamin had made the case for in his essays on technological reproducibility: that even though the reproduced object always carries with it this embedded history that is nonetheless 'petrified', it has an important role to play in the dissemination of works to a larger audience. But Adorno makes a more salient point here: he recognizes that the vinyl record's status as a reified object is also its greatest reason for existing. In other words, as we have seen, music serves a critical function in the world for helping people to mediate and understand the moment in which they live. Vinyl records, and all technologically reproduced items, transform that mediation into an object that in turn replaces authentic experience. Vinyl is a form of reification because it reduces and supplants the real aesthetic experience into a thing or an object and therefore undermines the artwork's articulation of its own sociohistoric production. As Adorno argues in relation to film in *The Dialectic of Enlightenment* (1944), there is great danger in not recognizing how social relations appear normalized when a reified object, like film, becomes mistaken as the experience of actual social relations.[12] However, he does not, therefore, reject vinyl outright, but prizes it for its ability to nonetheless accrete and distribute this reified mediation.

It is important to consider one more facet of Adorno's position on film. As Levin has argued, Adorno's critical take on film and the dangers of the reification of experience is not due to his rejection of its mode of technological reproduction. Levin notes how some try to claim that Adorno modulated his position later in his career in his 1966 essay 'Transparencies on Film.' Adorno's later readings mark a recognition 'of the progressive and critical potential of cinematic montage to transform even photographic mimesis into constellations, i.e., a type of writing, thus acknowledging that cinematic technique is not structurally excluded by its technology' (Levin, 1990, 25). In other words, even though cinema is yet another mode of art that reifies experience, it is not the case that it should be rejected because of this. Rather, Adorno argues that the process of montage creates a new level of mediation of the reified material. Levin goes on to argue how Adorno's reading of cinema is influenced by his understanding of vinyl, but I want to focus on the way that Adorno values the ability of the reified image to transform its status as petrified object through the process of montage – for montage is one of the key elements of Jeck's compositions.

Jeck's *Vinyl Coda IV* from 2001 is a 45-minute piece in which all of the elements that animate his work are reverberating. It begins with his trademark emphasis on the crackles and hisses of vinyl. To put it now in completely Adornian terms, Jeck's work opens by announcing and recognizing itself as the reified object that it is. This noisy by-product of technological reproduction signals to us not only some, perhaps nostalgic, historical distance but also openly signifies itself as an inexact facsimile. Or, perhaps more stridently, as an aesthetic manoeuvre that performs its open brokenness and separation from its original sources, the vinyl noise functions as a mediation of our own experience of Modernity. *Vinyl Coda IV* slowly builds as other unidentifiable slices and skips enter the fray: a skittering slice of jazz drum kit, pieces of voices singing parts of phrases, a separate percussive hit running in a different tempo than the established rhythm (run forward and backward several times), a repetitive two-note string refrain, and then, about 21 minutes in, all of these phrases gently but noisily careening off of each other, the Mormon Tabernacle Choir enters with 'The Little Drummer Boy'. The emergence of something seemingly holy (that is, structured in terms of a coherent or sound philosophical position and ontology) in the midst of the cacophony at first startles and, being slightly lower in pitch than the original, gives it an eerie quality. Jeck leaves the final 'rum-pum' to repeat and delay until it decays and disappears. Later, we recognize the entrance of a piece of Debussy's 'Clair De Lune', to hear it jostle against the other remnants of detritus that were established earlier in the song. Recontextualized within *Vinyl Coda IV* we hear only fragments of Debussy come and go and recognize it as one of many fragments of history subject to decay. More, Jeck's pieces refuse not only any narrative closure but also, in only deploying fragments of other works, his work becomes a site in which the idea of the unity of artworks is dashed.

This dismantling the idea of the unity of artworks mirrors the premium that Adorno places on modern art like Beckett's writing. In *Aesthetic Theory* (1997b), Adorno claims that:

> At ground zero, however, where Beckett's plays unfold like forces in infinitesimal physics, a second world of images springs forth, both sad and rich, the concentrate of historical experiences that otherwise, in their immediacy, fail to articulate the essential evisceration of subject and reality. This shabby, damaged world of images is the negative imprint of the administered world. To this extent Beckett is realistic. (Adorno, 1997b, 31)

Much like the case that Adorno made for the importance of Beckett's writing, Jeck's work registers this sense of the necessity of announcing its own inability to have a unity or cohesion with the world it mimetically represents.[13] Jeck's damaged and noisy soundscapes are a productive corollary to the kind of work that Adorno demanded in an 'administered world' – producing works that announce themselves as a world lost and a world irretrievable. Jeck's so-called nostalgia is one that is weighted with much that animates Adornian critical theory. Jeck's works dramatize the loss of aura that Benjamin elucidated and announce their status as works severed from any notion of something authentic. His works tirelessly create a montage of noise that reflects our fragmented mediation of the modern world.

# PART FOUR
# Approaching Noise Musics

# CHAPTER FIFTEEN

# Noise as Music: Is There a Historical Continuum? From Historical Roots to Industrial Music

*Joseph Tham*

### Introduction: noise music, a continuum?

Noise or noise music has been proposed by some critics as a non-genre; it is often referred to in terms of 'anomalous zones of interference between genres' (Brassier, 2009, 62) and the term is used as 'the expedient moniker for a motley array of sonic practices with little in common besides their perceived recalcitrance with respect to the conventions governing classical and popular musics' (Hegarty, 2007, ix–x). The history of noise has also been theorized as a composite history – or rather histories – of practices which, besides being an account of disruptions and disturbances, can only with hindsight have projected onto it the loose chronological connection(s) of the various strands of the avant-garde since the early twentieth century. In other words, there is no seemingly coherent continuum of an aesthetic development of noise as a genre (Cain, 2009, 29). However, Nick Cain, in his primer on noise music, posits that there is a transformation of this 'negativity' of noise as an existence defined by what it is not, of a series of 'attempts at cultural deprogramming conceived in opposition to then-dominant discourses' (Cain, 2009, 29), to something more self-consciously positive. He suggests that there has been a gradual evolution of noise as a musical language, a genre in and of itself, complete with codes, idioms and a historical narrative.

Like jazz and dance music, the definition and historical narrative of noise music is problematic. However Simon Reynolds has suggested a historical continuum of dance music in his book, *Energy Flash*, where he put forward a 'hardcore continuum' that is a narrative of a 'nexus where a number of attitudes and energies mesh: druggy hedonism, an instinctively avant-garde surrender to the "will" of technology, a "fuck art, let's dance" DJ-oriented "functionalism" [and] a smidgeon of underclass rage' (Reynolds, 2012, xxiii). A similar set of criteria can be used to describe a 'noise continuum' as 'sonic hedonism, an instinctively avant-garde surrender to and harnessing of the "will" of technology, a "fuck art, let's make some glorious din" outsider-oriented functionalism and a smidgeon of counter-cultural rage'. The similarities between the hardcore continuum and the noise continuum are striking, as both have clear historical precedents – noise having the lineage of Futurists, Dada, *musique concrète*, industrial music and so on, in the same way that hardcore dance music has Kraftwerk, and Detroit techno. They both share the compulsive drive to move forward aesthetically in exploring the musical unknown, and both have latter-day artists who acknowledge past practitioners' contributions to their musical output. As with any genre, therefore, the historical narrative would never be self-conscious and well-formed in its formative years but it is always a complex process of multiple strains of criss-crossing cultural and aesthetic developments coming together to generate a more coherent movement subsequently (Cooke, 1998, 7–24).[1] The following pages aim to trace the formation of such a progression of noise music by examining the earliest protagonists in the early twentieth century through various related composers and movements in the subsequent decades up to the early 1980s, when noise music as an established musical convention started to take self-conscious shape. This chapter is thus the first part of a larger history of noise music to come.

## Noise, but not noise: aestheticizing (1910s–1960s)

The twentieth century was the century of the avant-garde, the modernist age and the mechanical-technological milieu. With new sensibilities, fresh perspectives and unheard-of scientific paradigm shifts came new modes of creation and execution in literature, the arts and music. Arnold Schoenberg and the twelve-tone composition signalled the first modernist break with classical musical composition and expression and with the Futurists, the century started its fetish with dissonance and cultural rebelliousness which basically laid the foundation for the historical avant-garde. While the Viennese school of Schoenberg, Webern and Berg proposed a break or at least an unprecedented re-shuffling of the traditional tripartite hegemony of harmony, melody and rhythm, in turn forcing the art of music composition to the edge, the Futurists under the nominal leadership of Filippo Marinetti and his musical ideologue, Luigi Russolo, pushed the boundary of what music is, over the starboard.

The creation of the earliest noise machines – the *intonarumori* – by Russolo to simulate the sounds of the industrialized urban landscape and modern military hardware was all about roars, crashes, hisses, gurgles, creaks, scrapes, screeches, and more (Tisdall and Bozolla, 1977, 111–12). This was a seemingly novelty product of the attention-grabbing Futurists, designed in order to stake a claim in the consciousness of the West, as well as to celebrate the new-found freedom which urbanization and its accompanying rapid industrialization seemed to bring to the modern society. The noise machines were toured across Europe, and hundreds of spectators bore witness to them, but by the late 1920s, due to a lack of interest from the musical establishment to include the machines into their oeuvre and, more importantly, due to technological limitations, the *intonarumori* were not yet loud and raucous enough. Furthermore, the machines were bulky and unwieldy and there was no commercial impetus to manufacture them in huge quantities to effectuate any sea change in music/noise-making. The music establishment was still very much staunchly upholding the sacred principles of musical virtuosity via mastery of traditional musical instrumentation, and thus, despite the ground-breaking atonal works of Schoenberg, Webern and Berg, the *enfants terribles* trio of the Viennese school, harmony and melody were still the golden rules.

However, the avant-garde soldiered on, with the advent first of Dada in Zurich, Switzerland, where the irreverent group of cultural outsiders staged a theatrical and musical cabaret of the absurdist and iconoclastic sort. They aimed at destroying what the traditional art forms represented – the bourgeois separation of art from life, and its transformation into a mere spectacle – and they hoped, via the Cabaret Voltaire, to reintegrate the two. The Dada practitioners, however, were nihilists of the first degree, who wished to annihilate all art by making declamatory and denunciatory manifestos and broadsheets and sending them out to the unsuspecting world. Their dismantling of sounds, words and language, coupled with their use of clangorous noise-making makeshift contraptions during their acts, were early examples of the ur-performative nature of some modern noise musicians. The Dadaists, however, were anti-war and by rejecting certain aspects of urbanism, positioned themselves antithetically to the Futurists, whose obsession with all things militaristic and urban neatly marked the early history of noise. This thus gives us two convenient theoretical approaches to noise-making.

The Dada movement also brought the ideas of collage and chance into the arts; the non-narrative and non-linear juxtaposition of sounds, words and visuals, as well as the breakaway from a rational intentionality in both our daily and cultural acts, were rich reservoirs of inspiration for subsequent generations of avant-gardists, mavericks and refuseniks. For example, William S. Burroughs and Brion Gysin took collage to the literary extreme in their cut-ups in the 1950s and 1960s and subsequently noise musicians used this as a basis for their creation of sonic mash-ups and aurally disorientating and shocking 'music'.

Occurring simultaneously across the other side of the continent, Soviet Russia was going through both a socio-political revolution as well as a cultural avant-gardist one. The influence of the Italian Futurists was not so much a direct inspiration but something to react against. The already restless artists, literary types and poets picked up on the manifestos of the Futurists and issued even more nihilistic treatises. Variously known as the Russian Futurists and the Constructivists, the various cells of these individuals calling themselves Ego-Futurists, Nothingists, and so on, attempted to push the borders of revolutionary and modernist arts relentlessly forward. However, there were two pieces of composition that arose during this vibrant period of Russian experimentalism and avant-garde flowering, which equalled and, to some, might even top the Futurist *intonarumori*: Nikolai Foregger and his Orchestra of Noises performing for the iconoclastic proto-inter-media production of 'Mechanical Dances' and, more importantly, the monumental *Symphony of Sirens* by Arseny Avraamov, staged in the city of Baku, which mobilized thousands to perform an ambitious symphony to celebrate and glorify the October Revolution of 1917 (Alarcón, 2008, 19–21). The 'gesamtkunstwerk' scale of the piece predated other later noise-informed/infused works like Hermann Nitsch's *Das 6-Tage Spiel Des Orgien Mysterien Theaters* (Green, 1999, 171–7). An entire city came together and partook in a symphony of orchestrated noise, thus symbolizing the cathartic, insurrectionary and modernist nature and status of noise as an agent of change and the flag-bearer of the avant-garde.

Surrealism, a major art movement closely associated with Dada both in terms of the people involved as well as the strategies they used to push the boundaries of art and life further, contributed to the forward thrust of the avant-garde via automatic writing, Freudian psychoanalytical manifestations, and the core belief that life can be changed through art. In view of the ideological zero-sum political situation in Europe in the 1920s and 1930s, left-wing ideas also figured largely in the consciousness and motivation of the Surrealists. However, putting aside the reigning ideological context, the Surrealists and the Dadaists believed that the arts were true agents of change in all areas of humanity, and dissonance, or noise, was necessary. This establishes the neat equation of change/forward-looking/innovation with the idea of noise as a possible agent of change, challenge, and a foundational oppositional force to the old world order, the decadent capitalist system and the conservative establishments at all levels of society. (However, it must be noted that the leader of the Surrealists, André Breton, was resolutely anti-music.)

It would take a few individuals to show the rest more concrete ways to progress from the abstract realm of theory, polemic and manifesto to bringing the noise forth into music: namely Edgard Varèse and John Cage. Varèse can be seen as an associate of the Futurists, whom he admired with certain reservations, but once again, technological limitations meant he was not able to realize the new and exciting sounds which he heard in his head and so lived a life of frustration in the 1920s and 1930s. Nevertheless, he repeatedly articulated in print his hope for the emergence of new musical instruments and tools in the near future, for agitated composers like himself to actualize music filled with dissonance and novel sounds yet unheard-of. These new sounds would overcome the limited possibilities of traditional instrumentation to align with the modernist age. His dream was partially fulfilled when he completed some of the first few electronic compositional masterpieces, *Poème Électronique* (1957–58) and *Déserts* (1950–54), but that was only in the 1950s towards the end of his life. John Cage, on the other hand, liberated sounds from the oppressive hegemony of traditional musical establishment in more ways than one: his use of non-conventional musical tools like the phonogram and, in *4'33"* (1952), of the basic idea that that anything can be music, gave license to thousands after that to make noise. His aleatory compositions were a continual refinement of the ideas first expounded by Dada and Surrealism, to break the authoritarian hold of the composers over musical compositions. Both of them can be considered as beacons along the road to noise music but they had never professed to any concrete aesthetics which would be linked to the genre, as, ultimately, they were still part of the classical field – albeit inhabiting a more iconoclastic or fringe role. Noise's awakening as a musical genre would have to wait until the 1950s when a younger generation of artists in various fields, armed with the new technology available after the Second World War and the new socio-political climate of the 1950s and 1960s, moved closer to a more self-conscious and self-aware noise aesthetics.

## Legitimizing noise: 1950s–1960s

### Musique concrète/*electroacoustic music*

The tape recorder as a compositional tool became the departure point for the foregrounding of the non-musical elements around us: noise as music. With the post-war availability of the tape machine proliferating through

Europe and the USA, it was just a matter of time before someone would harness it extensively to create musical pieces of pure electronic provenance and texture from surrounding noises. Pierre Schaeffer and his assistant, Pierre Henry, composed the world's first tape/electronic work, *Symphonie pour un homme seul* (Symphony for a Man Alone) (1950), which signalled the final realization of the pre-Second World War sensibility and its imagination of combining the idea of modernity with a new music through the actualization of a truly modern art in the form of tape composition by the end of the 1940s in France. After this symphony, everyone who mattered in the modern classical world had to try their hands at it: Stockhausen, Cage, Berio, Boulez – the list goes on. Music had finally broken away from the presumptuous imitation of the natural world of sound in an abstract realm; the only limit is being constrained by the imagination and the tediousness of composing using tape. Other key *musique concrète* and electronic composers like Luc Ferrari and Bernard Parmegiani, who helped cultivate the sustained experimental legacy of the GRM,[2] produced pristinely beautiful but frequently aurally jarring pieces which incorporate sharp shards of electric spikes, dramatic soars and trawls of amplitude and an uncanny knack for inserting processed found sounds into the composition. This helped to reinvent music and invent a prototype language of noise along the way. Noise as a self-conscious musical form was thus born.

The subsequent setting up of centres devoted to the composition of tape-based works and electronic pieces was a sign of the euphoric acceptance by the musical avant-garde of this new mode of creativity. Some applied the principles of serialism (Pierre Boulez), some made use of the inherent asynchronous nature of two simultaneously playing tape machines (Steve Reich), and some, especially the axis around the GRM, reimagined the found sounds surrounding them and moulded futuristic and noisy sound *études*. But it would take the world quite a while to catch on and understand fully what this all meant. Right now, only with the coffers of the state and corporate sponsorship could one dream of doing likewise. Noise-making within the confines of traditional art music composition was still in the hands of the upper strata of society. However, the fact that the founding father of *musique concrète* was more of an engineer than a traditional composer with the relevant conservatory training and its attendant musical baggage, was a sign of things to come by the time noise became a fully established genre in its own right. Most noise artists are unable to sight-read or scribble musical staves but rely wholly on their need to create anew and concoct musical forms which defy notes, tones and musical conventions. They hijack the evolving technological forward thrust for their own sonic bliss and *jouissance* based on their intuition and the art of improvisation.

## *Henri Chopin and William Burroughs/Brion Gysin*

With the advent of tape machines, they soon became a tool to rewire the hegemony of language and poetry when various groups of literary types started deconstructing and building anew poems of another kind: concrete and sound poetry – in other words, text as noise. Poets, proto-sound artists and literary agitators cut up, sped up, sliced and spliced and even removed literal meaning from their poetry and introduced noise as disruption and a mode of compositional mindset into modern literature. Parallel to these, one must definitely acknowledge the collaboration of William S. Burroughs and Brion Gysin in picking up from where the Dadaists and Surrealists left off in the art of collage to re-examine the insidious influence and control of the word on humankind for the past few millennia. More importantly, the ideas and experiments of these two visionaries basically rewired the minds of subsequent musicians to treat noise, tapes and electronic equipment as powerful means to challenge the increasing hegemonic outreach of the capitalist monolith to reduce the populace to passive consumers who, in their view, were being brainwashed and rewired to become modern-day zombies. It was just a matter of time before the two groups of artists came together and terrorized the establishment with Henri Chopin's *OU Revue* magazine, a periodical curated and published by Chopin tirelessly for most of the middle of the twentieth century, which slowly changed and shook up the world of the arts. Burroughs and Gysin were often featured in the accompanying flexi-disc which came with each issue of the magazine, demonstrating their take on sound art using the art of the cut-up. Many from the Lettrist movement, the surviving Dada and Surrealist crowd, as well as younger generations of sound explorers like the Swedish experimentalist Ake Hodell and self-made DIY avant-savant Englishman Bob Cobbing were actively propounding their ideas of the interface of sound, words and art within and beyond the publication reaches of the *OU Revue*.

## *Performance art*

The connection between noise and the world of performance art and sound art is an erratic one, as some are clearly music precedents while others are more conceptual forebears: within the Fluxus and Fluxus-related group of artists, Yoko Ono with John Lennon released albums which combined her experimental take on voice while pushing the form of rock to its limits and thus foretelling the coming of No Wave and Noise Rock; Yasunao Tone's 'wounded CDs' in the 1980s and 1990s are also creative rethinkings of abusing the format of the then-new digital miracle music carrier, the CD, to make non-repetitive and unpredictable results in their noise/music production. Christian Marclay made a name for himself with his use/abuse of vinyl, and one can find noise artists working in similar vein in the works of Industrial Records associate Boyd Rice/NON and Japanese free jazz/improviser Otomo Yoshihide. All of them explored, questioned and interpreted the medium in their own ways in their noise-making.

Hermann Nitsch, the most established and recognized of all the Viennese Actionists, was a devotee of noise: his symphonies and his infamous *Des Orgien Mysterien Theaters* performances placed the cacophonous 'musical' accompaniments (noise) in the foreground as one of the key elements of the re-enactment of the Dionysian rite. He and the other Actionists like Gunter Brus, Otto Muehl and Rudolf Schwarzkogler were pushing performance art using the body and rituals while highlighting certain atavistic and primordial symbols and signs in their various actions, which during the 1960s in Vienna and Europe attracted police interference, legal actions, and smear campaigns from the press, as well as applause and support from like-minded audiences and fellow travellers. Subsequent noise artists are known to name-drop them or explain their noise aesthetics and performative foundations based on the actions and words of this group of taboo-breakers. Early Merzbow/Masami Akita releases used words like 'action' as a form of acknowledgement of his debt to them.

Other performance artists who were not so linked to noise-making and music became important influences on the later practitioners in their conceptual ideas and the execution of performances: Vito Acconci's theory of the power field and his various performance pieces which aimed at interrogating the domains of public and private in the late 1960s and early 1970s were conceptual avant-garde bullets which shattered the straitjacketed mindset of the public; Chris Burden's *Shoot Piece* (1971) totally destroyed the bourgeois construct of the separation of life and art when he was injured while, during the performance, he was supposed to be grazed by a bullet fired by his collaborator from a distance but instead more than what was expected was blasted off his body. Their transgressions were staples to the future generations of noise artists in their interrogation of the interface of body politics as well as the realm of the politics of power and their ramifications on the human psyche.

Younger generations of performance artists traversed the invisible demarcations between art, music and life with ease after the 1960s and 1970s, when the first generations of performance artists from both groups had successfully broken down initial societal barriers: John Duncan's *Blind Date* (1980) (he had sexual intercourse with a corpse, recorded and released the procedure and then he topped it off with a vasectomy) updated Acconci's *Seedbed* (1972) (the artist situated himself below the exhibition space, out of sight of the visitors and masturbated according to his associational fantasy of the sounds and voices he heard through the floorboards) (Goldberg, 2001, 156) and pushed it even further by wrapping it with ethical thorns to prick and question the audience about issues of moral standards and societal norms. Of course, he did not deny the fact that it was also a form of public psychoanalysis to interrogate his personal psyche and purge his demons in some of the works he enacted (Duncan, 2006, 16–17). Christof Migone, a Canadian artist, though not as outwardly transgressive, also used his body as a 'canvas' for noise and sound-making, from holding out his tongue as far as he could to the cracking and popping of the joints on the body. His art is more personal but never frivolous, as he often throws open the assumptions of body politics and its relation to modern-day existential struggle (Migone, 2005, 16–17). Even the notorious Haters are performance artists par excellence, who revelled in the joyful and iconoclastic physical destruction of fetish objects to attempt to break down modern materialist, consumerist thought processes as well as injecting a solid dose of vitriolic fun in their acts of smashing and drilling. The recordings these artists made, which blur the usually inviolable boundaries between previous non-contaminated fields, are precisely what noise is all about – a transgression of conceptual, creative and even ethical spheres, and questioning issues which most take for granted. Noise as performance art is thus a platform for examining and highlighting the existential rage of modern society expressed via the body, albeit an often disembodied one. The visual and audio aspects of these performance artists deepen the performative and expressive dimensions of noise 'compositions' and 'performances'; a prime example would be contemporary Swiss art-noise collective, Schimpfluche-Gruppe, which can be seen as successors to the Viennese Actionists.

## It must have been the ... 1960s (late 1960s–1970s)[3]

The technological spread of post-war audio and electronic gadgetry from the military and the musical establishment to the used goods and thrift shops across the USA and Europe was a decisive point in the empowerment of the uninitiated to make noise. The rapid development and mass production of audio and related technology in the increasingly entrenched recording industry, with its new flush of wealth through the explosion of rock, blues and soul music from the 1960s onwards, as well as the consumer demand for better sound delivery from their vinyl platter, allowed many youths and the young-at-heart to ravage these shops to pick up budget-priced guitars, pedals, drum parts, amplifiers, speakers and odd instrumental oddities like the revox recorder, oscillators, all sorts of sound generators and even exotic foreign instruments which began to stream into the West after the mass migration of ex-colonial subjects and Third World citizens seeking political asylum or simply a better life. A kind of junkyard aesthetic was gradually formed. The early days of the Stooges were rumoured to have Iggy Pop banging away atonally and joyously on an assortment of metallic knick-knacks, being one of the many examples of such rock and pop cultural informed attempts at proto-punk and do-it-yourself noise-making.

The following case studies are just a few of the more prominent historical precedents which took on and expanded this sensibility in creating their sound/noise/music identity and compositions. Many of them became inspirations to many noise practitioners in the 1980s and beyond.

## *Nihilist Spasm Band*

While many teenagers picked up guitars and drums to emulate their favourite British invasion groups, a few of them, albeit not so adolescent, began their decades-long music bashing in a Canadian town every Monday night. The Nihilist Spasm Band were formed by a group of amateur musicians and non-musicians, who just wanted to create a musical world all of their own with home-made kazoos and musical odds and ends, augmented with the basic band set-up. Within the band were members who held socially respected jobs like doctors and teachers in their twenties and thirties, who were influenced more by jazz, blues and traditional musical forms. They have been banging away joyously despite the passing of a couple of their key members since the 1960s, after the self-released debut record, entitled *No Record*, in the late 1960s. The lack of touring activities did not restrain the band from reaching out to a wider audience who were avid record collectors and fervent music fans around the globe: Surrealist sonic adventurers Nurse With Wound name-checked them on their album sleeve, while seminal Japanese collective Hijokaidan were big fans who were responsible for the release and availability of many later-year records of the band. In the 1990s there was even a series of noise festivals called No Music Festivals, curated to pay tribute to this group of absolutely non-commercially minded noise-niks and to gather noise and noise-infected acts from all over the world.

## *Suicide*

The legendary and influential New York duo was a necessary evolutionary stage of noise music's progress from the embryonic stage of its earlier decades to its fruition in the 1980s. Despite the relatively mild-sounding and more poppy musical output of Alan Vega and Martin Rev on their first two classic New York electro-punk albums, their early performances have attained mythical status, since no documentation exists or survived from the early 1970s when the two were at their most performance-art phase. This helped to push their total confrontational rock-noise to out-and-out noise freak-outs. Their later gigs, supposedly more toned down, were still of high intensity: their no-compromise and up-yours stance onstage was proven one time too many when they were very close to death-threatening situations of flying axes and audience death-threats (Nobakht, 2005, 111–12). They were the only group which the rebellious No Wavers respected among the first generation of New York punks, as they were consistently the most 'out-there', and putting their lives on the line for art, rock'n'roll and sheer noise. They managed to do all this with just a beat-up old keyboard and low-rent gadgets and Alan Vega's signature blood-curdling shrieks and screams of weird tales of modern-day urban Americana. The only significant parallel would come only later in the UK with Whitehouse in the late 1970s.

## *Los Angeles Free Music Society*

Noise-making of all kinds is the *raison d'être* of this sprawling collective which consists of many loose alliances and one-man sound crusades; some even became legendary 'noise-rock' outfits in their own rights, hailed by many in the noise circuit to be pioneers and prime movers. The Los Angeles Free Music Society (LAFMS) was not a uniform, monolithic entity, though; many involved might indulge in *outré* exotica compositions *à la* Tom Recchion, controversial extreme body-performance-art projects of John Duncan, neo-psychedelic Paisley Underground stalwart Dennis Duck and many more whose participation in the musical sojourns of the collective could be of a fleeting kind, dipping in and out with scant regard for mainstream 'rock group' allegiance. Purportedly starting its long and weird existence in an alternative record shop, Poo-Bah Records in the mid-1970s, the LAFMS was an umbrella association for outsiders, freaks and art-school types in the bland musical environment dominated by the post-Altamont West Coast escapist rock aristocrats of James Taylor and the Eagles.

Inspired by previous cohorts of noise-inflected artists and musicians like the Afro-American free jazzers and *musique concrète* composers, the various outfits and projects within the collective made use of various sound-making tools and instruments they could lay their hands on to produce home-spun sonic detritus, crude tape collages and atonal snippets, big-band junkyard rave-ups and gothic post-nuclear fallout torch songs. One of the most revered as well as the most consistent and persistent of them all, Smegma, set the precedent for noise-makers from the 1980s onwards with a sense of purpose, with anarchic communal overtone in the methodology of their survival, their devotion to joyous noise and the intentional opt-out of the straight society. Perhaps this was why they had to move from the increasingly Reaganite California to the more countercultural Northwest in the later part of their musical odyssey. Another equally important group, the Doo-dooettes, though dormant in recent years, were notorious for their idiosyncratic take on ur-rock of the most primitive kind; the discovery and subsequent release of their collaboration with Japanese psychedelic noise guitar welder Keiji Haino from the mid-1980s was a revelation and a key document which should have placed them squarely as the bridge between noise and psychedelia.

## Noise turns on its ugly head: late 1970s–early 1980s

The late 1970s signalled the pivotal turn of noise away from both academic conservatory 'lab coat experimentation' and junkyard art trash collectives to a self-reflexive, self-conscious movement of musical expression and rebelliousness against the society of spectacle – the final collapse of the optimistic 1960s with record-setting unemployment rates, the breakdown of Cold War *détente*, the entrance of hawkish and neoliberal politicians into the White House and 10 Downing Street and a growing cynicism felt by the youth towards this decadent world in the new decade. In most cases, the idea of the 'me' over everything else became the byword of daily existence for youth. On the other hand, alienation and existential angst was not uncommonly felt by those at the fringe towards the increasingly crass consumerism, mega-corporate domination and the renewed threat of a nuclear catastrophe. Now with ever more readily available musical tools (ironically this was due to the economics of scale of these big multi-national corporations to produce more of them and sell them more cheaply), the newer generation of 'noisicians' enjoyed a second flood of high-tech (albeit analogue) media equipment which served to enhance and bear fruit to the manifestation of their dystopian or Dionysian worldview.

### *Industrial music for ... industrial people*

The legacy of performance art continued in the singular vision of Genesis P-Orridge, Cosey Fanny Tutti, Chris Carter and Peter 'Sleazy' Christopherson after the shedding of skin of their previous extreme artistic manifestation as COUM Transmissions in 1976. The obstinately non-musicianship of Throbbing Gristle as well as their collective aim to forge a music devoid of musical conventions, record industry standards, and their puckish social intervention guaranteed them a crucial position in the historical continuum of noise music. Everything they produced was meant to be a statement, including the usage of pre-branding techniques and strategies, the setting-up of their own record label, the recording of every single gig they performed, the release of all of them as documentation, the purchase of the latest audiovisual equipment the market had to offer and the making of pre-MTV musical-video materials, all via Industrial Records. The underlining rationale for the existence of Throbbing Gristle was to re-educate the masses (thus the discarding of the performance art of COUM Transmissions for the 'popular' medium of the 'band') by channelling the writings of William S. Burroughs, media theory and certain strains of countercultural movements against the hegemonic domination of the industrial-militarypolitical complex.

Live, the members of the group were known to 'play' the instruments which they were least adept at or comfortable with to ensure their ideological purity and intent; volume and intensity in both sound and visual accompaniment during their sets were enforced and any form of compromise was disallowed. The only persons who could dictate the content of their harrowing presentation were themselves. Traversing through the eerie exotica, monotonous drones, sporadic bellows and wails, electronic guttural releases, death-raising horn blasts, electric shudders, crawling bass thumps to screeching six-string freak-outs, TG's noise and their rallying were picked up, rubbed off and emulated all over the world soon afterwards.

With like-minded souls like Cabaret Voltaire, NON, Z'ev, Monte Cezazza, Controlled Bleeding and SPK, as well as other similar but slightly later musical rupture in the early 1980s like Einstürzende Neubauten and Die Todliche Doris, industrial music became the dark side of the post-punk milieu of the late 1970s and early 1980s. The common influences of the cut-ups and the 'electronic revolution' of William S. Burroughs and Brion Gysin and the prophetic apocalyptic alternate worlds of J. G. Ballard (especially *The Atrocity Exhibition*) ensured the perpetuation of the continuum of influence and inspiration in noise. Cabaret Voltaire and Throbbing Gristle both ventured into video production which, they hoped, would serve as missives into the world out there, to be picked up by disaffected youths and alienated cells of individuals who were able to see through the capitalist-materialist illusions of the late twentieth century but yet powerless or alone in their solitary alienation.

## *Nurse With Wound/Coil/Current 93*

The term 'England's Hidden Reverse' was coined by David Keenan, the author of a retrospective historical and cultural account to describe this group of industrial-tinted individuals who are known to tap into both the long-running English esoteric underground since the angel-obsessed John Dee, as well as the urban decay of the modern British post-industrial monochrome. These three key groups of a slightly later second generation of noise-exponents formed a rallying point for many subsequent incarnations of English underground weirdness, anti-mainstream communitarianism and flip-side cultural cabal. The resolutely non-musical debut album of Nurse With Wound, *Chance Meeting On A Dissecting Table Of A Sewing Machine And An Umbrella* (1979), was given the now-legendary review rating of 'Yes-Isok' in one of the British music weeklies.[4] The fact that this gave it a much higher profile than it would have had otherwise led to its selling out in weeks, subsequently rapidly provided the group with a core group of fans. (More importantly, the main man behind this outfit, Steven Stapleton has a lifelong obsession with Viennese Actionists, Dada and Surrealism, and he often states that his compositions are surrealist. He has also shared in print the close relationship between his music with predecessors *musique concréte* and Futurism [Keenan, 2003, 52].)

The more-than-legendary Nurse With Wound list which was featured on the sleeve of their first two albums has now gained such pedestal status that any self-respecting fan of esoterica, underground, avant-garde and noise music has to get their hands on – or at least bear a cursory listening to – most, if not all, of the artists listed. Besides a few oddities, most of them have, in one way or the other, cued the advent and development of noise as a historical genre from John Cage to Jean Dubuffet, from Sperm to *Musica Elettronica Viva*. Noise as a genre absorbed, filtered and collaged their various influences into a cosmic mash, an atonal meltdown or an artistic agitation. The collagist mindset, whether due to the lack of proper musicianship, a deliberate defiance of established music practices or even a sheer Dionysian excess, can be traced to the Dada movement as well as to more recent junkyard consciousness of the 1960s and 1970s. Thus, together with Current 93's early foray into the ritualistic and the atavistic on albums like *Dog's Blood Rising* and *Nature Unveiled* (both 1984), Nurse With Wound's first few albums set the tone for an outsider altering of the ears and minds in the larger scheme of noise to come.

Coil, the third group in this tripartite of English underground, provided another path to noise in a less obvious manner. All convoluted bodily rhythms, otherworldly phasing, delay and distortion of vocals and electronic bleeps and blurts, noise can also be sidereal and mystical, and vaguely danceable if you want to, but ultimately mind-blowing and totally psychic tune-ins at their loudest. Albums like *Scatology* and *Horse Rotorvator* are an essential brew of sensual brain-churning of a less traditional male aggressive kind; instead they trade on their ability to eroticise noise. Coil's methodology is both a culmination of the queer aesthetics and Throbbing Gristle/Psychic TV's atavism. Coil's 'danceable' noise is both hypnotic and disturbing, seductive yet repulsive. They predated the recent sideways shift of some noise artists like Pete Swanson and Heatsick to a more 'dance'-oriented output.

## Power electronics: Whitehouse and Maurizio Bianchi

Throbbing Gristle (TG) left behind many inexhaustible traces in the post-punk landscape, but not all were welcomed by the purveyors themselves. Genesis P-Orridge was famous for dismissing the group Whitehouse in one of the interviews when he was asked about the legacy of TG. Infamous for the thematic glorification of mass murderers, Nazi death camps, amoral proclamations, socially untouchable taboos, and the musical see-saw of high pitch sine-like waves and often-hysterical declamations at a highly psychotic level, William Bennett and his co-conspirators like Philip Best and Peter Sotos were misunderstood, misrepresented and avoided by most. They themselves contributed to this near-pariah status, of course. The determined refusal to explain and rationalize the lyrical topics, artwork and album titles gave journalists and moralists of all sorts a field day to ostracize the group and their associated acts for most of the 1980s and 1990s. Even up to today, dismissive and harsh words can still be found in articles about the group.

They also spawned the noise-based genre power electronics, which took most of its musical cues from the modus operandi of Whitehouse and Sutcliffe Jugend and other pioneers of this movement like Maurizio Bianchi's idiosyncratic 'noise' *études*, and acts released by labels like Come Organisation (run by William Bennett) and Broken Flag (run by the main stalwart of another group immersed in the same scene, Ramleh). The fact that the industrial movement and the power electronics sub-genre attracted an entire horde of leather-clad, tattoo-donning and gothic touched-up acolytes was both a pro and a con. The ability for the industrial clangour to spread and to allow for more to get the messages of the likes of TG was a good thing, but like all movements, it built up its own sub-cultures of pretenders, posers and wannabes. The subsequent commercialization of the movement in the form of Nine Inch Nails and Ministry had, by the early 1990s, substituted the revolutionary ideas with Generation-X's obsession with self-centred existentialist issues and emoting.

# Conclusion

By the early 1980s, the various strands of avant-garde, experimental and electronic musics converged into what is known today as noise music. Despite the seemingly disparate roots of noise music from the state-sponsored art music of *musique concrète* to the regional junkyard-informed collectives, to the highly politicized dystopia-painting of industrial anti-music units, the underlying rationale behind the sound-making of these precedents is all about making sonic concoctions/compositions which challenged the conventions of the day and pushing the boundaries of musical form forward in whatever way possible. Putting aside normative musical knowledge and skills, these proto-noise artists gave to those who came after them the artistic license, freedom and legitimacy to continue the path of noise-making.

# CHAPTER SIXTEEN

# Noise as Material Impact: New Uses of Sound in Noise-related Movements

*Rafael Sarpa*

### Introduction

Transformations in sound during the twentieth century have mostly been prompted by the discussion, application and claims of several conceptions of noise. Noise has invaded daily life throughout the process known as modernity with the emergence of modern cities, in which profound technological exchanges have developed. These new technologies spread sounds of a different quality from those found in nature, once the mobilized levels of amplitude, spectral content and persistent forms of existence are compared. New technologies of control and sound generation have also made it possible to manipulate noise. The spreading of this new sound material was the theme of a series of musical expressions during the twentieth century, particularly through the Italian futurists, Edgard Varèse, John Cage, *musique concrète*, various forms of rock, punk and its sucessors, free jazz, industrial music and Japanese noise music, among others.

Several authors including Attali (1985), Kahn (2001), Hegarty (2007) and Tham (2012) have decided to focus on a broader definition of noise so as to include a wide range of practices, which also makes it possible to assess what singularities they might have proposed in contrast with one another. Thus, a history of the use, definition and incorporation of noise takes shape, while each one of the authors stresses the relevance of certain characteristics of noise, proposing common categories of rupture which link these accounts together. However, this chapter suggests a different approach. Instead of attempting to cover the entire set of practices which can be understood in terms of noise, this chapter aims at detecting the intrinsic features of so-called Japanese noise. Japanese noise, power electronics and, in many respects, the first wave of industrial music have added a new meaning to the term 'noise' which was not preponderant in other approaches to sound in the twentieth century.

These three genres have envisioned the possibilities for conceiving of a use of sound as a material impact; that is, they aim at exploring some of the intrinsic features of sound, which are able to offer themselves as a stimulus for the repulsive, excessive, or even destructive intentions directed at the bodies of their receptors. This leads to a second argument. In order to think and use sound for these purposes, it is necessary to address the one who receives this sound, although not only by considering the level of one's tastes or preferences, but also the level of one's physical and physiological apparatuses – that is, as a form of equipment that works under commonly limited configurations due to the biological constraints of the species. The key determinant for this proposal is considering how this impact has been explored in noise practices. This chapter claims that these genres affirm themselves as impact or affect through the exploitation of the features which emerge from the relations between a specific use of sound and the body. This is not only through a relation between affect and the meaning a listener might develop with regard to a certain set of sonorities, elements, musical materials, and so on. Hence, this chapter attempts to emphasize how much these genres seem to have dedicated a special attention to the possibilities of using sound in order to explore the material limits of bodies, as well as offering ways of understanding their relations according to these terms.

## Materialities

Positing an idea of affect based on the exploitation of bodily limits is not an easy task. First and foremost, it elicits the risk of undertaking an endeavour whose simple and almost literal correlation lies on the boundaries between the physiological and the symbolic fields. Such an endeavour – the starting point of socio-biological theories – is also a common practice among several theoretical currents with a neuro-cognitive approach. We are constantly confronted by statements from so-called scientists claiming they have managed to map brain regions, genes or biochemical activities considered responsible for a series of determinations expected to belong to human agency, to a matter of subjective taste or choice.[1] Nevertheless, there is another tendency of authors who became interested in researching the nature of the role played by material components – that is, the body and the technologies connected to it – in the shaping of cultural expressions, without, however, tracing such a strict correlation between both fields. Included in this group of approaches are the works of theorists such as Georg Simmel, Siegfried Kracauer, Walter Benjamin, the intellectual group known as the Toronto School of Communication (Harold Innis, Eric Havelock, Marshall McLuhan) and, more recently, Friedrich Kittler, Hans-Ulrich Gumbrecht, Siegfried Zielinski and Nicole Boivin, among others.

Instead of basing their arguments on some sort of single or primary cause within physico-chemical or physiological matter, such studies have aimed at investigating the kind of pressure these components exert upon the production and attribution of meaning. Assuming the possibility that both the body and technology are not neutral, that is, mere conduits which are freely malleable accordingly to their users' agency, leads to the realization that both the body and technology function within separable boundaries. Neither bodies nor technologies are infinitely plastic, and therefore they are not totally subjected to the desire of individuals or cultures. They function inside predetermined limits that privilege certain usages, excluding others as impossibilities – which can lead to the devising of new technologies in order to bring such impossibilities into the realm of the possible. A simple example would be the invention of the airplane, over a long-standing history of failed attempts and subsequent improvements, as a way to make it possible for the human body to fly.

Paying attention to these material factors means regarding them in the same manner as any other factors that might be involved in the formation of a cultural expression, connected to different domains such as those of a historical, economic, individual, geographic, political or stochastic order. The direct consequence brought about by such an approach is the possibility for expanding this list through considering the intrinsic features of technologies as well as the physiological and cognitive configurations of the bodies involved – although as these factors are usually interdependent, emphasizing both poles provides a more precise focus.

If, somehow, explanations based exclusively on material components cause instant rejection, the same does not occur with regard to the formulations of cultural studies, a field which is virtually based on the idea that understanding the human body and the human itself is only possible through discursive practices. From this idea stems the understanding that if we observe the world searching for meanings, all that can be found are the ways a culture or an individual organizes experience for their own purposes; in other words, the things can only carry the meanings attributed to them by mankind. The consequence of these assumptions is a picture of the world as composed of neutral things: things devoid of intrinsic qualities and properties that could motivate or inspire the uses people make of them.

According to what became known as the 'linguistic turn' by authors belonging to several theoretical currents during the twentieth century, an idea of language became fundamental for the understanding of cultural expressions, leading to an emphasis on meaning, the symbolic, representation, signification and interpretation. This theoretical trend borrowed some premises from both Saussure and Jakobson's linguistics, particularly the notion of the arbitrariness of a linguistic sign – that is, that there is no direct relation between the signifier used to refer to a thing or an idea and the meaning of this represented thing. Since culture's symbolic networks were understood as a kind of language according to these suppositions, the framing in terms of the signifier/signified relation was understood as follows: the things of the world acted as the arbitrary signifier to which cultures and individuals attributed meaning – the signified. Although things and bodies may have received great attention from some branches of cultural studies, they are often traversed by the attempt at verifying how they are socially or culturally constructed. According to Graves-Brown, these kinds of studies that could be grouped under the general term 'material culture studies' (2000, 7) normally ignore, or bypass, what is properly material in the objects of study, still focusing research more on the agent underneath their use than on their material potentialities.

Following a similar path, while tracing origins to a more distant past, Gumbrecht (2003) claims that one of the manners of distinguishing the history of metaphysics in the West was the way in which relating to something in the present, or something that presents itself as a tangible object within the reach of our bodies, has been enclosed into parentheses. This gesture would then become intensified due to the Cartesian notion of 'cogito', mediated by a belief in the distinction between body and soul, gradually bestowing the latter with priority. The 'spiritual' or 'mental' faculties provided man with a place of prominence and distinction above all the other things of the world, thus becoming that what distinguishes the human in contrast to everything else. The whole of existence could then be regarded as essentially dependent on the movements of the human mind. This would provide the body with a secondary place or as a consequence of the mind, while notions based in a certain substantiality of things and bodies would be restricted or even banned from the reflexions upon the human conditions. Hence, the key to understanding things would then be given, in spite of numerous manoeuvres and detours along this history, in the human faculties, and not directly resulting from the things of the world.

This belief in the possibility of a clear and radical distinction between body and soul lies in the core of the very distinction between subject and object, which provides the subject with the responsibility for expressing the existence of the object, or what is and is not appropriated in the understanding of the things of the world. Consequently, things and bodies are immediately regarded as insufficient – as a simple expression conveying meanings which are kept hidden precisely due to a lack in their intrinsic matter. The need to interpret derives from this strict insufficiency of expression itself. Its accomplishment relies upon an idea of meeting a 'depth'. In order to reach the deep meaning of the things of the world, the interpretative act requires that the observer must stand at a great distance from the observed things, for that is the only way to be detached from them. Although the formalization of this need was undertaken by Dilthey, in the foundation of 'hermeneutics' as a discipline, resulting in interpretation as a task for the recently created human sciences in the twentieth century, Gumbrecht notes that similar premises were already being used since the fifteenth century, when attempts to think the relationship between man and the world took place. Therefore, matter – whether of bodies or the things of the world – is permanently at a disadvantage or in the background, tending to be considered as deceptive, as though it concealed the 'true meaning', or, at most, acts as an expression unable to articulate itself.

That being said, the purpose of this chapter is to argue for the possibility of a material investigation of sound, body and noise, as it appears in the three genres here selected: Japanese noise, power electronics and the first wave of industrial music. To claim materiality as a focus of this investigation means understanding the organs of the senses and the whole body as partially autonomous realms that impose modes of operation with which any cultural expression needs to negotiate in order to be in the world. As Csordas states, it is not the case of replacing one determinist scheme for another, but to supplement cultural studies by inserting an 'added dimension of materiality to our notions of culture and history' (Csordas, 1995, 4). The extent to which a material factor plays a larger or smaller role will depend on the specific cultural expression being studied. It is claimed that an attention to the material conditions of sound and the body is paramount to the specific 'languages' of the three music genres that are being studied here.

When one observes the bodily mechanisms which can be affected by sound waves, it is possible to realize that the sounds received by the listener and identified as sound are only a fragment of these effects. Sound and the body interact in several other ways beyond the audible, constituting an effectively synaesthetic relationship. Some acoustic movements impinge upon bodies for reasons that certainly can be best explained by haptic experience, such as pressure, impact, touch, immersion, and so on. Sound's haptic attributes, once propagated in greater amplitude, become potentialized, making these attributes more important for reception. As Goodman states, the study of the dimension of vibration itself is justified for being both a prior to and independent from symbolic or cognitive hearing, meaning that vibrations interact with several bodily zones, ranging from sensing sound in the skin to the modulation of brain waves, and hormonal regulation, which interfere with the pulse, digestion and muscular tension (Goodman, 2009, 10). Besides this, our hearing apparatuses work within limits of sensitivity and tolerance, otherwise a certain amount of stimulus may generate either a temporary or a long-term hearing loss, causing lesions in sensorial cells or in the auricular nerve. The ear has inner mechanisms in order to be protected from sounds of a greater amplitude, but the functioning of these protections wears out the body due to the muscular tensing inside the middle ear.

Another relevant aspect explored in McLuhan-based studies is that the organs of the senses, as media, function according to specific modes that privilege certain attributes at the expense of others. The different ranges of operation through which the eyes and the ears capture stimulus is a classic example. The eyes only manage to see whatever the face is directed at in that moment, while the ears manage to receive stimulus propagated from any direction. Another important characteristic is the existence of eyelids, which unceasingly open and close all of the time, and are capable of being quickly activated whenever one wishes to block images from one's visual field. It is also easy to shift focus and avoid the presence of an image. The ears, however, do not have the same protection; it is necessary to use the hands to cover them or earplugs, in order to reduce the presence of a sound. And if we really want to get rid of unwanted sounds and it is not possible to mute the sound source, the only solution is to take the whole body away from its reach. This might vary from centimeters to hundreds of meters or even kilometers in the case of greater amplitude sounds.

Once these processes described above are kept in relative autonomy from cultural factors and from natural or acquired perceptive ones, functioning in a more automatic range of interactions between sound vibrations and the body, it is important to reaffirm that the meaning of sound as emphasized here differs from the one commonly used in the studies which involve sound wave reception. This current chapter is not very interested in the listener's attributions to the sounds that surround him/her, whether those are propagated by soundscapes, musical works, or specific agents, nor in the psychophysiological functions which allow the identification of parameters or patterns in the universe of sound. These features generated directly from the interaction between sound and the body make it possible, according to Goodman, to use sound as a sort of 'force' (Goodman, 2009, 10). This relative autonomy of the vibrational field in relation to the body is made clear in the limits of the body's resistance itself, whether on the verge of pain when receiving a stimulus, or upon the occurrence of temporary or permanent damage in the hearing organs. It is in this way that I propose to regard sounds working as a material affect – through the consideration of processes in which the body is submitted to physical impacts when exposed to specific sounds. Therefore, by focusing essentially on these responses, this chapter refuses conceptions according to which sound is simply regarded in relation with its symbolic possibilities.

Using sound as a kind of force means that it can be activated either as a repulsive or an attractive form. Despite the fact that these are 'model cases', and that it is rare that one of the forces appears without the other in a given context, sound expressions can tend more towards one pole than the other. According to Goodman:

> At opposite poles of the sonic warfare continuum then, two basic tendencies could be identified, two poles of the continuum of sonic force, perhaps two inverse modes or tactical tendencies. One is militarized. These extensive and intensive tendencies of audio-social radiation can also be usefully described as, on the one hand, centrifugal, efferent, repulsive, producing a movement that spirals out from source, and on the other hand, a centripetal, afferent, attractional power producing a movement that spirals in toward a source. Clearly one tactical deployment of sound is subordinated to the strategic aim of crowd dispersal, to the dissipation of a collective energy, to repulsion and dissolution of clusters, and to the individualization of the movement of bodies. On the other side, we have a tactical deployment whose objective is that of intensification, to the heightening of collective sensation, an attractive, almost magnetic, or vortical force, a force that sucks bodies in toward its source. (Goodman, 2009, 11)

Both kinds of impact reflect two different ways of thinking the entanglement between sound and power. As a repulsive force, sound is ruled by the same principle theoretically formulated by the Futurists, unceasingly repeated in Marinetti's texts – a principle that supposes a directly proportional relationship between sonic intensity and the amount of mobilized amplitude.[2] Futurism values the higher, faster, noisier stimulus. In turn, sound as an attractor understands force as a means to cause 'mobilization' and 'contagion', in the sense that it causes bodies to replicate the rhythms conveyed by the sound system. For Goodman, this trend corresponds to what he calls 'Afro-Futurism' – aesthetic currents which have promoted the union between dance and sound systems.

It is possible to identify a whole historical process as an example of the uses of sound as a repulsive force by the military and police units, as well as in a series of sound aesthetics from the twentieth century. In the first case, one might consider the uses of sound in torturing, military manoeuvres, or to disperse crowds. In the second case, one might consider several composers and aesthetic currents, ranging from Edgard Varèse, Galina Ustvolskaya or Iannis Xenakis to rock music in its numerous variants, taking into account that Italian Futurism is likely to be this tendency's first relevant expression. Nonetheless, the emergence of Japanese noise, this specific approach to sound and force, has reached levels of such importance as to profoundly resignify this model of sound mobilization. This understanding of sound as a repulsive force was largely the one explored in Japanese noise, power electronics and, from a different perspective, the first wave of industrial music manifestations. The productions of these genres seem to be searching for a dwelling place within the boundaries of the body's endurance of sound stimuli, acting as privileged territories in an attempt at communicating with the material limits of bodies.

Contrary to what one might suppose, it is not necessary to know these limits exactly in order to attempt to communicate with them. Although the responses to sound exposition are not the same for every body, neither for every culture, and that, besides, bodily damage related to hearing may take years to manifest itself, this does not prevent these practices from seeking – in dialogue with these limits – a reference regarding the production of their very expressions. If several listeners might not agree whether a durationally long sound within the range of 90dB is intense or not, there will hardly be as many listeners tending to disagree about a durationally long sound of 150dB.

It is true that, as Hegarty states, the question remains limited, and that if there were other ears, other brains, a different viscus, then it would be possible to map the functioning of this different system, proposing also a stimulation aimed at trespassing these mapped limits. However, is it reasonable to question (regardless of any concern with answering it here) whether the modes of exploration involved in the propositions of these noise genres are actually grounded in the limits set by the relationship between body and sound rather than in a concern about trespassing limits in general? Watching *Slaughtered Vomit Dolls* (2006),[3] listening to 'Pro-rapist',[4] reading *120 Days of Sodom*[5] and witnessing Herman Nitch's *6-Day Play*[6] can be understood in general terms as relating to the same kind of transgressive experience. Conversely, all these works engage in singular experiences, since they mobilize different concepts and different sensory interplays of affection. Could something similar be said about mixed martial arts competitions, sadomasochistic practices, police violence, war crimes, serial killers, and biotechnologies to come? If all of the above involve experiences concerning corporeal limits, would these limits then be the same? Do they cause impacts of the same kind? An investigation aimed at distinguishing sensorial experiences might further emphasize other qualities regarding limit-experiences, which could be suggested by the means of an augmented conception of materiality.

## Materially driven impacts

To advance towards the understanding of how bodies are affected by sounds it is necessary – in temporal terms at least – to reject the strong meaning of the concept of noise in Attali and some of the other authors previously mentioned. Attali describes noise at its most general level as the effects caused by a new practice within the core of an old one. It is a concept that goes beyond sound, even departing from it, being thus applicable to other fields and objects of study. Hence, any emerging practice would be taken as noise, according to this general meaning. However, a silent practice and one with great amplitude, also tending to the whole occupation of the audible spectrum, will greatly differ when the sensorial experiences they cause are considered. It is possible to consider an exaggerated use of silence as a limit-experience, for instance. Still, wouldn't these sensorial experiences be radically different?

Even if it can be argued that the categorization of certain works or artists can be very approximate, Japanese noise and power electronics do have some traits that are very recurrent throughout the artists' oeuvres. Let's take as an example 'Ultra Marine Blues', the fifth track of Merzbow's *Pulse Demon* (1996) album. During its seven minutes and 49 seconds there is almost not a single moment where sound spectra are not occupying the whole audible space, leaving the listener exposed in various ways to a huge white noise mass that never ceases to be present during the listening experience. Compression is extensively used, which creates a situation in which the listener is receiving sound constantly at the maximum volume. It is also important to mention that in any live presentation of almost any artist that can be linked to the Japanese noise or power electronics scenes, amplification is used beyond what would be normally tolerable considering the size of the usual concert hall. Other elements, such as rhythmic pulses, and filtering processes that select various frequency regions from the spectra, emerge – and this is also a typical Merzbow trait, also described by Hegarty[7] – making it more difficult to define a global form to the piece.

Let us move to the power electronics terrain, taking as an example 'Roman Shower', the first track of Prurient's *Black Vase* album. What it is noticeable during its fifteen minutes are very high-pitched oscillations around 3,000hz, where the human ear is very sensitive, which are also hyper-compressed, so to speak, as in the Merzbow example, not allowing time for the ears to rest. One interruption of this constantly changing, yet static frequency finally happens around the thirteenth minute – just to return right afterwards accompanied by a screaming voice. As with Merzbow, Prurient does not obviously restrict itself to these traits, and after the first seven minutes other materials start to appear.

This characterization is obviously reductive – there are several nuances typical of each artist. What to say, for example, of the rapprochement with nineteenth-century Romanticism that is present in Tetsuo Furudate and Zbigniew Karkowski's *World as Will* series? And given that we are now in 2012, such apellations are no longer restricted to Japan and it becomes more and more usual to rename the genre as 'harsh noise'. However the traits themselves are what is of interest here, more than the genre-defining categories as such. The referred-to traits are consistent with a consideration of the materiality of means and bodies as discussed above – as an attention to the use of sound to reach the body's limits of tolerance. They are typically very stressful to the body. They cause temporary auditive reduction, muscle fatigue and are dominating of our attention span, making it more difficult to pay attention to something else. Analytic listening – the separation of sections and understanding of music as articulate sound materials – is rendered problematic, inviting the listener to another experience, different from the ones the authors that were referred to at the beginning of the present chapter were discussing.

It is not being argued that by grouping these authors under the rubric of 'noise' they propose the same experience. However, the attention paid to materialities could be fruitful in that it could extract different properties of the aesthetics studied and merge these genres with other histories, different from the ones being privileged in the more common literature about noise. For example, taking as a basis the studies of materialities and noise as being characterized by 'material impact', could the resulting concept of noise enable a grouping of this genre in a history of modern music – from the second Viennese school, to free jazz, punk, bypassing Japanese noise, up to the new complexity school of composition and sound art? Is material affect also an important element of these other aesthetics? It is important to emphasize that the model proposed here should not be read as discarding alternative and conflicting models. All of them can be potentially accepted as good and interesting fictions. I do not intend to offer an emphasis on the materialities as being the correct or true one, which would be rather naïve on my part.

To focus on the irritation caused by noise, Hegarty (2009, 110) cites a visual example from Bataille – of the latter's response to an old photographic image of a Chinese man having his limbs cut off – in order to argue about the irritability generated by noise. Considered in this way, the experience of being exposed to a stimulus that reaches us as a noise would be condemned, by longer exposure, to have its impact on sensation dissolved. Since Hegarty is interested in proposing a general concept of noise, he can jump from visual irritation to sonic irritation without taking into account many constraints that could interfere in this identification between these experiences. However, things may be more complex concerning sound. It is possible that the fact that an image ceases to shock would never apply to shocking sounds, for they are two different sensorial experiences with distinct functions. The idea of shock being reduced by the means of the repetition of noise is likely to be more valid in the case of the languages of noise when applied to the senses that have been embraced by various avant-garde and experimental sonic movements. For instance, if the lack of a tonal discourse, with its harmonic, melodic, sectional and rhythmic conventions, on a dodecaphonic or any post-tonal piece irritates me, then maybe I will no longer remain irritated if I keep listening to it. The same does not apply to Japanese noise in terms of what is understood by this chapter as 'irritation'. When attempting to find correspondences to the Japanese noise experience in the field of visuality, maybe it is necessary, instead of considering the exposure to degrading images, to consider the exposure of the body to extreme luminosity.

Generally speaking, eliminating an irritating image is much easier than getting rid of an irritating sound. One might simply shift the position of the face or close one's eyes, for instance. Let us evoke the classic childish response to the violent scenes from a movie. In practical terms, you only need to turn your face away for an instant and that's all – if you dare to, of course. Thus, shock is easily averted. Things start to get really complicated when one needs to avert a haptic irritating contact – that is the path for committing physically violent and constraining acts. Without haptic constraints, threats would remain abstract or imaginary. When dealing with a sound used as power, we are not dealing with a stimulus which can affect us by mobilizing codes that have been banned from a culture, and cause a certain discomfort for this reason. It is a sound impact that, by exploring bodily, material limits, causes an experience that seems, as previously mentioned, related to para-symbolic or pre-symbolic communication regimes. The *noise* movements mentioned here are expressions that attempt at exploring sound frequencies where it is not very easy to relativize the sensation of being excessively mobilized. It is as if they are using sound to force a response from a body that could not remain numb in the presence of this set of stimuli.

It is important to stress the irony of the fact that a book like *Sonic Warfare*,[8] so clear in its open condemnation of the modes of exploration employed by the genres here described, could be so useful for the understanding of these very practices. But, in fact, this chapter's main divergence from the author are not related to his analyses, but rather the polarization he constructs. Simon Reynolds, like Goodman, also demonstrates the same harshness towards the noise genres this chapter is interested in. They both reduce all of them to just one more chapter in the history of the uses of the body in practices of power and domination. It is also possible that this might be the case. But even then, 'must we burn Sade'? Are we going to recover from the guilt of having colonized Africa by condemning musical genres? It is equally easy for any person to condemn a practice when one is not much interested in it. This is especially in the case when these practices seem to resonate with interests commonly considered despicable. Yet, as has been discussed by Hegarty (2009, 124), it is somewhat problematic to further develop an idea that considers such movements as a 'fascist mobilization of sound', since these practices are offered and not imposed. Considering this aspect, a greater power of imposition would obviously characterize expressions produced by mass practices, due to their economic power for repetition, their more extensive reach, and also the controlling effects of what they propose.

Reynolds himself states in his work with Joy Press (1995) that there is a clear understanding about the destructive potential of the mobilization of sound amplification, but this is acknowledged exclusively in the case of rock music. These authors bet on the impacting potentialities brought about by technology. So, it is necessary to stress that rock has a long list of respected deaf musicians. However, the emergence of Japanese noise may have deeply reconfigured what would become of the use of sound as a power, doing it in such a way as to make sound mobilizations in other aesthetic practices seem more a mere side effect than the main object in the scene. Even Krautrock is unable to abolish certain grammars. Besides that, the numerous genres related to rock convey a clear dichotomy between the impact provided by live performances and aseptically recorded albums, where the song must be always clear, and where the uses of sound effects should not transgress the similarity to instrumental sources, among other aspects.[9]

As previously mentioned, industrial music is a case apart. Industrial had an agenda of intensive exploration of components and themes considered taboo, while sound was just one among many strategic components used. Sound was mostly mobilized by this genre for the same reasons that were also applied to images. In order to fulfil this intention, it privileged the use of *samples* from the speeches of dictators and serial killers, as well as lyrics with violent content; recordings from simulated acts of violence or abuses being committed; the sounds of industrial machinery and several uses of noise as earlier avant-garde movements have understood it, as sounds with no defined pitch or form, refusing to work according to common patterns for song arranging; and purposefully editing and releasing poorly recorded and performed tracks, contrary to the high-fidelity rules strictly followed by the record industry, among other resources. The aspects mentioned above indicate an exploration of impact due to an emphasis on symbolic features. However, working on a project of this sort also made other explorations possible even if, at first glance, using a sonic model that would become purer and more intense later in power electronics and Japanese noise: the idea that sound could intensify affects when explored in its intrinsic materiality.

Whether working with these registers could have been a strategic decision resulting from a conceptual approach previously defined, or could be explained by a specific preference for the sonorities involved, could be discussed. Probably, musical development itself has played its part as well, but these two factors, instead of neutralizing one another, are indeed inseparable. Acknowledging a corresponding bodily register for the impact caused by these sounds does not deny the interests concerning the use of these same sounds. That is, I desire aggressive sounds and enjoy perceiving this ongoing process; I enjoy the way my body and someone else's body receives these sounds. The imaginary, then, has always been present here, finding in the body and technologies a way to be put into practice. However, the preponderance of one or the other factor should be examined in each case.

After analyzing the Whitehouse or the SPK cases, it is hard to say what is most relevant. In the former case, Philip Best and William Bennett's shock-fuelled lyrical content, before and after the participation of Peter Sotos, cannot be separated from this strategic level on which they function as aggressive agents. However, these propositions already imply a certain level of 'tympanic' fruition[10] that immediately relatively restricts the musical universe at the style's disposal. It is only possible to acknowledge levels of sonic exploration within this universe once one considers the point where bodies get extremely affected. In post-Japanese noise this is both essential and taken to extremes, which hardly allows for the identification of this strategic use of sound, or any other use besides the haptic-aesthetic fruition. Although the imaginary affect remains, when the artist decides to mobilize violent images on the album's cover or in music titles, however, every strategic objective almost fades away. That is why industrial music practitioners did not determine which musical materials should belong to the genre, for they had more strategic demands on their horizon. Obviously, the point aimed at by this article is that it was no coincidence or a mere aesthetic preference that Japanese noise, power electronics, and the first wave of industrial music, to name a few tendencies, have attempted to simultaneously occupy the whole audible frequency spectrum with as much amplitude as possible. It was no coincidence that power electronics has emphasized the emergence of high frequencies, a region in which human hearing capacities are extremely sensitive, recognizing these sounds as louder. It is hard to eliminate the sensation of pressure, the sensation of general bodily mobilization when facing such a stimulus. Probably, this impact will hurt. Perhaps, this might not hurt forever, and the stimulus repetition might replace pain with something else. Weariness, maybe? But it seems that what remains in these movements is the use of sound as mediator in an attempt at trying to communicate with the limits of the body, wherever they take place.

# CHAPTER SEVENTEEN

# Into the Full: Strawson, Wyschnegradsky and Acoustic Space in Noise Musics

## J.-P. Caron

Music offers a world, and inhabitability. Noise offers something more like dark matter which may be what allows a structure for everything else to exist.

(Paul Hegarty, 2007, 139)

### Construing the purely auditory world

Peter Strawson, in his classic 1959 study *Individuals*, offers a fascinating narrative in which he questions the possibility for the identification and re-identification of particular objects in a spaceless world. At first this may seem obscure, but it can be clarified by presenting Strawson's method of reasoning and the entangled questions he tries to answer. In his book, Strawson seeks to make the case for what he calls *descriptive metaphysics*. Its task would be 'to describe the actual structure of our thought about the world' (Strawson, 2006, 9), as opposed to *revisionary metaphysics*, which seeks to replace our structure with a better one. One could legitimately doubt the possibility of describing this so-called actual structure of our thought even while accepting some of Strawson's insights as one way among others of talking about our experience of things. This is the position implicit in this inquiry. I do not intend to defend Strawson's position as the true position, but rather to use his intuitions in an otherwise very different task: to offer a perspective in which some of the specificities of the acoustic space proposed by noise music can be examined.

Strawson proposes the idea that physical objects have priority in our picture of the world. That means that the way we construe our experience of the world takes physical objects as the somewhat primal basis on which experience is structured. Some basic features given by physical objects would be their spatio-temporal properties, and the possibility of identifying the subject (i.e. ourselves) as something different from its surroundings, or that which is not ourselves. For Strawson, the possibility of differentiating ourselves from the environment lies ultimately in our ability to locate objects (*to identify and reidentify concrete particulars*, in his more technical language) and to locate our body among these objects.

In the second chapter of his book, incidentally called *Sounds*, Strawson proceeds to interrogate himself about the possibility of maintaining a conceptual apparatus roughly like our own, albeit in a completely transformed system of coordinates. To this end, he proposes a thought-experiment in which a purely auditory world is proposed, as a paradigm case of what he takes to be a spaceless world. The idea is to find analogous structures to the ones we encounter in our ordinary experience in an environment devoid of most of the coordinates that shape our everyday world. That means, for Strawson, asking for the possibility of identifying and re-identifying particulars in a world devoid of spatial properties (the *no-space world*, as he calls it). Of course sound isn't as such a purely temporal phenomenon devoid of spatiality. We are used to locating diverse sound sources in space, for instance in an electroacoustic sound environment and, thus, the sounds they make are also localizable in their trajectories from left to right, from above to below, and from the front to the rear. Specific morphological traits also point to spatial qualities, such as intensity, which indicate distance from the hearer – the more distant, the lower the intensity of the sound, and vice versa. Hence, Strawson's no-space world could not just be a soundworld, since sound is perceived as having intrinsically spatial qualities, and originates in our everyday physical world as air pressure that is felt by our hearing apparatus. That is why Strawson calls his no-space world *a purely auditory world*: it must be stripped of all the dimensions which would be derived from any senses other than listening. This is an important distinction, since it clears up the possible objection stemming from the spatial character of sound: we are not referring here to sounds as such, but to the properties grasped only through listening. The underlying hypothesis is that spatial concepts would be construed by listening only as a derivation from visual or tactile concepts. For Strawson, spatial consciousness would be primarily derived from sight.

One could still argue here that we actually listen to sounds as coming from the left or from the right, so that a blind person would be able to locate sound trajectories in space even without visual support. Some authors, such as Casati and Dokic (1998), even hold that the identification of properties of the sound sources would be the defining feature of the sense of hearing: hearing would be a specific way of acquiring knowledge about the world, in which distance would play an important part. Both vision and odour share this same relationship to distance that hearing has, but in different ways; whereas colour, for instance, offers information about the surface of objects, and odour about its material composition, hearing captures what Casati and Dokic call 'the internal structure' of objects – the fact that they are simple or composed, or assembled from a number of different parts. Hearing, like odour, also gives us information about the material composition of objects; metal and glass sound very different, for example (Casati and Dokic, 1994, 32–3). This points to an intrinsically spatial and identifying function of hearing, thus making Strawson's inquiry seem almost futile.

This is true, but the no-space world Strawson proposes is still a far more radical scenario than the one just depicted; in this world, the whole existence of bodies would be put aside. Since we are depriving ourselves of all spatial concepts, the concept of a body itself is dispensed with. So our own self-consciousness as individuals possessing a body is therefore rendered problematic and, according to Strawson, our self-consciousness as something other than our surroundings is far from evident in such a scenario. For Strawson, this touches on the problem of solipsism, since he defines this notion not as the non-existence of the outside world, but as the impossibility of differentiating between that which is ourselves and that which is not ourselves. A consciousness that is capable of performing this differentiation is called a *non-solipsistic consciousness*.

> The question: Could there be reidentifiable sound-particulars in the purely auditory world? was raised as if it were a further question which had to be considered, over and above another question, viz.: Could a being whose experience was purely auditory make sense of the distinction between himself and his states on the one hand, and something not himself or a state of himself, on the other? But now it seems that these questions are not independent. An affirmative answer to the second entails an affirmative answer to the first. For to have a conceptual scheme in which a distinction is made between oneself or one's states and auditory items which are not states of oneself, is to have a conceptual scheme in which the existence of auditory items is *logically* independent of the existence of one's states or of oneself. (Strawson, 2006, 72)

Since our own identification as something that possesses thoughts that are different from the things around us lies in our identification of ourselves as a particular thing among others and, ultimately, in the possibility of identifying particulars in general, this very possibility becomes a question (the crucial one) in Strawson's philosophical fiction: can we identify particulars in a no-space world? Can we identify something as other-than-ourselves in this particular framework? And, finally, in Strawson's own words: is there any possibility for a non-solipsistic consciousness in the no-space world?

## From the empirical to the intrinsic

At this point the reader may be wondering what the relevance of all this would be to the study of noise music. The thought-experiment proposed by Strawson is relevant insofar as it opens up in a dramatic way the dimension of the intrinsic space of sounds, which is not reducible to the empirical space we experience when we think of the distance between physical objects, or even the distances we can infer by listening to the sounds they make. It is the 'space' we are referring to when we talk about higher- or lower-pitched sounds, when we speak of regular or irregular divisions of a given musical interval and of the different grades of our musical scales. Music proposes specific orders of time and (musical) space, and the questions Strawson asks can shed light on some of the processes entangled in music- or noise-making and listening. For now we shall continue following Strawson in his inquiry, prior to exploring a different model for thinking about sonic space.

For Strawson, the possibility of a non-solipsistic consciousness in a no-space world depends on the possibility for identification and re-identification of particulars in this scenario. To answer this question, Strawson imagines a number of different situations. Imagine that there is a single musical piece being played in two different rooms simultaneously by two different orchestras. Both orchestras reach approximately the same chord at the same time *t*. The listener located in room *A* would hear the same as the listener located in room *B*? Broadly speaking, yes, they would be listening to the same chord. But would that chord be the same in both pieces? Can we talk of an event that is *numerically* identical in both cases, that is, can we talk of *the same event, as the same particular*, as opposed to the same *type* of event, or the same *universal*? Strawson is interested in the re-identification of individuals, i.e. the re-identification of the same object and not of the same type or universal which different individuals exemplify. This issue remains tied to another: the possibility of re-identification is in turn linked to the possibility of considering an object as existing while we do not have any contact whatsoever with it, such as the chair we visualize in the room, then no more once we leave the room and then again once we return to that same room. We are able to re-identify the chair as the same one that was there previous to our leaving the room. This means that we consider the chair as an existing object throughout the time we were away. An analogous situation could be devised for sound in the following way: we are listening to a musical piece on the radio, it gets interrupted by interference, after which the programme returns and we re-identify the same piece that was playing before. We do so because we consider that the programme went on while the interference prevented us from listening to it. But still, in this situation we have information that is not purely auditory. Would it be possible to perform this same operation in a purely auditory world?

It is here that Strawson makes use of the morphological characteristics of sound in his inquiry. He imagines that each *identifier* (each 'person' in the purely auditory world) would have a specific sound with a specific timbre, so that we are always hearing *our own sound*. Once another sound comes closer, we hear it too. Loudness would offer the obvious analogy with distance. Yet, this is the case only because in our everyday world we already have spatial concepts and we already infer that differences of loudness often mean differences in the distances from the respective sound sources. How could one conclude, after all, *without the concept of a place*, that the sound is not being heard because it is too distant to be heard? Strawson proceeds to imagine a different scenario, with a new candidate for offering the adequate analogy of space: pitch.

> In other words, we want an analogy of distance – of *nearer to* and *further away from* – for only, at least, under this condition would we have anything like the idea of a dimension other than the temporal in which unperceived particulars could be thought of as simultaneously existing in *some kind of systematic relation to each other*, and to perceived particulars. (Strawson, 2006, 75)

This systematic relationship, which is given in the context of regular empirical space, is replaced in the world of Strawson by the hypothesis of a master-sound. This master-sound would be heard constantly, modulating in time in different ways. When the master-sound is at a given pitch $p$, a new sound would appear. The situation here would be roughly analogous to the aforementioned situation of listening to a radio, imagining that the master-sound here would fulfil the function of the knob, the different positions of the master-sound corresponding to positions of the knob in relation to different stations, and the appearance or disappearance of sound correlated to the positions of the master-sound would supply a perhaps sufficiently near analogue of the notion of *place*: every time the master-sound appears at pitch $p$, the same sound complex appears, so that with the aid of this device of the master-sound, one could be said to re-identify the same sound complex after an absence of contact, therefore considering it as *existent* while distant from any sensible contact.

Strawson leaves the question open as to whether this scenario satisfies the criteria for a non-solipsistic consciousness or not. However, he presents some important considerations: that it is integral to our self-awareness that we have bodies, and that these bodies are likely to take action; that a distinction between actions taken by our bodies and actions carried out independently of them is tantamount to the distinction between that which is ourselves and that which is not. The partial conclusion established is that, while it is not impossible to create in a purely auditory world some kind of analogue of our situation of being immersed in a world of four-dimensional coordinates, nothing could, on the other hand, guarantee (other than our own disposition in admitting so) that the conditions proposed here are sufficient to establishing a near-enough scenario to our everyday world.

## Into the full space of pansonority

I have already claimed that Strawson's philosophical fiction could serve as an especially dramatic heuristic device in opening up the possibility of thinking about musical space. However, I propose an inversion of the sense of the inquiry: Strawson sets out to find in the auditory world the analogues of our coordinate system; on the contrary, what if music has from the beginning been searching in our everyday world for the very conditions for its own structure? In this sense the narrative proposed by Strawson sheds light on the pretensions of musical structure, to the extent that it is characterized by fashioning procedures and creating a space that are, to some extent, similar to the predominantly visual relationships we find in our ordinary world. The reappearance of themes, melodies, notes, or musical objects in the midst of various traditional musical discourses could be read as providing the coordinates of the basic cognitive human understanding of oneself and others, of *here* and *there*, although we do not have guarantees of re-identification of individuals as much as of universals. The working hypothesis is the following: if the objectualities that we find in our musical world (notes, orderings, scales, themes, harmonies) would, in a sense, recreate the possibilities of orientations that we are able to grasp in our ordinary *empirical* world, noise music would, as a new radical musical break, recast these problems of organization of musical time and space on new basis. Let me, then, for purposes of comparison, consider a different theoretical fiction about the purported instrinsic space of sound (as opposed to the empirical space of everyday life). After this I will try and reap the richer consequences for a theoretical treatment of acoustic space in noise.

So far, a mainly *empty acoustic space* has been imagined, which is then filled with sonorous events, which can be identified and reidentified (at least as universals) in their basic properties: timbre, pitch, volume. What if we imagine the opposite: a *full sound space* in which all points would be sounding simultaneously, completely occupied from the bass to the treble?

This is precisely the image proposed by Ivan Wyschnegradsky in his work *La loi de la pansonorité* under the name of the 'total sound continuum'. This notion appears in the book as an operational limit for the constitution of *ultrachromatism*, as Wyschnegradsky calls his theory. Summarizing a bit, the author proposes a full musical space, which he proceeds to *divide* in equal parts, constituting the various different spaces that comprise the musical systems of *ultrachromatism*. One of these spaces is considered a specially important entity: the so-called 'relative sound continuum', comprised by all the audible musical space divided in 12ths of the whole tone, giving us 144 sounds per octave in the whole audible spectrum. The difference between the *total sound continuum* and the *relative sound continuum* lies in the fact that the first is *virtual*: that means, it cannot be actually heard, since one cannot be sure of having the absolute whole of the (humanly) audible space resonating at once. Its function is *operational*, it is a condition of possibility for the divisibility of space into no matter what different periodicities. As French composer Pascale Criton says: 'What interests Wyschnegradsky is the introduction of the idea of a non-structural plan of the sonic material, a non-"magnetized" and non-"tonalized" plan inside of which a spatial principle of free structuration (an action field) acts'[1] (Criton, 1996, 16).

The practical implications of this are several, starting with the construction criteria of the objects that compose the musical system in question. For Wyschnegradsky, consideration of an empty musical space entails that the only criteria for choosing the musical objects that would fill it are relations between the sounds themselves. This means that, from an initial sound taken as a fundamental (in the musical sense, the root of the scale), all other sounds would be deducted by relationships of closer and further acoustical affinity, taken as consonant relations – we can compare this as going up the harmonic series and choosing from it the sounds that would compose the gamut (see, for instance, Partch, 1973, for a treatment of this procedure). This is indeed what Wyschnegradsky called the *natural paradigm* of musical space, governed by consonant relations between the sounds of the system, and it corresponds to the traditional way of structuring musical sound. Even though temperament is used nowadays for the technical advantages of modulating between tonal centres, the basic configuration is historically derived from such thinking. *Pansonorité*, on the other side, considers the space as *filled* with sound from bottom to top, which means without gaps, such that one could divide it in any regular or irregular way. The procedure then becomes not deductive but *divisionary*; while the natural paradigm infers the acoustic gamut out of the acoustic affinities of the sounds themselves, in pansonority the *spatial* continuum is divided, generating unheard sound qualities different from the ones deducted from the acoustic properties of each sound in isolation. Thus, *space* is the most basic category of ultrachromatism, not sound. Once more, Criton says:

> The simultaneous conception of the set of all sounds of a harmony-scale opens itself to the idea of *space*, of specific sonorous environments, or of a sonic net, in which everything can sound at the same time, with no exclusivity and no hierarchy, unmaking the duality consonance-dissonance and permitting, thus [...] to liberate a qualitative conception of intervals.[2] (Criton, 1996, 16)

Wyschnegradsky's idea serves then for the construction of a number of different divisionary spaces. Even if the procedure is not based in the immanent nature of sound, being generated through rational construction, the method still answers a need for sounds to be located in space as a means to a meaningful musical discourse. In other words, it is still linked with the model of the *musical note*. However, its basic intuitions point to another direction.

> All of this is equivalent to the recognition of the explosive nature of sound. A latent force is present inside musical sound that tends to unfold to the maximum over all the extension of musical space, in principle, infinite and continuous, and to fill this infinity with a continuous sonority. Otherwise said, every chord, every interval, every isolated sound tends to become *pansonority*, that is, to transcend it's physical nature and to become the continuous whole.[3] (Wyschnegradsky, 1996, 125)

Not only the various spaces derivable from the *total continuum* could be articulated themselves as novel acoustic milieus, each creating its own harmonic and timbral environment, they can follow one another in time, in a logic more akin to sound masses than to individual notes. The *explosive nature of sound* accounts not only for increases in the densities of masses composed of individual punctual sounds layered on top of each other, but also for a densification of the single sound as such – that is, not divided into particulars, but just one huge sound mass that tends to occupy the whole of the audible spectrum, like the thickening of a point into a spot. It is my intuition that this is especially suitable for the understanding of the practice of noise.

## From the intrinsic to the empirical

Usually noise is understood negatively, as something fundamentally different from sound that is likely to organize (or be organized in) and articulate (or be articulated in) music. From the perspective proposed above, noise is not simply the *unwanted other* of sound, but that which makes (musical) sound possible. The two models of space as empty and as full set up two different metaphysics implicit in musical practice. The first clearly marks the difference between sounds and noises as the basis for selecting musical objects capable of ordered articulation. The second model redefines the roles of sound and noise, positing the latter as a difference of degree in relation to first, and even if we maintain the current notion of noise as an inharmonious sound conformation, it becomes the foundation of all possible soundworlds – the set from which every musical formation can be derived. Here we find the expression of Hegarty, the noise of the 'Dark matter which may be what allows the structure for everything else to exist' (Hegarty, 2007, 139).

One could legitimately ask whether the above considerations have any importance for noise music as such. After all, noise musicians are not philosophers asking for identification conditions for sound particulars, neither are they composers working in the Western tradition searching for theoretical ways in which to justify their new musical resources. As I have quoted elsewhere,[4] Zbigniew Karkowski says:

> To say that we do serious music suggests a probably rigorous scientific approach, whereas, on the other end of the spectrum, Japanese noise, which isn't a commercial popular music either, is a form of expression which is practiced without anyone in Japan either writing one line or formulating one question about the interest in doing it. On one side, method, language and formalization as work, on the other, the brute experience of a material which makes and remakes works by experimenting with the informal bruitism. Well, in the hard sciences, theory and experience go together. It's like noise was revealing without knowing a split between theory and practice, the unconscious Janus of the classical experience.[5] (Karkowski, 2009, 47)

Nevertheless, we are always influenced by the concepts we use, and if we understand the function of concepts in our human agency in this particular way, philosophical inquiry no longer seems so distant from actual practice. But so far this argument justifies prospectively the relevance of the proposed model for sound. Is it relevant *now*?

I think the adoption of a different way of grasping the phenomenon could influence our ways of hearing music. The adoption of a more comprehensive model for sound could therefore influence us into accepting or engaging with different ways of working with sound. When noise is no longer defined negatively, it certainly loses some of its more ideological contours – as a reaction against order or music itself – but on the other side, we are more able to understand the specific sound-world articulated within this practice. Since *it is sound, not just noise,* we are now obliged to understand it and accept it in that way, trying to recognize its specific perceptual patterns and configurations.

Building textures by stacking sound effects on top of each other is a very common procedure in noise music that results in a peculiar situation concerning the recognizability of sound. Take the typical noise set-up of pedals connected to one another. Imagine we have an oscillator, as is frequently the case, as the primary sound source, connected to a distortion pedal, connected to a reverb/delay pedal. The oscillator is always present, though in a concealed, hidden form. As we hear the sound distort, we can hear it acquire different characteristics, as if it was being heard in different environments (the reverb/delay pedal). Different frequencies of oscillation either result in different harmonic palettes or in different rhythmic patterns in the final result. This is all engulfed by the large amount of distortion, once, after a certain time, the basic oscillation suddenly makes itself heard again.

We are again confronted with the basic situation described in Strawson's no-space world, of different sound particulars or types appearing and disappearing again, after being engulfed in other effects. The principle would not be so different from the reappearance of a melody after a long absence. However, what happens here in practice is that noise music taps into a dimension in which the same sound source (or number of sound sources) is transformed in its timbre over time, having its identity revealed and hidden again. The very fabric of the work could be created as the transformations of either a single sound source, or a limited number of sources that are once present, then absent, then become present once again in perception. While we still recognize the specific morphological traits of its constitutive moments, the near-constant presence of saturated sound makes identification of one sound as *another sound, different* from the one before, problematic. The interrelation of the various effects produces a texture in which sounds are transformed to reappear again in their specific morphological profiles. And we can characterize individual style based on these morphologies: Whitehouse by the emphasis on control and permanence; Merzbow, conversely, by abrupt change and instability; Masonna by intensified concentration on individual information in a very limited time-span; K2 by the intervention of acoustic elements, such as metallic sounds and the relationship between attack and sustain of each sound; Vomir by the occupation of a range of noise that remains the same from start to end of each track; Maurizio Bianchi by the presence of melodies and their placement in a continuum that leads to noise and back to melody again.

In this particular view, the particular use of technology encountered in noise musics seem to reverse Hegarty's proposition. If the spaces articulated by noise music seem at first like impenetrable atmospheres of distant planets, this music *is inhabited* during performance. The physical gesture of making noise will engender always-new configurations, and each new gesture will then transform it anew, in an auditory dialogue with the sonorous space in which he sees himself immersed now and then. The use of high densities and amplitudes reveals a desire to dwell in sound, to the extent that it no longer unfolds as music different from the physical world, to be apprehended by the sensibility and intellect alone. The sound is now perceived as a physical presence that shapes our ways of accessing the perceived space. Not only the intrinsic space of sound is created by the densities generated in performance, but the very perception of the empirical performance space is modulated by these same sounds. As Thibaut Walter says in his introduction to G. X. Jupitter-Larsen's writings,

> The ecstatic experiences found once bodies are immersed in the decibels, where pain and pleasure melt, opens up a time-space specific to sound in general. In this production and in this hearing of sound as sound, of sound delivered from rhythmic, melodic, compositional and orchestral preoccupations and pushed to its saturated radicality, body and thought let themselves dilate, resound, contract, ramify and open up to an omni-dimensional space-time.[6] (Walter, 2010, 26)

Here there is necessarily a failure. For the intervention of noise in empirical space is unable to actually change it. But the vector remains the same: *to overflow musical space, through amplification and saturation, into empirical space.* In this way, Strawson's inquiry is reversed; whereas the no-space world was the place where one ought to encounter ways in which our habitual conceptual and sensible apparatus could survive, noise offers a total sonorous space that overflows our ordinary empirical physical world as the barrier between the empirical and the purely intrinsic is tentatively broken via amplification. Thus, at least in theory, the noise musician inhabits, along with his audience, the space he, himself, creates.

# CHAPTER EIGHTEEN

# Gossips, Sirens, Hi-Fi Wives: Feminizing the Threat of Noise

*Marie Thompson*

Noise is irrevocably political. It remains bound up with contestations of space, power struggles, acts of torture and acts of silencing. There are questions regarding who or what is the cause of noise, who are its gatekeepers, and who are its victims? What is excluded and what is permitted? The notion of noise as a threat or a challenge to the status quo, be it musical or social (see Attali, 1985), has lent itself to a rhetoric of rebellion; noise can subvert, overthrow, erase musical orders and, by extension, the socio-political orders in which both music and noise are embedded. As Anthony Iles states:

> There is strong field of attraction to the cultural space of noise for the politicized musician – a music that does not have a set code or form nor an expected mode of behaviour. Those packing a liberatory politics with their music often turn up here. (Mattin and Iles, 2009, 15)

However, my contestation is that before any liberatory agenda can be claimed for noise, its relationship with gendered bodies needs to be taken into account.

This chapter calls for an alternative politics of noise, which distinguishes itself from the legacies of both Futurist noise and Cagean silence. The former is explicitly masculinist, if not misogynistic; Futurism's 'scorn for women' is present from the outset – it is written as one of the principles of Futurism within Marinetti's founding manifesto.[1] The gendered connotations of the latter are perhaps less overt; Cage's silence, while a significant event within Western compositional and notational musical traditions, has often been treated as *the* dominant moment in experimental music – it is its beginning and its limit. In turn, Cagean silence has come to function as a silencing; despite his intentions to rupture hegemonic silences, Cage's silence, understood as the birth and endpoint of experimental music, has thus silenced the influences and innovations of other musical practices, including those by women and people of colour (Kahn, 2001; Rogers, 2010).[2] If we are to hear Cagean silence and Futurist noise as forming the foundations of (artistic) noise, as setting the axis against which all future explorations of noise are plotted, then it must be asked who is laying claims to the liberatory potential of noise and silence; on whose behalf do these sonic interventions act, and who, in the process, do they silence?

As a means of foregrounding the particular (and largely overlooked) connection between the female, the feminine and noise, this chapter will trace a non-linear narrative of women's noise and their silencing, in which the dualism of noise/silence has corresponded with a binary separating the archetypes of bad woman/good woman. The point is not to show women as ahistorically and essentially noisy but rather to draw attention to a recurring thematic, whereby noise has 'marked' female bodies and sounds within radically different socio-cultural contexts. However (feminized) noise is deemed unwanted because it threatens to disrupt and disturb; it is a transformative force. Consequently, this chapter will ask: if women's noise is dangerous, according to the ears of patriarchal orders, then does it contain a subversive potential? Can it interrupt and interfere with certain normative, molar categories that have worked to assure, and normalize, the inferiority of the feminine and feminized? It will consider such questions in relation to the notion of the molecular subject-in-process, made audible in the noisy vocal performances of Diamanda Galás as a means of speculatively pointing to an affirmative politics of noise.

\* \* \*

Women, it has often been stated, should exist in silence; they are to be seen and not heard. For Aristotle, woman, inherently inferior and defined in opposition to her male counterpart, is virtuous in her silence: 'silence is a woman's glory but this is not equally the glory of man' (Aristotle, 2008, 52). 'She' is defined in terms of absence and passivity. Woman's chaotic existence, her inconsistent, uncertain opinions, means that she is to be excluded from the *polis* and is not permitted to speak publicly in courts. Within the church, women's speech is considered improper and shameful: 'let the women keep silent in the churches; for they are not permitted to speak' (Corinthians 14.33-5). The archetypal silent woman has no voice within discourses of history, technology, politics or art; she has no voice within the canons of culture. She is *lacking*.

In more recent times, men too have come to be defined by their silence. Within the popular imagination, there is also a stereotype of masculine silence: the silence of the husband who veils himself behind the Sunday newspaper. He is 'the strong and silent type'. He keeps his innermost thoughts and emotions under wraps, hidden behind a stiff upper lip, where he deals with them calmly and rationally. He is never the provider of 'too much information'. A quiet dignity marks his activities. But his silence is different. The silence of masculinity is often elective; Aristotle's remarks bear witness to the fact that freedom of speech has all too often been the privilege of (white) men. The silence of women, by contrast, is all too often a silencing; regulated and policed by her male superiors. Her silence is not so much silence as noise-abatement. Woman, left undisciplined and unrestricted by her husband, her church, and society, embodies the threat of noise.

Throughout the history of Western thought, women and noise have frequently found themselves on the same side of philosophical dichotomies that have governed and legitimated their subordination. Like noise, 'she' has been constructed in terms of unreason, disorder, non-meaning and excess. She has been met with fear and degradation; she has been the perversion of reason, morally bankrupt and the abject defilement of the sacred and the pure. She has been constructed in the misogynistic imagination as sexually dangerous; her sexual allure brings with it the threat of death, reminding man of his corporeal, finite existence (see Landau et al., 2006). For Pythagoras, women are the creation of evil: 'there is a good principle that created order, light and man and a bad principle that created chaos, darkness and woman' (Beauvoir, 1997, 122). To be sure, it is 'woman' who is to be blamed for mankind's fall from grace. In the Judeo-Christian tradition, the birth of sin and the destruction of man's paradise comes about from a woman's chatter: it is Eve who listened to the undesirable sounds of the devil, coercing Adam into eating the apple in the Garden of Eden. Before Eve there was Zeus's creation of woman, Pandora. She too, with her 'weak willed' and 'curious' femininity, opened that which should never be opened. Her interference in matters deemed none of her business led to the unleashing of chaos and evil in the world.

Implicit within the admonitions of women's silence is a fear of her sonic presence. It is not so much that her silence is virtuous but that her noise is dangerous to the ears of patriarchal orders. In turn, female, or feminine, speech has often been branded as unwanted noise; their 'idle gossiping', their squeals of excitement, and their conversations are cast out as abject distractions; their unpredictable outbursts are to be controlled and abated. The imagined noise of women, of feminine speech and conversation, is marked within the languages of various cultures in derogatory and unflattering terms. In Japanese, there is the saying *onna sannin yoreba kasimasii* – 'three women together mean din'. In German, there is *Klatschen wie ein*

*Waschweib* – 'to chatter like a washer woman'. In a dictionary published by the Swedish Academy, sixteen compound nouns paired a word referring to talk with a word for woman, including the charming *skvallerkäring*, meaning 'gossip hag'. In Bedouin culture, the potential danger of women's noise is implied in the saying that men's talk is full, but women's is empty; whenever two women talk there is the devil between them (Romaine, 1998, 161).

Despite their associations with silence, women have often been represented as 'naturally' noisy in comparison to their male counterparts; within popular consciousness they are imagined to be more talkative, choosing to discuss the trivialities of life and surrounding themselves with a noisy, meaningless babble. However, as Suzanne Romaine suggests, feminine noisiness is tied to its expected abatement: 'perhaps it just seems that women talk a lot more because men expect women to be silent. When silence is your yardstick, any woman who talks at all seems to be talking too much' (Romaine, 1998, 161). Of particular offense to the ears of patriarchal order is the seemingly inviolable connection between women and gossip. Despite transcultural connotations of gossip as a feminine pastime,[3] it was not always the case. In his essay 'How the "Gossip" Became a Woman' (1977), Alexander Rysman traces gossip's etymological transformation from a positive term, referring to both men and women, to a pejorative term for women. Gossip is thought to originate from 'god sib', referring to a godparent or family friend, and has evolved over time to refer to 'idle talk' or a 'female tattler'.[4]

Women's gossip fulfils the function of noise. On one level, it is heard as meaningless, extraneous chatter; it is sonic excess, derived from the purported verbal incontinence of women. The notion of gossip as a sonic surplus devoid of meaning or function is also mirrored in the bodies of gossips. There is the characterization of gossip as unattractive, undesirable talk originating from the mouths of unattractive, undesirable women; the witches, crones and the 'gossip hags'. The 'old wives' of 'old wives' tales' are the women who have outlived their reproductive function and fertility, existing as a grotesque excess of feminine matter:

> Ugly talk comes from ugly women, unwomanly women beyond the age of childbearing, and is therefore unnatural. The woman who is no longer fertile outlives her purpose. Childbearing is redemption for woman's sin, for her sexuality and by implication for her speaking. (Romaine, 1996, 163)

However, as Rysman states: 'the major sin of "gossip" is to develop social ties outside the institutions of male dominance' (Rysman, 1977, 176). After all, there is the cultural archetype, from Pandora onwards, of women as *interfering*; they embody a threat of interruption to the well-laid plans of men.[5] The flows of information, carried in barely audible whispers, serve to cause trouble for those authoritative figures that seek to keep her in silence. Gossip carries with it the threat of exposure – details of wrongdoings or illicit affairs that work to undermine the moral superiority of those who hold power. To be sure, gossip carries with it the idea that 'women talking together make trouble for men' (Bastin, 2011, 18), since men and their wrongdoings are often suspected to be the subject of women's 'idle chatter'. Gossip is dangerous because it has the potential to rupture dominant orders; it can become an interruption within the channels of morality and society.

The feminine threat of noise is also embodied by the figure of the siren. The siren, like the characters of gossip, is an unwomanly or unnatural woman, associated with the non-human. The siren exists as a monstrous distraction; she is a hybrid of bird and woman. For Attali, noise carries with it the threat of death (Attali, 1985, 27). Similarly, the siren is a figure of death and corruption; her song is both seductive and fatal, both alluring and destructive. The siren causes death-by-music, or rather, death-by-noise. Sailors are lured to their deaths by the siren's song; her wailing voice guides them to shipwreck and demise on the rocky shores of her island. The figure of the siren has been imagined to be anthropophagous: like the gossip, she is imagined to feast on the downfall of men. The siren's noise serves to interrupt reason; hers is the voice of non-reason, the cause of madness in men. Ulysses, bound to the ship mast, is driven temporarily insane by the siren's song. While he succumbs to the madness brought by women, he resists their threat of death through premeditated self-control.

These feminine noises are thus instilled with conflicting values. On the one hand, notions of frivolity, triviality and pettiness mark the sounds characterized as feminine. Women's talk is degraded as extraneous and meaningless, likened to the non-verbal braying and clucking of animals. However, despite their apparent triviality and meaninglessness, feminine noises are also dangerous, wicked and damaging, serving to rupture moral and social orders. In turn, women's noises are to be abated; they are to remain veiled in silence, their sonic presence regulated by the masculinized structures of morality.

The threat of feminine noise to male authority has been met with gendered forms of torture and violence, directed at women deemed disorderly, rebellious and disruptive. It is striking, as Lynda Boose argues, that corporal punishment of women has been 'much more frequently targeted at suppressing women's speech than they are at controlling their sexual transgressions' (Boose, 1991, 184). The Scold's Bridle, for example, consisted of an iron muzzle with a bridle plate, sometimes with spikes, designed to physically restrain a woman's disruptive or disrespectful tongue. According to a 1675 English legal summary, women who are deemed scolds, defined as troublesome or 'angry' women who breach public peace and increase discord, should be subject to the cucking or ducking stool, submerging them in unclean water in front of an audience (Boose, 1991, 186). In medieval Germany and Austria, the Shrew's Fiddle was used to clamp the neck and wrists of women convicted of fighting or bickering, while they were mocked, jeered and humiliated by others. While these punishments worked to shame and physically restrain disruptive women, there have also been depictions of imagined methods that serve to physically alter threatening or disobedient women: a 1660 French print of the 'Skull Doctor' portrays a man who transforms the wives of dissatisfied husbands into docile and obedient women, by hammering their heads on an anvil. The anvil is inscribed with the phrase: 'strike hard on the mouth: she has a wicked tongue' (Romaine, 1996, 152).

In his 1886 novel *Tomorrow's Eve*, Auguste Villiers de l'Isle-Adam 'corrects' the feminine noise of fictitious or insignificant talk by replacing women with automata. The novel tells the story of Lord Ewald, who has fallen in love with a beautiful actress and singer, Miss Alicia Clary. However, although Miss Alicia is physically perfect, she is deemed to have an empty personality; she will say whatever others wish to hear, and lacks in emotion and character. While Ewald once loved her 'external' form – her body and sound of her voice, he is irritated by her 'internal' content – her soul, her thoughts and her conversation: 'my passion, which began as a craze for the figure, the voice, the perfume, and the EXTERIOR charm of this woman, has become absolutely platonic ... I am attached to her by nothing more than a painful admiration. What I would like would be to see Miss Alicia dead, if death didn't result in the effacing of all human features' (Villiers, 2001, 46). Alicia is an empty vessel that makes too much noise. What Ewald desires in Alicia is the silent beauty of her body; when she conceals her thoughts, rendering them inaudible, she becomes a glorious statue. Torn between her attractive form and vulgar content, Ewald is suicidal; although Alicia is imperfect, he feels he is incapable of loving another woman. His friend, the fictional Thomas Edison agrees to help by building a machine-woman with Alicia's form but without the noise of her irksome personality. Edison shows Ewald his prototype android, Hadaly, which was an effort to overcome the artificiality and flaws of a 'real' woman by replacing her with a perfect and more natural machine that was capable of bringing man true happiness. Edison modifies the prototype to emulate Miss Alicia's external features and installs it with recordings of her voice (Edison dupes Miss Alicia into thinking that she is auditioning for a theatrical role to get her to utter the android's words) to create a woman whose external beauty is matched by her character and conversation.

\* \* \*

Fast-forward from the mythical sirens, obedient androids, original sins, and medieval torture to the twentieth century, and the threat of feminine noise surfaces once again. Discourses on noise and domestic spaces have often focused on the constitution, intrusion and defence of territories through sound: the sonic relations of neighbours and cohabitants and the permeability of the border separating the private from the public. However, sonic relations within the domestic sphere can also be heard through the history of home audio technologies, which bring with them gendered discourses of noise, privacy, disruption and control. Kier Keightley's explication of the gendered values of home audio technologies between 1948 and 1959 reveals that contestations of volume, noise and disturbance were not simply markers of generational conflict, a sonic war initiated by the post-war youth culture against adult musical culture, but also involved conflict between adults, informed by assertions and reconfigurations of gender roles within domestic spaces. With the emphasis on values of 'togetherness' and communal living, and the correlative decline of masculine private spaces (i.e. the drawing room and the study) the hi-fi became involved in a struggle by white, middle-class men to reclaim domestic space from their wives.

In this context, hi-fi, or high fidelity, can be understood in numerous, related ways. High fidelity refers to a favourable signal-to-noise ratio in audio reproduction, in which intended messages or sounds are communicated clearly and accurately, unobscured by minimal noise and distortion levels, and aided by improved frequency bandwidth. Hi-fi audio quality is contrasted with lo-fi audio quality, in which sound recordings have high levels of unwanted artefacts, such as noise, background hum and distortion that disrupt the intended signal, drawing attention to the materiality of the medium. As well as identifying a particular quality of sound reproduction, hi-fi also referred to the sound-reproduction equipment, as well as referring to a cult of (male) audiophiles and hobbyists, who sought to remain informed with the latest developments in hi-fi, modifying and improving their home audio equipment accordingly.

There are (at least) two flows of noise within Keightley's historical account of the hi-fi. First, there is the notion of noise-as-(high)-amplitude; excesses of volumes and extremes of frequencies facilitated a transcendence of the domestic sphere through immersion in sound. The high volumes of the hi-fi abated the demands of the everyday, allowing the husband-listener to escape to 'his favourite seat in the concert hall' (Keightley, 1996, 153). The purported masculine preference for 'loud, "normal", proper volume' was coupled with an understanding of women as incapable of sharing such tastes (Keightley, 1996, 166). When the audiophile's spouse interacted with the hi-fi, they were responsible for placing the volume controls in the 'ignominious position', or, alternatively, the 'retrograde, or female position' (Keightley, 1996, 167). In his article 'On playing music LOUD', published in 1949, Edwin C. Buxbaum explains that a wife's resistance to high volumes may have a physiological grounding, since some 'medical men' suggest:

> The female is more sensitive to sound than the male, and that – like such familiar pets of our civilization (I hesitate to say other pets) as the cat and the dog – they are hypersensitive to the upper frequencies and simply cannot endure the blare and blast of the brass, the shimmer of tremolo on the E string, or any good long crescendo. (Buxbaum, 1949, 51)

Keightley draws attention to the cartoon illustration that accompanies Buxbaum's article. A couple is depicted lying in bed. While her husband sleeps peacefully, the wife is disturbed by a nightmarish scenario, in which she is tied to a chair, positioned in the firing line of an oversized speaker horn. The husband is depicted as gleefully controlling the volume knob of the hi-fi, subjecting his visibly distressed wife to the stream of sound. For the male audiophile, the hi-fi becomes a sonic weapon used, quite literally, to blast women out of the domestic space; she is silenced by its noise.

But why should the noise of the hi-fi be directed towards the wife? Within the misogynistic discourse of hi-fi, there is the threat of another noise: the noise of the wife. The noise that she embodies disturbs the husband's hi-fi experience. She is construed as the degradation of the audio signal; her voice and the sounds of her activities become interference in the channel. Her sonic presence within the (male-regulated) domestic space is the invasion of excess; that which should be hidden behind silence. Once again, the primary source of women's noise is her extraneous speech. She interrupts and disrupts the masculine 'silence' (which is, in fact, deafening) with her frivolous chatter and her scolding tongue. The hi-fi is thus engaged in a war of noises; it is presented as a means for husbands to (re)gain control over the domestic space by drowning out their spousal opponent.

These two noises, the noise of excessive volume and the noise of feminine interruption, are apparent in the 1958 *Hi-Fi and Music Review* article 'Must you shake the walls?' The article details how a man's house and marriage simultaneously collapse as both are subjected to the extreme volumes of his hi-fi. The article opens with the wife screaming at her husband to 'turn it down'. However, as Keightley states,

> While hi-fi is imagined as literally threatening to destroy conjugal domestic space (the ultimate transformation), it is the wife who is positioned as the source of the truly oppressive noise (the commanding shriek). (Keightley, 1996, 164–5)

According to these discourses, the wife's experience of the hi-fi as noise is ultimately false; it is only noise to her because of her lack of tolerance, her philistinism, her physiological inferiority, or her wishes to retain or regain control over the domestic space. To the masculinist audiophile, the genuine threat of noise within the domestic space comes from the feminine interruption of the 'irate wife'. She is the enemy of the hi-fi and, by extension, the masculine sonic order; she embodies the potential rupture of its truth and clarity. Her noise interrupts the transcendental moment of the hi-fi audio experience, dragging the husband-listener back to the everyday of problems and responsibilities.

Thus far, this chapter has explored the treatment of feminine or feminized sounds as noise. The historical understandings of 'her' sonic presence resonate with constructions of 'woman' as interfering, meddling, trivial and irrational. The voices of women are suspected to threaten the integrity of a variety of male-regulated spheres, from the church, the *polis* and the law, to the marital homes of post-war white, middle-class American audiophiles. In turn, 'feminine' speech has been condemned as meaningless, thoughtless, extraneous, frivolous, ugly and evil. 'She' is to be kept in silence, her noise abated and repressed, since her tongue is a disruption. Thus noise is not simply sound that is deemed unwanted. Noise is first that which disrupts, inducing a change in relations. Noise is feared, or labelled dangerous and unwanted because it is a transitional and transformative force. It is that which is considered to be out of place, or that which does not fit. Moreover, if these feminine noises are dangerous to the ears of patriarchal orders, if they threaten the integrity and authority of those who assume superiority over her, then do women's noises and their status as 'noisy' carry with them a subversive potential?

Within these narratives of feminine noise, the most dangerous women are themselves noises in the system. They refuse the rule of representation and fail to match up to the constructions of femininity that have been made for them. They respond not by asserting an alternative model of femininity but by remaining resolutely unresolved and transitional. Such beings (or more accurately, becomings) are the elusive and unstable shape-shifters, the anomalies; they are the monsters, the mutants, sirens, and cyborgs. They are dangerous because they are not what we expect them to be, nor do we know the extent of their powers, what they might be able to do. They fail to be accounted for within the orders of identity, existing not outside, as such, but within the grey areas and liminal spaces. The sounds of these shape-shifters disrupt the boundaries of normative dualisms, which function as scaffolding for (masculine) conceptions of social order; they are threateningly noisy and potentially subversive because they expose the permeability of these boundaries, rendering arbitrary the dichotomies that they support. As we have already seen, gossip is dangerous because it permeates the boundaries that separate the private from the public. Then again, according to patriarchal constructions, all women are monsters; their carnal existence conflates the molar distinction between inside and outside, consequently unsettling the notion of the bounded, unified self.

As a means of (speculatively) considering the potentially subversive relationship between noise and women, I would now like to draw attention to how this connection can be put to use through artistic pursuits – namely, in the noisy performance of a molecular and embodied subject-in-process. Such a subject is not constituted by an essence or soul; it bears little resemblance to the sovereign individual. Rather, the subject-in-process (or, more accurately, the body-in-processs) is constituted by its affective relations – its ability to affect and be affected. As such, the subject can be thought of as an open, ever-mutating assemblage rather than a closed, unified and autonomous subject.

A number of feminist and philosophical thinkers have examined the broader, ethico-political value of recognizing the (female) subject and/or body as a transitional, mobile assemblage (for example, Rosi Braidotti, Elizabeth Grosz, Donna Harraway, Moira Gatens and Gilles Deleuze and Felix Guattari) as well as the dangers and difficulties of seeking to undo traditional notions of identity and subjectivity. Braidotti succinctly voices the problem of deconstructing subjectivity and identity for feminist thinkers, specifically in relation to Deleuze and Guattari's notion of becoming-woman:

> One cannot deconstruct a subjectivity one has never been fully granted control over; one cannot diffuse a sexuality which has historically been defined as dark and mysterious. In order to announce the death of the subject one must first have gained the right to speak as one. (Braidotti, 2003, 51)

Nevertheless, inasmuch as 'the phallologocentric regime cannot be separated from the majority, that is, a material colonization of space ... [that starts] from the theft of the bodies of women and "others" and their confinement into a binary, Oedipalizing cage of negation', alongside liberalism's 'undue glorification of the self, given as both centralized, unitary and plural', the creation of new, desiring subjects, that require 'massive reorganizations and changes in the material fabric of society' (Braidotti, 2003, 61) remains potentially advantageous.

For our purposes, there are two sides to thinking the subject in such terms. First, it has the potential to render arbitrary the most 'natural' constructions of femininity, which rely on dualisms that organize relations between – and separate – male from female, culture from nature, subject from object, self from society, the Same from the Other, and so on. In making audible the processual dynamism of the subject and its irreducibility to binary categorizations, such hierarchical dualisms are revealed to be insufficient. Yet this is not just a critique. These (embodied) undoings, dismantlings and blurrings are productive, insomuch that they create new becomings, new differences and new affective capacities.

Given its associations with identity and (individual) subjectivity, it is interesting that within the realms of experimental and noise music, many female artists have chosen to explore the potentials of the voice. Mladen Dolar, for example, states that 'we can almost unfailingly identify a person by the voice, the particular individual timbre, resonance, pitch, cadence, melody, the peculiar way of pronouncing certain sounds. The voice is like a fingerprint, instantly recognizable and identifiable' (Dolar, 2006, 22). But the voice also has a particular capacity to evade and permeate material and symbolic boundaries; it is transitional, always in a state of in-between; existing on the threshold between inside and outside, caught in the space between 'me' and 'you'. On one hand it is resolutely embodied and on the other disembodied. For some artists, it is the voice's – especially the singing voice's – imbuement with gendered connotations that makes it such a fruitful site of exploration and experimentation. The composer, performer and sound artist Pamela Z has suggested that the long-standing association of women with insanity (and thus, by extension, unpredictability and irrationality) has, in terms of vocal production, permitted a degree of freedom: 'somehow it's more acceptable for a woman to do something that seems like losing her mind, being wild and being crazy with her body or her voice, either as a dancer or a singer' (Rogers, 2010, 222). Likewise, Nina Power has remarked upon the innovative use of the voice by the electronic noise musician Jessica Rylan in her account of the relationship between noise, machines and women. Rather than limiting herself to an 'imitative reproduction' of the 'juddering-by-numbers idea that noise should be as harsh and relentless as possible', Rylan uses the specifics of sound and noise to stage a Cyborgian exploration of the artificiality of the natural, outstripping and outdoing its simulation by 'plugging and unplugging her voice and body into the auto-circuits of an oneiric eroticism that weaves beguilingly amidst a series of disconcerting incongruities' (Power, 2008, 102).

Here, however, I would like to consider the comparatively well-known work of the American composer and vocalist Diamanda Galás,[6] who can be heard to give voice to a noisy, multiplicitous and transformative subject-in-process that, while veering closely to stereotypes of the madwoman, creatively and productively disassembles and reassembles relations between molar categorizations. Galás's vocal performances are noisy in the sense that they make use of abrasive, dissonant or harsh sonorities, evoking notions of incomprehensibility, ugliness and excess, and in the sense that they are disruptive, disturbing and, at times, threatening. Yet in her experiments with the voice and the producing body she also evokes the notion of noise as potential; noise as the new or the not-yet-categorized.

In her disruptive vocal performances, Galás foregrounds the voice's ability to permeate the (imagined) material borders of the embodied subject: 'here is a voice that refuses to pretend that it does not attack and invade the listener's ears' (Jarman, 2011, 132). For Galás, the voice 'has always been a political instrument as well as a vehicle for transmission of occult knowledge or power. It's always been tied to witches and shamanistic experience – the witch as transvestite/transsexual having the power of both male and female' (Galás and Juno, 1991, 11). Moreover, inasmuch as the subject-in-process is 'a mutant, the other of the Other; a post-Woman embodied subject cast in female morphology' (Braidotti, 2003, 45), Galás herself refuses to categorize herself in relation the male/female dichotomy: 'people ask me, "How do you feel as a woman onstage?" and I say, "a *what*? Woman, man – I am a fucking nigger, white person, lesbian, homosexual, witch, snake, vampire – whatever!" I don't think in any one of those terms – that's so limited!' (Galás and Juno, 1991, 11).

While Galás has a marked aesthetic commitment to notions of abjection, horror, madness, suffering and despair – those affective and emotional experiences that serve to rupture the sense of unified self – her work can be understood as an assemblage of influences, aesthetics, concepts and vocal and musical styles: 'I don't respect the boundaries of any art form; I certainly don't respect music's boundaries' (Galás and Juno, 1991, 17). Her diverse repertoire weaves between a number of genres, traditions and practices, stitching together blues, opera, Greek lament, *bel canto* singing, noise, ballads, spirituals, and avant-garde composition. To be sure, while never truly separable from one another – nor ever a straightforward generic emulation – Galás's voice contains within it a number of different voices that can be foregrounded; alongside the extreme and extended vocal style she is best known for, there is the blues/jazz voice of *The Singer* and *Guilty! Guilty! Guilty!*, and the more rock-oriented voice of *The Sporting Life*, a collaboration with Led Zeppelin's John Paul Jones. However, Galás primarily approaches the voice as a transformative sonorous-affective force; she has remarked that her music is not *about* something, but that it *is* something – the 'thing itself ... the sound of the plague, the sound of the emotions involved' (Galás and Juno, 1991, 14). Similarly, Chare writes:

> To hear Galás, is not to encounter a description of horror but to experience an incarnation of it. In Galás's work this incarnation is of a number of different bodies constructed as horrible by culture and made to endure the horrible effects of that construction, made to suffer its oppression. (Chare, 2007, 61)

Such a voice can be heard on Galás's unnerving recording debut, *The Litanies of Satan* (1982), where her use of extreme vocal techniques – screams, shrieks, grunts, growls, multi-phonics and exaggerated vibrato – twist her words and blur their comprehensibility. Here, there are none of the 'feminine virtues' of the fair tongue or graceful speech. In the second part of the recording, 'Wild Women with Steak Knives (The Homicidal Love Song for Solo Scream)', Galás makes use of a five-microphone set-up to give voice to different personalities and vocabularies of a schizophrenic woman (Galás and Juno, 1991, 8). Resolutely unstable, vocal lines flow and morph into each another, sometimes dominating, sometimes supporting and sometimes interrupting one another. Yet Galás is not entirely incoherent; rather, she veers between the absolute clarity of a furious monologue, extended screams, gibberish wails, and repulsive emulations of vomiting and suffocation.

During *Litanies of Satan*, as well as tracks such as 'Cunt', Galás's voice (or voices) contains a grotesque corporeality; the gargling sounds of her larynx, tongue, lips and saliva are made audible – the sounds of the body-in-action that are typically excluded from recordings of the voice but nevertheless lie behind the production of the voice. And yet there is nothing *natural* about this voice; this is not a return to an imagined, pre-symbolic and pre-social state. Although it is riddled with what would be conventionally understood as 'flaws', these noises are not accidental or erroneous. They are not extraneous to, but an integral part of the sonorous-vocal assemblage: mutating, disrupting and ultimately shaping other vocal sounds. Galás's extraordinary voice, pushed to its full three-and-a-half-octave range and coupled with her use of external, technological manipulations, is stretched and disfigured beyond recognition. It is simultaneously 'intensely bodily—when we hear orgasmic squeaks, squashed throaty groans, and breathy whispers—and intensely alien, as those sounds are so beyond what is normally expected from the voice' (Jarman, 2011, 128). In 'Litanies of Satan', for example, Galás's five vocal lines are layered at points to create walls of sound. EQ and tone control assist her extreme vocal range, allowing her heighten and lower the voice beyond 'natural', gendered registers; it is at once too shrill to be 'authentically' female and too low to be 'authentically' male. Freya Jarman states that

> ... the monstrous, the cyborg, and queer slip freely alongside each other in Galás's work, each of them committed to disrupting borders and rethinking connections and oppositions—the monster between human and nonhuman; the cyborg between human and machine; queer between sexual desire, chromosomal sex, and gender identity. (Jarman, 2011, 140)

It is Galás's vocal shape-shifting and its subsequent disruption of binary orders – natural/artifical, male/female, primal/alien, embodied/disembodied and also intended/extraneous, musical/unmusical – that makes her voice all the more unnerving.

Yet Galás plays a potentially dangerous role. There is a risk that Galás can be heard to affirm damaging and oppressive stereotypes of femininity. Her sounds resonate with the notion of women as irrational excess; she takes on the ranting, noisy voice of hysterical unreason. Then again, Galás's vocal performances are by no means a straightforward emulation of the masculine construction of feminine madness. As Susan McClary states,

> This is politically very different from the tradition of male composers projecting their own fantasies of transgression as well as their own fears onto women characters and performers. Galás is not interested in the narrative of raising the specter of the monstrous, flirting with madness, and then reimposing control – the narrative in which the double discourse of violation and protection at stake ... Her simulations are not peep shows. (McClary, 2002, 110)

But nor is this to suggest that Galás gives voice to a more 'genuine' feminine madness. Rather, Galás's noisy simulations of troubling constructions of femininity reveal them for what they are. For McClary, Galás can be heard to confront these stereotypes head-on; she reveals 'how very constructed the classic madwoman must have been – how sanitized, how made to conform to variable cultural fantasies and finally, how frameable' (McClary, 2002, 111). In short, Galás's articulations are thought to be too unclean, too piercing and, fundamentally, too noisy to match the masculine stereotypes of feminine madness.

Moreover, while the vocal utterances of the female, hysterical madwoman are imagined to be uncontrollable, Galás remains in complete control of her virtuosic voice and the performance materials. Her noisy, ugly, yet fascinating vocal tone is the outcome careful manipulations, informed by training and research. She has compared her vocal training to that of a warrior, insofar as it requires one to push beyond the expected limits of the body and the voice in order to take on new affective capacities:

> Training to be a singer is like training in the martial arts. A Japanese material artist once said that in my performance I use 'kill energy' because my singing involves superhuman uses of the voice [...] singing is not about the parlor room nuances of the [individual] personality, but a very concentrated energy – *the transformation of the body into a weapon*. It's about going *beyond* your self. (Galás and Juno, 1991, 9, my emphasis)

In turn, to only recognize Galás's work as a (negative) critique of pre-existing dualisms is to overlook the creative and productive (positive) dimension of exploring the permeability of such boundaries and the (quite literally) extraordinary status of her voice(s). Galás has stated that within her work there is a commitment to (immanent) freedom; for example, she considers insanity to carry with it a liberatory potential, insomuch that it offers a line of flight from the self. *Apropos* 'Wild Women with Steak Knives' she states:

I wanted to produce an immediate extroversion of sound, to deliver a pointed, focused message – like a *gun* ... the way I sing embodies the concept that diffraction of the personality provides an essential liberation from the self, thus extroverting the insanity. And when you extrovert the insanity you can live most of the time as a real person, yet be able to change your self and commit actions that your real self would not be capable of. (Galás and Juno, 1991, 8)

Notwithstanding the division between 'real' self and 'alternative' self seemingly suggested by Galás, the notion of an immanent and transformative escape seems crucial here. Yet this is an escape that has no prescribed endpoint or conclusion. Rather, what comes with Galás's escapes are new sonic and sensuous-affective experiences; new capacities to affect and be affected, and new vocal-bodily potentials that lie beyond what is expected of the female voice.

\* \* \*

The relationship between noise and the 'feminine'/'feminized' thus runs in (at least) two directions. On one side, we have a patriarchal politics of noise and silence, which tells of the subordination and suppression of women. Women's sounds have been abated in the name of order and reason; they are disruptive, extraneous and dangerous. On the other, we can understand this 'feminine' noise as having a potentially subversive capacity, in that it can disrupt molar categorizations. As we have seen, the most dangerous women according to patriarchal narratives are those characters who are themselves noises within the system; they are disruptive, transitional bodies that cannot be constituted in relation to normative dualisms. An open-ended, subject-in-process can be recognized in the noisy vocal performances of Diamanda Galás, which harness noise to create destabilizing and disruptive voices. Galás's voices reveal the insufficiency of hierarchical dualisms and the permeability of material-discursive borders in their pursuit of new escape routes from the binary grid system.

# CHAPTER NINETEEN

# Beyond Auditive Unpleasantness: An Exploration of Noise in the Work of Filthy Turd

*James Mooney and Daniel Wilson*

## Introduction

Filthy Turd is one of several monikers used by the UK-based noise artist Darren Wyngarde. Wyngarde's live performances as Filthy Turd are typically very loud – timbrally noisy – and sometimes involve nudity, acts of violence, masochism, scatophilia and other forms of subversive behaviour. The album art, track titles and promotional materials include references to vomit, faeces, acts of self-harm and sexual imagery. There are two Filthy Turd online blogs (Filthy Turd, 2009a, 2011) comprising a curious mixture of informative text and what appears to be complete gibberish. The following is a representative example of the latter:

> ksykin radiation radiation ckougcockttenccock.Unfortunatefilthyy cussi-hcking ckougcockttenccock.Unfortunatefilthyy taidationtaidation and ineim and radiation lucartilarhips tadiationdnd ckougcockttenccock. Unfortunatefilthyy rbfra ckougcockttenccock. (Filthy Turd, 2009a, 'Radiation Leg')

What exactly is one to make of all of this? Is there any artistic merit to be found here or is it simply obscene nonsense? And what of the music? One might expect it to be noisy – many of his releases are categorized under the genre of 'noise',[1] and Wyngarde himself has, on occasion, self-identified as a noise artist – but what does that actually mean? Is the music merely cacophonous – nasty to listen to, 'auditive unpleasantness', to borrow Hegarty's phrase – or is there more to it than that? And how, if at all, is the music itself related to other aspects of Filthy Turd's practice, to all of those behaviours and imagery that seem designed to provoke disgust?

'What we think of as [...] inherent to an idea of noise, its unwantedness, comes [...] with an undesirability that goes beyond the auditive unpleasantness of certain sounds' (Hegarty, 2007, 26). Here, Hegarty points to 'unwantedness' and 'undesirability' as fundamental characteristics of noise. Importantly, he also points out that noise 'goes beyond the auditive unpleasantness of certain sounds'; that is, noise should not be considered exclusively a sonic phenomenon. If noise is not exclusively a sonic phenomenon, then how best to generalize the territory that noise occupies? Jacques Attali generalizes noise as something that can exist within any system of inscription: 'Noise [...] does not exist in itself, but only in relation to the system within which it is inscribed' (Attali, 1985, 26). To combine Attali's and Hegarty's sentiments: noise is not (necessarily) sound, but *anything* that is unwanted or undesirable within a given context or system of inscription.

In this chapter we examine the work of Filthy Turd with a particular focus upon its relationship with noise, exploring the specific ways in which Wyngarde's practice can be considered 'noisy', as well as suggesting what this might tell us about the nature of noise itself. As our title suggests, we will show that, far from simply being a 'racket', the notion of noise is explored and presented here in several different ways that go beyond the superficial, 'common-sense' conception of noise as mere auditive unpleasantness. In doing so we will show how several disparate aspects of Filthy Turd's practice – nonsense text, repulsive imagery, graphic design, as well as some specific musical techniques – come together to form a coherent noise aesthetic. All of the Filthy Turd tracks referred to in this chapter are available online (see Discography), and the reader is encouraged to listen to them alongside reading our analysis.

## Timbral noise

Let's start with what is, probably, the most intuitive common-sense understanding of what noise is: something that we hear. Noise is sound. Specifically, noise tends to refer to particular types of sound: pneumatic drills, jet engines, traffic, heavy machinery, sirens, alarm bells. What these sounds have in common is that they are: (a) loud; and/or (b) harsh in timbre. (Sounds having a 'harsh' timbre tend to have broad frequency content, which in layman's terms means they are typically unpitched. 'White noise' – sound containing equal energy in all frequencies across the audible spectrum and sounding rather like radio static – is another example.) Generally, a sound is likely to be considered 'noisy' if meets either or both of these criteria. The sound examples just given all share these timbral characteristics and could, purely on the basis of those sonic characteristics, be categorized as noise-sounds. This kind of noise – where sounds are characterized as 'noisy' based purely on their spectral content – we will call 'timbral noise'. Much of Filthy Turd's work makes use of sonic materials that are timbrally noisy, *My Name is Filthy* (Filthy Turd, 2006b) being a good example. Here, the sound itself *is* the noise; it is '*a* noise'. Timbral noise is a subcategory of sound in general, and this is in contrast with the varieties of noise we will discuss later, which need not be directly concerned with sound at all.

## Affect, disgust, lust

Timbral noise has two significant by-products. Firstly, it can disrupt aural communication: imagine trying to have a conversation with somebody whilst standing next to a noisy pneumatic drill. (We will return to this during our discussion of 'medial' noise.) Secondly, it can cause us to experience visceral, bodily sensations. This kind of experience, known as 'affective response', is described by Goodman as follows: '[Noise] moves up through your body, constricting your internal organs until it is in your chest and throat, making it impossible to breathe' (Goodman, 2009, xiii). Huron, in his book on music and expectation, suggests that our affective response to loud sounds has to do with our biological predisposition toward increased alertness in situations where there is potential danger.

> Loudness is known to increase physiological arousal. There are good reasons for this connection: loudness is indicative of events in the environment that entail a large expenditure of physical energy. Whether physical energy is embodied in animate agents (such as a herd of elephants) or in inanimate objects (like boulders rolling down a slope), high levels of physical energy are more likely to pose a danger than low levels of energy. (Huron, 2006, 34)

Furthermore, the knowledge that no real danger exists (as is usually the case in music) cannot suppress the affective response (Huron, 2006, 6). The use of timbral noise in music, in other words, may serve to provoke an affective response in listeners – a heightened arousal – despite the knowledge that there is no real danger. Indeed, Huron goes on to suggest that the instinctive negative 'defence' response followed by the more gradual evaluation that no real danger is posed plays a significant role in the enjoyment of music generally. One can see why this effect might be particularly pronounced in music that makes extensive use of loud, timbral noise:

> [W]hen music evokes one of these strong emotions, the brain is simply realizing that the situation is very much better than first impressions might suggest. In this regard, music is similar to other forms of pleasurable risk-taking, such as hang gliding, skydiving, riding roller coasters, or eating chilli peppers. (Huron, 2006, 36)

Or dripping hot wax on oneself, as is sometimes the case in Filthy Turd's live performances (see Filthy Turd, 2006d, c. 4'10"). In the same performance (c. 4'30") Wyngarde sets fire to lighter fuel contained inside the bell of an upturned cymbal, which when struck causes flames to jump several feet in the air. This puts the audience in increased 'danger' – the presence of flames being likely to evoke similar kinds of affective response to the loud sounds – and hence increases the potential enjoyment of the performance further when an evaluation of 'no real danger' is reached.

Of the affective response known as disgust, Curtis and Biran state the following:

> The manifestations of disgust include a particular facial expression (wrinkling of the nose, pulling down the corners of the mouth), characteristic neurological signs (lowered blood pressure, lowered galvanic skin response, and nausea) and characteristic actions (stopping, dropping the object of disgust, shuddering or saying 'yuk!'). (Curtis and Biran, 2001, 18)

Curtis and Biran's research identifies numerous stimuli that are apt to provoke disgust. These include: bodily secretions such as blood, faeces and sexual fluids; dead bodies; things or people contaminated with disgusting material; certain animals including fish; poor hygiene; 'violations of the body envelope' such as the breaking of the skin or penetration of an orifice;[2] and what they term 'moral disgust [...] the type of disgust that is reserved for politicians, injustice [...] and abuse of power' (Curtis and Biran, 2001, 18–21). The name Filthy Turd itself evokes several of these images, of course. Consider also album titles such as *Piss Enema* (Filthy Turd, 2005; referring to bodily fluids and the violation of the body envelope), *Death Ray Orgasm/No Sexual Hygiene* (2007b; death, allusion to sexual fluids, poor hygiene), and *Death Ejaculations* (2009b; death, sexual fluids). Consider *Bloody Waters/Dirty Fucking/Slaves* (2007a), whose title references blood, dirt and sex and whose album art depicts people urinating on each other. *Power\*Control\*Lust* (2003) and *An Occult History Of The Midlands* (2010) both include death references (in the form of images of the grim reaper) in their artwork, the former also alluding to the 'moral disgust' associated with the abuse of power. *Kill The Women Rape The Men* (The Rita and Filthy Turd, 2005) features a track charmingly entitled 'The Fish-Woman Has Her Finger In Your Arse-Hole', the disgusting components here being the fish (identified by Curtis and Biran as a 'disgusting' animal) and the invasion of the body envelope. (Incidentally, note also the reversal of an unfortunate biblical turn of phrase in the title. This is a neat example of schematic noise, which will be discussed later.)

Last, but certainly not least, in Filthy Turd performances it is not unknown for Wyngarde to remove his clothes and smear his body in what appears to be excrement (see, for example, Filthy Turd, 2006c). When Curtis and Biran state that 'certain categories of [...] people are [...] found disgusting, notably those [...] contaminated by contact with a disgusting substance' (Curtis and Biran, 2001, 21), it is hard to imagine a more fitting example.

It will be clear from some of these examples that there are sexual undercurrents in much of Filthy Turd's work. Pornographic imagery is used in the album art for several releases, including *Love Hotel* (2006a), whose front cover depicts a man masturbating. Clearly there is a link between sexual behaviour and affective response. The response could be one of arousal or perhaps one of disgust, but in either case it is a definite affective response. There is also, of course, a sense in which these behaviours and types of imagery are 'undesirable' and 'unwanted' (recalling Hegarty) within the system (recalling Attali) of mainstream culture as a whole. In this sense they can be regarded as 'noisy', although not directly related to sound.

## Medial noise

We use the expression 'medial noise' to denote the occurrence of anomalies arising within a system or framework as a direct consequence of the design or architecture of that very framework. Elsewhere (Mooney, 2010) one of the authors discusses the 'affordances' of tools, which in plain English means 'the things they allow you to do'.[3] As the examples given will demonstrate, medial noise always occurs as a function of the affordances of the framework itself. Here we will discuss two phenomena – glitching and clipping – that are examples of medial noise in the digital audio domain, arising 'from within' the digital audio framework itself.

The conventional wisdom in digital audio is that edits should be made at zero-crossings, that is, at points where the sound wave crosses the horizontal axis when represented graphically. If an edit is made 'badly', at a point where the waveform has a large amplitude above or below the horizontal axis – in other words, not at a zero-crossing – this results in an unnaturally abrupt 'step' in the waveform, as shown in Figure 19.1, and a corresponding click or 'glitch' in the sound when it is played back. It is only because the digital audio paradigm allows us to dissect and re-order sonic events in time that it also, inherently, allows us to produce anomalous discontinuities like this. The glitch is an artefact that comes 'from within' the digital audio framework itself, and hence medial noise.

Now we turn to clipping. Digital audio represents sonic events as long sequences of numbers within a finite range (in Figure 19.1 the range is −1 to +1; every point on the waveform has a value within that range). It is not possible at any point for the digital audio signal to have a value outside this prescribed range. Loud sounds that would, hypothetically, result in a waveform that breaches this range are 'clipped', that is, forcibly restricted to the minimum and maximum allowed values. When this happens, it results in abrasive and rather unnatural-sounding distortions of the sound. In digital music production, therefore, the recording and manipulation of sound is typically undertaken in a way that avoids clipping. Again, the clipping is a direct consequence of the digital audio framework itself.

In 'God is Everywhere' (Filthy Turd, 2008), we can find examples of both clipping and glitching.[4] Figure 19.1 shows where an edit has been made without adhering to the zero-crossing rule. This results in a sharp discontinuity in the waveform and a glitch as described previously. Additionally, the signal has been overdriven, and we can clearly see the results of digital clipping, where the peaks and troughs of the audio waveform have been flattened.

The introduction of clipping – a form of medial noise – also happens to render the sound more timbrally noisy, since it results in an increase in frequency content that literally renders the sound closer to white noise. Medial noise in the audio domain can, in other words, actually *cause* timbral noise. The clipping technique can also be found elsewhere in Filthy Turd's work. 'Help Me Now Help Me' (Filthy Turd, 2008), for instance, makes extensive use of sampled material which has been overdriven to the point of distortion through signal processing (see Figure 19.2). This track will be discussed further in the section on 'schematic noise'.

Another example of medial noise can be found in 'c20h25n30', where some of the material contains glitches as though being played from a damaged CD. This is aesthetically reminiscent of the work of Yasunao

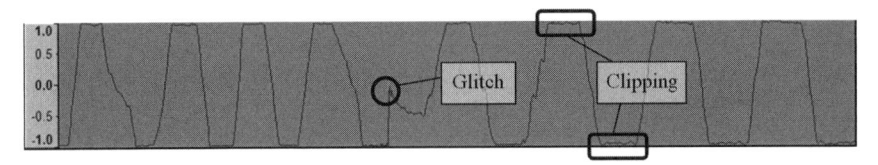

**FIGURE 19.1** *Extract from Filthy Turd's 'God is Everywhere' showing glitch where two samples have been joined together at a non-zero point in the waveform (approx. 0'59" in). Digital clipping is also present throughout the track, as evidenced in the flattened peaks in the waveform.*

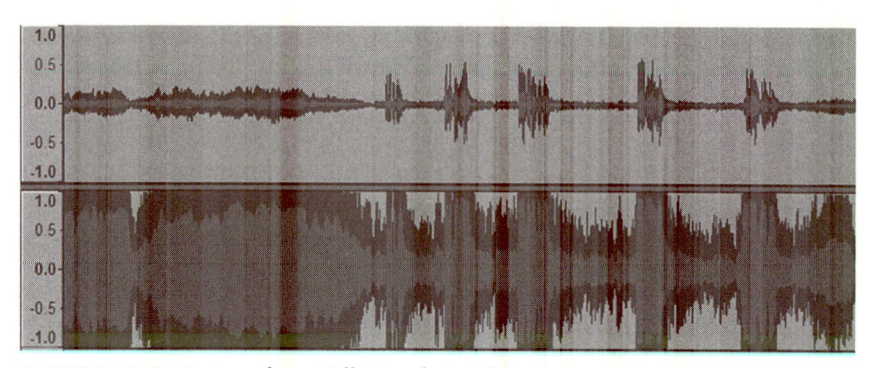

**FIGURE 19.2** *Extract from Telly Savalas's 'If' (upper waveform) compared with how it is quoted in Filthy Turd's 'Help Me Now Help Me' (lower waveform).*

Tone, whose *Solo for Wounded CD* (1997) is composed entirely from the sounds generated by deliberately damaged discs (Stuart, 2003). The deliberate hijacking of the CD player's error correction system is an example of medial noise, since the noise is an artefact of the playback medium itself. Agamben describes the production of medial noise as 'the exhibition of mediality: the process of making a means visible as such' (cited in Crocker, 2007). The compact disc is not used as a transparent carrier of content, but is itself exhibited as a latently noisy medium. The practice of appropriating a system such that it generates noise 'from within itself' is the defining characteristic of medial noise and, of course, a staple of the glitch aesthetic.[5]

**FIGURE 19.3** *Screenshot of Filthy Turd's website on MySpace (accessed 19 July 2010).*

Earlier we noted that noise need not necessarily concern sound, and medial noise can, naturally, occur outside of the audio domain. The digital image and video work of Rosa Menkman, for example, subverts the internal structure of video files, producing artefacts that are essentially the visual equivalents of audio glitching and clipping. Menkman (2010) includes a selection of screen shots illustrating the visual results of medial noise in digital images. For an example of an audiovisual work combining elements of medial noise in both video and audio domains, see Menkman and Wilson (2010). Similar visual characteristics can clearly be seen in the artefact-like background image used until recently in Filthy Turd's MySpace website (see Figure 19.3). Note also the unusually large font size, meaning that no more than three or four words can ever be seen on-screen at any time. The garish image and large font make the information on the website, to all intents and purposes, unreadable (though the layout and graphics have subsequently changed following restrictions imposed by MySpace).

Medial noise can also occur within the framework of digital text-formatting. If a text file (a word-processing document or the HTML code for a website, for example) is incorrectly 'parsed' – that is, if the computer for some reason ends up interpreting it incorrectly – then this can result in a scrambling of the text and, potentially, the introduction of erroneous characters. Again, this is analogous to the introduction of clipping and glitching artefacts in digital audio. The results can end up looking rather like the quasi-understandable gibberish-prose that we see on Wyngarde's Filthy Turd blog, quoted at the start of the chapter. Both of these Filthy Turd website examples – the oversized font with glitchy background image and the nonsense blog text – present information in such a way that it appears illegible. This can be regarded, in a sense, as a deliberate inhibition of communication. Recall that earlier, we identified the inhibition of communication as a potential by-product of the presence of timbral noise. Here, the same trope – the inhibition of communication – is evoked deliberately in the visual domain.

## Schematic noise

Let us return momentarily to 'Help Me Now Help Me', for medial noise and timbral noise aside, there is something else at work here. 'Help Me Now Help Me' quotes extensively from Telly Savalas's 1975 single 'If'. Although the original Savalas track has been quite heavily distorted, it is still clearly recognizable. 'Help Me Now Help Me' is, in effect, one long, uninterrupted quote: we hear the Savalas song almost in its entirety, from start to finish, in its original form, save for the introduction of distortion. Anybody familiar with the original song will have no trouble whatsoever in recognizing it, and – crucially – even those unfamiliar with that specific song are still likely to recognize it, generically, as fitting within the idiom of the pop song, with all its attendant characteristics. Thus, the listener is able to understand that a pop song normally would not – *should* not – sound like this. Pop songs do not usually contain distortion in this way; it comes across as erroneous.[6]

Consider another example that uses material sampled from a pop song: 'c20h25n30' (which samples Mungo Jerry's 'In the Summer Time'). Again, the quotes are lengthy: the first verse of the song is quoted in its entirety, followed by most of the second verse. There is no signal processing, and for about 50 seconds we hear the track exactly as in the original. Around 50 seconds in, the quoted music is abruptly interrupted by a glitch and jumps back to the beginning of the second verse. Since we hear two (almost) complete verses of 'In the Summer Time' – over 30 seconds of directly sampled, unaltered material – this establishes an expectation of continuity. We expect to hear the rest of the song, and the sudden anomalous glitch disrupts this expectation. Again, the listener does not necessarily need to be familiar with this specific song in order to experience this disruption of expectation. Any listener familiar with the Western pop song idiom in general will intuitively understand that discontinuity of this kind is a breach of the rules. The effect is one of surprise.

'Surprise', Huron states, '[...] arises from a discrepancy between an actual outcome and a highly practised schema' (Huron, 2006, 14). In this latest example (and also in the previous), the schema is that of the Western popular music song. This particular schema can be thought of as a generic template of all of the normal characteristics of pop songs. If the listener is familiar with pop songs (through conscious or unconscious cultural conditioning) then we can say that he/she is 'highly practised' in this schema. The quote from 'In the Summer Time' activates the expectations of the schema and the listener makes certain structural predictions based on it. The 'actual outcome', however, is at odds with the schematic prediction and the sudden glitch is therefore surprising. The same can be said of 'Help Me Now Help Me' (quoting Telly Savalas). It is schematic expectation that allows the listener to understand that there is something 'wrong' about the way the Telly Savalas song is presented: the pop-song schema (although the possibility of distortion almost certainly does figure somewhere within it) does not allow for distortion to be presented to the listener in this particular way. In both tracks, in other words, there is a difference between the schematic characteristics of pop songs and the ways in which the quoted material is presented by Wyngarde. We will therefore refer to this type of noise as 'schematic noise'.

In order for this to work, it is crucial that the sampled material be clearly recognizable as fitting within the pop-song schema. Huron alludes to this when he states that '[c]omposers must activate either normative schemas (such as styles) or commonplace clichés in their listeners if their violations of expectation are to have the desired effect' (Huron, 2006, 36). There is also a sense in which Wyngarde's use of material quoted from pop songs generates noise in relation to a different schema: that of noise music itself. Many noise artists base their practice predominantly on the use of timbral noise – materials that are noisy in the spectral sense described previously. By contrast, Filthy Turd's *Cock the Lights* (2008) album (although it does make some use of timbral noise) is notable in that many of the sounds presented to the listener, such as undistorted pop music samples, are *not* timbrally noisy. This, in some sense, represents a violation of the unwritten rules of the noise-music schema – if, that is, we regard timbral noise as one of the defining characteristics of that schema. In any case, this argument serves to demonstrate the fact that noise operates on multiple simultaneous levels in Wyngarde's work.

'A Call to Arms' (Filthy Turd, 2008) quotes from Nilsson's 'Everybody's Talkin'' and this time the quote takes the form of a loop, such that we repeatedly hear the phrase 'I'm going where the sun keeps shining through the pouring rain'. Or, at least, that is what we expect. In reality, the word 'rain' is cut slightly short, so what we actually hear is 'Through the pouring ra...' before the loop jumps back to the start of the phrase. The result is three-fold. First (and perhaps most obviously) there is a disruption of the lyrics. Secondly, there is a disruption of the meter of the song, that is, the rhythmic continuity. Nilsson's track, like many pop songs, has a metric rhythm in 4/4 time, but when cut short and looped in this way the meter is disrupted. We expect 4/4, but what we actually hear is a slightly truncated version of it that sounds rhythmically incorrect. Thirdly, the loop-points also happen not to occur at zero-crossings in the digital waveform, meaning that digital glitches are present when the loop jumps from the end back to the start. (A similar treatment can be found in 'God Is Everywhere', which includes sampled material from Freda Payne's 'Band of Gold'.) To summarize, there is schematic noise with respect to two different schemas: the linguistic schema, responsible for our surprise at the noisy truncation of the word 'rain', and the pop-song schema (or possibly a more generic metric-rhythm schema), which is surprised at the non-continuity of the expected 4/4 meter. There is also medial noise – in the form of glitching – in the digital audio domain. Once again, a close analysis reveals multiple forms of noise operating at multiple levels within the music.

Cutting short the word 'rain' creates schematic noise at a linguistic level. Although this is apt to cause surprise, it is unlikely to affect our understanding of the meaning of the lyrics, for in a sense we still hear the complete word 'rain' in our mind's ear. The syntactic integrity of the sentence, in other words, remains more or less intact. In 'Spiritual Filth (Reprise)' there is a more pronounced disruption of the linguistic schema. This track samples material from Paper Lace's 1975 single 'Billy don't be a Hero', and the quoted material is introduced part way through a word ('lovely'), which is itself part way through a sentence. The resulting sentence is as follows: '...ly fiancée. From where I stood I saw she was crying, and through her tears I heard her say, "Billy, don't be a hero, don't be a f...".' Clearly, the syntactic integrity of the sentence is destroyed, along with its linguistic intelligibility. 'c20h25n30' employs a similar technique, quoting from Lee Marvin's 'Wand'rin Star' to produce the following nonsense sentence: 'To pack, I've never seen a sight that didn't look better looking back. I was born under a wa...'.[7]

Schematic noise and medial noise can be (but are not always) related, and in order to demonstrate this we will return once more to the example of 'c20h25n30', where we hear Mungo Jerry's 'In the Summer Time' as though played from a faulty, glitching CD. The CD glitch – an example of medial noise – results in a disruption of the structure of the quoted pop song, which in turn results in the production of schematic noise within the pop-song schema. The schematic noise, in other words, is produced as a by-product of the medial noise; medial noise can *cause* schematic noise.

Earlier, we drew upon quotations from Attali and Hegarty to posit noise as that which is unwanted or undesirable within any given context or system of inscription. In recognizing that the glitch is unwanted and anomalous within the digital audio framework, and that the structural discontinuity is unwanted and anomalous within the pop-song schema, it is easy to make the transition to an understanding of noise as 'that which is unwanted' within *any* schema or framework. Furthermore, the fact that the unprocessed Mungo Jerry quotes are neither timbrally noisy nor normatively unpleasant neatly demonstrates that our understanding of noise 'goes beyond the auditive unpleasantness of certain sounds'.

## Conclusion: the Filthy Turd aesthetic

We have defined three different noise types: timbral, medial, and schematic, giving examples of each in Wyngarde's work. We have described some of the musical techniques, performance characteristics and thematic tropes present in the work: disgusting imagery and behaviour, pornographic material, nonsensical websites, and so on; and explained these in terms of the three noise types. What remains is for us to summarize how noise is used by Wyngarde to provide – despite first appearances – a coherent aesthetic in his work as Filthy Turd. In doing so, we will also allude to something more general about how the three noise types might be related to each other.

Earlier we identified two human consequences of noise: affective response and the inhibition of communication. These two central characteristics are key to our interpretation of Wyngarde's work. Most aspects of the music and its surrounding practice can, we argue, be interpreted as attempts to

# BEYOND AUDITIVE UNPLEASANTNESS

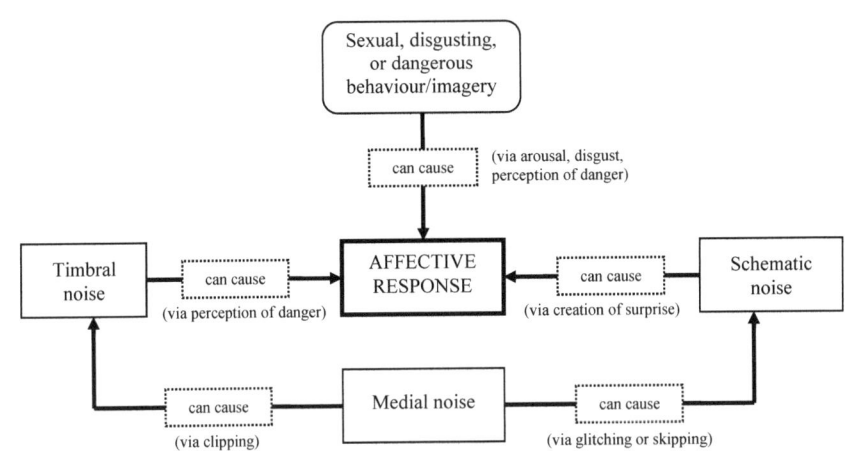

**FIGURE 19.4** *Diagram illustrating Filthy Turd's use of noise alongside sexual, disgusting or dangerous behaviour and imagery to produce affective response. This operates in parallel with the production of perceived inhibition of communication shown in Figure 19.5.*

invoke these two responses. The production of affective response and the production of a sense of inhibited communication usually happen simultaneously and in parallel, but for the sake of explanation it is clearer to illustrate these processes in two separate diagrams.

Figure 19.4 shows the mechanisms by which noise is used alongside sexual, disgusting or dangerous behaviour and imagery in order to produce affective response. Timbral noise invokes a perception of potential 'danger' (even if no real danger is present), resulting in a heightened affective state. Schematic noise, by confounding expectations, creates the affective response of surprise. Other, non-musical techniques, such as sexual, disgusting or dangerous behaviour and imagery, are used to produce or enhance affective responses of arousal, disgust, or the perception of danger. Medial noise can cause timbral noise, as happens in digital clipping, which enriches spectral content and renders sounds closer to white noise, in turn causing affective response. Medial noise can also cause schematic noise, for example where glitching and skipping interfere with linguistic, musical-structural or stylistic schema, in turn resulting in surprise.

Figure 19.5 shows how, in parallel, noise is used to give the impression of an inhibition of communication. Timbral noise (momentarily ignoring the reference in Figure 19.5 to 'visual noise') inhibits communication by 'drowning out': 'What did you say? I couldn't hear you because of that pneumatic drill.' Schematic noise inhibits communication by rendering materials structurally or syntactically incoherent. Medial noise can cause timbral noise, for instance where a vocal recording distorted by clipping

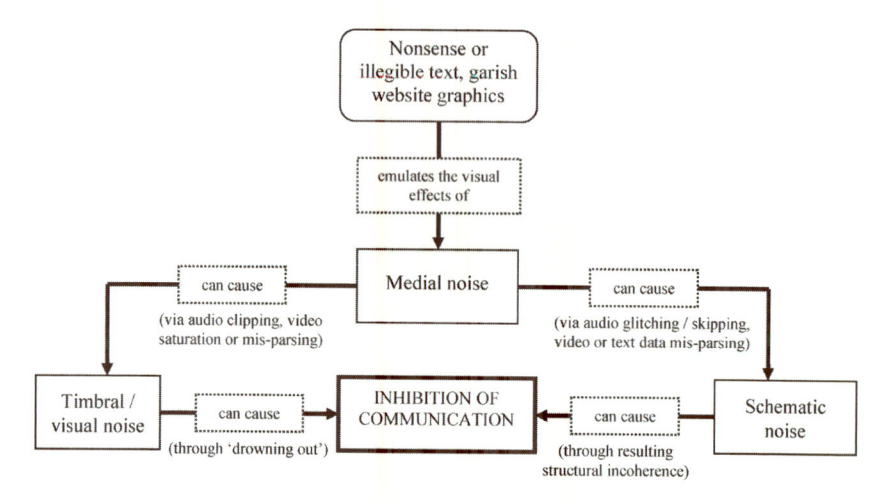

```
                    ┌─────────────────────┐
                    │   Nonsense or       │
                    │ illegible text, garish│
                    │  website graphics   │
                    └─────────┬───────────┘
                              │
                    ┌─────────▼───────────┐
                    │ emulates the visual │
                    │      effects of     │
                    └─────────┬───────────┘
                              │
   ┌──────────┐     ┌─────────▼───────────┐     ┌──────────┐
   │can cause │◄────│    Medial noise     │────►│can cause │
   └──────────┘     └─────────────────────┘     └──────────┘
(via audio clipping, video                    (via audio glitching / skipping,
 saturation or mis-parsing)                    video or text data mis-parsing)

┌───────────┐  ┌──────────┐  ┌──────────────┐  ┌──────────┐  ┌───────────┐
│ Timbral / │  │can cause │─►│ INHIBITION OF│◄─│can cause │  │ Schematic │
│visual noise│ └──────────┘  │COMMUNICATION │  └──────────┘  │   noise   │
└───────────┘                └──────────────┘                └───────────┘
           (through 'drowning out')    (through resulting
                                        structural incoherence)
```

**FIGURE 19.5** *Diagram illustrating Filthy Turd's use of noise alongside graphical and textual means to produce the impression of inhibited communication. This operates in parallel with the production of affective response shown in Figure 19.4.*

(medial noise) becomes denser in frequency content (timbral noise) and becomes unintelligible (inhibition of communication). Medial noise can also cause schematic noise, for example where skipping (or deliberately perverse editing) destroys the syntactic integrity – and hence intelligibility – of lyrics in a vocal recording. Wyngarde's use of nonsense text, and the garish, illegible nature of the Filthy Turd MySpace page (sadly now rendered legible through the enforcement of a standard layout template by MySpace administration) emulate the effects of medial noise in digital-text and digital-image frameworks, respectively.[8] Medial noise can cause visual as well as audible noise (returning now to the 'visual noise' in Figure 19.5), which in this context means the randomization of pixels or characters, a visual 'drowning out' analogous to white noise in the audio domain.[9] Medial noise can also cause schematic noise, for example where the improper parsing of digital text data results in sentences that are garbled and incomprehensible.

Filthy Turd is noisy in ways that go 'beyond the auditive unpleasantness of certain sounds' (Hegarty, 2007, 26). For certain, there are plenty of sounds that *are* auditively unpleasant – what we call timbral noise. But there are also plenty of sounds that are not of themselves timbrally noisy, such as sampled pop songs, which manifest themselves as *schematically* noisy because of the context and manner in which they are presented. There are uses of text and graphics that are noisy even though they do not produce any sound at all. There are hijackings of digital media systems that produce not timbral noise, but medial noise, ostensibly unwanted and undesirable. And there are dangerous and provocative behaviours, disgusting and sexual imagery, designed not just to amplify the effects of exposure to noise through the production of affective response, but also to be unwanted and undesirable – schematically noisy – within the framework of mainstream society as a whole. Noise is anything, sonic or otherwise, that is unwanted or undesirable within a given framework, and Filthy Turd exemplifies this in many ways.

## Acknowledgements

The authors would like to thank (in alphabetical order): Ben Charles (for introducing the authors to the work of Filthy Turd), Bob Davis, Michael Goddard, Benjamin Halligan, Sara Jansson, Stephen Kilpatrick, Jessica Maddams, Rosa Menkman, Nikos Stavropoulos, Marie Thompson, and finally, Darren Wyngarde for giving us something to write about.

# NOTES

## Introduction

1 Mattin's approach to noise is not from the theoretical standpoints, let alone genres, of contemporary music. And while noise is related to improvisation, in terms of aspirations for maximizing freedoms to break with conventions, even improvisation is radically problematized – related to neoliberal and immaterial labour forms that demand spontaneous creativity and total adaption to any situation from which something can be 'produced'. See Mattin, 2011, n.p. ('A single decision: Interview with Addlimb').

2 Bigger than Words, Wider than Pictures: Noise, Affect, Politics, convened by Michael Goddard and Benjamin Halligan, University of Salford, Summer 2010. The first volume arising from this event was *Reverberations: The Philosophy, Aesthetics and Politics of Noise*, edited by Goddard, Halligan and Paul Hegarty, and published by Continuum in 2012.

3 Menkman, like Mattin and Hegarty, was present to open dialogues with colleagues at the noise conference in these respects, as were colleagues from the groups Mogwai and The Telescopes.

## Chapter One

1 The satirist and cultural revolutionary, Oskar Panizza 'developed an ultimately tragic view of history, which postulated that genuine freedom – the ability to live according to the urgings of the Dämon – was possible only at times of chaos and upheaval' (Jelavich, 1985, 62).

2 The student revolution began with protests against the rules prohibiting visitors of the opposite sex visiting dormitory rooms at a suburban Paris campus. Within a few weeks it had taken hold with the student occupation of the Sorbonne, the citadel of French learning. The students were subsequently joined by 10 million workers, half the French labour force, so shutting down the economic machinery of France for several weeks. Other popular movements during the spring of 1968 included the US anti-Vietnam campaign, the Prague Spring and violence on campuses from Japan to Mexico. See http://histclo.com/country/fran/co-fran1968.html (accessed 15 June 2012).

3 To an extent, this can be traced back to the romantic anarchism of the Beats,

with its interest in Eastern mysticism, poetry, jazz and drugs and writers Jack Kerouac and Allen Ginsberg.

4   Although it is recognized that the fight against middle-class prurience led increasingly towards an explicit identification of sexual freedom with total freedom which, at its extreme, embraced pornography, including the so-termed 'velvet underground' advertisements for blue moves and classified ads, and *play power's* 'Female Fuckability Test' (Neville, 1971, 14). As such, while love was fundamental to the philosophy of the counterculture, there was nevertheless a marked difference between the transcendental spirituality promised to followers of the Maharishi Mahesh Yogi and the revolutionary liberation of the Yippie Party's Jerry Rubin and his symbolic call for patricide.

5   Jimi Hendrix, Fillmore East, New York City, New Year's Eve 1969 (cited in Shaar Murray, 1989, 22).

6   It is not insignificant that the choice of 'The Star Spangled Banner' as America's national anthem in 1931 provoked criticism by the Music Supervisors' Conference of America as reflecting a nation at war rather than a nation committed to peace and goodwill (Fuld, 1966, 434). Hendrix was not alone in his attack on the country's overt militarism.

7   Shaar Murray adds: 'It is appropriate that Francis Ford Coppola hired Randy Hansen, a young guitarist whose act used to consist of note-for-note Hendrix reproductions [...] to contribute sedulously Hendrix-derived overkill to the soundtrack of an ambush scene in his 1979 Vietnam exorcism *Apocalpyse Now*' (Shaar Murray, 1989, 24).

8   The illustration can be seen at http://www.beatles-history.net/beatles-monterey-pop.html (accessed 4 April 2011). It is interesting to note that Jimi Hendrix had also been invited, along with the Who, as part of the British contingent. The band performed their current UK hits, ending the set with Pete Townshend setting fire to his guitar before smashing it to pieces.

9   The *Marseillaise* was adopted as the French national anthem on 14 July 1795 and while it was subsequently banned by Napoleon I, Louis XVIII and Napoleon III, it was recognized as the anthem of the international revolutionary movement during the nineteenth and early twentieth centuries. It was reinstated as France's national anthem in 1879. See http://www.nationalanthems.info/fr.htm for additional information (accessed 5 April 2011).

10  I am grateful to Michael Hannan for his analysis of the sound design of 'A Day in the Life' (Hannan, 2008, 60–1).

11  Russell Reising and Jim LeBlanc note that psychedelic rock has used alarm clocks, chimes, bells, the effects of clocks ticking and other effects to signal psychedelic awakening (Reising and LeBlanc, 2008, 111).

12  It is also reported that McCartney's interest in the avant-garde, and his admiration for Stockhausen, led to the inclusion of an 'instrumental passage with a spiralling ascent of sound ... [starting] the passage with all instruments on their lowest note and climbing to the highest in their own time' (Martin and Pearson, 1994, 56).

13   Penderecki's 'Threnody to the Victims of Hiroshima' was featured in the British TV documentary *A Guide to Armageddon*, where the effects from the heat of the atomic bomb are shown.

14   The Beatles' inroads into popular culture in terms of such issues as politics, fashion, commerce, gender and sexuality, not least their challenge to embedded class defence, is discussed in my chapter 'The Beatles as zeitgeist' (Womack, 2009, 203–16).

15   As Jim DeRogatis (2002) writes, 'Strange as it seems in retrospect, the music industry thought revolution might be the next big marketing concept circa the late '60s, and MC5 were signed to Elektra (along with their younger "baby brother" band, the Stooges) by Danny Field (A&R) who later managed The Ramones.'

16   Sleeve note on 'MC5.1969 *Kick Out the Jams*' (compact disc), New York: Elektra.

17   My discussion of Sinclair and his affiliation with the MC5, Trans-Love Energies, and the White Panther Party draws on Bartkowiak (2007), Bartkowiak (2009) and Callwood (2010).

18   Simon Frith and Angela McRobbie define cock rock as 'an explicit, crude, and often aggressive male sexuality' (Frith and Goodwin, 1990, 374).

19   My discussion of the codes involved in noise and the association with the revolutionary ideology of the 1960s counterculture provided an opportunity both to return to my original thinking on the relationship between rock and the counterculture (1992) and to Richard Middleton's seminal discussion in *Studying Popular Music* (1990) which informed and influenced my thinking and conclusions.

## Chapter Two

1   In his 1975 album review for *Rolling Stone*, James Wolcott surmised: '*Metal Machine Music* isn't so much a knife slash at his detractors as perhaps a blade turned inward', describing Reed's creation as 'droning, shapeless' and 'hopelessly old-fashioned' (Wolcott, 1975).

2   See, for example, Reed's interview for *Sound on Sound* (Inglis, 2007).

3   A useful account of these terms may be found in Mertens (2004, 16–17).

4   On vinyl, a locked groove allows the final 1.3 or 1.8 seconds of music to repeat until the listener lifts the stylus away. The loop's duration is determined by one rotation of the record.

5   Reed emphasized this lineage in an interview promoting the Zeitkratzer DVD release: 'In the Velvet Underground, my guitar solos were always feedback solos, so it wasn't that big of a leap to say I want to do something that's nothing but guitar feedback, that doesn't have a steady beat and doesn't have a key' (Petrusich, 2007).

6    For a more comprehensive overview of these 'conditions of audibility', see Middleton (1990, 184).

7    Zeitkratzer (translation: 'Time Scraper') is a Berlin-based experimental chamber group directed by pianist Reinhold Friedl. They are renowned for their interest in noise, improvisation and contemporary music repertoire. Many of the original members who took part in the 2002 performance of *Metal Machine Music* have since left and been replaced and Ulrich Krieger himself departed in 2003.

8    Reed gave the following account of his disbelief: 'Ulrich Kreiger [...] got in touch with me and asked if they could perform it and whether he could transcribe it and I said that I didn't think it could actually be done ... So he said let me do five or ten minutes and let me see what you think and they did and I was [...] amazed by what he could do and what they could do' (Doran, 2010).

9    Further evidence of this can be found in Chris Jones's online review for the BBC (2007) and Dave Simpson's article for *The Guardian* (2007).

10   My previous reference to the score being a regression of sorts is to highlight the way in which this challenges the usual chronology whereby a score is a component of the compositional process preceding and hence informing a performance or recording. In many respects, the acts of scoring and then rearranging *MMM* constitute a bookending of the original work.

11   For example, Krieger was able to stress that the work was modal, based on a fundamental pitch resulting from the original tuning of Reed's guitars: 'All the string instruments in my arrangement are tuned to open fifth B-F# and play only these notes or overtones thereof [...] There are also tonal melodies played around that drone, if one listens closely – they are just "hidden" in the sonic eruption of *MMM*' (Inglis, 2007).

12   Reed, disillusioned with the content of his previous studio album *Sally Can't Dance* (released August 1974) quipped: '[t]he worse I am, the more it sells. If I wasn't on the record at all next time around, it would probably go to number one' (quoted in Bockris, 1994, 281). In his biography, Bockris appears to suggest that Reed's *MMM* was in part prompted by his desire to discard any outwardly imposed identity: 'In Jan 1975 Reed was desperate to find a new image that would free him from the prison of any image' (Bockris, 1994, 286).

13   The DVD footage of Zeitkratzer's performance directs the viewer's attention to these precise aspects: instances such as close-ups of the percussionist moving a bow across the edge of a cymbal promoting awareness of otherwise obscure timbral occurrences.

14   The term 'anaphone' derives from Philip Tagg's Sign Typology: 'anaphone is analogous to analogy [...] A sonic anaphone can be thought of as the quasi-programmatic, "onomatopoeic" *stylisation* of "non-musical" sound [...] Kinetic anaphones have to do with the relationship of the human body to time and space' (Tagg, 2003, 99–100).

15   MM3 was formed by Reed and Krieger in 2008 with Sarth Calhoun. Their

first performance was in Los Angeles in October 2008. Their use of digital processing is, of course, far more complex than the analogue effects employed in the original *MMM*, and live loops play a significant role in the improvised creations.

16   MM3's concert at the Royal Festival Hall, London (April 2010) began with guitars leant against amplifiers; the resultant feedback gradually increasing in dynamic while the audience entered.

17   Further recycling (sampling) of *MMM*'s contents may be found in Sonic Youth's *Bad Moon Rising* (1985) and TV on the Radio's *Return to Cookie Mountain* (2006).

## Chapter Three

1   For fuller discussion of this utilization of stereo sound, see Moore, 2001, 121–6; 2012, xvi, 395.

2   This is the 1966 album credited to John Mayall with Eric Clapton, typically known as the 'Beano' album. Mike Vernon produced and Gus Douglas engineered the album. The sound seems to have been a result of Clapton's unapologetic boosting of amplifier volume beyond the standard levels used for studio recordings, necessitating a rethinking of the positioning of microphones in relation to amplifiers, coupled with a tendency to try to record music live in the studio – pushing the recording philosophy more towards single takes rather than multiple tries. See 'Mike Vernon: Producing British Blues' at http://www.soundonsound.com/sos/dec10/articles/vernon.htm (accessed August 2012).

3   See Whiteley, 2004, 119, footnote 8. The year 1965 is also identified in the culturally significant 1972 compilation *Nuggets: Original Artyfacts from the First Psychedelic Era, 1965–1968*.

4   Jones visited the village of Jajouka in 1968 with Brion Gysin and the album *Brian Jones Presents The Pipes of Pan* was released posthumously in 1971; Jones died in obscure circumstances in 1969.

5   Macan is precise in this respect, subdividing the psychedelic period into three wings (1997, 19–20) in order to locate a Prog Rock pre-history in the psychedelic period in the 'three multimovement suites' in 1968 releases from Pink Floyd, the Nice and Procol Harum (Macan, 1997, 42).

6   The installation was modelled after the artist's first installation – literally an 'open house', where his bedroom in his parents' suburban house was thrown open to the public. The room was reassembled for the London Hayward Gallery Jeremy Deller retrospective of 2012 together with, in part, the artist's curating and reworking of other materials from the Acid House era.

7   See the interview in Reynolds for more on this intervention (Reyolds, 1990, 180–6).

8   The *Godstar* tracks were released in a number of formats, including *Godstar:*

*Thee Director's Cut by Psychic TV* (2004). Thompson also notes how early British imaginings of the Acid House sounds of Detroit and Chicago, even when 'getting them wrong', fed into and shaped British Acid House nonetheless (Thompson, 1998, 133).

9   For a discussion of this conception in respect to late 1970s 'disco' science fiction cinema and television, see 'Disco Galactica: Futures Past and Present' (Halligan, 2010, 81–109).

10  Where a line of direct influence is actually apparent from Dinosaur Jr., as with groups such as Catherine Wheel and Swervedriver, such groups were tellingly associated with the shoegaze scene while rarely actually releasing shoegaze music.

11  For further discussion of Moore's model, as applied to shoegaze, see Sangild (2004).

12  King notes that the term was coined by Alex Ayuli, half of the shoegazing-associated group A R Kane, and an advertising copy-writer (King, 2012, 306).

13  For the track 'Alzheimers' (from *American Whip* of 2004) the post-shoegaze group Joy Zipper sampled extracts from filmed interviews of elderly patients in the advanced stages of memory loss, and reproduced their characteristic grasping for words just beyond reach in the song's lyrics. The film sampled is *Complaints of a Dutiful Daughter* (Deborah Hoffman, 1994).

14  Macan notes this demographic as true of Prog Rock too (Anglican, private education- and university-orientated, and of a 'southeastern English youth-based subculture' [1997, 144]) – a genre which was, at the time of his writing, and until Hegarty and Halliwell's recent study (2011), déclassé on the grounds of apoliticism and elitism.

15  Shoegaze music then discretely persisted into the 1990s and beyond, as apparent in music from the Brian Jonestown Massacre (a band in part modelled on the 1960s counterculture) and Yo La Tengo. A brief phase of 'Nu-Gaze', of 2007–2008, was characterized by groups who tended to utilize the sonics of shoegazing but restored the centrality of a singer. Exceptions to this retrograde step include Amusement Parks on Fire, A Place to Bury Strangers and Serena-Maneesh. The late 2000s, however, were also a period of activity for shoegaze groups who had remained dormant for some years, including My Bloody Valentine, Chapterhouse and Swervedriver, and with the Telescopes embracing a higher visibility.

16  Such promos which were made specifically for terrestrial broadcast, as with the BBC's late 1980s alternative music programme *Snub TV*, and for release on compilation videos, rather than being entirely aimed at MTV terrestrial broadcast.

17  The promo video was made by Mike Mason, of the shoegaze group Swallow.

18  Wiseman-Trowse discusses the aesthetic of shoegaze covers in respect to the work of Vaughan Oliver and his v23 design studio (2008, 153–6), and finds in them '[…] an attempt to replicate the narcotized withdrawal that the music represents' (Wiseman-Trowse, 2008, 155).

19  Idiosyncratically, the released live version of 'Nefi + Girly' by Nu-Gaze group Asobi Seksu (on *Asobi Seksu*, 2007) ends with the explanation that the song is about the singer's cat and their dysfunctional relationship.

20  Reynolds and Press draw a parallel between abstract expressionism and the music of My Bloody Valentine in the ways in which 'the figure is obliterated' – the figure of the musician, and as discernible originator of sounds within the overall music (Reynolds and Press, 1995, 220).

21  Is it as a consequence that there is such a difference, now, between shoegazer CDs (often in good condition, as if well treated and carefully shelved) and Acid House CDs (typically scratched, the faded or foxed inlay reminiscent of cigarette smoke, the jewel case dirtied and cracked)? This suggests the utilitarian role of Acid House CDs (taken to parties, passed around, used as aids for cigarette-making) and the 'muso' fetishization of shoegaze CDs (kept at home as treasured possessions).

22  An urban legend persists that the transformation of Creation records from the modest home of shoegaze groups occurred with the agreement, at the instigation of Oasis, to drop Slowdive from the label. Creation shoegaze groups included the Telescopes, Ride and My Bloody Valentine and earlier signing included the Jesus and Mary Chain, whose use of feedback has been held to have been influential on shoegazing.

23  This was clearly more than a matter of confrontation; Shields seems aware of the affective nature of psychedelia in the 1960s: 'What I do is about consciousness, being conscious of a feeling in my whole body. The trouble with the attitude towards psychedelic music is that it's about your head only. And to me, and all non-Western people when they get into altered states of mind, it's the whole body that's involved' (quoted in DeRogatis, 2003, 491).

# Chapter Four

1  Both the stigma and the cultural impossibility of deafness in the context of music are expressed by Beethoven, writing in 1801: 'I have ceased to attend any social functions just because I find it impossible to say to people: I am deaf. If I had any other profession I might be able to cope with my infirmity; but in my profession it is a terrible handicap' (quoted in Hood, 1977b, 342).

2  The decibel scale is a logarithmic rather than linear form of measurement; a difference of 20 dB between two sounds means that the more intense one has 10 times the amplitude (100 times the power) of the softer. Generally for acoustics concerned with human hearing, dB measurements are 'A-filtered', which means that they focus on the mid-range frequencies our ears are most physiologically sensitive to. Mostly, as is conventional in much non-specialist writing about the subject, the dB ratings cited here are technically dB(A).

3  Nightclub sound systems, despite technical improvements in recent years, remain a further source of intense levels of music; see SCENIHR, 2008, 27.

4   Though see the 'rapid response' section of the journal, which includes for this article one from the splendidly named Dr Funk challenging Patton and McIntosh's findings: 'The assertion that concussion can result from an activity as benign as dancing defies common sense' (Funk, 2009, n.p.).

5   Let us acknowledge the irony that the youthful generation, the rock and rollers and the baby (sonic) boomers, have aged and deafened. As Pat Benatar puts it in a hearing impairment booklet: 'Our generation has helped shape American culture, especially since we're the first to be raised on rock 'n' roll. From Aerosmith to the Rolling Stones, our music defines us, but all those years of rockin' are beginning to take a toll' (quoted in HEAR, 2004, 2). If our music defines us it is because our music deafens us. Rock 'n' toll.

6   Pete Townshend has given an account of one small excessive aspect of the shortened musical life of Keith Moon, drummer with the Who, who died in 1978: 'On the stage once, I saw Keith Moon, who uses earphones to follow a drum track, I saw his earphones *catch fire*, on God's honour, *catch fire* on his head there was so much level ... and he's still going louder, louder, *louder*!' (quoted in Wilkerson, 2009, 249n. 2; emphasis added).

## Chapter Five

1   For more on this argument, see Ross, 2009.

2   Performance: *The Final Academy*, Brixton Ritzy (London, 1982), with William S. Burroughs, Throbbing Gristle, Cabaret Voltaire, 23 Skidoo. Commercially unavailable.

3   Performance: *Plan K* (Brussels, 1979), with William S. Burroughs, Joy Division, Cabaret Voltaire. Commercially unavailable.

4   For further on this, see Revill, 2000, 599.

## Chapter Six

1   *Die Nachgeborenen* is taken from Brecht's poem 'To those born later', 1936–38 (Brecht, 1995, 136). It is a familiar term in modern German Literature Studies often as 'Die Generation der Nachgeborenen', used for the German generation of artists born around or after 1945 who used their art to confront or come to terms with their discovery that their parents had been either perpetrators or victims of Nazism.

2   Bargeld had hoped to direct and perform the work with Heiner Müller but Müller died suddenly in December 1995 (personal interview, Berlin, 5 November 2004).

3   Bargeld stated that he had at this time a recording of Artaud's screams which, along with the text of *The Theatre and its Double*, was very influential on

the group (personal interview, Berlin, 5 November 2004). Jessamy Calkin, the group's tour manager during the 1980s, also said in interview that 'they were always quoting Artaud' (personal interview, London, July 15, 2008).

4  The work illustrates a key aspect of their philosophy of collapse; here was an actual as well as a metaphorical attack on the autobahn as a structure associated both with Hitler and, later, *Kosmische* musicians' route of escape. This urban-guerrilla artistic warfare is aptly captured by a photograph depicted on the back cover of Neubauten's first album, *Kollaps* (ZickZack, 1981). Here a black-clad Bargeld, flanked on either side by Einheit and Unruh (resembling a group of guerrilla street fighters) stand to attention between the Nazi-associated symbols of the Olympic Stadium towers; their found object instruments are ritualistically laid out as captured weaponry and a show of strength, ready to assault the Federal Republic's ears and musical/architectural structures with their noise-attack.

5  Neubauten's textual structuring and content are equally Artaudian. Their creation of texts from dreams, collections of lists, chance games (based on a card system) and surreal associations deconstructs the popular song's formula and its closed studio parentage. Similarly, the texts avoid what Artaud called 'psychological conflicts of man and battlefields of moral passions' (Artaud, 1970, 51) preferring his cosmic, scientific, biological and mythical themes.

6  He also helped to organize and curate Neubauten's first East Berlin concert in December 1989 (see Uli Schueppel's film *Von Wegen*, 2009).

7  The East German Deutsche Rundfunk Archiv (DRA) in Potsdam provided me with recordings of these three works; however, there is also a recording of *Hamletmaschine* on Ego, an independent label set up by Neubauten in 1991 as an outlet for its projects, both collective and individual.

8  See Andrew Spencer's paper 'Kopfarbeit or Theatre in your Head' (2000), which discusses Müller's metaphor of *die Fehler* (error) and references this to Neubauten's work (as in the skipped stylus mentioned above). Spencer quotes Müller saying that 'the only hope is in error because when all the technological systems work – we are lost' (Spencer, 2000, 208).

9  This is a technique which Neubauten have frequently used with spoken text; for example, *DNS Wasserturm* (1983) and *3 Thoughts* (1993).

10  The Germans' name for the Velvet Revolution 1989–90; it means 'turn/change'. It can also be applied to the sudden necessity for the East Germans to look in a different direction.

11  My approach to analysing Bargeld's Artaudian screams is to use Rudolph Laban's dance categories of Effort and Quality.

12  However, he remained dissatisfied with the outcome, maintaining that it had not been possible to create the fully desired painful effect with the lighting (personal interview, Hamburg, 28 October 2006).

13  Dieter Kranz, Frankfurter Rundschau: *Aus dem Nachlass*, 2 November 1994, sourced from NBOA, 27 November 2006. Other details from hand-written notes loaned to me from NBOA and from Unruh (personal interview, Berlin, 14 February 2007).

14  Personal interview, Berlin, 10 November 2005. Much of this work was created using a chance-based system called, by the group, 'Dave cards'.
15  George Brecht used this term when describing an aspect of Fluxus art performance in which elements could be so slight that they could be missed; however, they have still occurred (see Dezeuze, 2005).
16  Stories were abundant during the 1980s of on-stage accidents with fire and chain saws and near-misses with audience members; however, Neubauten have always stressed that their interpretation of 'cruelty' was in line with Artaud's as requiring a painful and difficult spectatorship, not deliberate harm visited on their own bodies as performance art or, by proxy, on their audience (see Maeck, 1996).
17  Neubauten's highly energized on-stage performance 'dance' provides another strand of their working Artaudian practice, as does the visual impact of their stage-set of machinery, found and constructed objects; these present the spectator with a fascinating pre-show sculpture, especially as the group always declare the process of working with the objects on-stage. One of the most effective Artaudian uses of stage-space was for the supporters' *Grundstück* concert (3 November 2004) in the condemned, degutted Palast der Republik; here the musicians worked around the central circle of supporters imitating Artaud's proposed hangar configuration.
18  The protagonist in *Von Wegen* (2007) hopes that the final emptiness, or breath, will come while he is still dancing, for – as with Artaud – the act of dancing in defiance of gravity's bounds remains a central positive state for Neubauten.

# Chapter Eight

1  Extra-sonic events, in this context, denotes factors beyond those of musical or non-musical sounds, or sound events that form part of an artist's work. This includes musical performance, the artistic use of voices and playing of musical instruments. In other words: extra-sonic events are not on the recording.
2  Arguably, Nouvelle Vague's lounge versions of punk and new wave hits have been quite successful in this respect.
3  For a fuller discussion, see Steinholt (2012).
4  See Letov (1994).
5  The not-so-reliable statistics of YouTube 'likes' and 'dislikes' confirm this. More importantly, the public debate following the band's two most recent performances testifies to the disenchantment of an increasing number of people previously sympathetic to Pussy Riot's actions.
6  An otherwise bold article by Sergey Chernov on Pussy Riot (Chernov, 2012) uses rather toothless English translations of the song titles: 'Clear up the Pavement' for 'Free the Cobblestone', and 'Putin Got Scared' for 'Putin Pissed Himself'. What may have motivated the desk at *St Petersburg Times* remains an open question.

7   Pussy Riot YouTube posting: 'Devchonki iz Pussy Riot zakhvatyvaiut transport'. Available at: http://www.youtube.com/watch?v=qEiB1RYuYXw&feature=plcp (accessed March 2012).

8   Pussy Riot YouTube posting: 'Gruppa Pussy Riot zhzhet putinskii glamur'. Available at: http://www.youtube.com/watch?v=CZUhkWiiv7M&feature=plcp (accessed March 2012).

9   Pussy Riot YouTube posting: 'Smert' tiurme, svoboda protestu'. Available at: http://www.youtube.com/watch?v=mmyZbJpYV0I&feature=plcp (accessed March 2012).

10  See, for example, the *Daily Telegraph* of 20 January, 9 and 14 March 2012, *The Guardian* of 6, 11 and 12 March, and 18 August 2012, and *The Observer* of 1 July and 19 August 2012. I keep the descriptions of these two actions brief, since they have already received considerable mention in English-language media.

11  Pussy Riot YouTube posting: 'Pussy Riot na krasnoi ploshchadi s pesnei "Putin zassal"'. Available at: http://www.youtube.com/watch?v=yqcmldeC7Ec&feature=plcp (accessed March 2012).

12  The Cathedral of Christ the Saviour was erected in the mid-1800s during the reign of Nikolai I to commemorate the 1812 victory over Napoleon. Following the revolution, it was emptied and used as a stable before Stalin had it demolished. The plan was to erect a Palace of the Soviets skyscraper on the site, but the fundament of the riverbank proved too weak to support it. Instead a public open-air swimming pool was constructed on the premises. The reconstruction of the cathedral began in 1990 and it was consecrated in 2000. It has become a symbol of the Russian Orthodox Church's return to glory in post-Soviet times.

13  Pussy Riot YouTube posting: 'Pank moleben "Bogoroditsa Putina progoni" Pussy Riot v Khrame'. Available at: http://www.youtube.com/watch?v=GCasuaAczKY&feature=plcp (accessed March 2012).

14  See, for example, Viktor Shenderovich in television interview on RTVi. Available at: http://www.youtube.com/watch?v=AIEiFvaobw8&feature=related (accessed March 2012).

# Chapter Nine

1   Amazingly this meagre record of the group has recently been supplemented by a digitized live recording – of surprisingly good quality – featuring no less than 24 tracks, even if not all of these are complete songs.

2   The Fall were a notable exception to this tendency, touring in 1982 at the crucial *Hex Enduction Hour* period of their development, and having a dramatic and provocative impact on some local groups, if more due to their uncompromising attitude than the formal properties of their music.

3   This is somewhat of an exaggeration as there was, to name two examples, a

resurgence of cultural activity around Maori culture in literature, music and art, as well as a new wave of filmmaking beginning with the seminal, and somewhat punk, *Sleeping Dogs* (1977) dealing with one man's battle against a future authoritarian regime in New Zealand. Nevertheless when it came to music, especially in cities like Dunedin, it was fair to claim, as record store owner Roy Colbert did, that 'there was no rock band of any substance ... before 1980' (Colbert, cited in Mitchell, 1996, 224), even if there had been various forms of folk, psychedelic, hippie and other forms of countercultural music in other places. Nevertheless the creative reception of punk and the DIY cultures it spawned was definitely a watershed of cultural assertiveness in New Zealand.

4   There have been some more recent updates to this, such as some of the chapters of the Graeme Downes co-edited volume *Dunedin Soundings* (2011) that examines a range of Dunedin musics from a compositional perspective, and the extensive research into a range of New Zealand music scenes conducted by Andrew Schmidt on his blog *Mysterex* and elsewhere: see http://mysterex.blogspot.co.nz/search/label/New%20Zealand%201980s%20Independent%20Music

5   The fact that the seminal Dunedin Double EP was recorded in Christchurch and not Dunedin only adds to this sense of mobility and interchange.

6   Eggleston's claim also attests to the perceived tribal affinities between Maori *iwi* (tribes) and Scottish clans.

7   A decade later this garage/surf aesthetic would be taken up much more successfully by King Loser, a band that explicitly distanced themselves from the Dunedin Flying Nun music scene.

8   Bannister claims that Knox's insistence on amateurism was not merely an economic necessity but a credo and a disingenuous one: 'there's a certain amount of pose in the whole amateur schtick' (Bannister, 2006, 119).

9   Interestingly enough, despite the score-settling already apparent in Bannister's earlier *Absolutely George Street* (1999) that is his anecdotal account of his own band Sneaky Feelings in the context of Flying Nun and Dunedin music, his later and more academic and purportedly transnational-focused book *White Boys, White Noise* (2006) still seems to be settling these same scores, despite its combination of New Zealand and international examples of indie guitar music. While a somewhat bizarre hybrid of men's movement feminism, critical theory and musicological analysis, the book is certainly one of the few to attempts to treat indie guitar music systematically, even if some of its conclusions about the relative value of jangly versus drony guitar music seems to derive less from its theoretical framework than from long-standing prejudices.

10  In addition to the already intimated influence of the Fall, who also made inroads into the New Zealand mainstream singles charts with 'Totally Wired' and 'Lie Dream of a Casino Soul', Joy Division were also relatively popular, with their single 'Love will Tear us Apart' not only reaching second place in the singles charts on its first release but also charting highly on each of the successive occasions it was re-released.

11 See Antonio Negri, 1991, 174–6. In this context, *disutopia* is used to describe Spinoza's move beyond Renaissance idealist thought as characterizing what he calls the 'Dutch Utopia' (22–44) toward a more radical materialist, ontological construction of the world, beginning with the behaviours of bodies rather than transcendent ideas. Despite these different contexts, Negri's description of the concept of disutopia does seem highly resonant with the aesthetic principles of the Dead C. and other Xpressway bands: 'If the metaphysical utopia was a transcription of the ideology of the market, the ethical disutopia is the proposal of the rupture of the market ... The Disutopia is the revelation of the real forces that move behind the rupture of the ideological perfection of the market ... it is the vindication of a project that ... has been able to limit itself and still conserve its power in its entirety' (Negri, 1991, 176).

12 See Alvin Toffler (1970). Alister Parker and John Halvorsen of the Gordons discuss the Future Shock EP on a recent 'Extended Play' documentary on Auckland's bFM: http://www.95bfm.com/assets/sm/205163/3/ExtendedPlay14.4.mp3. Interestingly, it turns out that the lyrics for 'Adults and Children', the third track on the EP, largely come from the instructions on a vial of prescription drugs, whereas usually it is taken to be about intergenerational conditioning.

13 This album was known as Volume II, and was in fact the Gordons Mark II, as the singer Alister Parker had become a born-again Christian and left the band to form a U2-influenced Christian rock band, New Man. John Halvorsen was never happy with the quality of the second Gordons album, which has never been released in digital form except as an even poorer quality bootleg; nevertheless it contains some of the Gordons' most startling and brilliant tracks.

14 The techno-futurism is strongly critiqued in Berardi (2009, 123–37; 2012, 17–68, 164–6), both of which culminate in a manifesto of post-futurism.

15 On Machinic Heterogenesis, see Guattari, 1995, 33–57.

# Chapter Ten

1 'Noise offers something more like dark matter which may be what allows a structure for everything else to exist (i.e. music, meaning, language, and so on, emerge from and against noise)' (Hegarty, 2007, 139).

2 See, for instance, *Wire* #207, 2001.

3 See, for example, the work of Keith Fullerton Whitman and Russell Haswell of the last few years, both of whom have shifted, if not from digital to analogue, then from computer-based to 'dirty electronics'-style practices.

4 The tracks entitled 'Acid in the Style of David Tudor' on the album of the same name seem to draw their inspiration from Tudor's *Neural Synthesis (1–9)* suite of recordings.

# NOTES

5   See 'Why Computer Music Sucks' by Bob Ostertag (Ostertag, 1998).
6   Quoted by the author at 'UF8: Sound Out Of Line', Urbanomic Falmouth, 27 June 2009.
7   I have no idea what 'Vlook' means, possibly a reference to array handling in computer programming.
8   The conception of granular synthesis is usually attributed to Xenakis for instance, but this fact doesn't monopolize the sound to the same degree.
9   See, for instance, Xenakis's questioning: 'what are the possible restrictive limits of human psychophysiology? What are the most general manipulations which may be imposed on the clouds and their transformations within psychophysiological limits?' (Xenakis, 1992, 47).
10  'What is the most economical way to create a plane wave in an amplitude-time space (atmospheric pressure-time), encompassing all possible forms from a square wave to white-noise?' (Xenakis, 1992, 289).
11  In *die Riehe*, a German journal of contemporary music, Herbert Eimert wrote: 'only in coming to electronic music can we talk of a real musical control of Nature' (Eimert, 1957).
12  GENDYN is the name of the program Xenakis wrote to produce dynamic stochastic synthesis. It stands for 'GENeration DYNamique'. For the purposes of clarity, this article has referred only to DSS.

## Chapter Eleven

1   At the time of viewing, this painting was on loan to the the Museum of Metropolitan Art from the Allen Memorial Art Museum, Oberlin College, Ohio.
2   Consider, for example, *Variations V* (1965), where, to a backdrop of manipulated television images, sound was prescribed by the movements of the dancers as they came into proximity with various antennae, or intersected the beams of the stage lights.
3   For a concert-goer who is already familiar with the repertoire, one could argue that this cognitive frame is pre-existing.
4   See, for example, Jonathan D. Kramer's 1988 study on musical time, or Robert Fink's (2005) disco-infused take on Reich and Glass.
5   In a similar fashion (and thinking back to the earlier discussion of Newman's minimalist series), Rosalind Krauss discusses the 'schizophrenic' nature of the grid in the visual arts, explaining that, 'logically speaking, the grid extends, in all directions, to infinity. Any boundaries imposed upon it by a given painting or sculpture can only be seen – according to this logic – as arbitrary. By virtue of the grid, the given work of art is presented as a mere fragment, a tiny piece arbitrarily cropped from an infinitely larger fabric. Thus the grid operates from the work of art outward, compelling our acknowledgement of a world beyond the frame. This is the centrifugal reading. The centripetal one

works, naturally enough, from the outer limits of the aesthetic object inward. The grid is, in relation to this reading a re-presentation of everything that separates the work of art from the world, from ambient space and from other objects' (1996, 18–19). Again (as with Littlefield and Mertens), the duality of the framing function is emphasized.

6   In 2004, English National Opera performed a 75-minute extract from Act III of *Die Walküre* on the main Pyramid Stage at Glastonbury Festival.

## Chapter Twelve

1   Elements of this essay appear in eldritch Priest's *Boring Formless Nonsense: Experimental Music and the Aesthetics of Failure* (London and New York: Bloomsbury, 2013).

2   There is obvious resonance here with Danto's argument *vis à vis* the 'artworld', with the salient difference that the concert form has far more material specificity (or, put differently, its specificity stems from its material construction as much as its discursive movements). See Danto, 1964.

3   The term 'backgrounded music' is used here to indicate that the previously discrete category of original artist recordings is increasingly used in settings that background it. Simply put, all recorded music is potentially background music.

4   As we discuss below, the listening techniques of the concert performance that produce the exaggerated effect of music as something-to-be-listened-to are supplanted, and perhaps even accelerated, by recording technology that decouples the circumstances of performance from the circumstances of listening to recreate the sense of music as a thing apart from the material world.

5   The term 'sound' is here used in place of the German '*Geräusch*'. While the latter literally translates as 'noise', Lachenmann points out that the German does not have the negative connotations of its English counterpart. For example, he says that one 'would describe the sound of wind blowing as *Geräusch*, to imply that it's a beautiful and natural sound' (Lachenmann, in Schmidt, 2004, 118).

6   To be clear, *Burrow Music* is a composed work built around acoustic instruments that is not intended to be performed live, but instead exists only as a recording.

7   This is technologist Linda Stone's expression which she coined to capture the way one often feels 'a desire to be a LIVE node on the network', which is to say, a desire to be connected. Arguably, for the contemporary subject, this desire is existential. To be continuously connected is to maximize one's opportunities of being engaged, and the sense of being busy or continuously engaged has itself come to express the sense of being alive. See Linda Stone, 'Continuous Partial Attention', at http://lindastone.net/qa/continuous-partial-attention

8  Thus, for example, recordings are not insulted by speaking over them, nor do they have the preciousness of an ephemeral event, and are always-already repeated and repeatable in any case.
9  These include: melodica; sopranino, alto, and bass recorders; Casio D[igital]-H[orn]-100; alto and baritone saxophones; trumpet; trombone; electronic panpipes...
10  For a detailed discussion of the infinity series and Nørgård's application of it in his music, see Christensen (2004).
11  See Walter Benjamin's essay, 'The Work of Art in the Age of Mechanical Reproduction' (also translated as 'The Work of Art in the Age of Its Technological Reproducibility') (2002).

## Chapter Fourteen

1  See especially the first two chapters of Hegarty's *Noise/Music* (2007).
2  See not only the large tome of their collected letters in which this intellectual relationship was fomented, *The Complete Correspondence 1928–1940* (2001), but also, among others, Giorgio Agamben's analysis of their exchange in *Infancy and History* (2007) and Susan Buck-Morss's *The Origins of Negative Dialectics* (1979).
3  As Krzysztof Ziarek (2005) unfolds in his work on Benjamin: the moving of art into the digital realm questions art's own force as separable from the technology that produces it. I have also made the case elsewhere that digital sound has a completely different relationship to its original source (see Hertz, 2001).
4  Martin Jay's important early book on Adorno (*Adorno*, 1984) devotes much time to what he calls his 'Atonal philosophy'.
5  See Alexander Stewart's important essay on the origins of funk, 'Funky Drummer: New Orleans, James Brown and the Rhythmic Transformation of American Popular Music' (2000).
6  There are many places where Adorno makes this argument, but it is probably best developed in his *Philosophy of New Music* (2006).
7  Adorno would return later to refine this argument in *Aesthetic Theory* (1997b), but his argument about Kafka is to be found in 'Notes on Kafka', collected in *Prisms* (1983).
8  See Robert Hullot-Kentor's reading of Adorno's time at the Darmstadt School of Composition in his 'Popular Music and "The Aging of the New Music"' (2006).
9  As Kahn notes in *Noise Water Meat* (2001), it is important to recognize the noisy possibilities at several levels, not just the vinyl and the needle, but then also the amplification that is required to make those sounds legible.
10  Profiles on glitch artists or glitch music have yet to mention any nostalgia.

See, for example, Rob Young's excellent 'Worship the Glitch: Digital Music, Electronic Disturbance' (2002). If glitch music, like Markus Popp's work as *Oval*, enhances the technological fallibility of the supposedly superior CD format, it has yet to register as a nostalgic moment, but could easily be addressed in the same manner now that MP3 technology has quickly taken over from the CD.

11  If one of Tony Wilson and Factory's greatest 'punk' moves was to create a sandpaper album cover for the Durutti Column's first album (1980's *The Return of The Durutti Column*), so that it would damage the albums around it, then the noise equivalent of that would be to create an album cover with sandpaper on the inside so that the album would be worn down as it was repeatedly removed and returned.

12  See especially how he and Max Horkheimer address the problem in relation to the Hollywood Culture Industry in the chapter 'Enlightenment as Mass Deception', in *The Dialectic of Enlightenment* (2002).

13  References to Beckett riddle Adorno's work, especially in *Aesthetic Theory* (1997), but Adorno focuses exclusively on Beckett in his essay 'Trying to Understand *Endgame*' (1991). See also Benjamin Halligan's essay (2012), which also closes with Beckett as a certain endpoint of modernity, when words fail and noise is all that remains.

## Chapter Fifteen

1  The history of jazz is a case in point which many critics throughout history have issues with – not just the narrative of its continuum and historico-aesthetical development, but also the fundamental definition of the term itself. For many, they even reject the word as racially biased or derogatory.

2  GRM, which stands for Groupe de Recherches Musicales, was formed by Pierre Schaeffer in 1958 to further the research and composition of *musique concrète*. It continues today as INA GRM.

3  For some, the Velvet Underground and Krautrock seem to be part of this genealogy of noise in the late 1960s and 1970s, but I would like to propose that VU and Krautrock, with a few exceptions like Faust, did not have direct bearings on the development of noise music. These groups were mainly using feedback and noise as an exploration of the technology available then to enhance the rock form using guitars and electronic equipment. Noise is more about anti-expression expression or even the obliteration of meaning in experience and expression. Most Krautrockers are musician-types to begin with – for example, Jaki Liebezeit is an accomplished drummer and Manuel Gottsching is a revered guitarist. John Cale is classically trained and his bandmates might not share his musical pedigree, but Lou Reed and Sterling Morrison are adequate musicians at the very least. Noise musicians very often discard such virtuosity, if they have any to begin with, by using unconventional instruments or using instruments unconventionally to make noise.

4   The music weekly is *Sounds* and the review was published in the summer of 1979.

## Chapter Sixteen

1   As though science used to be one unequivocal and simple act to be accomplished and has not been marked by a history of shifts in key concepts (Koyré), or as if there existed a well-delimited field for science (Chalmers), or as if it was not subjected to political interests of all sorts (Latour), among other issues.
2   As in the 'Futurist Manifesto' (1909).
3   A 2006 film directed by Lucifer Valentine.
4   Fifth track of Whitehouse's *Right to Kill* album (1983).
5   Marquis de Sade (1785) *Les 120 journées de Sodome ou l'école du libertinage.*
6   A performance by Hermann Nitsch first staged in 1998 at Schloss Prinzendorf, Austria.
7   For a more detailed analysis of Merzbow, see Hegarty (2009), Chapter 10.
8   As it is also ironic that the recent Whitehouse 'afro' incursion (also as Cut Hands) could promote a synthesis between such polarities.
9   These genres are previous to the emergence of the movements emphasized in this chapter, since several manifestations related to rock are found in previous decades, when this distinction would be blurred, or rather when the exploration of impact would happen by different means, as in no wave, black metal, drone/doom, shoegaze and its successors.
10  I am loosely adopting here a concept of the 'tympanic' as proposed by Caesar (2007). The author proposes it in the context of acousmatic music, playing on a reference to 'retinal art' – an art too compromised by the idea of creating images for the eyes – as Marcel Duchamp used to describe visual arts before the advocacy of an art more interested in the interplay of concepts and ideas – what became known as 'conceptual art'. The use of tympanic proposed here in this chapter aims to separate in two poles proposals that are more interested in developing specific sounds and those more focused on exploring general strategies that are not necessarily aural. As an example, in analyzing Whitehouse's work from their early beginnings to later developments, there is a certain sonic identity which is preserved as a very specific and restricted sonic terrritory of explorations, even if there are definitely some changes between 'You don't have to say Please' (from 1985's *Great White Death* album) to 'Wriggle like a fucking eel' (from 2003's *Bird Seed*). In the case of Throbbing Gristle, this sonic territory would be considerably expanded and more unpredictable, since their general strategies demanded leaving sonic possibilities less defined. Such a separation should be taken more in its reflexive possibilities than as a clear distinctive dichotomy since it could

## Chapter Seventeen

1. 'Ce qui intéresse Wyschnegradsky, c'est d'introduire l'idée d'un plan a-structural du matériau sonore, plan "démagnetisé" et "détonalisé" dans lequel agit un principe spatial de libre structuration (champ d'action).'
2. 'La conception simultanée de l'ensemble de tous les sons d'une échelle-harmonie s'ouvre sur l'idée d'espace, de milieu sonore spécifique, ou de réseau sonore, dans lequel tout peut sonner ensemble, sans exclusive ni hierarchie, défaisant le dualisme consonance-dissonance et permettant ainsi [...] de libérer une conception qualitative des intervalles.'
3. 'Tout ceci équivaut à la reconnaissance de la *nature explosive du son*. Une force latente est présente au sein du son musical qui tend à se déployer au maximum sur toute l'étendue de l'espace musical, en principe infini et continu et à remplir cette infinité d'une sonorité continue. Autrement dit, chaque accord, chaque intervalle, chaque son isole tend à devenir pansonorité, c'est-à-dire, à transcender sa nature physique et à devenir le tout continu.'
4. See Caron (forthcoming).
5. 'Dire que l'on fait de la musique savante suggère un accompagnement "scientifique" probablement rigoureux, or à l'autre bout du spectre, la *noise* japonaise qui n'est pour autant une musique commerciale populaire est une forme d'expression qui s'est faite sans que personne au Japon n'écrive une ligne ou ne formule la moindre question sur l'intérêt de faire cela. D'un côté, la méthode, le language, la formalisation comme oeuvre et de l'autre, l'experience brute du matériau qui défait et refait oeuvre par la mise en experience de l'informe bruitiste. Or, dans la science dure, théorisation et expérience vont de pair. C'est comme si la noise avait accru/révélé sans le savoir une déchirure entre théorie et pratique, le Janus inconscient de l'experience classique.'
6. 'Les experiences extatiques recherchées une fois le corps plongés dans les decibels, où douleurs et plaisirs se mêlaient, ouvraient un espace-temps proper au son en general. Dans cette production et cette écoute du son pour le son, d'un son délivré des soucis rythmiques, mélodiques, compositionnels et orchestraux et poussé dans sa radicalité saturée, le corps et la pensée se laissent dilater, résonner, contracter, ramifier et ouvrir à un espace-temps omnidimensionnel.'

## Chapter Eighteen

1. Marjorie Perloff has argued that Marinetti's 'scorn for women' has been misunderstood; given Marinetti's later publication, she reads this as 'scorn' for traditional bourgeois marriage arrangements. She also points to an interview that shortly followed the publication, in which Marinetti paid homage to the 'magnificent elite of intellectual women' in Paris, in contrast with their 'less enlightened Italian counterparts' (Perloff, 2007). Others, however, are less forgiving of what appears, at first glance at least, to be Marinetti's blatant misogyny. Clara Orban has argued that while Marinetti later went on to acknowledge the potential for women in non-reproductive roles, in the first manifesto women play two roles: mother and outcast (Orban, 1995, 54). Neither of these roles are radical departure from traditional representations, irrespective of the futurist agenda to break free of the past. Nevertheless, women did partake in the futurist movement, in spite of its creation of an overtly and openly misogynistic environment.

2. Cage's attempt to separate sound from signification can be also heard to silence the politics of sound. Kahn argues that Cagean silence, in its attempts to hear sounds in themselves, has silenced the world that can be heard in sound; in short, the social in sound: 'the sound and the fury never signify nothing, or rather, just nothing. What such auditive states have proven to drown out are the social in sound' (Kahn, 2001, 4). Similarly, Rogers states: 'Cage's body of work was innovative in the context of Eurological compositional traditions, but it has been taken up by some academics and journalists to define what constitutes "experimental" music in the broadest sense. This has worked to deny the influence of comparably influential music practices by women and people of colour. Thus, despite Cage's own efforts to disrupt hegemonic silences, the centrality of his work in subsequent electronic and experimental music histories has often had the effect of silencing others' (Rogers, 2011, 10).

3. Suzanne Romaine notes, with reference to the work of Margaret Mead, that among the Tchambuli people of Papua New Guinea, gender roles are potentially reversed; it is men who are associated with gossip and bickering (Romaine, 1998, 162).

4. Rysman states that the idea of gossip as idle talk is relatively recent; there is no use of the term in this way prior to the nineteenth century in the Old English Dictionary. Gossip is a contraction of the old English phrase 'God sib', for family, friend or godparent of either gender (Rysman, 1977, 176–7).

5. Giselle Bastin has explored how Pandora became a cultural archetype for gossip, having let loose that which should have been kept inside. She notes that women's bodies and sexuality have historically been connected with women's language, subject to characterizations as 'open, leaky, and wasteful' repositories. As such they have been the 'natural' culprits of spreading destructive information (Bastin, 2011, 22).

6. While many may label her as a performance artist, Galás herself has rejected the term: 'I would never use that word for myself … yes I compose the music

and I perform the music and I compose the libretto and I design the lights until I turn it over to a professional lighting designer. But Wagner did that, too! People who call this performance art do it out of sexism – any woman who organizes a *Gesamtkunstwerk* is condemned to this territory' (quoted in Jarman, 2011, 129).

## Chapter Nineteen

1  See http://www.discogs.com/artist/Filthy+Turd (accessed August 2012).
2  For further reading, see McNally (2002).
3  The concept of affordance was first introduced by Gibson (1966) and has subsequently been elaborated by Gaver (1991), Norman (2002), and others. It is applied to the use of musical tools by Mooney (2010).
4  All the tracks from *Cock the Lights* are available online for download or streaming playback.
5  For a brief summary of glitch see Cascone (2002).
6  Our analysis assumes that the listener is culturally familiar with Western pop songs. If this is not the case then it is unlikely, we suggest, that the listener would have the kind of aesthetic experience we describe.
7  These nonsense sentences might almost make sense to readers familiar with the lyrics of these songs. For those who are not, an internet search for the complete lyrics may help to better illustrate the point.
8  Whether the nonsense text, garish graphics – or indeed any 'noisy' artefacts in Wyngarde's work, sonic or otherwise – are the *bona fide* results of actual medial noise processes or simply engineered emulations designed to look or sound similar is a moot point, really, since the end result from the point of view of an audience member is the same in either case.
9  The analogy is not a perfect one, but hopefully it is strong enough to show that analogous processes are at work across multiple modalities.

# BIBLIOGRAPHY

Ades, D. (ed.) (2006), *The Dada Reader: A Critical Anthology*. London: The University Of Chicago Press.
Adorno, T. (1983), 'Notes on Kafka' in *Prisms*, trans. S. M. Weber. Cambridge, MA: The MIT Press, pp. 243–71.
—(1991), 'Transparencies on Film' in *The Culture Industry*. London and New York: Routledge, pp. 179–86.
—(1997a), 'Trying to Understand Endgame' in *Notes to Literature* Vol. 1, R. Tiedemann (ed.), trans. S. W. Nicholsen. New York: Columbia University Press.
—(1997b), *Aesthetic Theory*, trans. R. Hullot-Kentor, Minneapolis: University of Minnesota Press.
—(1999), 'Music and Technique' in *Sound Figures*, trans. R. Livingstone. Stanford: Stanford University Press, pp. 197–214.
—(2002a), 'The Form of the Phonograph Record' in *Essays on Music*, R. Leppert (ed.), trans. S. H. Gillespie. Los Angeles and London: University of California Press.
—(2002b), 'The Aging of the New Music' in *Essays on Music*, R. Leppert (ed.), trans. S. H. Gillespie. Berkeley, CA and London: University of California Press.
—(2006), *Philosophy of New Music*, trans. R. Hullot-Kentor. Minneapolis: University of Minnesota Press.
Adorno, T. and W. Benjamin (2001), *The Complete Correspondence: 1928–1940*, H. Lonitz (ed.). Cambridge, MA: Harvard University Press.
Adorno, T. and M. Horkheimer (2002), *Dialectic of Enlightenment*, trans. E. Jephcott. Stanford: Stanford University Press.
Agamben, G. (2007), *Infancy and History*. London: Verso.
Alarcon, M. (2008), *Baku: Symphony Of Sirens – Sound Experiments In The Russian Avant Garde: Original Documents And Reconstructions Of 72 Key Works Of Music, Poetry And Agitprop From The Russian Avantgardes (1908–1942)*. London: ReR Megacorp.
Allen, M. (2006), 'Pentecostal Movement Celebrates Humble Roots', *The Washington Post*, 15 April. Available at: http://www.washingtonpost.com/wp-dyn/content/article/2006/04/14/AR2006041401421.html (accessed July 2012).
Anon. (2006), 'Who Guitarist's Deafness Warning'. Available at: http://news.bbc.co.uk/1/hi/entertainment/4580070.stm (accessed October 2008).
Aristotle (2008), *Politics*, trans. B. Jowett. New York: Cosimo.
Arnold, M. (1995), 'Observations About, Around and Beside "Burrow out; Burrow in; Burrow Music"', unpublished PhD thesis, University of Victoria.

Artaud, A. (1970), *The Theatre and its Double,* trans. V. Corti. London: Calder and Boyars Ltd.
—(1974), *Collected Works, Volume Four,* trans. V. Corti. London: Calder and Boyars Ltd.
—(1995), *Pour en finir avec le jugement de dieu* (To Have Done with the Judgement of God). Brussels: Sub Rosa, SR92 [CD].
Ashley, R. et al. (2007), *Yasunao Tone – Noise Media Language.* Canada: Errant Bodies.
Attali, J. (1985), *Noise: The Political Economy of Music,* trans. B. Massumi. Minneapolis: University of Minnesota Press.
Auslander, P. (2008), *Liveness: Performance in a Mediatized Culture* (2nd edn). London and New York: Routledge.
—(2009), *Performing Glam Rock: Gender and Theatricality in Popular Music.* Ann Arbor: University of Michigan Press.
Azerrad, M. (2001), *Our Band Could Be Your Life: Scenes from the American Indie Underground 1981–1991.* New York, Boston and London: Back Bay Books/Little, Brown and Company.
Bachelard, G. ([1958] 1994), *The Poetics of Space,* trans. M. Jolas. Massachusetts: Beacon Press Books.
Ballard, J. G. ([1957, 1960] 2006), 'Venus Smiles', 'The Sound Sweep' in *Complete Short Stories: Volume 1.* London: Harper Perennial.
Bangs, L. (1976), 'The Greatest Album Ever Made', *Creem,* March. Available at: http://www.rocknroll.net/loureed/articles/mmmbangs.html (accessed August 2012).
—(1981), 'A Reasonable Guide To Horrible Noise', *The Village Voice,* 30 September. Available at: http://music.iupui.edu/faculty/albright/BangsReview1.html (accessed July 2012).
Bannister, M. (1999), *Positively George Street: A Personal History of Sneaky Feelings and the Dunedin Sound.* Auckland: Reed.
—(2006), *White Boys, White Noise: Masculinities and Indie Guitar Rock.* Aldershot: Ashgate.
Barnes, M. (2009), 'Come On, Feel the Noise', *The Guardian* (Film and Music section), 9 January, 3.
Bartkowiak, M. (2007), *Rock and Revolution: The MC5 and Music's Political Life.* Michigan: Michigan State University Press.
—(2009), *The MC5 and Social Change: A Study of Rock and Revolution.* Jefferson, NC: McFarland.
Bastin, G. (2011), 'Pandora's Voice Box: How Woman Became the "Gossip Girl"' in *Women and Language: Essays on Gendered Communication Across Media,* M. Ames and S. Himsel (eds). North Carolina: McFarland & Company, pp. 17–29.
Battles, J. (2008), 'Noise A Major Threat to Health of City Dwellers', *The Sunday Times,* 12 October. Available at: http://www.timesonline.co.uk/tol/news/world/ireland/article4926766.ece (accessed January 2011).
Baudrillard, J. (1988), *The Ecstasy of Communication,* trans. B. and C. Schutze. New York and Boston: Semiotext(e)/The MIT Press.
Baumeister R. F. (1984), 'Acid Rock: A Critical Reappraisal and Psychological Commentary', *Journal of Psychoactive Drugs,* 16(4), October–December, pp. 336–45.

Baxter, B. B. (1959), *What is the Church of Christ?* Available at: http://web.archive.org/web/20060616071601/http://woodsonchapel.com/coc.cfm (accessed July 2012).
BBC (2007), *25 Year Party Palace.* Available at: http://www.bbc.co.uk/manchester/content/articles/2007/05/17/210507_hacienda_facts_feature.shtml (accessed July 2012).
Beauvoir, S. (1997), *The Second Sex*, trans. H. M. Parshley. London: Vintage.
Bell, C. (2002), 'Vinyl Redemption', *The Wire*, #221 July.
Bendrups, D. and Downes G. (2011), *Dunedin Soundings.* Dunedin: Otago University Press.
Benjamin, W. (2002), 'The Work of Art in the Age of Its Technological Reproducibility' in *Selected Writings. Volume 3: 1935–38.* Cambridge, MA: Harvard University Press.
Berardi, F. (Bifo) (2009), *Precarious Rhapsody*, E. Empson and S. Shukaitis (eds), trans. A. Bove et al. London: Minor Compositions/Autonomedia.
—(2011), *After the Future*, G. Genosko and N. Thoburn (eds). Edinburgh, Oakland and Baltimore: AK Press.
Berke, J. (2009), 'It Had to Happen. iPhone/iPod Touch Becomes a Hearing Aid'. 7 July. Available at: http://deafness.about.com/b/2009/07/07/it-had-to-happen-iphoneipod-touch-becomes-a-hearing-aid.htm (accessed July 2010).
Bernard, J. W. (1993), 'The Minimalist Aesthetic in the Plastic Arts and in Music', *Perspectives of New Music*, 31(1), Winter, pp. 86–132.
Bez (1998), *Freaky Dancin'.* London: Pan Books.
Bockris, V. (1994), *Lou Reed: The Biography.* London: Hutchinson.
Boivin, N. (2008), *Material Cultures, Material Minds: The Role of Things in Human Thought, Society and Evolution.* Cambridge: Cambridge University Press.
Bolter, J. and R. Grusin (2000), *Remediation: Understanding New Media.* London: The MIT Press.
Boose, L. (1991), 'Scolding Brides and Bridling Scolds: Taming the Woman's Unruly Member', *Shakespeare Quarterly*, 42(2), pp. 179–213.
Boulez, P. (1968), *Notes on an Apprenticeship*, trans. H. Weinstock. New York: A. A. Knopf.
Bracewell, M. (1997), *England's Mine: Pop Life in Albion from Wilde to Goldie.* London: HarperCollins.
—(2007), *Remake/Remodel: Art, Pop, Fashion and the Remaking of Roxy Music, 1953–1972.* London: Faber and Faber.
Braidotti, R. (2003), 'Becoming Woman: or Sexual Difference Revisited', *Theory, Culture and Society*, 20(3), pp. 43–64.
Brassier, R. (2009), 'Genre Is Obsolete' in *Noise and Capitalism*, Mattin and A. Iles (eds). San Sebastián: Arteleku, pp. 61–71.
Brecht, B. (1995), *Bad Time for Poetry*, J. Willett (ed.), trans. J. Willett et al. London: Methuen.
Brent, P. (1969), 'Crow's Nest', *Creem* 1(1) cited in (2000) *On Record: Rock, Pop and the Written Word*, S. Frith and A. Goodwin (eds). London: Routledge, p. 57.
Bromwell, N. ([2000] 2002), *Tomorrow Never Knows: Rock and Psychedelics in the 1960s.* Chicago and London: University of Chicago Press.

Brus, G. (2010), *Bodyanalysis: Actions 1964–1970* [DVD]. Berlin: Edition Kröthenhayn.
Buck-Morss, S. (1979), *The Origin of Negative Dialectics*. New York: Free Press.
Budofsky, A. (2011), 'Drumming with Maureen Tucker', *Modern Drummer Online*. Available at: http://www.moderndrummer.com/web_exclusive/900001118/Maureen Tucker (accessed April 2011).
Bull, M. (2005), 'No Dead Air! The iPod and the Culture of Mobile Listening', *Leisure Studies* 24(4), pp. 343–55.
Burroughs, W. S. (2007), *Thee Films 1950s-1960s* [DVD]. London: Cherry Red.
Buxbaum, E. C. (1949), 'On Playing Music LOUD', *Saturday Review of Literature*, 25 June, p. 51.
Caesar, R. (2007), 'As grandes orelhas da escuta (entre a teoria e a prática)' in *Notas. Atos. Gestos*, S. Ferraz (ed.). Rio de Janeiro: 7 Letras, pp. 31–52.
Cage, J. (1937), '"The Future of Music Credo", delivered as a lecture in Seattle'. Available at: http://www.ele-mental.org/ele_ment/said&did/future_of_music.html (accessed April 2011)
—(1961), *Silence*. Connecticut: Wesleyan University Press.
—(1982), 'So that Each Person is in Charge of Himself', interviewed by W. Mertens [CD], G. Branca (2007), *Indeterminate Activity of Resultant Masses*. Atavistic Records.
Cain, N. (2009), 'Noise' in *The Wire Primers*, R. Young (ed.). London: Verso, pp. 29–36.
Callwood, B. (2010), *MC5 Sonically Speaking: A Tale of Revolution and Rock 'n' Roll*. Detroit: Wayne State University Press.
Caplow, T., H. M. Bahr, J. Modell and B. A. Chadwick (1991), *Recent Social Trends in the United States 1960–1990*. Montréal: McGill-Queen's University Press.
Carballo, M. (1999), 'Religion In The World At The End Of The Millennium', *Gallup International*. Available at http://www.gallup-international.com/ContentFiles/millennium15.asp (accessed January 2011).
Carcano, E. (ed.) (2002), *Henri Chopin's Revue OU: Complete Recordings Box Set* (booklet). Milan: Alga Marghen.
Caron, J. P. (forthcoming), 'The World as Noise and Representation: Karkowski's and Furundate's *World as Will* Trilogy', in *Order is an Exception*.
Casati, R. and J. Dokic (1998), *La Philosophie du Son*. Paris: Jacqueline Chambon.
Cascella, D. et al. (2004), *John Duncan – Work 1975–2005*. Berlin: Errant Bodies.
Cascone, K. (2000), 'The Aesthetics of Failure: "Post-Digital" Tendencies in Contemporary Computer Music', *Computer Music Journal*, 24(4), pp. 12–18.
Chalmers, Alan (1999), *What is This Thing Called Science?* (rev. edn) Queensland: University of Queensland Press.
Chare, N. (2007), 'The Grain of the Interview: Introducing Diamanda Galás', *Parallax* 13(1), pp. 56–64.
Charles, R. (n.d. [2004?]), Interview, available at: www.raymovie.com/raycharles/the_man_ray_charles_interview.html. (accessed May 2010).
Chaves, M., Hadaway, K. and Marler, P. (1993), 'What the Polls Don't Show: A Closer Look at U.S. Church Attendance', *American Sociological Review*, 58 (December), pp. 741–52.

Chernov, S. (2012), 'Female Fury', *St Petersburg Times*, No. 1693, 1 February, p. 1.
Christensen, E. (2004), 'Overt and Hidden Processes in 20th-Century Music', *Axiomathes*, 14(1–3), pp. 97–117.
Clover, J. (2009), *1989: Bob Dylan Didn't Have This to Sing About*. Berkeley, CA and London: University of California Press.
Cole, J. (2007), *Zeitkratzer – Metal Machine Music (Asphodel)*. Album Review, Music OMH. Available at http://www.musicomh.com/albums/zeitkratzer_0907.htm (accessed October 2012).
Connell, J. and C. Gibson (2003), *Sound Tracks: Popular Music, Identity and Place*. London and New York: Routledge.
Conrad, T. (2004), 'LYssophobia: On Four Violins', in *Audio Culture: Reading in Modern Music*, C. Cox and D. Warner (eds). London: Continuum, pp. 313–18.
Cooke, M. (1998), *Jazz*. London: Thames and Hudson.
Cotner, J. S. (1992), 'Pink Floyd's "Careful with That Axe, Eugene": Toward a Theory of Textual Rhythm in Early Progressive Music', in *Progressive Rock Reconsidered*, K. Holm-Hudson (ed.). New York and London: Routledge.
Critchley, M. and R. A. Henson (eds) (1977), *Music and the Brain: Studies in the Neurology of Music*. London: Heinemann.
Criton, P. (1996), 'Wyschnegradsky, théoricien et philosophe' in *La Loi de la Pansonorité*, I. Wyschnegradsky. Geneve: Contrechamps, pp. 9–54.
Crocker, S. (2007), 'Noises and exceptions: Pure Mediality in Serres and Agamben'. Available online at http://www.ctheory.net/articles.aspx?id=574 (accessed August 2012).
Cross, I. (2005), 'Music and Meaning, Ambiguity and Evolution' in *Musical Communication*, D. Miell, R. MacDonald and D. Hargreaves (eds). Oxford: Oxford University Press, pp. 27–43.
Csordas, T. (1994), *Embodiment and Experience: The Existential Ground of Culture and Self*. Cambridge: Cambridge University Press.
Cunningham, D. (2003), 'A Time for Dissonance and Noise: On Adorno, Music, and the Concept of Modernism', *Angelaki*, 8(1), pp. 61–74.
Curtis, V. and A. Biran (2001), 'Dirt, Disgust, and Disease: is Hygiene in Our Genes?', *Perspectives in Biology and Medicine*, 44(1), pp. 17–31.
Cutler, C. (1991), *File Under Popular: Theoretical and Critical Writings on Music*. London: November Books.
Daniel, E. (2007), 'Noise and Hearing Loss: A Review', *Journal of School Health* 77:5 (May), pp. 225–31.
Danto, A. (1964), 'The Artworld', *Journal of Philosophy*, 61(19), pp. 571–84.
Davis, L. J. (1995), *Enforcing Normalcy: Disability, Deafness and the Body*. London: Verso.
—(ed.) (1997), *The Disability Studies Reader*. London: Routledge.
Davis, M. with Q. Troupe (1989), *Miles: The Autobiography*. London: Picador.
Deleuze, G. (2002), *Cinema 1: The Movement-image*. London: Continuum International Publishing Group.
Deleuze, G. and F. Guattari (1987), *A Thousand Plateaus: Capitalism and Schizophrenia*, trans. B. Massumi. Minneapolis: University of Minnesota Press.

DeLio, T. (1981), 'Avant-Garde Issues in Seventies Music' in *Breaking the Sound Barrier: A Critical Anthology of the New Music*, G. Battcock (ed.). New York: Elsevier-Dutton Publishing.
DeRogatis, J. (2002), 'The Great Albums: The MC5, Kick Out the Jams'. Available at http://www.jimdero.com/News2001/GreatAug4MC5.htm (accessed July 2012).
—(2003), *Turn On Your Mind: Four Decades of Great Psychedelic Rock*. New York: Hal Leonard Corporation.
Dezeuze, A. (2005), 'Brecht for Beginners, George Brecht events: A Heterospective', *Papers of Surrealism*, no. 4, Winter. Available at www.surrealismcentre.ac.uk (accessed August 2007).
Dick, P. K. (2001), *The Man in the High Castle*. New York: Penguin.
Dickinson, P. (2006), *Cage Talk: Dialogues With & About John Cage*. New York: University of Rockhampton Press.
Diederichsen. D. (2011), 'Power of Intensity, People of Power: The Nietzsche Economy', in *Are You Working Too Much? Post-Fordism, Precarity, and the Labor of Art*, J. Aranda, B. K. Wood and A. Vidokle (eds). Berlin: Sternberg Press/e-flux journal, pp. 8–29.
Dolar, M. (2006), *A Voice and Nothing More*. Cambridge, MA: The MIT Press.
Doran, J. (2010), 'Lou Reed Interview: Metal Machine Music Revisited', *The Quietus*, 7 April. Available at http://thequietus.com/articles/04037-lou-reed-interview-metal-machine-music (accessed July 2012).
Eimert, H. (1957), 'What is Electronic Music', in *Die Reihe*, Vol. 1. Available at: http://www.scribd.com/doc/7396247/Herbert-Eimert-What-is-Electronic-Music-Die-Reihe-Vol1-1957 (accessed May 2011).
Elder, M. (2012), 'How Russians Finally Changed Their Tune and Backed Jailed Pussy Riot Trio', *The Observer*, 1 July, p. 21.
Emmerson, S. (1986), *The Language of Electroacoustic Music*. Hampshire: Palgrave Macmillan.
Eshleman, C. and B. Bador (1995), *Watchfiends and Rack Screams*. Boston: Exact Change.
European Commission (2005), *Special Eurobarometer 225/ EC Wave 63.1 June 2005 – TNS Opinion & Social Survey*, June. Available at: http://ec.europa.eu/public_opinion/archives/ebs/ebs_225_report_en.pdf
Felder, R. (1993), *Manic Pop Thrill*. New Jersey: The Ecco Press.
Filthy Turd (2003), *Power*Control*Lust*. CDr, Verato Project: verazität 020.
—(2005), *Piss Enema*. Cassette, Hospital Productions: HOS-126, 2005.
—(2006a), *Love Hotel*. CDr, Turgid Animal: TA209.
—(2006b), *My Name is Filthy*. CDr, Smell the Stench: no catalogue number. Available at: http://rapidshare.com/files/269601030/Filthy_Turd_-_2006_-_My_Name_Is_Filthy.rar (accessed August 2012).
—(2006c), *Filthy Turd at De Hondenkoekjesfabriek 2006*. Available at http://www.youtube.com/watch?v=95H6H_-MeUk (accessed April 2011).
—(2006d), *Filthy Turd Live in Bristol 08/04/06*. Available at: http://www.youtube.com/watch?v=hbyW3h1h_us (accessed April 2011).
—(2007a), *Bloody Waters/Dirty Fucking/Slaves*. CDr, Dead Eternity Records: DE02.
—(2007b), *Death Ray Orgasm/No Sexual Hygiene*. Cassette, Spacelessjam: SPACE07.

—(2008), *Cock the Lights*. CDr and mp3, Dadaist Audio: DADA151. Available at: http://www.archive.org/details/DADA151 (accessed August 2012).
—(2009a), 'Filthy Turd Blog on Myspace'. Online blog at http://www.myspace.com/filthyturd/blog (accessed March 2011).
—(2009b), *Death Ejaculations*. Cassette, Knife In The Toaster: kt086.
—(2010), *An Occult History Of The Midlands*. CDr, Fragment Factory: [FRAG05].
—(2011), 'Filthy Turd'. Online blog at http://filthyfilthyturd.blogspot.com (accessed April 2011).
Fink, R. (2005), *Repeating Ourselves: American Minimal Music as Cultural Practice*. Berkeley, CA: University of California Press.
Ford, S. (1999), *Wreckers Of Civilisation: The Story of COUM Transmissions and Throbbing Gristle*. London: Black Dog Publishing.
Fried, M. (1998), *Art and Objecthood*. Chicago and London: University of Chicago Press.
Friedel, H. et al. (1998), *Hans Hofmann*. New York: Hudson Hills.
Frith, S. (1996), *Performing Rites: Evaluating Popular Music*. Oxford: Oxford University Press.
—(2000), 'Rock and Popular Culture', *Radical Philosophy*, 103, September/October.
Frith, S. and A. McRobbie (1990), 'Music and Sexuality', in *On Record: Rock, Pop and the Written Word*, S. Frith and A. Goodwin (eds). London: Routledge, pp. 317–32.
Fuld, J. (1966), *The Book of World Famous Music: Classical, Popular and Folk*. New York: Crown Publishers Inc.
Funk, J. R. (2009), 'The Kids are Alright: Head Banging Poses No Special Risk of Neck or Head Injury', in 'Rapid Responses' to Patton and McIntosh a2825, *British Medical Journal*, 26 February. Available at: www.bmj.com/cgi/eletters/337/dec17_2/a2825#209459 (accessed June 2010).
Gabowitch, M. (2009), 'Fascism as Stiob', *Kultura* 4, pp. 3–7.
Galás, D. and Juno, A. (1991), 'Diamanda Galás' in *Angry Women*, A. Juno and V. Vale (eds). California: Re/Search Publications.
Gaver, W. W. (1991), 'Technology Affordances', in *Proceedings of the SIGCHI Conference on Human Factors in Computing Systems: Reaching Through Technology* (CHI91), pp. 79–84.
Gayou, E. (ed.) (2009), *Pierre Schaeffer: Polychrome Portraits*. Paris: GRM/INA.
GegenSichkollektiv (2012), 'Anti-Self: Experience-less Noise' in *Reverberations: The Philosophy, Aesthetics and Politics of Noise*, M. Goddard, B. Halligan and P. Hegarty (eds). London: Continuum, pp. 193–206.
Gibson, J. (1966), *The Senses Considered as Perceptual Systems*. London: Unwin Bros.
Glass, P. (1987), *Music by Philip Glass*, R. T. Jones (ed.). New York: Harper and Row.
Goldberg, R. (2001), *Performance Art: From Futurism To The Present*. New York: Thames and Hudson.
Goldstein, R. (1967), 'I Blew My Cool Through the *New York Times*', *New Times and the Village Voice*, 20 July, pp. 173–4; reproduced in *The Penguin Book of Rock and Roll Writing* (1992), C. Heylin (ed.). New York: Penguin, pp. 541–7.

Gololobov, I. (2011), 'Punk, Law, Resistance... War and Piss', *Critical Legal Thinking*, 8, March. Available at: http://www.criticallegalthinking.com/?p=2473 (accessed March 2012).

Goodman, S. (2009), *Sonic Warfare: Sound, Affect, and the Ecology of Fear*. Cambridge, MA: The MIT Press.

Gosch, A. (1984), 'Will the Real Ted Nugent Please Stand Up?', *Stars and Stripes*, 5 March. Available at: www.stripes.com/news/from-the-s-s-archives-will-the-real-ted-nugent-please-stand-up-1.49746 (accessed June 2010).

Gracyk, T. (1996), *Rhythm and Noise: An Aesthetics of Rock*. London: I. B. Tauris.

Grahame, K. ([1908] 2008), *The Wind in the Willows*. London: Puffin.

Grauerholz, J. and I. Silverberg (eds) (1998), *Word Virus: The William Burroughs Reader*. New York: Grove Press.

Graves-Brown, P. (2000), *Matter, Materiality and Modern Culture*. London: Routledge.

Green, M. (ed.) (1999), *Brus Muehl Nitsch Schwarzkogler: Writing Of The Vienna Actionists*. London: Atlas Press.

Griffiths, P. (1994), *Modern Music: A Concise History*. London: Thames and Hudson.

Guattari, F. (1995), *Chaosmosis: An Ethico-Aesthetic Paradigm*, trans. P. A. Bains and J. Pefanis. Sydney: Power Publications.

Gumbrecht, H. U. (2003), *Production of Presence: What Meaning Cannot Convey*. Stanford, CA: Stanford University Press.

H.E.A.R. (2004), 'It's Hip to H.E.A.R.: Survival Guide: A Lifestyle Guide to Hearing Health'. Available at: www.hearnet.com/images_site/energizer/hip_to_hear_survival_guide.pdf (accessed June 2010).

Hainge, G. (2013), *Noise Matters: Towards an Ontology of Noise*. London and New York: Continuum.

Halligan, B. (2009), 'Please Ensure That Your Mobile Phone Is Switched Off': Theatre Etiquette in an Age of Outsourcing', *Studies in Theatre and Performance*, 29(2), pp. 56–8.

—(2010), 'Disco Galatica: Futures Past and Present', in *Battlestar Galactica: Investigating Flesh, Spirit and Steel*, R. Kaveney and J. Stoy (eds). London: I. B. Tauris, pp. 81–109.

—(2012), '"As if From the Sky": Divine and Secular Dramaturgies of Noise', in *Reverberations: The Philosophy, Politics and Aesthetics of Noise*, M. Goddard, B. Halligan and P. Hegarty (eds). London and New York: Continuum, pp. 101–20.

Hannan, M. (2008), 'The Sound Design of Sgt. Pepper's Lonely Hearts Club Band', in *Sgt. Pepper and the Beatles*, O. Julien (ed.). Aldershot: Ashgate, pp. 45–62.

Hardt, M. and A. Negri (2001), *Empire*. Massachusetts and London: Harvard University Press.

Hawkins, S. (2002), *Settling the Pop Score: Pop Texts and Identity Politics*. Aldershot and Burlington: Ashgate.

Heartbeats website. (n.d.), Available at: www.monstercable.com/productdisplay.asp?pin=5596 (accessed June 2010).

Hegarty, P. (2007), *Noise/Music: A History*. London and New York: Continuum.

—(2008), 'Just What Is It That Makes Today's Noise Music So Different, So Appealing?', *Organised Sound*, 13(1), pp. 13–20.

—(2012), 'A Chronic Condition: Noise and Time', in *Reverberations: The Philosophy, Aesthetics and Politics of Noise*, M. Goddard, B. Halligan and P. Hegarty (eds). London: Continuum, pp. 15–25.

Hegarty, P. and M. Halliwell (2011), *Beyond and Before: Progressive Rock since the 1960s*. London and New York: Continuum.

Heister, H.-W. (1992), 'Music in Concert and Music in the Background: Two Poles of Musical Realization', in *Companion to Contemporary Musical Thought*, J. Paynter (ed.). London: Routledge, pp. 46–71.

Hennion, A. (2003), 'Music and Mediation: Toward a New Sociology of Music', in *The Cultural Study of Music*, M. Clayton, T. Herbert and R. Middleton (eds). London: Routledge, pp. 80–91.

Hensley, C. (1999), 'The Beauty of Noise: An Interview with Masami Akita of Merzbow', in *Audio Culture: Readings in Modern Music*, C. Cox and D. Warner (eds) (2004). London and New York: Continuum, pp. 59–61.

Herr, C. (2009), 'Roll-over-Beethoven: Johnnie Ray in Context', *Popular Music* (special issue on disability), 28(3), pp. 323–40.

Hertz, E. (2001), 'Rethinking Aura Through Temporarility: Benjamin and "Industrial" Otherness', in *Benjamin's Blind Spot: Walter Benjamin and the Premature Death of Aura*, L. Patt (ed.). Topanga, CA: The Institute for Cultural Inquiry, pp. 100–9.

Heslam, D. (ed.) (1992), *The NME Rock 'n' Roll Years*. London: BCA.

Hicks, B. (2000), 'Jimi Hendrix: A Memorial (Northwest Passage, 29th September 1970)', in *The Jimi Hendrix Companion: Three Decades of Commentary*, C. Potash (ed.). New York: Schirmer.

Hicks, M. (1999), *Sixties Rock: Garage, Psychedelic, and Other Satisfactions*. Urbana and Chicago: University of Illinois Press.

Holtzman, S. (1978), 'A Description of an Automatic Digital Sound Synthesis Instrument', in *DAI research report*. Edinburgh: Department of Artificial Intelligence, 59.

Hood, A. J. (1977a), 'Psychological and physiological aspects of hearing', in *Music and the Brain: Studies in the Neurology of Music*, M. Critchley and R. A. Henson (eds). London: Heinemann, pp. 32–47.

—(1977b), 'Deafness and Musical Appreciation', in *Music and the Brain: Studies in the Neurology of Music*, M. Critchley and R. A. Henson (eds). London: Heinemann, pp. 323–43.

Hosokawa, S. (1990), *The Aesthetics of Recorded Sound*. Tokyo: Keiso Shobo.

Howard, D. N. (2004), *Sonic Alchemy: Visionary Music Producers and Their Maverick Recordings*. Milwaukee: Hal Leonard.

Hullot-Kentor, R. (2006), *Things Beyond Resemblance*. New York: Columbia University Press.

Huron, D. (2006), *Sweet Anticipation: Music and the Psychology of Expectation*. Cambridge, MA: The MIT Press.

Ingham, C. (2007), Sleeve notes to Slade album *Till Deaf Do Us Part* [1981].

Inglis, S. (2007), 'Lou Reed and Zeitkratzer', *Sound on Sound*, December. Available at: http://www.soundonsound.com/sos/dec07/articles/metalmachine.htm (accessed July 2012).

Jackson, B. and N. Jeffrey (2008), *The Cellarful of Noise*. Available at: www.hannahbarry.com/exhibitions/the_cellarful_of_noise/ (accessed October 2012).

Jarman, F. (2011), *Queer Voices: Technologies, Vocalities and the Musical Flaw*. Basingstoke: Palgrave Macmillan.
Jay, M. (1984), *Adorno*. Cambridge, MA: Harvard University Press.
Jelavich, P. (1985), *Munich and Theatrical Modernism: Politics, Playwriting and Performance, 1890–1914*. Cambridge, MA: Harvard University Press.
Jenkins, M. (1995), 'The Way We Slammed: Fifteen Years of Punk, Art, and Commerce at the 9:30 Club', *Washington City Paper*, 15 December. Available at: http://www.washingtoncitypaper.com/articles/7981/the-way-we-slammed-fifteen-years-of-punk-art-and-commerce-at-the-930-club (accessed July 2012).
JLIAT [website], http://www.jliat.com/ (accessed October 2012).
Johnson, B. (2009a), 'From John Farnham to Lordi: The Noise of Music', *Altitude*, 8, pp. 1–25.
—(2009b), 'Low-Frequency Noise in Urban Space', *Popular Music History*, 4(2), pp. 177–95.
—(2009c), 'Cultural Theory – Who Needs It?'. Available at: http://www.tagg.org/xpdfs/TheoryWhoNeedsIt.pdf (accessed March 2012).
Johnson, B. and M. Cloonan (2009), *Dark Side of the Tune: Popular Music and Violence*. Aldershot and Burlington: Ashgate.
Johnstone, N. (2005), *Lou Reed 'Talking'*. London: Omnibus Press.
Jones, C. (2007), BBC Review: *Is Lou Reed Still Taking the Mickey? Only you can decide...* Available at: http://www.bbc.co.uk/music/reviews/fzn8 (accessed October 2012).
Juman, S., C. S. Karmody and D. Simeon (2004), 'Hearing loss in steelband musicians', *Otolaryngology: Head and Neck Surgery*, 131(4), pp. 461–5.
Kähäri, K., G. Zachau, M. Eklöf and C. Möller (2004), 'The Influence of Music and Stress on Musicians' Hearing', *Journal of Sound and Vibration*, 277, pp. 627–31.
Kahn, D. (2001), *Noise, Water, Meat: A History of Sound in the Arts*. Cambridge and London: The MIT Press.
Kalb, J. (1998), *The Theatre of Heiner Müller*. Cambridge: Cambridge University Press.
Karkowski, Z. (2009), *Physiques Sonores*. Lausanne: Van Dieren.
Keenan, D. (2003), *England's Hidden Reverse: A Secret History Of The Esoteric Underground*. London: SAF Publishing.
—(2009), 'Guerilla Media', *Audio Poverty » Podcasts*. Available at: http://audiopoverty.de/?page_id=840 (accessed May 2011).
Keightley, K. (1996), '"Turn it Down!" She Shrieked: Gender, Domestic Space, and High Fidelity 1948–59', *Popular Music*, 15(2), pp. 149–77.
Keizer, G. (2010), *The Unwanted Sound of Everything We Want: A Book About Noise*. New York: Public Affairs.
Keysar, A. and B. Kosmin (2009), 'Summary Report', *American Religious Identification Survey (ARIS 2008)*. Available at: http://commons.trincoll.edu/aris/files/2011/08/ARIS_Report_2008.pdf (accessed July 2012).
Kincaid, J. (2009), 'Hear That? It's the Sound of your New Hearing Aid, the iPhone' (7 July). Available at: http://techcrunch.com/2009/07/07/hear-that-its-the-sound-of-your-new-hearing-aid-the-iphone/#comments (accessed July 2010).

King, R. (2012), *How Soon is Now? The Madmen and Mavericks who Made Independent Music, 1975–2005*. London: Faber and Faber.

Kittler, F. (1990), *Discourse Networks 1800/1900*. California, CA: Stanford University Press.

Koyré, A. (1985), *Études d'histoire de la pensée scientifique*. Paris: Gallimard.

Kramer, J. D. (1988), *The Time of Music: New Meanings, New Temporalities, New Listening Strategies*. New York: Schirmer.

Krapp, P. (2011), *Noise Channels: Glitch and Error in Digital Culture*. London: University of Minnesota Press.

Krauss, R. E. (1996), *The Originality of the Avant-Garde and other Modernist Myths*. Cambridge, MA and London: The MIT Press.

Kromhout, M. (2006), *'This was made to end all parties': An Investigation of the Work of Einstürzende Neubauten between 1980 and 1990*. University of Amsterdam: unpublished BA Thesis.

LaBelle, B., M. Spinelli and A. S. Weiss (2005), *Christof Migone – Sound Voice Perform*. Berlin: Errant Bodies.

Landau, M. J. et al. (2006), 'The Siren's Call: Terror Management and the Threat of Men's Sexual Attraction to Women', *Journal of Personality and Social Psychology*, 90(1), pp. 129–46.

Landy, L. (2006), 'Electroacoustic Music Studies and Accepted Terminology: You Can't Have One Without the Other' in *Proceedings of the EMS: Electroacoustic Music Studies Network*. Beijing.

Lane, H. (1997), 'Constructions of Deafness', in *The Disability Studies Reader*, L. J. Davis (ed.). London: Routledge, pp. 153–71.

Laruelle, M. (2009), *In the Name of the Nation: Nationalism and Politics in Contemporary Russia*. New York: Palgrave Macmillan.

Latour, B. (1979), *Laboratory Life: The Social Construction of Scientific Facts*. Beverly Hills: Sage Publications.

Lefebvre, H. (2004), *Rhythmanalysis: Space, Time and Everyday Life*. New York: Continuum.

Letov, E. (1989), *Voina*. Misteriia zvuka.

—(1994), Speech at the Unification of Leftist Forces. Available at: http://www.youtube.com/watch?v=HJPtQ0NZsYg (accessed March 2012).

—(2001), *Ia ne veriu v anarkhiiu*. Moscow: Skit International.

Levin, T. Y. (1990), 'For the Record: Adorno on Music in the Age of Its Technological Reproducibility', *October*, 55, Winter, pp. 23–47.

Littlefield, R. (1998), 'The Silence of the Frames', in *Music/Ideology: Resisting the Aesthetic*, A. Krims (ed.). Amsterdam: G & B Arts International, pp. 213–32.

Lucas, R. (2010), 'Dreaming in Code', *New Left Review*, 63, March–April, pp. 125–32.

Lyon, E. (2008), 'Articulated Noise', in *Proceedings of the ICMC, Belfast 24–29 August*. San Francisco: ICMC.

—(2008), 'A Computer Music Retrospective', *Organised Sound*, 13(3), pp. 209–16.

Macan, E. (1997), *Rocking the Classics: English Progressive Rock and the Counterculture*. Oxford and New York: Oxford University Press.

Macdonald, I. (2005), *Revolution in the Head: The Beatles' Records and the Sixties*. London: Pimlico.

Macdonald, M. (2003), *Varèse: Astronomer In Sound*. London: Kahn and Averill.
Maeck, K. (1996), *Hör mit Schmerzen*. Berlin: Die Gestalten Verlag.
Mann, P. (1999), *Masocriticism*. Albany, NY: State University of New York Press.
Marcus, G. (ed.) (1991), *Psychotic Reactions and Carburettor Dung by Lester Bangs*. London: Minerva.
Marcus, R. (2010), Music Review: 'Lou Reed – Thirty-Five Years of *Metal Machine Music*'. Available at: http://blogcritics.org/music/article/music-review-lou-reed-thirty-five/ (accessed October 2011).
Marsh, D. (1970), CD liner notes for MC5: *Back in the USA*. New York: Atlantic Records.
Martin, G. and W. Pearson (1994), *Summer of Love: The Making of Sgt. Pepper*. London: Macmillan.
Matossian, N. (2005), *Xenakis*. Lefkosia: Moufflon Publications.
Mattin (2011), *Unconstituted Praxis*. La Coruña and Brétigny-sur-Orge: CAC and Taumaturgia.
Mattin and A. Iles (eds). (2009), *Noise and Capitalism*. San Sebastián: Arteleku.
McClary, S. (2002), *Feminine Endings: Music, Gender, Sexuality*. Minneapolis: University of Minnesota Press.
McGonigal, M. (2007), *Loveless*. New York and London: Continuum.
McKay, G. (2005), *Circular Breathing: The Cultural Politics of Jazz in Britain*. Durham, NC: Duke University Press.
—(2009), '"Crippled with Nerves": Popular Music and Polio, with Particular Reference to Ian Dury', *Popular Music* (special issue on disability), 28(3), October, pp. 341–65.
—(1996), *Senseless Acts of Beauty: Cultures of Resistance since the Sixties*. London: Verso.
—(2013), *Shakin' All Over: Popular Music and Disability*. Ann Arbor: University of Michigan Press.
McLuhan, M. (1964), *Understanding Media: The Extensions of Man*. New York: McGraw-Hill.
McNally, R. J. (2002), 'Disgust Has Arrived', *Journal of Anxiety Disorders*, 16(5), pp. 561–6.
Menkman, R. (2010), 'A Vernacular of File Formats: A Guide to Databend Compression Design', sporadically available online (accessed April 2011).
Menkman, R. and D. Wilson (2010), *Digital Ate the Cassette Tape*. Available at: http://vimeo.com/14449814 (accessed April 2011).
Mertens, W. (2004), *American Minimal Music*. London: Kahn & Averill.
Metcalfe, S. (1997), 'Ecstasy Evangelists and Psychedelic Warriors', in *Psychedelia Britannica: Hallucinogenic Drugs in Britain*, A. Melechi (ed.). London: Turnaround, pp. 166–84.
Middleton, R. (1990), *Studying Popular Music*. Milton Keynes: Open University Press.
Millard, A. (2005), *America on Record: A History of Recorded Sound* (2nd edn). Cambridge: Cambridge University Press.
Mitchell, T. (1996), *Popular Music and Local Identity: Rock, Pop and Rap in Europe and Oceania*. London and New York: Leicester University Press.
Monster website (n.d.), Available at: www.monstercable.com/headphones/ (accessed June 2010).

Mooney, J. (2010), 'Frameworks and Affordances: Understanding the Tools of Music-Making', *Journal of Music, Technology and Education*, 3(2–3), pp. 141–54.
Moore, A. F. (2001), *Rock: The Primary Text: Developing a Musicology of Rock* (2nd edn). Aldershot: Ashgate.
—(2012), *Song Means: Analysing and Interpreting Recorded Song*. Aldershot: Ashgate.
Moore, T. (2008), 'Conversations with Thurston Moore: No Wave': interview by B. Sisario. Available at: http://charmicarmicat.blogspot.com/2008/06/conversations-with-thurston-moore-no.html (accessed July 2012).
Moravia, A. et al. (1989), *Pier Paolo Pasolini: A Future Life. A Cinema of Poetry*. Rome: Fondo Pier Paolo Pasolini.
Morley, P. (2010), 'Paul Morley on Music: Lou Reed's *Metal Machine Music*', *The Observer*, 11 April. Available at http://www.guardian.co.uk/music/2010/apr/11/morley-lou-reed-metal-machine (accessed May 2012).
Nasmyth, P. ([1985] 1997), 'MDMA We're All Crazy Now: Ecstasy's Arrival in Britain', in *Night Fever: Club Writing in 'The Face', 1980–1997*, R. Benson (ed.). London and Basingstoke: Boxtree, pp. 74–8.
Nattiez, J. (1993), *The Boulez-Cage Correspondence*. Cambridge: Cambridge University Press.
Neal, C. (1987), *Tape Delay*. London: SAF Publishing.
Negri, A. (1991), *The Savage Anomaly*, trans. M. Hardt. Minneapolis: University of Minnesota Press.
Neville, R. (1971), *Play Power*. London: Paladin.
Newlove, J. (1998), *Laban for Actors and Dancer*. London: Nick Hern Books.
Nitsch, H. (2006), *The Action Art Of Hermann Nitsch: From Past To Present* [DVD]. Berlin: Edition Kröthenhayn.
Nobakht, D. (2005), *Suicide: No Compromise*. London: SAF Publishing.
Norman, D. A. (2002), *The Design of Everyday Things*. New York: Basic Books. (Originally published 1988 as *The Psychology of Everyday Things*. New York: Basic Books.)
Nunes, M. (ed.) (2012), *Error: Glitch, Noise and Jam in New Media Cultures*. New York and London: Continuum.
Nuttall, J. (1970), *Bomb Culture*. London: HarperCollins.
O'Grady, T. (1983), *The Beatles: A Musical Evolution*. Boston: Twayne Publishing.
Omel'chenko, E. and N. Min'kova (2012a), 'Pussy Protest', MySpace. Available at: http://myplacefp7.wordpress.com/2012/02/02/121/ (accessed March 2012).
—(2012b), 'Pussy Riot have Steamed Everyone', MySpace. Available at: http://myplacefp7.wordpress.com/2012/03/14/pussy-riot-have-steamed-everyone/ (accessed March 2012).
ONEMENT-LABEL [website], http://onement-label.com/ONE-HOME.html (accessed June 2010).
Orban, C. (1995), 'Women, Futurism and Fascism', in *Mothers of Invention: Women, Italian Fascism and Culture*, R. Pickering-Lazzi (ed.). Minneapolis: University of Minnesota Press, pp. 52–74.
Ostertag, B. (1998), 'Why Computer Music Sucks.' Available at: http://www.bobostertag.com/writings-articles-computer-music-sucks.htm (accessed October 2012).
Page, T. (1981), 'Framing the River: A Minimalist Primer', *High Fidelity* (Musical America Edition), 31(11), November, pp. 64–8.

Pape, G. (2002), 'Iannis Xenakis and the "Real" of Musical Composition', *Computer Music Journal*, 26(1), pp. 16–21.
Pareles, J. (2010), 'Lou Reed's "Machine": Now More Strings, Less Metal', *The New York Times*, 8 February. Available at: http://travel.nytimes.com/2010/02/09/arts/music/09fireworks.html?_r=0 (accessed August 2012).
Partch, H. (1973), *Genesis of a Music*. New York: Da Capo Press.
Paton, G. (2008), 'Intelligent People "Less Likely to Believe in God"', *The Daily Telegraph*, 11 June. Available at: http://www.telegraph.co.uk/news/uknews/2111174/Intelligent-people-less-likely-to-believe-in-God.html (accessed July 2012).
Patton, D. and A. McIntosh (2008), 'Head and Neck Injury Risks in Heavy Metal: Head Bangers Stuck Between Rock and a Hard Bass', *British Medical Journal* 337, a2825 (17 December). Available at: www.bmj.com/cgi/content/full/337/dec17_2/a2825 (accessed June 2010).
Penzin, A. (2012), *Rex Exsomnis: Sleep and Subjectivity in Capitalist Modernity*. Ostfildern: Hatje Cantz Verlag.
Perloff, M. (2007), 'The First Futurist Manifesto Re-visited', in *Rett Kopi dokumenterer fremtiden*, K. Nygård and E. Prestsæter (eds). Available at: http://marjorieperloff.com/articles/marinetti-revisited/ (accessed August 2012).
Pete, R. M. (n.d.), *The Impact of Holiness Preaching as Taught by John Wesley and the Outpouring of the Holy Ghost on Racism*. Available at: http://www.revempete.us/research/holiness/ (accessed July 2012).
Petrusich, A. (2007), 'Lou Reed Interview', *Pitchfork*, 17 September. Available at http://pitchfork.com/features/interviews/6690-lou-reed/ (accessed April 2012).
Pierce, J. (1980), *An Introduction to Information Theory: Symbols Signals and Noise*. New York: Dover Publications Inc.
Power, N. (2008), 'Woman Machines: The Future of Female Noises', in *Noise and Capitalism*, Mattin and A. Iles (eds). San Sebastián: Gipuzkoako Foru Aldundia-Arteleku, pp. 97–103.
Priest, E. (2013), *Boring Formless Nonsense: Experimental Music and the Aesthetics of Failure*. London and New York: Continuum-Bloomsbury.
Prilepin, Z. (2010), *Grekh i drugie rasskazy*. Moscow: AST Astrel.
Pussy Riot (2011a), 'Osvobodi bruschatku'. Available at: http://pussy-riot.livejournal.com/5497.html (accessed March 2012).
—(2011b), 'Kropotkin-vodka'. Available at: http://pussy-riot.livejournal.com/5164.html (accessed March 2012).
Rapp, T. (2009), *Lost and Sound: Berlin, Techno und der Easyjetset*. Berlin: Suhrkamp Verlag GmbH.
Redhead, S. (1990), *The End-of-the-Century Party: Youth and Pop Towards 2000*. Manchester: Manchester University Press.
Reich, S. (2002), *Writings on Music: 1965–2000*, P. Hillier (ed.). New York: Oxford University Press.
Reising, R. (ed.) (2002), *'Every Sound There Is': The Beatles' Revolver and the Transformation of Rock and Roll*. Aldershot: Ashgate.
Reising, R. and J. LeBlanc (2009), 'Within and Without: Sgt. Pepper's Lonely Hearts Club Band and Psychedelic Insight', in *Sgt. Pepper and the Beatles*, O. Julien (ed.). Aldershot: Ashgate, pp. 103–20.

Revill, G. (2000), 'Music and the Politics of Sound: Nationalism, Citizenship, and Auditory Space', *Environment and Planning D: Society and Space*, 18, pp. 597–613.

Reynolds, S. (1990), *Blissed Out: The Raptures of Rock*. London: Serpent's Tail.

—(1997), 'Back to Eden: Innocence, Indolence and Pastoralism in Psychedelic Music, 1966–1996', in *Psychedelia Britannica: Hallucinogenic Drugs in Britain*, A. Melechi (ed.). London: Turnaround, pp. 143–65.

—(2004), 'Noise', in *Audio Culture: Reading in Modern Music*, C. Cox and D. Warner (eds). London: Continuum, pp. 55–8.

—(2005), *Rip It Up And Start Again: Post-Punk 1978–1984*. London: Faber and Faber.

—(2007), *Bring the Noise: 20 Years of Writing about Hip Rock and Hip-Hop*. London: Faber and Faber.

—(2012), *Energy Flash: A Journey Through Rave Music and Dance Culture*. Berkeley, CA: Soft Skull Press.

Reynolds, S. and J. Press (1995), *The Sex Revolts: Gender, Rebellion and Rock'n'Roll*. London: Serpent's Tail.

Richter, H. (1997), *Dada: Art and Anti-Art*. London: Thames and Hudson.

Riddell, S. and N. Watson (eds) (2003), *Disability, Culture and Identity*. Harlow: Pearson.

Ringen, J. (2005), 'Music Making Fans Deaf?', *Rolling Stone*, 18 November. Available at: www.rollingstone.com/news/story/_/id/8841090 (accessed April 2008).

Rita, The and Filthy Turd (2005), *Kill The Women Rape The Men*. CDr, Voltagestress*r: Voltagestress*r 021.

RNID [Royal National Institute for Deaf People] (n.d.), 'Hearing Matters. That's Why You Should Take Our Hearing Check Today.' Available at: www.rnid.org.uk/howwehelp/hearing_check/ (accessed June 2010).

Roads, C. (2010), 'Interview with Curtis Roads by Anthony Cornicello', *SEAMUS newsletter*, April/May (2).

Rogers, T. (2010), *Pink Noises: Women on Electronic Music and Sound*. Durham: Duke University Press.

Romaine, S. (1998), *Communicating Gender*. Mahwah: L.E. Associates.

Ross, A. (2009), *The Rest is Noise*. London: HarperCollins.

Roszak, T. (1970), *The Making of a Counter Culture: Reflections on the Technocratic Society and its Youthful Opposition*. London: Faber and Faber.

Russell, B. (2009), *Left-Handed Blows: Writing on Sound 1993–2009*. Auckland: Clouds.

—(2012a), 'Exploding the Atmosphere: Realizing the Revolutionary Potential of "the Last Street Song"', in *Reverberations: The Philosophy, Aesthetics and Politics of Noise*, M. Goddard, B. Halligan and P. Hegarty (eds). London and New York: Continuum, pp. 244–59.

—(2012b), *Time to Go: The Southern Psychedelic Moment: 1981–86*, CD liner notes.

Russell, B. with R. Francis and Z. Drayton (2012), *Erewhon Calling: Experimental Sound in New Zealand*. Auckland: Audio Foundation and CMR.

Russolo, L. (1986), *The Art of Noises*. New York: Pendragon Press.

Rysman, A. (1977), 'How the "Gossip" Became a Woman', *Journal of Communication*, 27(1), pp. 176–80.

Sacks, O. (2007), *Musicophilia: Tales of Music and the Brain*. London: Picador.
Sangild, T. (2004), 'Noise – Three Musical Gestures: Expressionist, Introvert and Minimal Noise', *The Journal of Music and Meaning*, 2, Spring. Available at: http://www.musicandmeaning.net/issues/showArticle.php?artID=2.4 (accessed September 2012).
Saunders, N. (1997), *Ecstasy Reconsidered*. Exeter: Nicholas Saunders/Turnaround.
SCENIHR [Scientific Committee on Emerging and Newly-Identified Health Risks] (2008), *Scientific Opinion on the Potential Health Risks of Exposure to Noise from Personal Music Players and Mobile Phones Including a Music Playing Function*, 23 September. Available at: http://ec.europa.eu/health/ph_risk/committees/04_scenihr/docs/scenihr_o_018.pdf (accessed July 2010).
Schmidt, A. (2012), *Mysterex*. [Blog]. Available at: http://mysterex.blogspot.co.nz/ (accessed October 2012).
Schmidt, E. (2004), 'Mahler contra Lachenmann', *Contemporary Music Review* 23(3–4), pp. 115–23.
Scholes, P. A. (1970), Entry in *The Oxford Companion to Music* (10th edn), J. O. Ward (ed.). Oxford: Oxford University Press.
Schwartz, H. (2011), *Making Noise – From Babel to the Big Band and Beyond*. Cambridge, MA: The MIT Press.
Scott-Hill, M. (2003), 'Deafness/Disability: Problematising Notions of Identity, Culture and Structure', in *Disability, Culture and Identity*, S. Riddell and N. Watson (eds). Harlow: Pearson, pp. 88–104.
Shaar Murray, C. (1972), 'Teen Outrage in Croydon', *Cream*, March. Available at http://makemyday.free.fr/cream.htm (accessed April 2011).
—(1989), *Crosstown Traffic: Jimi Hendrix and Postwar Pop*. London: Faber and Faber.
Shakespeare, T. (2006), *Disability Rights and Wrongs*. London: Routledge.
Shannon, C. and W. Weaver (1998), *The Mathematical Theory of Communication*. Urbana, Illinois: University of Illinois Press.
Shapiro, P. (2002), 'Deck Wreckers: The Turntable as Instrument', in *Undercurrents: The Hidden Wiring of Underground Music*, R. Young (ed.). New York and London: Continuum, pp. 163–80.
Shaviro, S. (1997), *Doom Patrols: A Theoretical Fiction About Postmodernism*. London and New York: Serpent's Tail/High Rick Books.
Shenfield, S. (2001), *Russian Fascism: Traditions, Tendencies, Movements*. London and New York: M. E. Sharpe.
Siebers, T. (2008), *Disability Theory*. Ann Arbor: University of Michigan Press.
Simpson, D. (2007), 'An Impossible Noise', *The Guardian*, 7 September. Available at http://www.guardian.co.uk/music/2007/sep/07/popandrock1 (accessed October 2012).
Simson, W. (1999), *15 Theses*. Available at: http://www.housechurch.org/basics/simson_15.html (accessed July 2012).
Slackman, M. (2008), 'A City Where You Can't Hear Yourself Scream', *The New York Times*, 14 April. Available at: http://www.nytimes.com/2008/04/14/world/middleeast/14cairo.html (accessed 30 July 2012).
Slates, H., (2009), 'Prisoners of the Earth Come Out!', in *Noise and Capitalism*, Mattin and A. Iles (eds). San Sebatián: Arteleku, pp. 151–64.

Smith, M. E. with A. Collings (2009), *Renegade: The Lives and Tales of Mark E. Smith*. London: Penguin.

Sokolov, M. (2006), 'Natsional-bol'shevikskaia partiia: ideologicheskaia evoliutsiia i politicheskii stil'', in *Russkii natsionalizm: ideologiia i nastroenie*, A. Verkhovskii (ed.). Moscow: SOVA, pp. 139–64.

Spencer, A. (2000), 'Kopfarbeit or Theatre in your Head', in *Probleme und Perspektiven: H.M. Bath Symposion*. Amsterdam: Rodopi, pp. 203–21.

Stack, O. (1969), *Pasolini on Pasolini: Interviews with Oswald Stack*. London: Thames and Hudson/Cinema One.

Steenhuisen, P. (2004), 'Interview with Helmut Lachenmann – Toronto', *Contemporary Music Review*, 23(3–4), pp. 9–14.

Steinholt, Y. (2005), *Rock in the Reservation: Songs from the Leningrad Rock Club 1981–86*. Bergen and New York: MMMSP.

—(2012), 'Siberian Punk Shall Emerge Here: Egor Letov and Grazhdanskaia Oborona', *Popular Music*, 31(3), pp. 401–15.

Stewart, A. (2000), 'Funky Drummer: New Orleans, James Brown and the Rhythmic Transformation of American Popular Music', *Popular Music*, 19(3) October, pp. 293–318.

Strawson, P. (2006), *Individuals. An Essay in Descriptive Metaphysics* (rev. edn). London: Routledge.

Strickland, E. (1993 [revised 2000]), *Minimalism: Origins*. Bloomington and Indianapolis: Indiana University Press.

Stuart, C. (2003), 'Damaged Sound: Glitching and Skipping Compact Discs in the Audio of Yasunao Tone, Nicolas Collins and Oval', *Leonardo Music Journal*, 13, pp. 47–52.

Stubbs, D. (2009), *Fear of Music: Why People Get Rothko But Don't Get Stockhausen*. Winchester, United Kingdom: Zero Books.

Svenonius, I. F. (2006), *The Psychic Soviet*. Chicago: Drag City Inc.

Tagg, P. and Clarida, B. (2003), *Ten Little Title Tunes: Towards a Musicology of the Mass Media*. New York and Montreal: MMMSP.

Taylor, T. D. (2001), *Strange Sounds: Music, Technology and Culture*. New York: Routledge.

Tham, J. (2010), 'Noise as Music: Is there a Historic Continuum?' Paper presented at 'Bigger than Words, Wider than Pictures: Noise, Affect, Politics', international conference, University of Salford, Greater Manchester.

Thompson, B. (1998), *Seven Years of Plenty: A Handbook of Irrefutable Pop Greatness 1991–1998*. London: Phoenix.

Thompson, D. (2012), '*Metal Machine Music*: Live at the Berlin Opera House.' Available at http://www.allmusic.com/album/metal-machine-music-live-at-the-berlin-opera-house-mw0001989803 (accessed July 2012).

Thompson, M. (2012), 'Music for Cyborgs: The Affect and Ethics of Noise Music', in *Reverberations: The Philosophy, Aesthetics and Politics of Noise*, M. Goddard, B. Halligan and P. Hegarty (eds). London and New York: Continuum, pp. 207–18.

Throbbing Gristle (2007), *TGV: The Video Archive Of Throbbing Gristle* [DVD]. London: Industrial Records/Mute Records.

Tisdall, C. and A. Bozzolla (1977), *Futurism*. London: Thames and Hudson.

Toffler, A. (1970), *Future Shock*. New York: Random House.

Tone, Yasunao (1997), *Solo for Wounded CD*. CD, Tzadik: TZ7212.
Toop, D. (1999), *Exotica*. London: Serpent's Tail.
—(2010), *Sinister Resonance*. London and New York: Continuum.
Toth, C. (2009), 'Noise Theory', in *Noise and Capitalism*, Mattin and A. Iles (eds). San Sebastián: Arteleku, pp. 25–37.
Unterberger, R. (1998), *Unknown Legends of Rock'n'Roll: Psychedelic Unknowns, Mad Geniuses, Punk Pioneers, Lo-Fi Mavericks and More*. San Francisco: Miller Freeman.
US Census Bureau (2010), *Statistical Abstract of the United States: 2010* (129th edn). Washington, DC: US Census Bureau.
Vale, V. and A. Juno (1982), *RE/Search #4/5: William S. Burroughs/Brion Gysin/ Throbbing Gristle*. San Francisco: Re/Search Publishing.
—(1983), *RE/Search #6/7: Industrial Culture Handbook*. San Francisco: Re/Search Publishing.
Villiers, A. (2001), *Tomorrow's Eve*, trans. R. M. Adams. Illinois: University of Illinois Press.
Vogel, I., J. Brug, C. P. B. van der Ploeg and H. Raat (2007), 'Young People's Exposure to Loud Music: a Summary of the Literature', *American Journal of Preventive Medicine*, 33(2), pp. 124–33.
Waksman, S. (1998), 'Kick Out the Jams!: The MC5 and the Politics of Noise', in *Mapping the Beat, Popular Music and Contemporary Theory*, T. Swiss, J. Sloop and A. Herman (eds). Malden, MA: Blackwell Publishers Inc, pp. 47–75.
Waldberg, P. (1997), *Surrealism*. London: Thames and Hudson.
Walter, T. (2010), 'Introduction', in *Saccages: Textes (1978–2009)*, G. X. Jupitter-Larsen and V. Dieren (eds). Lausanne: Lausanne Underground Film & Music Festival and Rip on/off, pp. 10–37.
Ward, F., M. C. Taylor and J. Bloomer (2002), *Vito Acconci*. London: Phaidon.
Watson, B. (2009), 'Noise as Permanent Revolution or, Why Culture is a Sow Which Devours its Own Farrow', in *Noise and Capitalism*, Mattin and A. Iles (eds). San Sebastián: Arteleku, pp. 105–20.
Weingarten, C. (2005), *Poisson d'Avril: Skzzz! [dispatch 001]: JUSTICE YELDHAM. poisson d'avril*. Available at: http://aprilfish.blogspot.com/2005/08/skzzz-dispatch-001-justice-yeldham.html (accessed May 2011).
Whiteley, S. ([1992] 2004), *The Space Between The Notes: Rock and the Counter-Culture*. London: Routledge.
—(1997), 'Altered Sounds', in *Psychedelia Britannica: Hallucinogenic Drugs in Britain*, A. Melechi (ed.). London: Turnaround, pp. 120–42.
—(2009), 'The Beatles as Zeitgeist', in *The Cambridge Companion to The Beatles*, K. Womack (ed.). Cambridge: Cambridge University Press, pp. 203–16.
Whyton, T. (2010), *Jazz Icons: Heroes, Myths and the Jazz Tradition*. Cambridge: Cambridge University Press.
Wickström, D.-E. and Y. Steinholt (2009), 'Visions of the (Holy) Motherland in Contemporary Russian Popular Music: Nostalgia, Patriotism, Religion and Russkii Rok', *Popular Music and Society*, 32(3), pp. 313–30.
Wilkerson, M. (2009), *Who Are You: The Life of Pete Townshend*. London: Omnibus.
Willis, P. E. (1978), *Profane Culture*. London: Routledge & Kegan Paul.
Wilson, L. (2012), 'Physical Spectatorship: Noise and Rape in Irreversible', in

*Reverberations: The Philosophy, Aesthetics and Politics of Noise*, M. Goddard, B. Halligan and P. Hegarty (eds). London and New York: Continuum, pp. 121–32.

Winseman, A. L. (2003), 'Does More Educated Really = Less Religious?', *Gallup*, 4 February. Available at: http://www.gallup.com/poll/7729/does-more-educated-really-less-religious.aspx (accessed July 2012).

Wise, T. (2003), 'Arrangement', in *Continuum Encyclopedia of Popular Music of the World*, J. Shepherd et al. (eds). London and New York: Continuum, pp. 630–31.

Wiseman-Trowse, N. (2008), *Performing Class in British Popular Music*. London: Palgrave-Macmillan.

Wolcott, J. (1975), Review of *Metal Machine Music*, *Rolling Stone*, 14 August. Available at http://www.rollingstone.com/music/albumreviews/metal-machine-music-19750814 (accessed June 2012).

Wyschnegradsky, I. (1996), *La Loi de la Pansonorité*. Geneva: Contrechamps.

Xenakis, I. (1992), *Formalized Music: Thought and Mathematics in Composition*. Mid Glamorgan: Pendragon Press.

—(2009), 'Total Immersion', Barbican Event Programme, 7 March. London: Barbican Centre.

Young, R. (2002), 'Worship the Glitch: Digital Music, Electronic Disturbance', in *Undercurrents: The Hidden Wiring of Modern Music*, R. Young (ed.). London and New York: Continuum.

Yurchak, A. (2006), *Everything Was Forever Until It Was No More: The Last Soviet Generation*. Princeton and Oxford: Princeton University Press.

Ziarek, K. (2005), 'The Work of Art in the Age of Its Electronic Mutability', in *Walter Benjamin and Art*, A. Benjamin (ed.). London and New York: Continuum, pp. 209–2.

Zuckerman, P. (2007), 'Atheism: Contemporary Numbers and Patterns', in *The Cambridge Companion to Atheism*, M. Martin (ed.). Cambridge: Cambridge University Press, pp. 47–65.

# INDEX

23 Skidoo 88, 333n. 2
808 State 49

Acconci, Vito 264
Acid House 47, 48–9, 50, 52, 59, 190, 192, 330n. 6, 331n. 8, 332n. 21 *see also* rave
acid use 45, 47, 48, 51, 87, 188 *see also* LSD
acousmatic music 188, 189, 343n. 10
acoustic space 111, 129, 286, 287, 291
Actionism (Viennese) 264, 265, 270
adorable 58
Adorno, Theodor 72, 242–9, 251–4, 341nn. 4, 6–8, 342n. 13
affect 22, 37, 41, 43–7, 52, 63–4, 111, 120, 121–2, 129, 142–3, 144, 186, 209, 211, 218–19, 221, 243, 274, 277, 278, 280, 282–5, 306, 308, 310–11, 314–16, 322–5, 332n. 23
affordances 210, 216, 316, 346n. 3
Agamben, Giorgio 318, 341n. 2
algorithmic music 224
ambient 49, 54, 81, 188
ambient sound 16, 90, 93, 211, 216, 217, 340n. 5
Amusement Parks on Fire 331n. 15
Antonioni, Michelangelo 90
  *Blow-Up* 90
  *Zabriskie Point* 44, 51
Aphex Twin 231 *see also* James, Richard
Apple company, the 70, 76
Arbeit, Jochen 100, 106
A. R. Kane 49, 54, 331n. 12
Arnold, Martin 209, 210, 215, 216–19, 221

arrhythmic 26, 27, 196, 204, 242
Artaud, Antonin 95–106
articulated noise (compositional strategy) 224, 231, 232, 234, 235, 236–7, 241
Asobi Seksu 332n. 19
atonality 81, 143, 222, 245, 259, 266, 267, 270, 341n. 4
Attali, Jacques 6, 14, 22–3, 85, 96, 107, 111–12, 273, 280, 297, 301, 313, 316, 322
auditive unpleasantness 282, 313, 322, 324
Auslander, Philip 32, 34, 40, 59, 60
Autechre 81
avant-garde, the 4, 9, 19, 27, 31, 36, 50, 56, 58, 60, 61, 63, 82, 85, 87, 116, 125, 143, 146, 184, 245, 249, 257, 258–9, 260, 262, 264, 270, 271, 282, 284, 308, 327n. 12

background music 207, 340n. 3
Bailter Space 134–5, 140–3, 144, 145, 147, 148
Balanescu Quartet, the 35
Ballard, J. G. 82, 87–8, 142, 269
Band of Susans 52
Bangs, Lester 19, 25, 32, 35, 120
Bannister, Matthew 146–7, 337nn. 8, 9
Bargeld, Blixa 97–100, 102–6
Barrett, Syd 41, 43
Barron, Lois and Bebe 90
Bataille, Georges 282
Bats, the 137
Baudrillard, Jean 142
BBC (British Broadcasting Corporation) 4, 89, 331n. 16

Beatles, the 16, 18, 44, 45, 72, 82, 86, 87, 121, 137, 138, 328n. 14 *see also* Paul McCartney
Beats, the 96, 326n. 3
Beckett, Samuel 253–4, 342n. 13
Beethoven, Ludwig van 68, 90, 245, 332n. 1
Benjamin, Walter 95, 104, 146, 148, 220, 243–4, 252, 254, 275, 341nn. 3, 11
Bennett, William 271, 285
Berg, Alban 245, 259
Berio, Luciano 203, 262
Berlin 24, 29, 30, 56, 95, 97, 104, 329n. 7
Bernard, Jonathan W. 205–6
Best, Philip 271, 285
Bez 51
Biafra, Jello 125
Bianchi, Maurizio 271, 295
Bleach 58
Blind Mr. Jones 58
Boo Radleys, the 57, 58
Boulez, Pierre 223, 248, 262
Bowie, David 50, 70
Bracken, Cory 234
Branca, Glenn 116–17
Brassier, Ray 8, 36, 119, 184, 257
Brian Jonestown Massacre, the 331n. 15
Britpop 59, 60, 85
Burden, Chris 195, 264
Burgess, Anthony 88
Burroughs, William S. 82, 88, 90, 260, 263, 269, 333nn. 2, 3
Butler, Samuel 138
Butthole Surfers 118
buzz 3, 130, 147, 192, 196
Byrds, the 42

C-86 (music genre) 52, 61
Cabaret Voltaire 83, 84, 89, 91–2, 109, 259, 269, 333nn. 2, 3
Cage, John 81, 86, 87, 88, 89, 95–6, 113, 117, 119, 147, 194, 198, 201, 202–3, 206, 209, 212, 214, 222, 223, 249, 261, 262, 270, 273, 297–8, 345n. 2

*4' 33"* (composition) 203, 207, 212, 261
Cain, Nick 257
Cale, John 27, 207, 342n. 3
Captain Beefheart 86
Carlos, Wendy/Walter 90
Cascone, Kim 186–7, 188–9
Catherine Wheel 57, 331n. 10
Chapterhouse 58, 331n. 15
Charles, Ray 64, 67
Chills, the 137–8, 149
chillwave 185
Chopin, Henri 263
Chris and Cosey 154, 166
Christ, Jesus 113, 114, 121
Christchurch 137–8, 140–1
Christ the Saviour Cathedral (Moscow) 131, 336n. 12
Cisneros, Roc Jiménez de 188, 189
Clapton, Eric 38–9, 40, 42, 52, 61, 330n. 2
Clean, the 138, 141, 149
Clock DVA 88
Cocteau Twins, the 52, 54
Coil 270
Coleman, Ornette 86
Coley, Byron 136
computer music 183, 187, 188–90, 193, 223, 224, 339n. 5
Comsat Angels 88
Conceptual Art 43, 263, 264, 343n. 10
concert hall, the 201, 204, 208, 210, 216, 244, 281, 303
Coppola, Francis Ford 90–2, 327 n7
*Conversation, The* (Coppola) 90–2
Cosloy, Gerard 136
COUM Transmissions 268–9
Crass 125
Creation Records 63, 332n. 22
*Creem* 19, 21
Criton, Pascale 292–3
Cunningham, David 245–6
Cunningham, Merce 201
Cure, the 52
Current 93 270
Curve 54, 57
cyborgs 140, 143, 305, 307, 309

## INDEX

Dada 84, 93, 98, 105, 258, 259, 260–1, 263, 270
Davis, Lennard J. 66, 69, 72
Davis, Miles 49, 50, 67
*Day the Earth Stood Still, The* (Wise) 90
Dead C., the 134, 135, 145–8
deafness 64, 66–9, 71–2, 75, 76, 284, 332n. 1, 333n. 5
Deleuze, Gilles 197 *see also* Deleuze and Guattari
Deleuze and Guattari 62, 190, 220, 306
Deller, Jeremy 47, 330n. 6
Denny, Martin 87, 88
depression 112, 123, 125, 143
Derbyshire, Delia 50
DeRogatis, Jim 45–6, 49, 328n. 15
Detroit 19–20, 22, 258, 331n. 8
Dick, Phillip K. 88, 142–3
Dinosaur Jr. 52–3, 147, 331n. 10 *see also* Mascis, J
discord, discordance 13, 14, 81, 246, 301
disgust 314, 315–16, 322, 323, 325
dissonance 4, 14, 17, 23, 27, 42, 81, 245, 247, 258, 260, 261, 293
distraction 209, 210, 215, 220, 299, 301
distress 70, 101, 130, 304
disutopia 135, 140, 148, 338n. 11
DJ, the (disc jockey) 4, 48, 51, 74, 84, 188, 249, 258
Dolar, Mladen 307
Doo-dooettes, the 268
Downes, Graeme 337n. 4
drone 4, 26, 27, 33, 40, 42, 46, 61, 83, 85, 87, 98, 99, 102, 104, 129, 130, 146–7, 192, 193, 198, 204, 242, 269, 238n. 1, 329n. 11, 343n. 9
Duchamp, Marcel 93, 343n. 10
Duncan, John 264–5
Dunedin 136–9
'Dunedin Double' (EP) 137–8, 337n. 5
'Dunedin sound', the 136–9
Durutti Column, the 342n. 11
Dylan, Bob 6, 40, 50, 121

dynamic stochastic synthesis (DSS) 190–2, 197, 339n. 12

earplugs 62, 70, 74, 278
Earth 54
Ecstasy ('E') 48, 49
'Edison, Thomas' (fictional character) 302
Eggleston, David 137
Einstürzende Neubauten 81, 95–106, 108, 109, 269
electricity, electrification 17, 21, 27, 30, 32, 36, 39, 47–8, 50–1, 89, 90, 121, 130, 132, 135, 147–8, 184, 187, 188, 189, 193, 196, 207, 213, 220, 222, 223, 238, 262, 269
electroacoustic music 187, 188, 189, 193, 223, 261, 287
electronic dance music (EDM) 47, 49, 50, 51, 52, 54, 55, 58, 60, 63, 193
electronica 4
electronics (equipment, sound) 48, 187, 271, 274, 277, 279, 281, 284, 285, 338n. 3
empirical space 289–90, 291
Eno, Brian 35, 50, 207
exhaustion 120, 123, 185, 188
extreme computer music (ECM) 183, 187, 188–9, 190

Fall, the 139, 336n. 2, 337n. 10
Faust 86, 146, 342n. 3
*Faust* (Schwab) 103
feedback 1, 4, 15, 16, 19, 21, 22, 23, 25, 26, 27, 29, 33, 35, 39, 40, 130, 144, 146, 186, 251, 328n. 5, 330n. 16, 332n. 22, 342n. 3
feminine noise 298, 299–302, 304–5, 311
feminism 127, 337n. 9
fetishization 185, 186, 332n. 21
Filthy Turd 154, 156, 312–25
Fireworks Ensemble, the 30, 33
Flowered Up 50
Fluxus 87, 96, 263, 335n. 15
Flying Nun (record label) 134, 135,

136–9, 140, 141, 144, 145, 146, 148–9
folk music 1, 42, 44, 70, 99, 121–3, 147, 184, 185, 337n. 3
*Forbidden Planet* (Wilcox) 89, 90
*Forced Exposure* (fanzine) 136
Foregger, Nikolai 260
Fourier analysis 190–1
framing 198, 200, 201–2, 203–4, 206, 207–8, 340n. 5
Frank Zappa and the Mothers of Invention 44
Freud, Sigmund 54, 260
Friedl, Reinhold 31, 32, 329n. 7
Frith, Simon 23, 31, 83, 219, 328n. 18
FulangchangandI 154, 168
funk 49, 137, 245, 246, 341n. 5
Furudate, Tetsuo 281
Fushitsusha 154, 168, 185, 186, 188
futurism 140, 143, 270, 279, 297
Futurists 222, 242, 248, 258–9, 260–1, 273, 279, 297, 298

Galás, Diamanda 298, 307–11
 *The Litanies of Satan* 308–9
 'Wild Women with Steak Knives' 308–9, 310
Galaxie 500 52
Gibbons, Walter 249
Gidal, Peter 218
Glass, Philip 204–5, 206, 339n. 4
glass, smashing and acoustics of 99, 102, 104, 195, 288
glitch 8, 81, 186, 187, 188, 189, 316–19, 320, 321, 322, 323, 341–2n. 10, 346n. 5
glossolalia 53, 118
Gnod 154, 157
God (Judeo-Christian deity) 101, 107, 108, 112, 113, 114, 117–18, 119, 120
Goodman, Steve 8, 277, 278, 279, 283, 314
'Gordonaut' 140
Gordons, the 134, 135, 140–2, 144, 146, 147, 148, 149
gossip (women's) 299–301, 305
Goth 53, 267, 271

gramophone, the 243, 244, 249
Grazhdanskaia Oborona ('GrOb') 123–7, 133
Groupe de Recherches Musicales (GRM) 262
Guattari, Félix 143 *see also* Deleuze and Guattari
Gum Takes Tooth 154, 158
Gumbrecht, Hans-Ulrich 275, 276–7
Gun Cleaner 154, 159
Gysin, Brion 260, 263, 269, 330n. 4

Halligan, Benjamin 3, 326n. 2, 331n. 9, 342n. 13
Halvorsen, John 141, 338nn. 12, 13
Happy Mondays, the 47, 50, 56
*Hard Day's Night, A* (Lester) 2
Hardt and Negri 46–7, 48
harmony 4, 6, 23, 37, 38, 60, 111, 146, 245, 246, 247, 248, 259, 293
Haswell, Russell 193, 338n. 3
Haters, the 81, 265
head banging 72
'head music' 43, 44, 48, 49, 50, 146
Hecker, Florian 183, 188, 189, 190
Hegarty, Paul 6, 32, 36, 46, 97, 109, 117–18, 154, 174, 184, 185, 242, 246, 273, 280, 281, 282, 283, 286, 294, 295, 313, 316, 322, 326n. 3, 331n. 14
Heino, Keiji 154, 170
Hendrix, Jimi 14, 15–16, 19, 39–40, 42, 86, 327n. 5–8
Herzog, Werner 82, 91
hi-fi (high fidelity) 303, 304–5
Hijokaidan 266
hip-hop 113, 249, 251
Hitchcock, Alfred 194
Hood 54
House of Love, the 57
hum 25, 88, 99, 102, 104, 105, 124, 192, 193, 217–18, 251, 303
Hypnagogic pop 185

improvisation 5, 9, 24, 36, 38, 49, 51, 67, 145–8, 195, 217, 222, 223, 235–8, 241, 262, 264, 326n. 1, 329n. 7, 330n. 15

indeterminacy 5, 17, 25, 31, 195, 223, 235
industrial music 29, 257, 258, 264, 268, 269, 273, 274, 277, 284, 285,
Industrial Records Ltd 264, 269
Industrial Tapes (company) 136
I Polly Touch 154, 169
iPod, the 65, 68, 70, 74, 75–6, 207
intonarumori (machines) 259, 260
Ives, Charles 222

Jack The Tab 49–50 *see also* P-Orridge, Genesis
Jagger, Mick 18, 51 *see also* the Rolling Stones
James, Richard 81 *see also* Aphex Twin
jangle 61, 137, 138, 146, 337n. 9
Japanese noise 109, 188, 193, 273, 274, 277, 279, 281–5, 294
jazz 19, 29, 38, 49, 67, 71, 76, 123, 145, 184, 218, 242, 253, 258, 264, 266, 267, 273, 282, 308, 327n. 3, 342n. 1
Jeck, Philip 242–4
Jefferson Airplane 44
Jeffries, Graeme 143–4
Jeffries, Peter 143–4
Jerry, Mungo 320, 322
Jesus and Mary Chain, The 52, 146, 332n. 22
JLIAT 207
Jones, Brian 40, 49, 51, 320n. 4
Joy Division 88, 137, 139, 143, 145, 333n. 3, 337n. 10
Joy Zipper 331n. 13
Jung, Carl 153
jungle 4, 15, 50, 53

Kafka, Franz 101, 247, 341n. 7
Kahn, Douglas 6, 96, 248, 273, 341n. 9, 345n. 2
Kak 39
Karkowski, Zbigniew 29, 281, 294
Keenan, David 185–6, 269
Keightley, Kier 303–4
Keller, Hans 43

Kilgour, Hamish 141
King Loser 337n. 7
Kirk, Richard 92
Kitchens of Distinction 55, 58
KLF, the 49
Knox, Chris 137–8, 144, 337n. 8
Kraftwerk 35, 258
Krautrock 60, 146, 284, 342n. 3
Krieger, Ulrich 24, 29–31, 33, 35–6, 329nn. 7, 11, 15
Kubrick, Stanley 82, 90

Lachenmann, Helmut 209, 213–14, 340n. 5
Laibach 108, 109
Lash Frenzy 154, 160
Lawrie, Stephen 63 *see also* the Telescopes
Leary, Timothy 16, 48
Leckey, Mark 59
Led Zeppelin 72, 185–6, 308
Lennon, John 16, 17–19, 87, 121, 263
Letov, Egor 123–7, 133
Levin, Thomas Y. 243, 252
'linguistic turn', the 275–6
Littlefield, Richard 199–200, 201–3, 204–6, 208, 340n. 5
'locked groove' 26, 27, 29, 328n. 4
lo-fi 136, 138, 139–40, 144, 146, 303
Loop 52, 58
loops 51, 86, 87, 99, 146, 186, 196, 242, 251, 321, 328n. 4, 330n. 15
Los Angeles Free Music Society 267–8
loudness 62, 69, 70, 71–4, 147, 192, 290, 314
LSD use 39, 44, 45, 46, 48, 57 *see also* acid use
Lush 58
Lyman, Arthur 82, 87
Lynch, David 82, 90
Lyon, Eric
  *Diagonal Noise* 232–4
  *Noise Concerto* 235–6, 237
  *Three Melodies for Vibraphone* 234

*Three Noises for Violin and Piano* 224–6

machinism 143
MacKay, George 47, 48
Malkmus, Stephen 136
Mancini, Henry 91
mantra 40, 104, 105, 106, 143
Marclay, Christian 249, 263–4
Marinetti, Filippo 259, 279, 297, 345n. 1
Marshall amplifiers 16, 23
Martin, George 16, 72, 82
Marvin, Hank 42
Mascis, J 53 *see also* Dinosaur Jr.
Mason, Mike 331n. 17
Masonna 111, 295
Master Musicians of Jajouka, the 40, 330n. 4
material impact 273, 274, 282
materialities 90, 113, 209, 210, 212, 213–14, 221, 274–5, 277, 280, 282, 303
Mathew, Max 189
Mattin 3, 5, 8, 326nn. 1, 3
Mayall, John 39, 40, 330n. 2
MC5, the 14, 19–23, 52, 328nn. 15, 16, 17
McCartney, Paul 17, 18, 87, 327n. 12 *see also* the Beatles
McLuhan, Marshall 275, 278
medial noise 212, 314, 316–19, 321, 322, 323–4, 346n. 8
mediation 32, 36, 147, 212, 216, 219, 242, 244–5, 247–8, 249, 252–3, 254
Mego (label) 188
Menkman, Rosa 8, 319, 326n. 3
Mertens, Wim 117, 119, 205–6, 328n. 3, 340n. 5
Merzbow 29, 81, 111, 184, 197, 264, 281, 295
Metal Machine Trio, the (MM3) 24, 34, 36, 329n. 15, 330n. 16
Migone, Christof 265
minimalism 31, 102, 143, 144, 148, 198, 200, 201, 204, 207, 208, 339n. 5

Ministry 271
Mitchell, Tony 137–9, 146–7
Modernism and modernity 190, 247, 253, 262, 273, 242n. 13
Mogwai 6, 54, 143, 326n. 3
Moloko 88
montage(s) 88, 194, 252–3, 254
Moose 58
Morley, Michael 144, 145, 149
Moroder, Giorgio 50
MP3 technology 69–70, 75, 342n. 10
Müller, Heiner 96, 98, 101–2, 333n. 2, 334n. 8
musical space 289, 291, 292, 293, 296
musical structure 134, 140, 141, 145, 224, 231, 291
musical template code 226–8
musicology (disciplines, discourse and exponents of) 6, 37, 183, 189, 198, 337n. 9
*musique concrète* 86, 87, 96, 184, 213, 246, 258, 261–2, 267, 270, 271, 273, 342n. 2
Mutual Extermination Club 154, 161
My Bloody Valentine 6, 53–4, 58, 60, 61–3, 70, 143, 147, 331n. 15, 332nn. 20, 22

nausea 117, 122, 153, 315
Nazareth 72
Nine Inch Nails 271
Negri, Antonio 140, 148, 338n. 11 *see also* Hardt and Negri
Nelsh Bailter Space 140, 141
neoliberalism 3, 109, 120, 268, 326n. 1
New Blockaders, the 185
Newman, Barnett 200, 201
New York 15, 116, 117, 120, 142, 145, 200, 249, 266–7
nightclubs 68, 69, 75, 332n. 3
Nihilist Spasm Band, the 266
Nilsson, Harry 321
Nitsch, Hermann 260, 264, 343n. 6
Noble, Ward, Moore 154, 171
Nocturnal Projections 143
noise music 5, 8, 9, 36, 64, 95, 108, 109, 111, 116, 117, 118, 119,

120, 134, 140, 183, 184, 185, 186, 187, 193, 214, 243, 257–8, 259, 260, 261, 263, 266, 268, 270, 271, 273, 287, 289, 291, 294, 295, 296, 306–7, 321, 342n. 3
noise rock 4, 52, 263, 267
Noise Quartet, the 237–8, 240, 241
noisiness 123, 124, 141, 185, 192, 193, 242, 246, 251, 300
NON (Boyd Rice) 264, 269
Nørgård, Per 217, 341n. 10
Norris, Richard 49 see also Jack The Tab
nostalgia 37, 54, 126, 251, 253, 254, 341n. 10
No Wave 116, 145, 263, 267, 343n. 9
nu-gaze 331n. 15, 332n. 19
Nugent, Ted 72, 73–4
*Nuggets: Original Artyfacts from the First Psychedelic Era, 1965–1968* 52, 330n. 3
Nurse with Wound 185, 266, 269–70

Oasis 72, 332n. 22
Onement (record label) 207
One Unique Signal 154, 172
Ono, Yoko 19, 263
Orb, the 49
Osbourne, Ozzy 72
Oval 187, 194

Pale Saints, the 58
pansonority 291, 292, 293
Paper Lace 321
Parker, Alister 141, 338n. 12 –13
Pavement 136, 139
Pentecostalism 108, 113–15, 117, 119–20
percussive 16, 70, 146, 229, 242, 246, 253
*Performance* (Roeg and Cammell) 51
Pin Group, the 137
Pink Floyd 41, 42, 44, 45, 49, 51, 330n. 5
pitch 16, 21, 26, 27, 33, 45, 61, 65, 97, 98, 104, 118, 191, 192, 193, 213, 216, 217, 226, 230, 233,
271, 281, 284, 289, 290, 291, 307, 329n. 11
Place to Bury Strangers, A 331n. 15
Pollock, Jackson 84, 188, 197
P-Orridge, Genesis 49, 268, 271
post-digital, the 186, 187, 188, 189
postmodernism 4, 58, 60, 188, 204, 205, 207
power electronics 271, 274, 277, 279, 281, 284, 285
praxis 5, 148, 190
Prog Rock 44, 46, 48, 218, 330n. 5, 331n. 14
Prurient 193, 281
psychedelia 4, 37–8, 44–6, 48–52, 55, 63, 138, 139, 149, 268, 332n. 23
Psychic TV 270, 331n. 8
Public Image Ltd 109
punk 116, 121–5, 127–9, 131–3, 135, 137, 138, 140–2, 149, 282, 335n. 2, 337n. 3, 342n. 11
Pussy Riot 127–32, 133, 335nn. 5, 6, 336nn. 7–9, 11, 13
Putin, Vladimir 122, 127, 129, 130, 131, 132, 335n. 6

Quicksilver Messenger Service 42

radical contingency 145, 147
Radio Luxembourg 85
randomness 25, 26, 97, 98, 148, 153, 223–32, 236, 238–41, 242, 324
rave 3, 37, 47, 48, 49, 51, 54, 56, 57, 58, 59, 62, 246 see also Acid House
recontextualizing sound 245, 253
Reed, Lou 24–36, 50, 342n. 3, 328nn. 1–2, 5, 329nn. 8, 11–12, 15, 342n. 3
  *Metal Machine Music* (MMM) 4, 24–36, 50, 328n. 1, 329nn. 10–12, 15, 329n. 7, 330n. 17
Reich, Steve 33, 204, 205, 206, 246, 262, 339n. 4
repetition 17, 26, 27, 40, 42, 46, 51, 101, 117, 140, 142, 192, 219, 236, 282, 283, 285
Rev, Martin 266

*Reverberations: The Philosophy, Aesthetics and Politics of Noise* (Goddard, Halligan, Hegarty) 8, 145, 326n. 2
Reynolds, Simon 8, 25, 28, 49, 146, 246, 258, 283, 284, 330n. 7, 332n. 20
rhythm 27, 42, 81, 85, 92, 105, 106, 116, 135, 144, 146, 217, 223, 245, 246, 253, 270, 279, 321
rhythmic/rhythmically 26, 72, 104, 105, 116, 124, 141, 187, 204, 213, 223, 224, 225, 226, 230, 232, 233, 245, 246, 281, 282, 295, 296, 321
Ride 56, 57, 332n. 22
Riot Grrl 127, 129
Roads, Curtis 194
Rohame 154, 173
Rolling Stones, the 18, 19, 38, 44, 333n. 5
Romaine, Suzanne 300, 302, 345n. 3
Roxy Music 86
Russell, Bruce 139, 145, 147–9
Russian Orthodox Church 131–2, 336n. 12
Russkii Proryv 125–7
Russolo, Luigi 81, 222, 242, 259
Rylan, Jessica 307
Rysman, Alexander 300, 345n. 4

Sacks, Oliver 65, 75
Safe 154, 174
sampling/samples 4, 29, 49, 50, 99, 143, 189, 284, 317, 320, 321, 330n. 17
Sangild, Torben 26, 27–8, 33, 331n. 11
Sargent, Lol 249
Schaeffer, Pierre 81, 85, 87, 96, 262, 342n. 2
schematic noise 316, 317, 319, 320–4
Schmickler, Marcus 189
Schoenberg, Arnold 81, 222, 223, 245, 247, 258, 259
Scipio, Agostino Di 193
score, the 5, 24, 28, 29, 30, 31, 35, 90, 96, 189, 205, 212, 213, 217

Scott, Raymond 89
'Second Summer of Love', the 4, 47, 63
Serena-Maneesh 331n. 15
serial music/serialism 223, 245, 262, 213
Shaar Murray, Charles 15–16, 18–19, 21, 22, 327n. 7
Shadows, the 42
Shepherd, Roger 136
Shields, Kevin 53, 54, 70, 332n. 23 *see also* My Bloody Valentine
shoegaze 4, 37, 49, 52, 53, 54–6, 58–60, 61–2, 141, 331nn. 10–11, 13, 15, 17–18, 332nn. 21–2, 343n. 9
Shoes This High 135
silence 3, 5, 21, 69, 81, 103, 111, 124, 144, 193, 198, 199, 201–4, 206–8, 226, 281, 297–8, 299, 300, 301, 304, 305, 311, 345n. 2
Silver Apples 50
Sinclair, John 19–22, 328n. 17
Skeptics 142
Skullflower 154, 162
Slade 72–3
Slowdive 53, 57, 332n. 22
Sly and the Family Drone 154, 175
Sneaky Feelings 138, 149, 337n. 9
Snow, Michael 57, 218
Soft Machine 88
Sonic Youth 52, 81, 116, 118, 139, 141, 143, 145, 330n. 17
'sound-box', the 38, 42, 53
sound clipping 187, 316, 317, 319, 323
sound continuum 292
soundscape 29, 37, 42, 53, 118, 254, 278
sound synthesis 5, 188, 189, 190, 191
*Space Between the Notes: Rock and the Counter-Culture, The* (Whiteley) 13, 44
Stapleton, Paul 235, 236, 238
Steely Dan 88
stochastic 184, 190, 191, 197, 222, 224, 339n. 12

Stockhausen, Karlheinz 81, 87, 88, 223, 246, 248, 262, 327n. 12
Stooges, the 52, 138, 266, 328n. 15
Stravinsky, Igor 35, 81
Strawson, Peter 286–91, 295, 296
Strickland, Edward 201
Stubbs, David 82, 84
subject-in-process 306
Suicide 266
'Summer of Love', the 46, 51, 63
Sun Ra 86
SuperCollider code 226, 232
Surrealism 260, 261, 270
Suzuki, Damo 154, 155
Svenonius, Ian 48–9, 112, 113
Swans 117, 118, 119, 154, 176
Swervedriver 54, 57, 331nn. 10, 15
Swirlies, the 58
Synecdoche 209, 211

Tagg, Philip 329n. 14
Tall Dwarfs 137, 144
tape recorders 32, 33, 86, 112, 138, 261
techno 4, 48, 49, 50, 83, 84, 123, 183, 188, 189, 231, 258
technological reproduction 242, 244, 252, 253
technologies 1, 4, 5, 8, 24, 25, 32, 48, 49, 50, 51, 64, 65, 66, 68, 69, 74, 75, 76, 83, 90, 91, 112, 140–1, 143, 147, 148, 186–7, 190, 209, 214, 216, 219, 242–4, 248, 249, 252, 253, 258, 259, 261, 262, 265, 273, 275, 280, 284–5, 295, 298, 303, 309, 340nn. 4, 7, 341n. 3, 342nn. 3, 10
Teenage Jesus and the Jerks 116
teleology 26, 198, 204–5, 206
Telescopes, the 6, 54, 58, 61, 63, 154, 163, 177, 178
*Teorema* (Pasolini) 5–6, 7
Test Department 81
Theater of Eternal Music 27, 204, 207
This Kind of Punishment 134, 135, 143–5, 148

Thompson, Marie 25
Throbbing Gristle 88, 108, 109, 141, 154, 179, 268–9, 270, 271
timbral noise 313–15, 317, 319, 321, 323–4
timbre 17, 18, 33, 50, 192–3, 194, 196, 217, 240, 245, 290, 291, 295, 307, 313
tinnitus 68, 70, 71, 74
tonality 116, 222, 223, 245–6
Tone, Yasunao 187, 263
Toop, David 93
Toy Love 137
Trans-Love Energies organisation (TLE) 19–20, 328n. 17
tremolo 25, 33, 42, 304
Trinh, T. Minh-ha 218
Tudor, David 96, 188–9, 190, 338n. 4
turntablism 4, 249
TV on the Radio 330n. 17
Twee Pop 52
Twilit Grotto 154, 164

Unruh, Andrew 98–9, 100, 103, 105, 106
University of Salford, the 77, 326n. 2

v23 design studio 331n. 18
Vaggione, Horacio 194
Vandewalle, Daan 234
Varèse, Edgard 222, 261, 273, 279
Vega, Alan 266–7
Velvet Underground, the 27, 40, 52, 83, 86, 137, 139, 141, 328n. 5
Venitucci, Luca 24, 29–30
Verlaines, the 138, 148
Vernon, Mike 330n. 2
vibration 21, 46, 65, 97, 104, 119, 277–8
Villiers de l'Isle-Adam, Auguste 302
vinyl 8, 29, 85, 112, 139, 242, 244–5, 249, 250, 251–3, 264, 265
virtuality 8, 38, 54, 83, 202, 210, 212, 214, 292
voice 186, 188, 192–3, 196, 197, 217, 232, 253, 263, 264, 281, 298, 301–2, 304, 305, 307–11
Voltiegers 154, 165

Vomir 295
Vorticism 143

Walkman, the 65, 68, 69, 74–6
'wall of sound' 61, 147
Webern, Anton 245, 259
Wellington 135, 138, 142
Wessel, David 189
Whitehouse 267, 271, 285, 295, 343n. 4
white noise 8, 63, 85, 147, 192–3, 224, 229, 235, 281, 314, 317, 323, 324
Whiteley, Sheila 13, 44–5, 49, 330n. 3
Who, the 68, 69, 327n. 8, 333n. 6
Whyton, Tony 30
Wilson, Brian 82, 85
Wilson, Tony 56, 342n. 11
Wise, Tim 30
Wiseman-Trowse, Nathan 54, 56, 60, 62, 331n. 18
Woodstock music festival 14–15

World of Twist 50
Wreck Small Speakers on Expensive Stereos 149
Wyschnegradsky, Ivan 292–3

Xenakis, Iannis 96, 190–1, 193, 194–6, 222–3, 279
  *S.709* (composition) 190, 195–6
Xpressway (cassette label) 136, 139, 144, 146–7

Yardbirds, the 44
Yeldham, Justice 195
Yo La Tengo 331n. 15
Yoshihide, Otomo 264
Young, La Monte 27, 85, 87, 198, 201, 204
YouTube 128, 335n. 5

Z, Pamela 307
Zeitkratzer 24, 28–9, 30, 31–4, 35
Zen Buddhism 113, 120